BASIC
REFERENCE
SOURCES

A Self-Study Manual

Third Edition

MARGARET T. TAYLOR
and RONALD R. POWELL

The Scarecrow Press, Inc. Metuchen, N.J., & London   1985

BASIC REFERENCE SOURCES

A Self-Study Manual

Third Edition

MARGARET T. TAYLOR
and RONALD R. POWELL

The Scarecrow Press, Inc. Metuchen, N.J., & London   1985

Library of Congress Cataloging in Publication Data

Taylor, Margaret, 1930-
   Basic reference sources.

   Includes index.
   1. Reference books--Problems, exercises, etc.
I. Powell, Ronald R.   II. Title.
Z1035.1.T35   1985   028.7'076   84-13880
ISBN 0-8108-1721-7

CONTENTS

LIST OF SOURCES

Note: The sources listed below include all of the titles mentioned in this manual. Titles are listed in the section in which they first appear. The starred titles are covered in detail in the manual. The other titles are noted more briefly, in a supplementary or comparative manner, usually with only a single question or a single reference in an answer.

Brief titles only are given. Following each title is a reference to its listing in Sheehy's Guide to Reference Books (Chicago, American Library Association, 9th ed., 1976; Supplements, 1980 and 1982), where more complete citations may be found. (A "1" before the Sheehy number refers to the first, 1980 supplement, and a "2" refers to the second, 1982 supplement.) If a title is not included in Sheehy, the full citation is given in this list. Also indicated, for the starred titles only, are the dates of the editions or issues used in preparing the manual and to which the answers are keyed. The symbol ■ is placed after the citations for those sources which are available in online, computer-accessed versions, as far as could be determined as of May 1984.

The student should have access to the starred titles, preferably in the editions noted. It is helpful but not necessary that he/she should have access to the supplementary titles. See Introduction for comments on adaptation of this list to specific course requirements.

Section 1a: National bibliographic records, U.S., current

*Publishers' Trade List Annual (AA472) 1982
*Books in Print (AA473) 1982-83 ■
 Publishers, Distributors, and Wholesalers of the United States: A Directory (New York, Bowker, 5th ed., 1983) ■
*Subject Guide to Books in Print (AA474) 1982-83 ■
 Books in Print Supplement (see AA473) ■
 Forthcoming Books (AA475) ■
 Subject Guide to Forthcoming Books (AA476) ■
 Paperbound Books in Print (AA471)
 Children's Books in Print (AA466)
 Subject Guide to Children's Books in Print (AA467)
 Scientific and Technical Books and Serials in Print (EA38)
 Medical Books and Serials in Print (EK26)
 Business and Economics Books and Serials in Print (CH105, 1CH47)
 Religious Books and Serials in Print (2BB3)
 Large Type Books in Print (AA470, 1AA98, 2AA62)
 El-Hi Textbooks in Print (AA469)
 Law Information (New York, Bowker, 2nd ed., 1983)
 Associations' Publications in Print (New York, Bowker, annually) ■
 Alternatives in Print (New York, Neal-Schuman Publishers, 6th ed., 1979)

Section 1b: National bibliographic records, U.S., current

 Publishers Weekly (AA477)
*Weekly Record (see AA477) 1983 issues
*American Book Publishing Record (BPR), monthly (AA463) 1983 issues
*American Book Publishing Record (BPR), cumulative, annual (AA464/465) 1982
*American Book Publishing Record Cumulative 1950-1977 (2AA58)
*American Book Publishing Record Cumulative 1876-1949 (2AA57)
 Reader's Adviser (AA339, 1AA68)

Section 1c: National bibliographic records, U.S., current

*Cumulative Book Index (AA461, AA468) 1983 issues
*Vertical File Index (AA479) 1983 issues

Section 2a: National bibliographic records, U.S., retrospective

*United States Catalog (AA460, see also AA461) 4th ed., 1928
*American Catalogue of Books (AA459) 1880-1911 or reprints
*Kelly: American Catalogue of Books (AA457) 1866-71 or reprints
*Roorbach: Bibliotheca Americana (AA456) 1852-61 or reprints

Section 2b: National bibliographic records, U.S., retrospective

*Sabin: Dictionary of Books Relating to America (AA451) 1868-1936 or reprints
 Molnar: Author-Title Index to Sabin's Dictionary (1AA96)
*Evans: American Bibliography (AA445/446/447/449/450) 1903-59 or reprints
 Shipton and Mooney: National Index of American Imprints (AA448)
*Shaw and Shoemaker: American Bibliography (AA453) 1958-66
*Checklist of American Imprints (AA454/455, 2AA60) 1964+

Section 3: Search strategy and review

Section 4: National library catalog and union list

 Library of Congress/National Union Catalog "author lists" 1942-1957 (AA92/93/94)
 National Union Catalog 1952-1955 Imprints (see AA94/95)
*National Union Catalog "author lists" 1958[1956]-1982 (AA94/95)
*National Union Catalog Pre-1956 Imprints (Mansell) (AA96, 1AA22, 2AA9)
 National Union Catalog 1956-1967 (Rowman and Littlefield) (AA97)
*Subject Catalog (Library of Congress catalogs) (AA99, 2AA11)
 Monographic Series (Library of Congress catalogs) (1AA21)
 National Union Catalog Register of Additional Locations (AA98, 2AA10)
 National Union Catalog. Books (Washington, D.C., Library of Congress, 1983+; on microfiche)
 National Union Catalog. U.S. Books (Washington, D.C., Library of Congress, 1983+; on microfiche)
 Music, Books on Music, and Sound Recordings (Library of Congress catalogs) (BH54/55)
 National Union Catalog. Audiovisual Materials (Washington, D.C., Library of Congress, 1983+; on micro-
    fiche)
 Audiovisual Materials (Library of Congress catalogs) 1953-1982 (BG116/117, 2AA51)
 National Union Catalog. Cartographic Materials (Washington, D.C., Library of Congress, 1983+; on micro-
    fiche)
 National Union Catalog of Manuscript Collections (DB39)
 National Register of Microform Masters (AA123, 1AA32)
 Catalog of Copyright Entries (AA478, 2AA63)

Section 5: Bibliographic sources for serials--current lists

*Ulrich's International Periodicals Directory (AE10) 21st ed., 1982 ■
 Ulrich's Quarterly (1AE4) ■
*Irregular Serials and Annuals (AE8) 8th ed., 1983 ■
 Sources of Serials (1AE3) ■
*Standard Periodical Directory (AE29) 8th ed., 1983-84
*Ayer Directory of Publications (AE24) 1983
 Editor and Publisher International Yearbook (AE25)
 Working Press of the Nation (AE30)
*International Directory of Little Magazines and Small Presses (AE5, 1AE2) 18th ed., 1982-83

Section 6: Bibliographic sources for serials--union lists

*Union List of Serials (AE133) 3rd ed., 1965
*New Serial Titles (AE134) 1982 issues
 New Serial Titles Classed Subject Arrangement (AE135)
*New Serial Titles 1950-70, Subject Guide (1AE34) 1975
*Gregory: American Newspapers ... a Union List (AF16) 1937 or reprints
*Brigham: History and Bibliography of American Newspapers (AF19) 1947 or reprints
*Newspapers in Microform (AF10, AF25/26, 2AF1, 2AF5)

Section 7: Indexes to serials--indexing services

*Readers' Guide to Periodical Literature (AE169) 1983 issues
 Abridged Readers' Guide (AE170)
*Humanities Index (AE172) 1983 issues
*Social Sciences Index (AE173) 1983 issue
 Social Sciences and Humanities Index/International Index (AE171)
 Applied Science and Technology Index (EA80)
 General Science Index (1EA11)
 Education Index (CB83)
 Art Index (BE31)
 Library Literature (AB10)
*Public Affairs Information Service Bulletin (PAIS) (CA34, 1CA12, 2CA9) 1983 issues ■
 Alternative Press Index (AE177)
 Access (1AE43)
 New Periodicals Index (1AE49)
 Popular Periodical Index (1AE50)
 Index to Periodical Articles by and about Blacks (AE187, 1AE47)
 Magazine Index (2AE23) ■
 Index to Little Magazines (AE184)
 Index to Commonwealth Little Magazines (AE185)
 Information Science Abstracts (AB13) ■
 Library and Information Science Abstracts (AB11/12) ■
*Poole's Index to Periodical Literature (AE164/165/166) 1891-1908 or reprints
*Nineteenth Century Readers' Guide (AE168) 1944
 Annual Magazine Subject Index (AE180/181)
 Annual Literary Index (AE178)
 Annual Library Index (AE179)
 Catholic Periodical Index (AE182/183)
 Subject Index to Periodicals (AE174)
 British Humanities Index (AE175)
*New York Times Index (AF67/68, 1AF13/14) 1983 issues
 Christian Science Monitor, Subject Index (AF64)
 National Observer Index (AF65)
 Wall Street Journal, Index (AF70)
 Newspaper Index (Bell and Howell) (AF69, 1AF15/16/17/18)
 National Newspaper Index (2AF13) ■
 Index to the [London] Times (AF76/77, 1AF23, 2AF15)

Section 8: Bibliographic sources for government publications

*Monthly Catalog of U.S. Government Publications (AG25, 1AG10, 2AG9) 1983 issues ■
 United States Government Manual (CJ72)
 Schmeckebier and Eastin: Government Publications and Their Use (AG13)
 Morehead: Introduction to United States Public Documents (1AG5)
 Boyd and Rips: United States Government Publications (AG9)
 Cumulative Subject Index to the Monthly Catalog (AG26)
 Publications Reference File (Washington, D.C., U.S. Government Printing Office)
 GPO Subject Bibliographies (2AG10)
 U.S. Government Books (Washington, D.C., U.S. Government Printing Office)
 New Books (Washington, D.C., U.S. Government Printing Office)
*Catalog of the Public Documents (Document Catalog) (AG24) 1896-1945
*Poore: Descriptive Catalogue of the Government Publications (AG20) 1885 or reprints

*Ames: Comprehensive Index to the Publications (AG21) 1905 or reprints
 Greely: Public Documents of the First Fourteen Congresses (AG19)
 Checklist of United States Public Documents (AG23)
 Numerical Lists and Schedule of Volumes (AG27)
 CIS U.S. Serial Set Index (1AG7)
*Index to U.S. Government Periodicals (1AE48) 1982 issues
*Congressional Information Service, Index to Publications (CIS Index) (CJ83/84, 1CJ56, 2CJ48) 1982 an-
     nual volumes
*Newsome: New Guide to Popular Government Publications (2AG5)
 Leidy: A Popular Guide to Government Publications (AG11, 1AG4)
 Jackson: Subject Guide to Major U.S. Government Publications (AG10)
*Monthly Checklist of State Publications (AG47) 1983 issues
 Parish: State Government Reference Publications (1AG14)

Section 9: Bibliographic sources for dissertations and theses

*Dissertation Abstracts International (AH14/15, 1AH5) 1983 issues ■
*American Doctoral Dissertations (AH13) 1980-81 volume
*Comprehensive Dissertation Index (AH10) 1973+ ■
 Lum: Asians in America; A Bibliography.... (CC139, 1CC150)
 Reynolds: A Guide to Theses and Dissertations (1AH4)
*Master Abstracts (AH18) 1983 issues
 Black: Guide to Lists of Master's Theses (AH17)

Section 10: Bibliographic records for other countries--Great Britain, France, Germany

*British Books in Print (AA673) 1983
 British Paperbacks in Print (see AA674)
 Bookseller (AA671)
 Whitaker's Books of the Month and Books to Come (AA670)
*Whitaker's Cumulative Book List (AA668/669) 1982
*British National Bibliography (AA667, 1AA125) 1983 issues
 English Catalogue of Books (AA666)
 Lowndes: Bibliographer's Manual of English Literature (AA639)
 Watt: Bibliotheca Britannica (AA640)
*Pollard and Redgrave: Short-Title Catalogue (AA647, 1AA123) 1st ed., 1926; 2nd ed., 1976-
*Wing: Short-Title Catalogue (AA660/661) 1st ed., 1945-51; 2nd ed., 1972-
*British Library, General Catalogue of Printed Books (AA100/101, 1AA23, 2AA12/13) 1959+
 Great Britain. Stationery Office. Catalogue of Government Publications (AE87/88/89)
 Répertoire des Livres de Langue Française Disponibles (AA618)
 Les Livres Disponibles (1AA118, see AA614)
 Bibliographie de la France (AA612/613, 1AA117)
 Livres-hebdo (2AA74)
*Les Livres de l'Année--Biblio (AA616/617) 1979
 Librairie Française, Catalogue Général (AA615)
*Biblio (AA611) 1969
 Quérard: La France Littéraire.... XVIIIe et XIXe siècles (AA606)
 Quérard: La Littérature Française Contemporaine, 1827-49 (AA607)
*Catalogue Général de la Librairie Française (Lorenz) (AA609) 1867-1945 or reprints
 Vicaire: Manuel de l'Amateur de Livres du XIXe siècle (AA610)
*Bibliothèque Nationale, Catalogue Général ... Auteurs (AA105/106, AA596, 1AA24) 1900+
 Deutsche Bibliographie (AA632, 1AA121) 1983 issues
*Deutsche Bibliographie; Halbjahres-Verzeichnis (AA633) 1982
*Deutsche Bibliographie; Fuenfjahres-Verzeichnis (AA634) 1956-60
 Deutsche Nationalbibliographie (AA627, 1AA120)
 Jahresverzeichnis der Verlagsschriften (AA630, see AA629)
 Deutsches Buecherverzeichnis (AA631, 2AA77)
*Heinsius: Allgemeines Buecher-Lexikon (AA622)
*Kayser: Vollstaendiges Buecher-Lexikon (AA623) 1834-1911 or reprints
*Hinrichs: Fuenfjahres-Katalog (AA624)
*Gesamtverzeichnis des Deutschsprachigen Schrifttums (GV) (1AA119, 2AA79/80)
 Verzeichnis Lieferbarer Buecher (AA636)

<u>Section 11:   Review of Part I</u>

<u>Section 12:   Dictionaries</u>

*Webster's Third New International Dictionary (AD10) © 1961 or later
  6,000 Words (1AD16)
*Webster's New International Dictionary (2nd ed.) (AD9) © 1934 or later
*Funk and Wagnalls New Standard Dictionary (AD7) © 1964 or later
*Random House Dictionary (AD8) © 1966 or later
  Century Dictionary and Cyclopedia (AD5)
*Oxford English Dictionary (AD25/26/27, 1AD5) 1888-1933 or reprints
*Dictionary of American English (Craigie) (AD105) 1936-44
  American College Dictionary (AD11)
  American Heritage Dictionary, standard or new college ed. (2nd) (AD12)
  Doubleday Dictionary (1AD2)
  Funk and Wagnalls Standard College Dictionary (AD13)
  Random House College Dictionary (AD14, 1AD3)
  Scribner-Bantam English Dictionary (1AD4)
  Thorndike-Barnhart Comprehensive Desk Dictionary (AD15)
  Webster's [9th] New Collegiate Dictionary (AD16)
  Webster's New World Dictionary, 2nd college ed. (AD17)
  New Century Dictionary (AD6)
  Shorter Oxford English Dictionary (AD28)
  Cassell's English Dictionary (AD29)
  Concise Oxford Dictionary (AD30, 1AD6)
  Kister: Dictionary Buying Guide (1AD1)

<u>Section 13:   Supplementary language sources</u>

*Fowler: Dictionary of Modern English Usage (AD58) 2nd ed., 1965; reprint ed., 1983
*Evans: Dictionary of Contemporary American Usage (AD56) 1957
  Nicholson: Dictionary of American English Usage (AD62)
  Horwill: Dictionary of Modern American Usage (AD61)
*Follett: Modern American Usage (AD57) 1966
  Morris and Morris: Harper Dictionary of Contemporary Usage (1AD14)
*Webster's New Dictionary of Synonyms (AD102) © 1978
*Roget's International Thesaurus (AD100) 4th ed., 1977 or (AD99) 1965
*Roget's II: The New Thesaurus (New York, Houghton Mifflin, 1980)
  Webster's Collegiate Thesaurus (1AD21)
*Wentworth and Flexner: Dictionary of American Slang (AD93, 1AD18) 2nd sup. ed., 1975
*Berrey and Van den Bark: American Thesaurus of Slang (AD87) 2nd ed., 1953
*Partridge: Dictionary of Slang and Unconventional English (AD91) 7th ed., 1970
*Mathews: Dictionary of Americanisms (AD106) 1951
*De Sola: Abbreviations Dictionary (AD34, 1AD7) 6th ed., 1981
*Acronyms, Initialisms, and Abbreviations Dictionary (AD36, 1AD8) 8th ed., 1983-84
  Bernstein's Reverse Dictionary (1AD19)
*NBC Handbook of Pronunciation (AD73) 3rd ed., 1964
  Kenyon and Knott: Pronouncing Dictionary of American English (AD76)
*Wood's Unabridged Rhyming Dictionary (AD84) 1943

<u>Section 14a: Encyclopedias</u>

*Encyclopedia Americana (AC1) © 1983
*New Encyclopaedia Britannica, 15th ed. (AC3) © 1983
*Collier's Encyclopedia (AC5) © 1983
*Academic American Encyclopedia (2AC1) © 1980 ■
*New Columbia Encyclopedia (AC6, 1AC2) 4th ed., 1975
*Lincoln Library (AC7) © 1982
  Random House Encyclopedia (1AC3)
*Compton's Pictured Encyclopedia (AC17) © 1983

*World Book Encyclopedia (AC20) © 1983
*Chambers's Encyclopaedia (AC4) © 1968
 Everyman's Encyclopedia (London, Dent, 1978)
 New Caxton Encyclopedia (London, Caxton, 1979)
 Subscription Books Bulletin Reviews (AA400)
 Reference and Subscription Books Reviews (AA401)
*Encyclopedia Buying Guide (1AC4) 3rd ed., 1981
 Britannica Junior (AC16)
 Merit Students Encyclopedia (AC19)

Section 14b: Foreign language encyclopedias

*Encyclopaedia Universalis, 1968- (AC34, 1AC8)
*La Grande Encyclopédie, 1971- (AC38, 1AC7)
 La Grande Encyclopédie, 1886-1902 (AC37)
 Larousse: Grande Dictionnaire Universel du XIXe siècle (AC39)
*Brockhaus Enzyklopaedie, 17th ed., 1966- (AC43, 1AC9)
*Meyers Enzyklopaedisches Lexikon, 9th ed., 1971- (AC47, 1AC10, 2AC4)
 Der Grosse Brockhaus (AC42)
*Enciclopedia Italiana di Scienze, Lettere ed Arti (AC57) 1929-37
*Enciclopedia Universal Ilustrada Europeo-Americana (Espasa) (AC82, 2AC11) 1907?-33
*Bol'shaia Sovetskaia Entsiklopediia, 3rd ed. (AC72, 1AC12, 2AC9) 1970-
*Great Soviet Encyclopedia (AC73, 1AC13, 2AC10) 1973-

Section 15: Yearbooks and almanacs

*Americana Annual (AC11) 1983
*Britannica Book of the Year (AC12) 1983
*Collier's Year Book (AC14) any recent edition
*World Book Year Book (see AC20) 1983
 Chambers's Encyclopaedia Yearbook (AC13a)
*Annual Register of World Events (DA50) 1982
 Appleton's Annual Cyclopaedia (AC10)
*Facts on File (DA51, 1DA16) 1982 and 1983 issues ∎
 News Dictionary (Facts on File, annually)
*Keesing's Contemporary Archives (DA52) 1982 issues
*World Almanac (CG75) 1983
*Information Please Almanac (CG66) 1983
 Reader's Digest Almanac (CG67)
 People's Almanac (1CG15, 2CG17)
 Negro Almanac (1CC142)
 Women's Action Almanac: A Complete Resource Guide (2CC168)
 Whitaker's Almanac (CG130)
 Canadian Almanac and Directory (CG98)
*Statesman's Year-Book (CG45) 1982-83
 Europa Year Book (CJ62)
 Municipal Year Book (CJ118a, 1CJ76)
 Book of the States (CJ118)
 Britannica Yearbook of Science and the Future (EA43)
 Science Year; the World Book Science Annual (EA44)
 Yearbook of Agriculture (EL50)

Section 16: Yearbook supplements: statistics

*Statistical Abstract of the United States (CG69) 1982/83
*Historical Statistics of the United States (CG71, 1CG18) 1975
*County and City Data Book (CG70, 1CG17) 10th ed., 1983
 State and Metropolitan Area Databook (2CG19)
 Statistical Abstract, India (CG141)
*Statistical Yearbook (of the United Nations) (CG40) 1979/80

Demographic Yearbook (CG35, 1CG2)
*Statistics Sources (CG52, 1CG9, 2CG13) 7th ed., 1982
 Guide to U.S. Government Statistics (CG57)
 Bureau of the Census Catalog of Publications (CG59, 1CG12/12a, 2CG21)
 Directory of Federal Statistics for Local Areas; a Guide to Sources (CG77, 1CG21)
 Directory of Federal Statistics for States; a Guide to Sources (CG78)
 American Statistics Index (CG76, 1CG19)

Section 17: Handbooks and manuals

*Kane: Famous First Facts (New York, Wilson, 4th ed., 1981)
*Guinness Book of World Records (New York, Sterling, 21st ed., 1983)
*Benét: The Reader's Encyclopedia (BD32) 2nd ed., 1965
*Brewer's Dictionary of Phrase and Fable (BD67) 1981
 Walsh: Handy Book of Curious Information (BD73)
 Ackermann: Popular Fallacies (BD66)
*Bartlett: Familiar Quotations (BD98, 2BD22) 15th ed., 1980
*Stevenson: Home Book of Quotations (BD106) 10th ed., 1967
*Evans: Dictionary of Quotations (BD101) 1968
*Hatch: American Book of Days (2CF12) 3rd ed., 1978
*Gregory: Anniversaries and Holidays (1CF15, see CF49) 4th ed., 1983
 Chases' Calendar of Annual Events (Flint, Michigan, Apple Tree Press, annual)
*Steinberg: Historical Tables (DA47, 2DA7) 10th ed., 1979
*Langer: New Illustrated Encyclopedia of World History (DA42, 1DA15) 6th ed., 1975
*Everyman's Dictionary of Dates (DA36) 6th ed., 1971
 New Emily Post's Etiquette (see CF60)
 McCaffree and Innis: Protocol: The Complete Handbook (1CF16)
 Menke's Encyclopedia of Sports (CB230, 1CB69)
 Robert's Rules of Order (CJ231)
 Scott's Standard Postage Stamp Catalogue (BF118)
 Occupational Outlook Handbook (CH498)
 How-to-Do-It Books: A Selected Guide (CB219)
 Nueckel: Selected Guide to Make-It, Fix-It, Do-It Yourself Books (CB221)

Section 18: Directories

*Encyclopedia of Associations (CA67) 17th ed., 1983 ■
*Foundation Directory (CA56/57, CB197, 1CA29, 2CA28) 8th ed., 1981 ■
*Research Centers Directory (CA68/69, EA180/181) 8th ed., 1983
*Yearbook of International Organizations (CK214) 1983/84
*Guide to American Directories (CH140, 1CH64, 2CH57) 11th ed., 1982
 Directory of Directories (2CH56)

Section 19: Biographical sources: universal

*Webster's Biographical Dictionary (AJ31) © 1980
*Chambers's Biographical Dictionary (AJ19) © 1968 or © 1969
 Lippincott's Biographical Dictionary (AJ29)
*New Century Cyclopedia of Names (AJ24) 1954
 Webster's Dictionary of Proper Names (BD93)
*International Who's Who (AJ35) 1983-84
 Who's Who in the World (AJ38)
*Current Biography (AJ34) 1982 issues
 New York Times Biographical Service (AJ37, 1AJ9)
 New York Times Obituaries Index (AJ25, 2AJ12)
 Annual Obituary (New York, St. Martin's Press, 1982)
 Pseudonyms and Nicknames Dictionary (2AA18)

Section 20: Biographical sources: national and subject

*Who's Who in America (AJ57) 1982-83 ■
*Marquis Who's Who Publications: Index to All Books (1AJ4)
 Who's Who Among Black Americans (1AJ27)
*Who Was Who in America (AJ51/52, 1AJ23) 1942+
*Who's Who (AJ178) 1983
*Who Was Who (AJ176) 1929+
 Who's Who in France (AJ152)
*Dictionary of National Biography (AJ165, AJ167) 1908+
*Concise Dictionary of National Biography (AJ166) 1953-61
*Dictionary of American Biography (AJ41, 1AJ16) 1928+ or reprints
 Concise Dictionary of American Biography (AJ42, 1AJ17)
 Appleton's Cyclopaedia of American Biography (AJ40)
*National Cyclopaedia of American Biography (AJ43/44, 1AJ20, 2AJ16) 1892+
 Van Doren and McHenry: Webster's American Biographies (1AJ21)
 Australian Dictionary of Biography (AJ79, 1AJ33)
*American Men and Women of Science (EA222, CA93, 1EA38, 1CA42) 15th ed., 1982 ■
*Directory of American Scholars (AJ63, 1AJ25, 2AJ15) 8th ed., 1982
 Who's Who in American Art (BE111)
 Dictionary of American Library Biography (1AB13)
 Biographical Directory of Librarians in the United States and Canada (AB88)
 Who's Who in Librarianship and Information Science (AB93)
 Who's Who in Library and Information Services (Chicago, American Library Association, 1982)
*Biography Index (AJ4) 1979-83 issues
*Biography and Genealogy Master Index (Detroit, Gale Research, 2nd ed., 1980) ■
 Performing Arts Biography Master Index (Detroit, Gale Research, 2nd ed., 1981)
 Biography Almanac (Detroit, Gale Research, 1981)
 Bio-Base (Detroit, Gale Research, 2nd ed., 1981) ■

Section 21: Geographical sources: gazetteers and guidebooks

Note: the first half of this section deals with the approach to geography as a subject area, and the
use of Sheehy, Wright and Platt, and Brewer, plus other basic bibliographic sources from Part I of this
manual, to locate bibliographies, dictionaries, encyclopedias, yearbooks, handbooks, directories, etc., in
that subject area. Many geographical titles other than those listed below are mentioned in the answers
as examples of these types of reference sources; the annotations in Sheehy, or in Wright and Platt or
Brewer, are sufficient for use of this manual.

*Wright and Platt: Aids to Geographical Research (CL5) 2nd ed., 1947
*Brewer: The Literature of Geography (CL1, 2CL1) 1973
*Columbia Lippincott Gazetteer of the World (CL56) 1962
*Webster's New Geographical Dictionary (CL61) © 1980
 United States Board on Geographical Names, publications (CL118/119)
 Permanent Committee on Geographical Names for British Official Use, publications (CL115/116/117)
 Stewart: American Place Names (CL126)
 Sealock, Sealock and Powell: Bibliography of Place-Name Literature (see CL120)
 Neal: Reference Guide for Travellers (CL267)
 Nueckel: Selected Guide to Travel Books (1CL68)
 Heise, Jon O. and Dennis O'Reilly: The Travel Book: Guide to the Travel Guides (New York, Bowker,
      1981)
*California (American Guide Series) (see CL268) 1967
 Post, Joyce A. and Jeremiah B.: Travel in the United States: A Guide to Information Sources (Detroit,
      Gale Research, 1981)
*Hotel and Motel Red Book (CL270) 1983-84
 Official Guide of the Railways (CL272)

Section 22: Atlases

*Rand McNally Cosmopolitan World Atlas (CL219, 2CL39) 1971, 1978, or 1981
 Rand McNally New International Atlas (2CL37)

National Geographic Atlas of the World (CL211, 1CL54)
*Hammond Medallion World Atlas (CL207, 2CL35) 1971, 1979, or 1982
*Goode's World Atlas (CL204) 15th ed., 1978
*Rand McNally Commercial Atlas and Marketing Guide (CL218a) 1983
*Times Atlas of the World, Comprehensive Edition (CL201, 1CL53, 2CL40) 1983
*Times Index-Gazetteer of the World (CL57) 1965 or 1966
Lock: Modern Maps and Atlases (CL166, see 1CL2)
Alexander: Guide to Atlases (CL165, 1CL45)
International Maps and Atlases in Print (1CL47)
Kister: Atlas Buying Guide (Phoenix, Arizona, Oryx Press, 1984)

Section 23: Review of Part II

PREFACE

The origin and development of this self-study manual has been recounted by Ira Harris in the Preface of the 1973 (first) edition. As stated there, it began in 1967 at the Graduate School of Library Studies, University of Hawaii, with the idea that expertise with bibliographic and information sources might be taught on a self-study, self-paced basis by leading students to the sources themselves instead of by the then more common approach of presentation and discussion of the sources in class.

Some preliminary units of a self-study approach were written and tested; the results were promising enough that, under a grant from the Grolier Foundation, units for an entire first semester basic reference course were subsequently written and tested. The testing, as discussed in the Harris Preface (1973), showed that the students who used the self-study approach did at least as well as those who were more conventionally taught, and student response was consistently enthusiastic. The entire sequence, as written by Margaret Taylor, was published by Scarecrow Press in a "preliminary" edition in 1971, and the manual has since been used in a variety of ways in library education programs. A revised edition, incorporating suggestions from users and up-dating the material, was published in 1973, as the "first" edition. A second edition came out in 1981, with Ronald Powell as co-author.

As with the second edition, our main concern with this revision for the third edition has been to bring the material up to date, rather than to make structural or conceptual changes in the manual itself or in the types and titles of sources included. Information about the sources and the answers to the search questions have been up-dated to the editions (or issues in the case of on-going publications) available as of December 1983. A few titles published since 1980 seemed to be useful additions. In the main, however, we were guided by the principle that the manual should consist of a limited, selective list of titles which could be examined in some detail and which could be expanded as a result of the student's increasing ability to compare titles and to use resources such as Sheehy's Guide to Reference Books. The number of starred titles, those which are considered in the manual in detail, is the same as in the second, 1981 edition (166). Again, we increased our inclusion of supplementary titles in this edition (361 as compared with 332 in 1981).

A problem which we faced with this revision was how to handle the online, computer-accessed versions of reference/information sources. The nature of this manual has been that of a "hands-on" approach to reference sources rather than a descriptive text. While this approach is feasible for printed sources, the machine-accessed, constantly-changing nature of the online versions precludes their treatment in the same way. We concluded that the best that we could do at this stage to acknowledge the increasing availability and importance of these online versions was to note, in the List of Sources, those titles which, so far as we could determine in May 1984, were available online, and to comment upon them in the Introduction.

It would have been impossible for us to have accomplished the task of this revision without the help of other people and the resources of libraries. Our primary resources were the libraries of The University of Michigan in Ann Arbor; we also used the Ann Arbor Public Library, some of the school libraries of the Ann Arbor Public Schools, and the Center of Educational Resources of Eastern Michigan University in Ypsilanti.

Specifically, we would like to thank our research assistants, who carried much of the tedious but necessary burden of library checking, locating materials, etc.: Kathy Tezla, Barbara J. Wilson, Margaret M. Benson, Anne Baker Jones, and Patricia E. Sumner. We would also like to acknowledge the continuing suggestions and support from our students at the School of Library Science of The University of Michigan.

We believe that the self-study approach provided by this manual offers substantial benefits in the teaching of reference/information sources, whether used in library science education programs, or in continuing education and staff development. The manual leads students to direct contact with the sources themselves, and provides reinforcement and feedback at the point of contact. It allows students to proceed at their own pace. It can free class time for discussion of other aspects of reference services and communications skills. We hope that it will continue to be a useful resource for our colleagues.

Margaret T. Taylor
Ronald R. Powell

June 1984

INTRODUCTION

Information for students using the manual

With this self-study manual, you will be guided
through a careful examination of a list of specific
reference sources. The manual consists of a
long series of questions relating to the examination, use, and comparison of these sources. The
question pages allow you enough room to jot down
your answers as you proceed. The answers to
these questions are given on separate pages
following the questions, so that you may check
your own answers to determine whether you are
finding the correct information and using the
sources correctly. The questions are designed
so that the correct answer to a question often
depends upon an understanding of the answers
to preceding questions; therefore, you should
check your answers frequently.

Since you have been given the answers,
you may be tempted to go immediately from the
question to the answer without trying to work
out the answer for yourself. You could learn
something from doing only this. The point of
this type of exercise, however, is not to give
you another textbook to read, or another annotated list of reference sources, but to provide
a method by which you can seek out the information yourself. The questions and answers
are set up to give you information about the
sources (bibliographic details, arrangement,
scope, etc.). More importantly, the questions
are also set up to help you learn a technique
of examination and evaluation of reference
sources which you can use for some actual
experience in search strategy, in using these
sources in the most efficient way. Both of
these skills are necessary for effective library
research/reference work, and you can gain
experience in these skills through working out
the answers to the questions in this manual.

As part of this learning process, it will be
necessary for you to refer to and use the actual
reference sources in order to work out the
answers to the questions; therefore you must
plan to work with the self-study manual in a
library where you have access to these sources.
Preceding this introduction is a "List of
Sources," giving all of the titles considered
in the manual. You should have access to
the starred titles. It is helpful but not essential to have access to the other titles.
The answers in the manual are keyed to the
editions noted in the source list. If possible,
and particularly if you are inexperienced, you
should work with those editions. If it is necessary to work with other editions, you must expect some variations from the answers in the
manual.

Also used extensively throughout this
manual as resource guides are Guide to Reference Books, edited by Eugene Sheehy (Chicago,
American Library Association, 1976, and Supplements, 1980 and 1982) and ALA Glossary of Library and Information Science (Chicago, American Library Association, 1983). You should have
access to these titles as you do the questions.

The manual is set up to be worked in sequence; each section is dependent upon information established in preceding sections. You
should start at the beginning and work through
each section in order. If you omit sections or
parts of sections, you must keep in mind that
there may be references in following sections,
particularly in the review questions and review
sections, to the material you have omitted.

It is not necessary to work through the
entire sequence at one time, of course. The
questions have been divided into several sections, with an average estimated time of two to
five hours each. You should try to work
through as much of each section at one time
as is possible.

One of the purposes of the self-study approach is to allow you to cover this material at
your own pace. Previous experiences in libraries or with the material, plus differences in
reading speed and ability to integrate details,
all contribute to the time variation among students. This manual has been set up to accom-
modate, so far as possible, a variety of learning and background differences, and it therefore includes much elementary material as well
as some repetition of material. If some of the
sequence seems unnecessarily simplified or
repetitive to you, you may want to make some
adjustments in your use of the material to fit
your own specific needs and background. You
may find that you can skip over some of the
questions quickly because the answers will seem
obvious to you; you may find that you can work
out some of the questions in your head rather
than referring back to the sources; you may
find that you do not need much help in determining bibliographic details, scope, arrangement, etc., and that the search and review
type questions will be most helpful to you. A
few suggestions have been made in the manual
itself about skipping and reviewing; otherwise

it is up to you to judge to what extent you can modify it for your own purposes. Keep in mind the basic importance of actual use and handling of the sources.

You will probably find that your progress will seem slower at the beginning, until you become familiar with the method and the material. Also keep in mind the possibility that the slower you are in working your way through the manual, the more you may be in need of--and therefore the more you may benefit from--this detailed, repetitive, reinforced type of guidance.

If you are working through this manual on your own, rather than as a course assignment under the direction of an instructor, you may find it helpful to do some preliminary reading on library reference services and information sources, such as are found in Introduction to Reference Work (vols. 1-2) by William A. Katz (New York, McGraw Hill, 4th ed., 1982) and/or Fundamental Reference Sources by Frances N. Cheney and Wiley J. Williams (Chicago, American Library Association, 2nd ed., 1980). Both Katz and Cheney include references to further reading, and both list other bibliographies of reference materials, similar to Sheehy, which you will find useful to explore to extend your knowledge of available sources beyond the scope of this manual.

An ever-increasing number of these printed sources are becoming available in online, computer-accessed versions. Use of the online versions of these sources is discussed in the various texts and readings on reference sources/services as noted above. Those sources in this manual which were determined to be available in online versions as of May 1984 have been designated with a ∎ in the main list of sources preceding this Introduction.

Information for instructors

This self-study manual is designed to be self-explanatory and self-contained when used in conjunction with the sources to be examined and with such aids as Sheehy's Guide to Reference Books and the ALA Glossary. Therefore it is possible for the manual to be used without any additional textbook assignments or classroom sessions, and is itself sufficient for purposes of teaching students (library school or otherwise) about the availability, examination, and use of basic reference materials. It is expected, however, that its use in a library school reference course would be as a teaching resource or tool to cover certain aspects of the course and to be used with other resources such as readings, lectures, discussions, projects, written assignments, case studies, etc. The manual does not attempt to cover such areas as reference services, the reference interview/encounter, selection and acquisition of reference sources, compiling bib-

liographies, etc. It is hoped that the use of the manual, through the self-study approach, can free more class time to cover these areas, as well as present the instructor and students with more options in handling the presentation and scheduling of course material.

The specific titles covered in this manual are not meant to suggest a definitive list. Some of the titles were obvious choices; others were included because they lent themselves well to this type of treatment, because they were useful in pointing out an arrangement common to several other sources, because they appeared to be generally available, etc. Such a specific list of titles will always be at some variance with course requirements. The nature of the programmed self-study approach requires that the student follow the program with a minimum of deviations, but some flexibility is possible and some suggestions are given here for adapting the manual to course requirements.

Preceding this Introduction is a List of Sources which includes all of the titles touched upon in the manual. The starred titles are covered in detail; the remainder are noted more briefly, in a supplementary or comparative manner, usually with only a single question or a single reference in the answer. It is not necessary for the student to examine these unstarred titles for purposes of the sequence of the manual; and any or all of them could be omitted.

On the other hand, additional supplementary titles can also be presented, either in a class session, or by encouraging the students to examine such titles on their own, using the technique developed in the self-study manual.

Some entire sections could be omitted if necessary. Sections 8 (government publications), 9 (dissertations), 10 (foreign bibliographic sources), 14b (foreign encyclopedias), and possibly 4 (national library catalog and union list) could be dropped with the least disruption of the sequence itself. In lieu of completely omitting a section, the students could be told to read the manual instead of working it for a particular section. Since the manual is set up on a self-study basis, the student could return later, after the course or while on the job, to work through any omitted sections.

If sections or titles are omitted, the student and instructor should keep in mind that there may be references to the omitted material in following sections, particularly in the review questions and review sections.

The answers in the manual are keyed to editions of sources as noted in the List of Sources. Preferably, students should have those editions to work with. If it is necessary for them to work with other editions, they should be warned of possible variations from the answers given in the manual. It is especially important that students have access to the correct editions in the early sections of the manual; as they progress, they should gain enough knowledge to make judgments on variations in the editions.

As discussed in the Preface, there are no exercises in this manual in the use of online, computer-accessed versions of these sources. Those which have been determined to be available online, as of May 1984, have been noted with a ■ in the List of Sources. Students should be made aware of the increasing availability and importance of such online versions through other aspects of the course in which this manual is used.

Since this manual was written so that it could be used by a completely inexperienced library school student, or by a student working alone, it must necessarily include a lot of material which may seem elementary or redundant to some library school students (such as: definition of terms, determination of titles and editions, etc.). It may be necessary for the instructor to emphasize this point in class and to encourage the more experienced students to use the material selectively. It may also be necessary to suggest that students ask for help if they feel they are working too slowly or if they need clarification on any aspects of the manual.

A few suggestions are given in the manual on compiling charts for review purposes. Otherwise, note-taking on the sources may be encouraged or discouraged by the individual instructor as desired. The manual does include some repetition/reinforcement/review material but not enough to provide instant recall on all details for most students.

This edition of the manual has been prepared with pages perforated so they may be easily removed, and with pre-punched holes so the pages may be put into a notebook, to provide students with some flexibility in their use of the manual.

PART I

BASIC BIBLIOGRAPHIC SOURCES

Section 1a

NATIONAL BIBLIOGRAPHIC RECORDS (U.S.)--CURRENT

Questions #1a/1--1a/67

With this first set of problems, you will begin your examination of the major sources which make up the current and retrospective bibliographic record of publications for the United States. While doing the questions and examining the sources, you should keep in mind the extent of the overall bibliographic coverage of U.S. publications, and the aims and objectives of bibliographic control itself.

1a-1 First of all, how would you define "a bibliography" or "a bibliographic source"?

1a-2 From this definition, and from what you may know or may have read about bibliographies, try to think of as many reasons as you can why you--either as a librarian or as a user of a library, as a user of bibliographic sources--would turn to these sources for information. What would some of these information needs be?

Before you begin examining the sources in this unit, you may find it helpful to read the brief survey of current publishing practices which is included at the end of this section (Appendix A). Then, keeping in mind that survey, and keeping in mind the potential information needs from your answer to #1a-2, you should go on to examine carefully your first group of sources. Starting with the current sources, the first group to examine consists of:

Publishers' Trade List Annual (PTLA) (AA472)
Books in Print (BIP) (AA473)
Subject Guide to Books in Print (AA474)

You should first locate the titles, then if possible sit down with or near them so that you can look at them together. The letter and number symbols following each title are item references to Sheehy's Guide to Reference Books (9th edition and supplements).

1a-3 Take Publishers' Trade List Annual (PTLA) first, and note the basic physical characteristics about the set itself. For example, how many volumes does it contain?

1a-4 It was already mentioned in the brief survey of publishing (see Appendix A) that each individual publisher is likely to issue, probably annually, a catalog or list of the firm's publications which are still "in print." What does "in print" mean?

1a-5 These catalogs are themselves available directly from the publisher. PTLA is, in fact, a collection of such catalogs. How often does PTLA come out (how often is it published)? (You can get this simply from the title of the set.)

3

1a-6   Who is the publisher of PTLA itself?

1a-7   How recent is the set you are looking at (what is its date of publication)?

1a-8   So far, then, you've established the basic bibliographic information about PTLA: its full title, its publisher, the fact that it comes out annually, the number of volumes, and which edition you are looking at. The next step in examining the source would usually be to determine the "scope" or content of the source. You have already established that PTLA is a collection of publishers' catalogs, but in addition you should find out such things as: what catalogs it includes, whether it has comprehensive coverage, whether it includes catalogs for all publishers in the United States, whether it includes catalogs for publishers other than in the United States. These are not easy problems to answer at this point, so begin by thinking: where might you look to find such information?

1a-9   Do any of the three possibilities listed for the answer to #1a-8 in fact give you an answer?

1a-10   Does PTLA contain a list of publishers whose catalogs are included?

1a-11   The next step is to determine the "arrangement" of the source. You have already established that PTLA is a collection of publishers' catalogs. How are these catalogs arranged? (In the set as a whole.)

1a-12   Is this single alphabetical arrangement of catalogs by publisher the only alphabetical listing in the set?

1a-13   Does the Index to Publishers tell you more than simply the names of the publishers?

1a-14   Can you find the catalog of Grune and Stratton, Inc.? Where is it located in PTLA?

1a-15   What about Quarterdeck Press of California?

1a-16   The University of California Press has published a book by Philip A. Munz called A Flora of Southern California. Is this still in print and if so, what is its price?

1a-17   Is a book titled Art of Southern Fiction still available from Southern Illinois University Press?

1a-18   The Walter H. Baker Company has published a collection of plays by Roger Cornish. Can you find out if it is still in print?

1a-19   Time-Life Books has published over the years several series of books, a series in this case be-
        ing a group of books with separate titles, and usually different authors, but on the same gen-
        eral topic, and with the same general physical format. One of the earliest of the Time-Life Books'
        series, beginning in 1968, was titled "Foods of the World." What are the titles and the authors
        of the first two books in this series?

1a-20   A book titled Imagination's Chamber by Alice Bellony-Rewald and Michael Peppiatt was published
        by the New York Graphic Society in 1982. What can you find out about the subject and the con-
        tents of this book?

1a-21   You established earlier (see #1a-11) that PTLA itself is arranged alphabetically by the name of
        the publisher, with special supplementary sections in the front. How are the items arranged
        within the catalogs themselves?

1a-22   Do most of the catalogs list books by subject?

1a-23   Thus far, then, you have been able to determine the arrangement (although not yet the scope)
        for PTLA. Can you make a brief, concise, succinct statement of the arrangement of PTLA?

1a-24   Using PTLA only, can you find out whether a book is in print if you know only its author and
        title? For example, if you knew only that the book Art of Southern Fiction was written by Fred-
        erick Hoffman, could you have found its in-print status and price as you did in #1a-17?

1a-25   What do you need to know about a book or publication in order to use PTLA?

1a-26   Therefore, what would you need to have in PTLA in order to answer #1a-24?

1a-27   Who is the publisher of BIP, how often is it published, what edition do you have, and how many
        volumes is it?

1a-28   What is BIP exactly? Is there any relationship between BIP and PTLA? Look at what Sheehy
        has to say about this, and then check it out in the source (BIP) itself. In BIP, look at the
        cover and title page, and at the introductory or prefatory material in the first volume.

1a-29   Has PTLA always had BIP to serve as an index? You will probably have to go to Sheehy for
        this one.

1a-30   What is the scope of BIP? Considering the sometime relationship between BIP and PTLA, can you establish the scope of BIP any more clearly than you could that of PTLA (see #1a-8 and #1a-9)?

1a-31   What is the arrangement of BIP?

1a-32   Look up Art of Southern Fiction by Frederick J. Hoffman in both sections (author and title) of BIP. Is it listed in both sections? Is the same information given in both sections, or does one section refer you to the other section for fuller information?

1a-33   What does "ISBN 0-809302683" refer to in the BIP entry for Art of Southern Fiction?

1a-34   The Better Homes and Gardens Books publishing company has published a number of comparatively inexpensive books on sewing and needlework. If you knew only this much about the publications, and did not know the authors, or the correct or specific titles, how would you find out what these books are and how much they cost, so that you could purchase them, or consider them for purchase?

1a-35   Is Glory and Lightning by Taylor Caldwell still in print? What is the publisher and price?

1a-36   Since you found it listed in BIP, would you then have to check as well in PTLA?

1a-37   Why, then, is it ever necessary to have or to use PTLA if you have BIP?

1a-38   Is Samuel Eliot Morrison's The Maritime History of Massachusetts (first published in 1979) still in print? What is the publisher and price? BE CAREFUL.

1a-39   Where are at least two places that you can find the address of the Bethany House Publishers?

1a-40   What is the in-print status, price, and publisher of Goya and His Sitters, by Elizabeth du Gue Trapier?

1a-41   On the previous question, the author was listed under Du rather than any other part of the name. If this had confused you and you had wondered what to search under--du, Gue, or Trapier--what could you have done?

1a-42   What is the full name and address of the publisher of Goya and His Sitters?

1a-43   The Denoyer-Geppert Co. is a publisher of maps and other geographical aids. Would you expect to find their maps included in BIP?

1a-44   Can you, however, find the address for Denoyer-Geppert Co.?

1a-45   BIP gives you author and title access to PTLA. What is a third major access you might need to have for bibliographic searching? In other words, what is a third kind of information you might have about any particular book or publication for which you are searching?

1a-46   Do you have this third type of access through BIP, or PTLA itself?

1a-47   Could you, then, find out what books are still in print in the U.S. on, for example, "data processing" or "air pollution"?

1a-48   What is the basic bibliographic information you need to know about the Subject Guide to Books in Print?

1a-49   Has BIP always had a "subject guide"? Where would you look to find this? (See #1a-29.)

1a-50   The "scope" of the Subject Guide to BIP would, presumably, be the same as that of BIP and PTLA. Are there, however, any omissions?

1a-51   What is the arrangement of the Subject Guide to BIP?

1a-52   What books are in print in the U.S. on the subject of data processing?

1a-53   The assigning of subject headings is a major part of library cataloging procedures, and libraries generally use a standard list of subject headings so that there will be some uniformity and consistency. The two major lists in use are the Sears List of Subject Headings (Sheehy, AB178) and the Library of Congress List of Subject Headings (Washington, D.C., Library of Congress, 1979; 9th ed.). Does the Subject Guide to BIP make use of either of these lists?

1a-54   Would this be of help to librarians?

1a-55   Will the books in Subject Guide to BIP be listed under only one subject heading?

1a-56   In #1a-34, you used the publisher's catalog in PTLA to find the specific titles and prices of some books on sewing and needlework published by Better Homes and Gardens Books. Can you find these publications listed in the Subject Guide to BIP?

1a-57   What is the publisher and price of Old China Trade by Foster R. Dulles?

1a-58   If you wanted to find a listing of all the editions currently in print of Mark Twain's Tom Sawyer, would you expect to find such a list in Subject Guide to BIP?

1a-59 There are some listings in Subject Guide to BIP under the heading of Clemens, Samuel Langhorne. What are these then, if Subject Guide to BIP does not include fiction entries?

1a-60 Where and how would you find such a list of all the editions currently in print of Mark Twain's Tom Sawyer?

1a-61 Look in the correct source for a listing of all the editions currently in print of Mark Twain's Tom Sawyer. How many places would you have to look to be sure to cover all of the editions?

1a-62 Since these are all editions of the same book by the same author, why is it necessary to look in so many places? Why aren't they all listed in the same place? (Refer back to the last part of the answer to #1a-41.)

1a-63 What is a pseudonym?

1a-64 In #1a-60, the problem was to find a list of all editions currently in print of Tom Sawyer. Where would you look to find a list of all the editions which have ever been published of Tom Sawyer?

1a-65 Where would you look to find out if such an author bibliography exists?

So far you have examined carefully three major bibliographic sources: Publishers' Trade List Annual, Books in Print, and Subject Guide to Books in Print. These three sources are, in fact, very closely inter-related. You have examined each for the basic bibliographic information, the scope, the arrangement, and special features such as address lists. You have compared these three sources. You have also had several opportunities to use these sources, to search for information in these sources; often it is the search for information itself which gives you added clues about the scope and arrangement of the source. Keep these sources in mind as you proceed through the following sections of this manual, because you will have reason to refer back to them again. Now that you understand these three sources fairly well, you can use them for purposes of comparison when you examine other similar sources.

1a-66 BIP and the Subject Guide to BIP appear annually, once a year. New books are published and go out of print continually, all year around. Is there any way in which BIP and Subject BIP are updated more frequently than once a year? Where would you expect to find this information?

1a-67 In addition to the BIP Supplement, the introductory material in BIP also mentions two similar publications titled Forthcoming Books and Subject Guide to Forthcoming Books. From the BIP introduction, what can you tell about the purpose and scope of these sources?

There are a number of other sources supplementary to and very similar to the basic ones you have just examined. Most of these are published by the Bowker Company, and are mentioned in the introductory material to BIP (in the section titled "Data Bases and Publications of the Department of Bibliography"): Paperbound Books in Print (see Sheehy item AA471), Children's Books in Print (AA466), Subject Guide to Children's Books in Print (AA467), Scientific and Technical Books and Serials in Print (EA38), Medical Books and Serials in Print (EK26), Business and Economics Books and Serials in Print (CH105, 1CH47), Religious Books and Serials in Print (2BB3), Large Type Books in Print (AA470, 1AA96, 2AA09), El Hi Textbooks in Print (AA469). Two newer but similar publications from Bowker not listed in the BIP preface are Associations' Publications in Print (not in Sheehy), and Law Information (not in Sheehy). As you can see from just the titles, these are basically subject-oriented (or form, in the case of Paperbound BIP and Large Type BIP). You should be aware of the existence of such supplementary sources, but it is probably not necessary to examine them in any detail at this stage. Since they are published by the Bowker Company, you can expect them to be similar in format to the sources you have already examined.

A similar source is Alternatives in Print (not in Sheehy; 6th edition published by Neal-Schuman Publishers, Inc., New York, N.Y.; subtitled: "an international catalog of books, pamphlets, periodicals and audiovisual materials," and advertised as giving "information on the print and nonprint publications of the small press, the counter-culture, the Third World, and the dissident press").

Note to student/user of self-study manual

So far, if much of this is new to you, you may have had considerable difficulty in coming up with the correct answers to these questions. This in itself is not too surprising. If you have understood the answers when you turned to them in this manual, and if you have understood fairly well where you got off the track in trying to locate the answers yourself, then you can expect to continue working your way through the questions and profiting from your experience. But if you still feel very confused and uncertain at this point, then it is time to consult with your instructor to see what the problem is.

BRIEF SURVEY OF U.S. PUBLISHING

Before you can make much sense out of the bibliographic records which you will examine in this section, it would be helpful for you to have some very elementary background information about the publication and distribution of books.

Books are produced by business firms called publishers. There are literally thousands of publishers in the United States. Each publisher is responsible for the publication of individual titles, ranging in number from two or three to several hundred. (The word "title" is used here as distinct from "copy"; e.g., the title, Mistral's Daughter, by Judith Krantz, was published in over 10,000 copies). In general, except for classic works which are no longer protected by copyright, publishers have exclusive rights to those titles which they have published; in other words, Mistral's Daughter in its hardcover edition is published only by Crown, not also by Doubleday or Simon and Schuster.

For each new title which he/she publishes, a publisher will have printed the number of copies which he/she expects or hopes to sell. This is usually called a "printing"; it may also be called an "edition." If the publisher's stock of printed copies is sold out, he/she may or may not--depending perhaps on demand --decide to have another printing run off. Presumably these second, third, etc. "printings" will be done without changing the content or the text or the format of the publication. If the publication is changed in any real way, it should therefore constitute another "edition," rather than "printing." Usually, publishers will indicate these changes by such terms as "second edition," "new edition," "revised edition," etc. The term "edition" has a number of other uses as well. A "reprint" may mean simply a "second printing" following directly on the first printing; or it may mean that the title has been re-set and reprinted, usually at a much later date than the original printing. Unfortunately, publishers do not use these terms of "printing," "edition," "new edition," "reprint," etc., as consistently or as carefully as we would like; it is sometimes a major bibliographic problem to figure out what changes, if any, have been made.

As long as a publisher still has copies in stock of a title, or as long as he/she continues to have new printings, or reprintings, made available as needed, then the title or the book is considered to be "in print." When the title is no longer available from the publisher's stock, and he/she does not intend to have another printing made, the title is considered to be "out of print" or "o.p."

The books, when in print, are available directly from the publisher who publishes them. (Some publishers may have other, usually larger, publishing firms act as agents or distributors for them.) Books are also sold, or distributed, through book stores or book dealers, who stock copies of titles from a large variety of publishers. The book dealers must, of course, get their copies directly from the publishers or from wholesalers.

The "book trade" is made up of the publishing industry, which produces the books, and the book dealers or book stores, which sell the books. Books sold through book stores to the general public (such as novels, poetry, cookbooks, travel books, etc.) are generally referred to as "trade" books. "Non-trade" publications, therefore, are most items not usually carried in the stock of most book stores; for example, textbooks, materials published by the government on any level, encyclopedias, etc. The distinction between "trade" and "non-trade" or "in the trade" and "out of the trade" is not always clear, and some types of publications have moved from one category to another. (For example, books published by university presses have in the past been considered as "non-trade," but now they are commonly carried "in the trade.") It is a useful distinction to be aware of, however, since it is often a criterion for inclusion or exclusion of materials in many bibliographies.

The "book trade" is certainly just as dependent as librarians--perhaps even more so--on complete, up-to-date, and accurate information--or bibliographic control--of books and other publications. Many of our bibliographic records, therefore, will be compiled primarily by and for the book trade itself. This does not, of course, necessarily make them any the less useful to librarians.

All new books, or new titles, are not published on the same day, or at the same time of year. New titles are published every day of the year, although there are a few seasonal surges, such as before Christmas. Advance information about new titles is given in Publishers Weekly, a periodical published by and for the book trade (and therefore referred to as a "trade publication," which is a somewhat different use of this term than the trade/non-trade distinction mentioned previously). Announcement of the actual publication of the title (meaning that it is "out" and therefore now available) is, in effect, its listing in the Weekly Record; you will be examining this Weekly Record as one of the bibliographic sources.

    In addition to announcements, advertisements, and listing in such book trade journals as <u>PW</u>, publishers also mail out advertisements and announcements, and often issue at various intervals throughout the year lists of new and/or forthcoming books. Publishers also issue from time to time, usually annually, lists or catalogs of their complete stock, older titles which are still in print/in stock/available (their backlist), as well as new titles. It is essentially these annual stock catalogs or lists which make up the volumes of the <u>Publishers' Trade List Annual</u>, which you will also examine. The only way in which you can definitely determine whether a particular title is still in print (available) is by writing to the publisher to inquire, or by looking it up in the publisher's stock catalog.

    This brief survey of the "book trade" has been quite elementary and simplified in order to give you some kind of working background for your examination of the bibliographic sources. There are many more complex aspects of the publishing and distribution of books, some of which may become clearer to you as you proceed through this course.

    Additional reading about the process of publishing may be found in several sources; see, for example, <u>Book Publishing: What It Is, What It Does</u> by John Dessauer (NY, Bowker, 2nd ed., 1981), and <u>Carter & Bonk's Building Library Collections</u> by Arthur Curley and Dorothy Broderick (Metuchen, N.J., Scarecrow Press, 6th ed., 1984).

NATIONAL BIBLIOGRAPHIC RECORDS (U.S.)--CURRENT

Answers #1a/1--1a/67

1a-1: If you do not feel you can give an answer to this from your own knowledge or experience, then you should begin by trying to look it up, either in any standard English language dictionary, or in a more specialized dictionary like the ALA Glossary, or in the text you are using for this course or in any readings you have been assigned on bibliography. Actually, the definitions of the term bibliography vary somewhat from source to source, and it may be necessary to read several different writers on the subject, and examine and work with many bibliographies over a period of time before the definition becomes really clear to you. However, for purposes of starting this manual, we can begin by defining a bibliography simply as a list of publications, which has some unifying element (such as: by a specific author, on a specific subject, published in a specific country....) and is organized in some systematic manner (such as: alphabetically by name of author, by subject, by date of publication....).

1a-2: For example: to find out what books have been published and are available; for book selection for the library collection, or for recommendation to readers; to find out the prices of such materials, and their sources of purchase; to verify and identify publications; to compile bibliographies of authors or subjects; to locate materials for interlibrary loan; etc.

1a-3: The 1982 edition (published in the fall of 1982) contains 15 volumes. Other editions may vary somewhat.

1a-4: Still available from the publisher (refer to Appendix A).

1a-5: Annually (once a year). Title: Publishers' Trade List Annual.

1a-6: R.R. Bowker Company in New York (and London). This appears on the title page.

1a-7: Again, this appears on the title page, as part of the title itself: Publishers' Trade

List Annual, 19__. It also appears as part of the copyright statement (Copyright © 19__) on the verso of the title page. It also appears on the spine. In the set issued in the fall of 1982, the date on the title page is 1982, and the date in the copyright is 1982. The answers to the following questions about PTLA are keyed to the 1982 edition. You should use this edition if it is available to you. If you are using earlier or later editions, you should keep in mind that the answers you get may vary somewhat from those given here. The structure of the source--its scope and arrangement-- should not vary greatly, but the specific information found within it will change from year to year, which is of course the point in having it re-issued each year.

1a-8: There are a number of possibilities: a) the title page; b) the preface; c) the annotation in Sheehy (item AA472).

1a-9: The title page is no help. The short preface tells you (as of the 1982 edition) that it is a "source of bibliographic data about in-print books and related products" and includes the catalogs of those publishers who "contractually elect inclusion." The Sheehy annotation tells you that it is a collection of publishers' catalogs and seems to imply that fewer publishers are electing inclusion. The actual scope of PTLA is never clearly stated, beyond "a collection of catalogs," but it is generally considered to include catalogs from major American publishers, plus some of the minor or smaller publishers as well.

1a-10: Yes, the "Index to Publishers" in the yellow pages section in the front of volume 1.

1a-11: Alphabetically by the name of the publisher. This should be quite obvious simply by glancing through the volumes themselves, but it is also pointed out in the annotation in Sheehy. This is

one of the reasons why it is very important to realize that the set consists of
more than one volume.

1a-12: No. Besides the major alphabetical section running (on white pages) through
all the volumes of the set, there are several alphabetical lists in the yellow pages
in the front of volume 1 (in the 1982 edition). There is the "Index to Publishers"
as noted in #1a-10, a Subject Index to
Publishers, and an Index to Publishers'
Series. There is also the section of "Yellow Pages Booklists," a collection of shorter lists which are not exactly arranged
alphabetically.

1a-13: Yes, it tells you where you will find the
catalog: i.e., in the regular alphabetical
order, or in the Yellow Pages Booklists.

1a-14: Yes. It is in the regular alphabetical order (the symbol *** in the Index to Publishers indicates this), in volume 2, between the catalogs of Grove Press and
Hacker Art Books, Inc. (in the 1982 edition).

1a-15: Yes. This one is in the yellow supplement
section. Since the Supplement is not in
strict alphabetical order, you have to look
in the Index which appears at the beginning of vol. 1, which tells on which page
of the Supplement you will find the Quarterdeck Press catalog (p. 430 in the 1982
edition).

1a-16: As of the 1982 edition of PTLA, it is still
in print (that is, it is still listed in the
publisher's catalog as being available).
The price is $32.50. (The lower case "s"
following the price is a code explained on
the verso of the first page of the University of California Press catalog: "short
discount" to the trade.) The original
date of its publication was 1974. The
number (02146-0) is part of the ISBN
number which will be explained later (see
question #1a-33 of this manual).

1a-17: As of the 1982 edition of PTLA, it is
still in print and the price is $7.95. The
publisher's catalog for Southern Illinois
University Press appears in the regular
order alphabetized under S. Here you
had only the title, not the author's name,
but this publisher's catalog provides both
author and title listings. In the title
index, the author is given as Hoffman.
To find the price, you must then look
in the author listing under Hoffman,
Frederick J.

1a-18: As of the 1982 edition of PTLA, it is
still in print and the price is $3.00.
The title is Short Plays for the Long
Living. The Baker catalog (located in
the Yellow Pages Booklists, p. 37) lists
by title only, and you did not have the
title, only the author, but the catalog
itself is only one column long, and you
can easily go through it to search out the
likely title by that author.

1a-19: The publisher's catalog will usually give
series information and will usually list
books in series under the series title as
well as under the individual titles. Since
Time-Life Books publishes primarily series
of this type, its catalog lists the series
titles, each series title followed by a list
of individual titles with the series.
The first two books in the "Foods of the
World" series were The Cooking of Pro-
vincial France, by M.F.K. Fisher, and
The Cooking of Italy by Waverly Root.
As a series title, "Foods of the World"
also appears in the series index in the
front of volume 1, with reference to the
publisher, Time-Life Books. (1982 edition.)

1a-20: The New York Graphic Society catalog
is included in PTLA (1982) edition).
The book is listed in the catalog (under
title) with a short annotation, from which
you can see that the book "covers the
history of the artist's studio from antiq-
uity to the present" as well as insight
into the creative process.

1a-21: They vary from publisher to publisher.
University of California Press had an
author listing only; Southern Illinois
University Press books are listed by author and title; Walter H. Baker Company
listed by title only. Time-Life Books
are listed by series title only.

1a-22: You'll have to glance through the set
at several of the catalogs to determine
this. Actually, most of these do not,
but some do: W.H. Freeman and Company, and Schenkman Books are examples of two which do list books by subject. There is (since 1978) a "Subject
Index to Publishers" in the front of the
PTLA set, but this is only a general
guide to publishers who publish in certain areas, not to specific books.

1a-23: Catalogs arranged alphabetically by
name of publisher. Shorter lists are
in the Yellow Pages Booklists in the
front of volume 1. The location is
shown by the index preceding these

booklists. The arrangement within catalogs varies from publisher to publisher.

1a-24:   No, you couldn't.

1a-25:   The name of its publisher.

1a-26:   An author or title <u>index</u> or both. Or at
least you need some sort of a listing by
author and/or title which will tell you
the <u>name of the publisher</u>. Which brings
you to the next title you are to examine,
Books in Print (BIP).

1a-27:   The publisher is the Bowker Company
(same as PTLA), it is published annually (same as PTLA), and the 1982-83
edition has six volumes: volumes 1, 2,
and 3 are "authors" and volumes 4, 5,
and 6 are "titles." This information is
all on the title pages of the volumes.
(A third set which may be shelved near-
by is the Subject Guide to Books in Print,
not part of BIP itself and to be considered later.) Both BIP and PTLA usually
"come out" or appear or are published
in the late fall of the year, and are
presumed then to contain listings of
books in print from the various publishers through the late summer, or about
July, of that year. Thus, the 1982-83
edition of BIP was available in about
October of 1982, and was presumed to
contain a listing of books in print as of
about July 1982. And therefore, from
January 1983 through October or November of 1983, you would be using the 1982-
83 edition of BIP. The answers to the
following questions about BIP are keyed
to the 1982-83 edition of BIP. If you are
using earlier or later editions, be aware
that the answers you get may vary somewhat from those given here.

1a-28:   The Sheehy annotation (AA473) to BIP
shows it as an index to PTLA, and indeed its subtitle is given there as "an
author-title-series index to" PTLA. However, since the 1973 edition of BIP,
Bowker has ceased subtitling BIP as an
index to PTLA, and now clearly states
in the introductory material that BIP is
not limited to information in PTLA. See,
for example, the first three paragraphs
of the major section titled "Data Bases
and Publications...." (p. v of 1982 edition), and the section on "Types of
Publications not fully represented in
BIP" (p. x of 1982-83 edition). Keeping
in mind that there may not be an abso-
lute correlation between the two sources,
BIP may in fact still be used as an author-title index to PTLA, in that it will

give the name of the publisher for those
items which it does include.

1a-29:   No. PTLA began annual publication in
1873, and BIP did not begin publication
until 1948. The Sheehy annotation to
PTLA (AA472) tells you clearly that from
1873 until 1948, there were no indexes,
except briefly in 1902-04.

1a-30:   Since the Sheehy annotation still treats
BIP as an index to PTLA, thereby sharing its vague statement of scope, it would
be best to go directly to the source itself
on this one, and see if the introductory
material is any more help. Use the same
references from the introductory material that you used in #1a-28 to establish
the current relationship between BIP and
PTLA. In the section called "How to
Use...." under "Types of publications
not fully represented in BIP," you can
see that, as of the 1982-83 edition, BIP
includes "listings of some 13,900 publishers," that it is not limited to information
in PTLA, that the BIPS Data Base includes "regular contributors" and depends upon contact with publishers, that
books listed must be "available to the
trade," that "no attempt was made to
include things other than books, such
as...," etc. Some specific exclusions
are given, such as free material, government publications, etc. It is almost
easier to say what is <u>not</u> in BIP than
what <u>is</u> in it.

1a-31:   Alphabetically by author and title.
These have been separated into two
alphabetical lists in the 1982-83 set, in
six volumes, with authors in volumes
1, 2, and 3 and titles in volumes 4, 5,
and 6, rather than mixing authors and
titles together into one alphabetical list.
This information can be seen from the
spines or the covers themselves, or in
the introductory material. Note that
volume 16 also contains an alphabetical
list of U.S. publishers with addresses.
There is now also a separately published
(by Bowker) list of publishers, titled
Publishers, Distributors, and Wholesalers of the United States: A Directory.

1a-32:   Yes, both author and title sections list
it, and both give the same information.
See BIP prefatory material regarding
this ("Information included in author
and title entries," p. ix of 1982-83
edition). BIP usually gives author,
title, publisher, date of publication,
ISBN, price. Less consistently, other
information may be given

1a-33:   This is the International Standard Book Number. See the prefatory material to BIP titled "ISBN, International Standard Book Number" (p. viii of the 1982-83 edition) for an explanation.

1a-34:   You do not know the authors or the titles of these books. You know only the publisher (Better Homes and Gardens Books) and the subject. You could not use BIP. Here your best source would be to go directly to the publisher's catalog in PTLA and see what is listed there. You would probably have to go through all of the titles listed in the catalog, but usually the publisher's catalog would be a less imposing list to go through than the entire title section of BIP. If the publisher's catalog did not happen to be included in PTLA, then you could write to the publisher for a copy of the catalog.

     In the 1982 PTLA, Better Homes and Gardens Books' list of publications is included in the Supplement section in volume 1; the list is one page long and easy to go through. The books in question are listed under "Sewing and Crafts"; most are $4.95 each and no authors are given.

1a-35:   Yes (as of the 1982-83 BIP). It is listed in BIP (Authors, under Caldwell, or Titles, under Glory....). The price is $10.00 ($3.50 paper); the publisher is Doubleday (Fawcett, paper) and the date of publication is 1974 (1982, paper).

1a-36:   Theoretically, no. BIP, of course, is subject to errors, as are all bibliographic sources, and if you wanted to be doubly sure, you could also check the publisher's catalog as well, but this is probably not necessary.

1a-37:   As you could see from your answers to #1a-19 and #1a-34, sometimes it is more direct to go to the publisher's catalog itself when you are not sure of authors or titles. And as you could see from your answer to #1a-20, the publisher's catalog itself in PTLA may give you more complete information than is found in BIP.

1a-38:   BE CAREFUL. Yes, as of the 1982-83 BIP, it is still in print ($7.95, Northeastern University Press). In this case, the name you were given was misspelled. The correct spelling of the author's name is Morison. This is a far more common hazard than you might think, and you should always be on guard for it. If you were aware that Morison is one of our foremost historians and that therefore his book would not be likely to have gone out of print so soon, you might have suspected either a misspelling or a mistake in BIP. In either case, double checking under the title entry would have answered your problem. Or possibly you might have glanced at Morison as an alternate spelling in BIP-authors at the same time you looked under Morrison. Eventually (after you've been misled by enough errors), such automatic consideration of alternate possibilities should be second nature to you. Of course, if you had looked in the title volume first, you would have found it, but don't forget that you could similarly have been given an incorrect title.

1a-39:   In the publisher's catalog itself in PTLA, and in the list of publishers at the end of volume 6 of BIP (remember your answer to #1a-31 about the arrangement of BIP). Also in the separate publication, Publishers, Distributors, and Wholesalers of the United States: A Directory, as noted in #1a-31.

1a-40:   In the 1982-83 edition of BIP-Authors, under Du Gue Trapier (filed letter by letter, as if it were spelled "Duguetrapier"), it is listed as in print, from "Hispanic Soc," at $10.00. It would also be correct to look in BIP-Titles, under Goya.

1a-41:   You could have looked under all three possibilities till you either found the correct one or eliminated all three; you could also have looked it up under title, since you had the title. In this case, BIP-Authors (1982-83) does give you a cross-reference from Trapier to Du Gue Trapier. See BIP introductory material on listing of cross-references and variant forms of authors' names ("Special Note on How to Find an Author's Complete Listing," p. ix of 1982-83 edition).

1a-42:   Hispanic Society of America, 613 W. 155th St., New York, NY 10032. The BIP entry gives only "Hispanic Soc" and you have to refer to the "Key to Publishers' Abbreviations" to find the full name and the address.

1a-43:   Probably not, since the BIP introductory material tells you that "no attempt was made to include things other than books" which would seem to exclude maps, at least those maps not bound together in a book. (See #1a-30.)

1a-44:   Yes, in the full list of U.S. publishers in the end of volume 16 of BIP.

1a-45:   Two pieces of information you might have about a book are the author and the title. Other pieces of information are the date of publication and the publisher, but probably they will not be as important to you as the possibility that you would be searching for a book or publication because of its subject matter. (For example, you might want to find a book on the subject of air pollution.) So you can then say that the three major accesses you need for bibliographic information, or for bibliographic control, would be: author, title, subject.

1a-46:   BIP does not have a subject index. In #1a-22, you noted that some of the publishers' catalogs in PTLA included subject listings, but not all, and that PTLA now contains a very general "Subject Index to Publishers," a list of broad subject headings under which publishers have indicated they wish to be listed.

1a-47:   Not from BIP or PTLA as such, unless you wanted to go through all of the titles they include to pick out those dealing with data processing. The third item in your list of sources to examine--the Subject Guide to Books in Print--is just the sort of thing you want.

1a-48:   Publisher: Bowker. How often published: annually, as with BIP. How many volumes: the 1982-83 edition has three volumes.

1a-49:   As with #1a-29, you would most easily check in Sheehy, and find that the Subject Guide has existed only since 1957, although BIP has existed since 1948. At this stage, such information may seem superfluous to you; you may not see the point of knowing when, for example, the Subject Guide began, since you are unlikely to use it for any but the current year. However, it is a very revealing aspect of the overall picture of bibliographic control in this country that such sources do not spring fullblown into existence, but rather develop in stages over the years, as a need for specific tools or for another access to such tools is demonstrated. This is particularly evident with the current bibliographic sources; their structure-- their scope and arrangement--may change from year to year, even from month to month or from week to week; it is important in using these sources to realize

that such changes are being made and to try to keep up with them.

1a-50:   The introductory material titled, "How to Use Subject Guide to Books in Print," following the title page, tells you about specific omissions, both from the BIP listings (i.e., most fiction, poetry and drama, and, in general, those books for which "the Library of Congress has not assigned subject headings," (p. ix of the 1982-83 edition), and for the same statement of omissions you found in BIP itself (p. xi-xii of the 1982-83 edition).

1a-51:   As you might expect, it is alphabetically by subject, and the introductory material (which you should read) gives you a good deal of information on the various types of subject entries or "subject headings" which are used, and how they are alphabetized.

1a-52:   The entry "data processing" in the 1982-83 Subject Guide to BIP refers you to other words used: electronic data processing, information storage and retrieval systems, and punched card systems. You would need to check under all headings. One of the problems with subject headings is that they tend to change from year to year as new terminology and new emphases come into being. You should always keep in mind as many different possibilities as you can, and hope that your source will give you sufficient references to the headings or entries which are actually used.

1a-53:   Yes, it follows the Library of Congress List of Subject Headings. See the "How to Use...." section.

1a-54:   Yes, because it uses a list which is likely to be familiar, and they can expect some consistency of headings, perhaps, with those used in their own card catalogs.

1a-55:   No, since Library of Congress subject cataloging may assign more than one subject heading, the Subject Guide to BIP will list titles under all assigned subject headings. This also is in the "How to Use...." section.

1a-56:   Since you do have the subject of these books, you could use Subject Guide to BIP and locate them, but this is still not as easy or as thorough as going directly to the publisher's catalog in PTLA. In Subject Guide to BIP 1982-

83, under the subject heading "needle-work," you would find at least two of these books listed (with the author entry as Better Homes and Gardens), but you would have to search under a large variety of headings (appliqué, quilting, rugs, etc.) to find all of them.

1a-57: AMS Press, $19.50 (as of 1982-83). Where do you go to find this? You could perhaps have found it under "China--Commerce" in Subject Guide to BIP, but why bother? You had the author and the title, and no reason to think either was incorrect, so BIP is much more direct. Also the title does not clearly indicate whether the subject is China the country or china as in porcelain.

1a-58: No, since Subject Guide to BIP specifically excludes most fiction listings (see the "How to Use...." section).

1a-59: Biographical and critical works about Clemens (Twain), which are included, and which would be listed under the author as the subject.

1a-60: You want to find a list of in-print titles; therefore you go to BIP. You could look under author or title.

1a-61: Look in BIP. In the author section, under Twain, there are several editions listed (20 in the 1982-83 edition of BIP). Under Clemens, Samuel Langhorne (Mark Twain is Clemens' pseudonym), there are some more editions. There is (as of 1982-83 edition) a reference from Clemens to Twain, but not one from Twain to Clemens. In the title volume, under Tom Sawyer, there are 6 editions listed (in the 1982-83 edition), with a reference to Adventures of Tom Sawyer where you will find 23 editions listed.

1a-62: BIP lists authors and titles as given by the publishers or their catalogs, and these may not be consistent. Publishers' listings may vary in use of the author's full name, or use of pseudonyms, or in complete titles. You cannot count on complete cross-referencing, so you should always be careful to check under all possibilities which occur to you. See again the section on "Special note on how to find an author's complete listing" in the BIP introductory material (p. ix of the 1982-83 edition), which you have already looked at for #1a-41.

1a-63: See the ALA Glossary or a dictionary.

(Mark Twain is Samuel Langhorne Clemens' pseudonym.)

1a-64: Probably an "author bibliography"--that is, a bibliography which attempts to give a complete listing of all the publications or writings by a particular author--for Clemens/Twain, if one exists. If such a bibliography is not recent, you might then have to supplement it by searching through more current bibliographic sources such as those you are examining in this unit.

1a-65: You might look to see if one is listed in the Subject Guide to BIP, under Clemens (or Twain) as the subject, in the same way that you found biographical and critical works about Clemens listed there in #1a-59. This, of course, would tell you only about whatever bibliography(ies) happened to be in print. You might also consider looking in a source such as Sheehy, which lists reference books (since an author bibliography is, of course, a reference book); it appears that Sheehy does not include bibliographies of individual authors, but Sheehy does list other guides to reference books which might be helpful--see the section titled "Reference Books" under General Reference Works, Bibliography, Selection of Books, p. 33-36 of the 9th edition.

1a-66: Information about up-dating of a particular source is likely to be found in Sheehy (or similar guides to such material) or in the prefatory/introductory material of the source itself. For a source which comes out as often as BIP does, it would probably be more accurate to see what the latest edition of the source itself says on this subject. The introductory material in the first volume of BIP, under "Other Bibliographic Publications to Supplement Books in Print" (p. xi of the 1982-83 edition), at the very end of the "How to Use...." section, tells you that a Books in Print Supplement is published in April of each year with updates for the six months since publication of BIP itself in the prior October (including some publications only announced as well as those actually published). The BIP Supplement up-dates authors and titles for BIP and subjects for Subject Guide to BIP in one volume. If you have access to it and can examine it, you will see that the entries themselves are similar to those found in BIP and Subject Guide to BIP. (The Sheehy annotation for

BIP also notes the half-year Supplement.)

1a-67: Forthcoming Books is published bimonthly
        (every other month). It is sub-titled
        "now including new books in print," and,
        like the BIP Supplement, it updates BIP
        but on an even more frequent (bimonthly)
        basis. Like BIP, it lists books by author
        and title. The Subject Guide to Forthcom-
        ing Books simply provides the subject ac-
        cess to Forthcoming Books, as the Sub-
        ject Guide to BIP does for BIP. Since all
        of these publications come from the same
        Bowker Company data base (as discussed
        in the introductory material in BIP, see
        particularly the section titled "Data Bases
        and Publications of the Department of Bib-
        liography"), you would expect that the
        amount of bibliographic information and
        the format for each entry would be similar
        in all of them. If you have access to
        Forthcoming Books and its companion Sub-
        ject Guide, you can examine them quickly
        and see that in fact the entries are sim-
        ilar to those of BIP and its companion
        Subject Guide.

NATIONAL BIBLIOGRAPHIC RECORDS (U.S.)--CURRENT

Questions #1b/1--1b/57

1b-1   Assume that you need to find ordering information for a book on photography which you think was published within the past few weeks. You know what the author and title are. You need to know the name of the publisher, the price, the extent of the illustrations, and you need to know that it has actually been published, not just announced for publication. Would you expect to find this information in BIP or the other sources which you examined or read about in the previous section of this manual?

1b-2   Are there sources even more current than BIP, the BIP Supplement, and Forthcoming Books which record new books upon publication? (In trying to answer this question, think: where did you look to get your information about Forthcoming Books?)

These sources given in the BIP introductory material as providing "a record of the new books as actually published," are the second group of titles to be examined, and are as follows:

Weekly Record (see AA477)
American Book Publishing Record (BPR), monthly (AA463)
American Book Publishing Record (BPR) Cumulative, annual (AA464, AA465)
American Book Publishing Record Cumulative 1950-77 (2AA58)
American Book Publishing Record Cumulative 1876-1949 (2AA57)

Again, it would be easiest to try to examine these titles together. Since both the Weekly Record and the American Book Publishing Record are periodicals, try to get together several recent issues rather than simply one issue or just the most recent issue.
     The first source to examine is the Weekly Record. Note from the Sheehy annotation that until 1974, the Weekly Record was published as part of Publishers Weekly, a journal (periodical) published by and for the "book trade." Publishers Weekly was discussed briefly in the introductory material to BIP, and in the "Brief Survey of U.S. Publishing" (Appendix A) following section 1a of this manual.

1b-3   It should be quite obvious that the Weekly Record comes out weekly; this is part of the bibliographic information which you should note. See if you can find the date, volume, and issue numbering on any recent issue, and see if you can find the statement (the masthead) which tells you how frequently WR is published, how much it costs, who publishes it, etc. Who does publish WR and what else does that company publish?

1b-4   What is the "scope" of the Weekly Record? (Use the cover page of the source for this.)

1b-5   What does "conscientiously" mean in this context?

1b-6   Are there any specific exclusions noted in the scope of the Weekly Record? That is, what are the limits which the Bowker Company has set for this listing?

1b-7   Would you expect the list to include such things as maps, films, records, globes, etc.?

1b-8   An important part of the "scope" for bibliographies is the amount of information given for each entry, or for each citation, within the bibliography itself. What does the introductory paragraph tell you to expect in each individual citation in the Weekly Record?

1b-9   Look at the sample page (p. 21) from Weekly Record, at the citation for Against the Night, the Stars by John Hollow. The elements of the citation are as follows:

>   author entry (HOLLOW, John)
>   title (Against the Night, the Stars)
>   sub-title (the science fiction of Arthur C. Clarke)
>   author statement (John Hollow)
>   edition (1st ed.)
>   place of publication (San Diego)
>   publisher (Harcourt Brace Jovanovich)
>   date of publication (c1983)
>   paging (197 p.)
>   size (22 cm.)
>   contents information (Bibliography: p. [193]-197)
>   Library of Congress Classification number ([PR6005.L36Z69 1983])
>   Dewey Decimal Classification number (813'.914) (located in upper right corner of entry; "19"
>   in the body of the entry indicates that the 19th edition of Dewey was used)
>   International Standard Book Number (ISBN 0-15-103966-6)
>   price ($14.95)
>   catalog tracings for subject headings (1. Clarke, Arthur Charles, 1917--Criticism and inter-
>   pretation. 2. Science fiction, English--History and criticism.) and added entries (I.
>   Title.)

Compare this with the citations in BIP, for example. Was all of this information given to you in BIP?

1b-10   Look at the entry on page 21 for Special Sisters by Arthur Frederick Ide. Who is the publisher? What is the price? Was the book ever published elsewhere?

1b-11   Review: If the citation does not give you the address of the publisher, where would you look to find the address of the publisher?

1b-12   Look through some recent issues. Besides author names, do you see any "corporate author" entries (such as conferences, institutions, organizations, associations, etc.)? Do you see any title entries?

1b-13   Do you see any subject entries?

1b-14   Do you see any cross-references from title to author? Choose any item entered under author and check to see if there is also an entry under title.

1b-15   What is the arrangement of the entries in the Weekly Record? Is this similar to BIP?

See question #1b-9.

Social conditions—Case studies. 3. Villages—China—Case studies. I. Title.

HOLDEN, Donald. 702.3'73
Art career guide : a guidance handbook for art students. teachers, vocational counselors, and job hunters / by Donald Holden. 4th ed., rev. and enl. New York : Watson-Guptill Publications, 1983. 322 p. ; 24 cm. Includes index. [N8350.H6 1983] 19 82-24701 ISBN 0-8230-0252-7 : 14.95
1. Art—Vocational guidance. I. Title.

HOLLANDER, Paul. 301
The faces of socialism : essays in comparative sociology and politics / Paul Hollander. New Brunswick [N.J.] : Transaction Books, [1983] p. cm. Includes bibliographical references and index. [HM22.U5H625 1983] 19 82-19458 ISBN 0-87855-480-7 : 29.95
1. Sociology—United States—Addresses, essays. lectures. 2. Socialism—Addresses, essays. lectures. 3. Comparative government—Addresses. essays, lectures. 4. Totalitarianism. I. Title.

HOLLENWEGER, Walter J., FIC
1927-
Conflict in Corinth ; & Memoirs of an old man : two stories that illuminate the way the Bible came to be written / Walter J. Hollenweger. New York : Paulist Press, c1982. 79 p. ; 21 cm. Translation of: Konflikt in Korinth. Bibliography: p. 65-79. [PT2668.O445K613 1982] 833'.914 19 82-80165 ISBN 0-8091-2455-6 (pbk.) : 3.95
I. Hollenweger, Walter J., 1927- Memoirs of an old man. 1982. II. [Konflikt in Korinth.] English III. Title. IV. Title: Memoirs of an old man.

HOLLOW, John. 813'.914
Against the night, the stars : the science fiction of Arthur C. Clarke / John Hollow. 1st ed. San Diego : Harcourt Brace Jovanovich, c1983. 197 p. ; 22 cm. Bibliography: p. [193]-197. [PR6005.L36Z69 1983] 19 82-23366 ISBN 0-15-103966-6 : 14.95
1. Clarke, Arthur Charles, 1917- —Criticism and interpretation. 2. Science fiction. English—History and criticism. I. Title.

HOOBLER, Dorothy. 910'.92'4 B
The voyages of Captain Cook / Dorothy and Thomas Hoobler. New York : Putnam, c1983. p. cm. Includes index. Bibliography: p. [G420.C73H66 1983] 19 83-3263 ISBN 0-399-20975-1 : 10.95
1. Cook, James, 1728-1799—Juvenile literature. 2. Voyages around the world—Juvenile literature. 3. Explorers—Great Britain—Biography—Juvenile literature. I. Hoobler, Thomas. II. Title.

HOOVER 016.973916'092'4
Institution on War, Revolution, and Peace.
Herbert Hoover, a register of his papers in the Hoover Institution archives / compiled by Elena S. Danielson and Charles G. Palm. Stanford, Calif. : Hoover Institution Press, Stanford University, c1983. xix, 216 p. ; 29 cm. (Hoover Press bibliographical series ; 63) [Z6616.H588H66 1983] [E742.5.H66] 19 82-80158 ISBN 0-8179-2631-3 : 75.00
1. Hoover, Herbert, 1874-1964—Archives—Catalogs. 2. Hoover Institution on War, Revolution, and Peace—Catalogs. 3. World War, 1914-1918—Civilian relief—Sources—Bibliography—Catalogs. 4. World War, 1939-1945—Civilian relief—Sources—Bibliography—Catalogs. 5. United States—Politics and government—1929-1933—Sources—Bibliography—Catalogs. I. Danielson. Elena S., 1947- II. Palm, Charles G. III. Title. IV. Series.

HOPKINS, Keith, 305.5'2'0937
1934-
Death and renewal / Keith Hopkins. Cambridge [Cambridgeshire] ; New York : Cambridge University Press, 1983. p. cm. (Sociological studies in Roman history ; v. 2) Includes bibliographies and indexes. [JC83.H76 1983] 19 82-17887 ISBN 0-521-24991-0 : 39.50
1. Rome—Politics and government—265-30 B.C. 2. Rome—Politics and government—30 B.C.-284 A.D. 3. Heads of state—Rome—Succession. 4. Elite (Social sciences)—Rome. 5. Gladiators. 6. Funeral rites and ceremonies—Rome. 7. Mourning customs—Rome. I. Title. II. Series.

HOPPEL, Joe. 796.357'0973
The Sporting News baseball trivia book / co-editor-writer, Joe Hoppel ; co-editor-researcher,

Craig Carter. 1st ed. St. Louis. Mo. : Sporting News Pub. Co., c1983. 286 p. : ill. ; 23 cm. [GV863.A1H66 1983] 19 83-135401 ISBN 0-89204-103-X (pbk.) : 9.95
1. Baseball—United States—Miscellanea. I. Carter, Craig. II. Sporting news. III. Title. IV. Title: Baseball trivia book.

HOSPITAL 362.1'1'068
departmental profiles / edited by Alan J. Goldberg (Group Systems Engineering Program, Massachusetts Hospital Association). Chicago, Ill. : Hospital Management Systems Society of the American Hospital Association, c1982. v, 136 p. ; 28 cm. Bibliography: p. 127-136. [RA971.H5933 1982] 19 82-6250 ISBN 0-87258-356-2 : 25.00
1. Hospitals—Administration. 2. Industrial engineering. I. Goldberg, Alan J. II. Massachusetts Hospital Association. Group Systems Engineering Program.

HOW it works : 603'.21
the illustrated science and invention encyclopedia. International ed. Westport, CT : H.S. Stuttman, [1983] p. cm. Includes indexes. [T9.H74 1983] 19 82-19610 ISBN 0-85685-522-7 : 299.50
1. Technology—Dictionaries. 2. Science—Dictionaries. 3. Technology—Dictionaries, Juvenile. 4. Science—Dictionaries, Juvenile.

HOW to deal with 343.7306'4
pension plans and compensation for the small business employer under the Economic Recovery Act of 1981 : ALI-ABA video law review study materials. [Philadelphia, Pa.] (4025 Chestnut St., Philadelphia 19104) : American Law Institute-American Bar Association Committee on Continuing Professional Education, c1982. x. 388 p. ; 28 cm. [KF6449.Z9H67 1982] 347.30364 19 82-150682 Price unreported
1. Pension trusts—Taxation—Law and legislation—United States. 2. Deferred compensation—Taxation—Law and legislation—United States. 3. Small business—Taxation—Law and legislation—United States. I. American Law Institute-American Bar Association Committee on Continuing Professional Education.

HOW to value marital 346.7304'2
property in divorce, the difference it can make : ALI-ABA video law review study materials. [Philadelphia, Pa.] (4025 Chestnut, St., Philadelphia 19104) : American Law Institute-American Bar Association Committee on Continuing Professional Education, c1982. x. 84 leaves ; 28 cm. "Q108." Bibliography: leaves 84-85. [KF524.Z9H68] 347.30642 19 82-137755 Price unreported
1. Separate property—Valuation—United States. 2. Community property—Valuation—United States. 3. Divorce—Law and legislation—United States. I. American Law Institute-American Bar Association Committee on Continuing Professional Education.

HUMAN needs 3 and the 610.73
nursing process / edited by Helen Yura, Mary B. Walsh. Norwalk, Conn. : Appleton-Century-Crofts, c1983. xvii, 288 p. ; 23 cm. Includes bibliographies and index. [RT42.H753 1983] 19 82-20580 15.95
1. Nursing. 2. Need (Psychology) 3. Nursing—Philosophy. I. Yura, Helen. II. Walsh, Mary B. III. Title: Human needs three and the nursing process.

HUMPLE, Carol Segrave, 658.3'042
1942-
Management and the older workforce : policies and programs / Carol Segrave Humple, Morgan Lyons. New York : AMA Membership Publications Division. American Management Associations, c1983. 71 p. : ill. ; 23 cm. (AMA management briefing) Bibliography: p. 71. [HD6279.H85 1983] 19 82-22791 ISBN 0-8144-2287-X : 10.00 ($7.50 to members)
1. Aged—Employment. 2. Age and employment. 3. Industrial management. I. Lyons, Morgan. 1942- II. Title. III. Series.

HYPOXIA, man at 616.9'893
altitude / [edited by] John R. Sutton, Norman L. Jones, Charles S. Houston. New York, N.Y. : Thieme-Stratton ; [Germany] : G. Thieme, 1982. xv, 213 p. ; 26 cm. Proceedings of the 2nd Banff Hypoxia Symposium, sponsored by the Arctic Institute of North America. Includes bibliographies and index. [QP82.2.A4H95 1982] 19 81-84773 ISBN 0-86577-048-4 pbk. : 24.95
1. Altitude, Influence of—Congresses. 2. Anoxemia—Congresses. I. Sutton, John R., M.D. II. Jones, Norman Longden. III. Houston, Charles S. IV. Banff Hypoxia Symposium (2nd : 1981) V. Arctic Institute of North America.

IDE. Arthur Frederick. 305.4'094
Special sisters : Woman in the European Middle Ages / by Arthur Frederick Ide. 4th ed., rev. and expanded. Mesquite. Tex. : Ide House. 1983. 115 p. : ill. ; 22 cm. Rev. ed of: Women in the European Middle Ages. 1981. Includes bibliographical references and index. [HQ1147.E85I29 1983] 19 82-23352 ISBN 0-86663-097-X (lib. bdg.) : 15.95 ISBN 0-86663-096-1 (pbk.) : 10.95
1. Women—Europe—History—Middle Ages. 500-1500. I. Title.

ILLINGWORTH. Ronald 613'.0432
Stanley. 1909-
The normal child : some problems of the early years and their treatment / Ronald S. Illingworth. 8th ed. Edinburgh : Churchill Livingstone. 1983. p. cm. Includes bibliographies and index. [RJ101.I4 1983] 19 82-9420 ISBN 0-443-02618-1 : 37.50
1. Infants—Care and hygiene. 2. Children—Care and hygiene. I. Title.

THE Illustrated 621.388'3'029473
video equipment encyclopedia, 1983. Shawnee Mission, KS (P.O. Box 2056, Shawnee Mission 66201) : B. Daniels Co., 1983. 958 p. : ill. (some col.) ; 28 cm. (Equipment catalogs) Cover title: Video. Spine title: Video encyclopedia. [TK6650.I353 1983] 19 83-128137 75.00 (pbk.)
1. Television—Apparatus and supplies—Catalogs. I. Title: Video equipment encyclopedia. II. Title: Video. III. Title: Video encyclopedia.

IMMUNE mechanisms in 616.6'1079
renal disease / edited by Nancy B. Cummings, Alfred F. Michael, and Curtis B. Wilson. New York : Plenum Medical Book Co., 1983 printing. xxviii, 564 p. : ill. ; 26 cm. Includes bibliographies and index. [RC903.I42 1983] 19 82-15135 ISBN 0-306-40948-8 : 65.00
1. Kidneys—Diseases—Immunological aspects. I. Cummings, Nancy B. II. Michael, Alfred F., 1928- III. Wilson, Curtis B.

INMAN, Don. 001.64'43
Assembly language graphics for the TRS-80 color computer / Don Inman and Kurt Inman with Dymax. Reston, Va. : Reston Pub. Co., c1983. viii, 280 p. : ill. ; 24 cm. Includes index. [QA76.8.T18I354 1983] 19 82-16548 ISBN 0-8359-0318-4 : 22.95 ISBN 0-8359-0317-6 (pbk.) : 14.95
1. TRS-80 color computer—Programming. 2. Assembler language (Computer program language) 3. Computer graphics. I. Inman. Kurt. II. Dymax (Firm) III. Title.

INTERNATIONAL 599'.019'24
Conference "Kinin 81 Munich" (1981)
Kinins—III / edited by Hans Fritz ... [et al.]. New York : Plenum Press, c1983. 2 v. (xxi, 1222) : ill. ; 26 cm. (Advances in experimental medicine and biology ; v. 156) Proceedings of the international conference held Nov. 2-5, 1981, in Munich. Includes bibliographies and index. [QP552.K5I53 1981] 19 82-19009 145.00
1. Kinins—Congresses. I. Fritz, H. II. Title. III. Series.

INTERNATIONAL Conference 662'.8
on Biomass (1st:1980: Brighton, East Sussex)
Energy from biomass : 1st E.C. Conference : proceedings of the International Conference on Biomass held at Brighton, England. 4-7 November 1980 / edited by W. Palz, P. Chartier, and D.O. Hall. London : Applied Science Publishers, c1981. xxiii. 982 p. : ill. ; 23 cm. Includes bibliographical references and index.

1b-16 Could you locate in the Weekly Record a book if you knew only its title? Such as a novel called Random Winds?

1b-17 You must therefore know, or be able to make an educated guess at, the main entry of the item in order to locate it. In #1b-13 you noted that there were no subject entries as such in the Weekly Record. However, do you have any subject access at all to the Weekly Record?

1b-18 In #1b-1, you had the problem of finding information about a book on photography published in the last few weeks, which might not be in BIP. Now, where and how would you go about finding it?

1b-19 The Weekly Record is published weekly, therefore 52 times a year. Suppose you had to find, in WR, the listing for a title which you knew had to be published last year but did not know what part of last year. Would you then have to go through every weekly issue of WR to a possible total of 52 issues?

1b-20 Look at a recent issue of American Book Publishing Record (BPR), and read the introductory note on the inside front cover. What connection does BPR have with WR?

1b-21 Has the Weekly Record always had this monthly cumulation? In other words, when did American Book Publishing Record begin?

1b-22 What is the scope of BPR?

1b-23 And as a further aspect of the scope, what (how much) information will be included in the individual entries or citations in BPR?

1b-24 What is the arrangement of BPR? Is it the same as the Weekly Record?

1b-25 If you are looking in BPR for a book for which you have the author (Wheeler, Daniel D.) and the title (A Practical Guide for Making Decisions), could you find it without determining the subject area? (This is a made-up title so don't try to look it up.)

1b-26 BPR is arranged by subject. Is it therefore alphabetically by subject?

1b-27 How would you find books on education in a recent issue of BPR? What about books on business? Library science?

1b-28 BPR, then, is a classified subject arrangement with a specific subject index. How would you find fiction in BPR?

1b-29 What title have you examined previously which was arranged by subject?

1b-30 Is the subject arrangement of BPR similar to the Subject Guide to BIP?

1b-31 In BPR, books on the subject of "pottery" are listed in the 730's, within the broad subject division of "The Arts," the 700's. Are they therefore listed in proximity to all of the books on crafts, regardless of whether these books are on the subject of pottery, weaving, woodcraft, leather work, etc.?

1b-32 Is a similar arrangement followed in Subject Guide to BIP?

1b-33 The scope of BPR then is the same as Weekly Record, but the arrangement is classified (by Dewey Decimal Classification) with author/title indexes. What are two basic differences between Weekly Record and BPR?

1b-34 Does Weekly Record have a subject approach? Does BPR have a subject approach? Therefore, can you look in Weekly Record and find all books published on education as easily as in BPR?

1b-35 In #1b-19, you found that in order to locate the listing for a title published last year, you would have to go through each weekly issue of Wekely Record to a possible total of 52 issues. Now that you know about BPR, what advantage would you have?

1b-36 What then are two advantages of BPR over Weekly Record?

1b-37 What is one advantage of Weekly Record over BPR? Does this tell you anything about the possible uses of Weekly Record in a library?

1b-38 When did BPR begin publication and what does this tell you about access to Weekly Record information prior to that time?

1b-39 Review: what information does the BPR/WR citation give you which you do not get from BIP? (See #1b-8)

1b-40 You have seen that the weekly issues of Weekly Record cumulate or combine citations into a monthly listing in BPR. Do the monthly issues of BPR further cumulate or combine?

1b-41 How often does the BPR Cumulative come out, and how far back does it go?

1b-42 Presumably, the BPR Cumulative has exactly the same scope and arrangement as BPR; what, then, is its specific use?

1b-43 The next source to examine, American Book Publishing Record Cumulative 1950-1977, goes back to 1950, but BPR itself only began in 1960 (see #1b-21). How then can this new cumulation go back further than BPR itself? Where do the listings of materials published from 1950-1959 come from? Where will you need to look to find this out?

1b-44 What is the scope of American Book Publishing Record Cumulative 1950-1977?

1b-45 What is the arrangement of ABPR Cumulative 1950-1977?

1b-46 What was the publisher and date of publication of a book titled The Elite Press by John C. Merrill?

1b-47 Hilda Boden is the author of a number of novels for children, published in the 1960's. How would you find the titles and dates of these novels?

1b-48 A book by Ray Pelfrey titled The Passing Game (about football) was published in Iowa in 1956. This was prior to the first publication of the American Book Publishing Record monthly issues in 1960. Can you locate an entry for this book in ABPR Cumulative 1950-1977? What was the name of the publisher of this book, and who helped Pelfrey write it?

1b-49 How would you find out what books have been published in the past 25 years or so on the cost of medical care in the U.S.?

1b-50 A second major cumulation titled American Book Publishing Record Cumulative 1876-1949 (in 15 volumes) was published by the Bowker Company in 1980. Since BPR only began in 1960, where do these particular listings of materials come from? Where will you need to look to find this out?

1b-51 In 1939, the Metropolitan Museum of Art in New York published a catalog, titled Life in America, of an exhibition of paintings. How many copies of this catalog were printed? (Use the American Book Publishing Record Cumulative 1876-1949.)

1b-52 Again using American Book Publishing Record Cumulative 1876-1949, how would you go about locating the title of a book by E. Flynn, published in the 1930's, on the subject of traveling to Australia by yacht?

1b-53 Of all the sources you have had so far, where could you look to find the publisher of Getting More Done in Less Time by Mike Phillips, published in 1982?

1b-54 You could get that information from either BIP or BPR Cumulative 1978. What does BIP tell you that BPR Cumulative does not?

1b-55 Where would you look to find out how many new editions of Shakespeare's plays appeared (in the U.S.) in 1982?

1b-56 Where would you look to find a list of all the different editions of Shakespeare's plays which are in print?

1b-57 Would the listing in BIP give you enough information to distinguish sufficiently between the various versions or editions? Suppose you wanted to make a choice between editions, for purchase, or for recommendation to a reader. Where would you go to find further information?

1b-1: Not necessarily. It would depend somewhat on what time of year you happened
to be using BIP. BIP itself is published
in the late fall of the year and would not
include listings for titles published after
that date, although it might include them
with an indication that they are "due" on
a particular date. The BIP Supplement,
published in the spring of the year, would
bring this up to date for the next six
months, again with some titles listed
which are "due." Forthcoming Books
(and Subject Guide to Forthcoming Books)
also updates BIP on a bi-monthly basis,
and specifically includes large numbers
of books announced for publication in the
coming five month period.

1b-2: See Sheehy; or the introductory material
in BIP, as you did in #1a-66, specifically
in the "How to use...." section of BIP,
under "Other bibliographic publications to
supplement BIP." In addition to those
sources noted in the end of section 1a,
the BIP introductory material gives Publishers Weekly (AA477) as a source of information about new books coming up, and
then gives both the Weekly Record (see
annotation to Sheehy AA477) and the
American Book Publishing Record (Sheehy
AA463) as providing a "record of the new
books as actually published."

1b-3: The date, volume and issue numbering
appear on the front cover, just below the
title. The masthead statement also appears on the cover, in the lower left
corner. The publisher is the Bowker
Company which also publishes BIP, PTLA,
Subject Guide to BIP, Paperbound Books
in Print, etc.

1b-4: See the paragraph at the top of the cover
page of each week's list: "... which
conscientiously lists current American
books and foreign books distributed in
the United States." It is not so stated
but it has always been assumed that the
list records new books as they are actually published--that is, that books listed
in the Weekly Record of July 4, 1983,

were published on or about that week.
You should be able to assume that titles listed in WR have in fact been published, not just announced for publication.

1b-5: That's hard to tell--basically it means
that they will try to be all-inclusive
(within the limits they have set) but
do not count on it--because actually the
Bowker Co. is dependent upon the individual publishers to contribute information, as it is with PTLA/BIP.

1b-6: Yes, there are specific exclusions.
This is set forth in the introductory
paragraph to each week's listing: x
"These listings do not include...."

1b-7: No. "Book" publication is specifically
stated. Also, these items have been
excluded from listing in BIP (see #1a-
30). Who publishes WR? Who publishes BIP?

1b-8: Cataloging, done either by the Weekly
Record staff or the Library of Congress, and price if available.

1b-9: No. BIP gives author, title, publisher, date of publication, ISBN, and
price (and by implication, the in-print
status). Less consistently, BIP may
give other information such as binding, language, illustrations, etc.
(Sometimes fuller information is given
in the publisher's catalog in PTLA.)
Note that although BIP sometimes gives
the LC catalog card order number, it
does not give the LC classification number.

1b-10: Publisher is Ide House. Price is $10.95.
This 1983 Ide House publication is a re-
vised edition of the title Women in the
European Middle Ages published in 1981.

1b-11: You have three possibilities so far:
the list of publishers in the back of
the last volume of BIP; the separate
Bowker publication titled Publishers,

Distributors, and Wholesalers of the United States: A Directory; the publisher's catalog in PTLA, if it is included. (See #1a-31.)

1b-12: Yes to both. (On the sample page [p. 21] for #1b-9, How It Works and The Illustrated Video Equipment Encyclopedia are examples of title entries; "Hoover Institution on War, Revolution, and Peace," and "International Conference on Biomass" are examples of corporate body or corporate author entries.)

1b-13: No.

1b-14: No on both counts.

1b-15: Basically, the entries are listed alphabetically by main entry only; that is, they are listed under whatever the cataloging entry is, whether author, or corporate author, or title, with no cross-references. This differs from the arrangement of BIP. BIP had entries under both author and title with some cross-references.

1b-16: No, not unless it happened to be entered under title, which is certainly unlikely for a novel.

1b-17: In a way, but awkwardly. The Dewey Decimal number in the upper right corner of each citation is a clue to the subject, and you could, for example, locate all the medical books in a week's listing by running down the right side of the columns and looking at every item with a 610 number. (This is not quite the same thing as a "subject entry," noted in #1b-13. A "subject entry" would mean that the subject itself would be used as the key element in the citation--for example, the subject word "Medicine" would be used as the entry word for the citation, and the citation would be filed alphabetically under "medicine." In general, a subject access would have to be through a subject entry, but you can see from this example of the Weekly Record that it is possible to have other types of access.)

1b-18: You would have to search through the weekly issues of Weekly Record, probably starting from the most recent you had on hand and working back, looking under the author's name (main entry), until you found the citation.

1b-19: Yes, you would, if you were using the Weekly Record only. However, your task is made much easier by the existence of the next bibliographic source on your list of titles to examine: the American Book Publishing Record (BPR).

1b-20: It is, of course, also published by the Bowker Co., but more than that, BPR is a "... cumulation of Weekly Record listings for this month"; that is, the weekly entries from WR are cumulated (added together, or combined) once a month to form the BPR.

1b-21: See Sheehy. It began in 1960, so prior to that time there was no monthly cumulation of the Weekly Record.

1b-22: Same as Weekly Record from which it is taken (except that it comes out only monthly instead of every week).

1b-23: Same as Weekly Record again, since the citations are taken directly from the Weekly Record. (See your answer to #1b-20.)

1b-24: No, it is not the same as the Weekly Record. BPR is "arranged by subject," as is stated on the cover of the 1983 issues.

1b-25: Yes. Each monthly issue of BPR has an author index and a title index.

1b-26: No, it follows the scheme of the Dewey Decimal Classification itself, and is therefore arranged by classification number. It is necessary to know where your subject falls in the classification scheme in order to locate it in the monthly listing. Once you have established that religion is 200, you can go to the 200 section, numerically, and see all in one place all the books on religion. A list of the major, broadest categories of the Dewey classification is given on the first page of the listings in each issue; there you can see that 200 represents religion, 300 represents social science, etc.

1b-27: What you need is a specific subject index to get you into the classification scheme. As of 1983, the BPR monthly issues have a "Subject Guide" which more or less serves this purpose. Access to the published schedules for the Dewey Decimal Classification would also help.

        Education is not one of the broad Dewey classifcations listed on the first page of the listings for BPR. You could guess that it would fall within the social science classification (300's). In the Subject Guide, a series of specific headings beginning with "education" refer you to the appropriate Dewey class numbers (and Library of Congress Classification numbers as well); the major Dewey number for education appears to be 370. The Dewey numbers in the Subject Guide under subject headings beginning with "business" are mainly within the 300's also, but some are in the 600's. Library science and other library-related headings refer mainly to the 000's.

1b-28: Fiction is listed separately, after the 900's, arranged alphabetically by author. Authors and titles are also both in the indexes.

1b-29: Subject Guide to Books in Print.

1b-30: No, not really. Subject Guide to BIP is arranged alphabetically by Library of Congress subject headings. BPR is arranged numerically by Dewey Decimal Classification with broader subject divisions than in Subject Guide to BIP.

1b-31: Yes.

1b-32: No. In Subject Guide to BIP (1982-83), books on pottery are listed alphabetically under the subject heading "Pottery," between "Potters' Marks" and "Potting Electronics." Books on weaving are under "Weaving," between "Weathervanes" and "Webb, Beatrice."

1b-33: The frequency of appearance, and the arrangement.

1b-34: Weekly Record does not really have a subject approach, except in the most awkward way by checking all the Dewey decimal numbers in the upper right corner of each and every listing. See #1b-16. BPR does have a subject approach; once you have established that the Dewey classification number for education is 370 (as you did in #1b-27), then you can simply look there and find all the books published on education (for that period) listed in one place.

1b-35: You could go through each monthly cumulation, in BPR, to a possible number of 12 issues--searching by author, as you have noted in #1b-25.

1b-36: (1) Basic subject access; (2) one list (monthly) compared to four or five lists (weekly) in Weekly Record.

1b-37: More frequent, up-to-date information. (Since Weekly Record comes out once a week, compared with BPR's monthly, you will get the information on new books faster or sooner.) Libraries such as major research libraries or special libraries which have a need for bibliographic or ordering information as soon as it is available will find the WR very useful; other libraries may find that the once-a-month publication of BPR is fast enough.

1b-38: 1960. (Sheehy again.) Prior to 1960, there was no monthly cumulation of the Weekly Record entries, and searching would have to be done through the entire 52 issues. Furthermore, prior to 1960, there was no reasonable--or quick--subject access to the entries in Weekly Record (refer back to #1b-17).

1b-39: Cataloging information, basically: LC classification number, Dewey classification number, added entry and subject tracings, etc. (See #1b-8 and #1b-9.)

1b-40: Into the American Book Publishing Record (BPR) Cumulative, the next title on your list to examine. Again, you might be a jump ahead of the titles, seeing a need and looking for a bibliographic tool or source which fills that need.

1b-41: See Sheehy annotation or figure it out from what you have on the shelves. BPR first cumulates into an annual volume (Sheehy AA464) and has, in the past, further cumulated quinquennially (every five years) (Sheehy AA465). Thus your library might have a cumulation for 1960-64, for 1965-69, for 1970-74, for 1975-79, plus annual cumulations for 1980, 1981, 1982, etc. In 1979, Bowker published a major cumulation of this set, titled American Book Publishing Cumulative 1950-1977 (Sheehy 2AA58), which is the next source you will examine. (It should be noted that libraries which decided not to purchase the 1950-77 cumulation may still have the 1960+ quinquennial and annual cumulations, and those libraries which did purchase the 1950-1977 cumulations may have discarded the 1960+ cumulations. The 1978+ annual and quinquennial cumulations will still be needed, of course.)

1b-42: Mainly that it is much easier to look in one alphabetical or subject list (annual cumulative) rather than in 12 separate monthly lists. This is the basic principle behind "cumulation" and it is one which is very useful to the construction of reference sources, particularly bibliographies.

1b-43: See the Sheehy annotation (2AA58). The title page also gives you some information and it is further explained in the Preface. Sheehy and the first page of the preface indicate that "Thousands of titles from the National Union Catalog for the years 1950 to 1968 and from the Library of Congress MARC tapes for the years 1968 to 1977 that have not appeared in previous cumulations of the American Book Publishing Record are included." (The Library of Congress/National Union Catalog sources will be covered in Section 4 of this manual.) And remember that although BPR has existed only since 1960, the Bowker Company has been publishing this information in the Weekly Record since 1876.

1b-44: Again, see the Preface. The scope is similar to BPR, of course; books published and distributed in the United States, with similar exclusions of governmental publications, subscription books, dissertations, etc. But one can expect the 1950-1977 cumulation to include titles which were not in BPR 1960-. See the statement quoted from the Preface in the answer to the previous question, #1b-43.

1b-45: Again, see Sheehy or the Preface if you cannot figure this out by looking at the source itself. The arrangement is similar to BPR, basically by subject (Dewey Decimal Classification) with author and title indexes, and a specific subject index to some extent through the "Subject Guide" (vol. 15).

1b-46: Since you have no date of publication, ABPR Cumulative 1950-1977 is especially useful here because it covers, in one alphabet, such an extensive period of time. This set has author and title indexes, so you can approach it either way for this question. The author index (vol. 13) lists, under Merrill, John Calhoun, seven Dewey Decimal Classification numbers. You need to check each of these out in the main classified arrangements (vols. 1-10) to find the entry for the particular book you want. In this case, the fourth Dewey number listed (070.9) is the one you want. (You might have guessed from the title of the book that the subject was journalism, and you might have known that in

Dewey, journalism is classified as 070 so that you could have checked out that reference first.) Actually, this particular entry is much easier to find from a title approach. The title index (vol. 14) lists only one Dewey number for this title, so you can go directly to the entry you want.

If you did not have access to the 1950-1977 cumulation of BPR, you could have searched through the various quinquennial and annual cumulations of BPR (1960-64, 1965-69, 1970-74, 1975-79, etc.) to locate the entry. Presumably it would have been in the 1965-69 cumulation, but you wouldn't have known that to begin with since you didn't have the date.

1b-47: The author index of the ABPR Cumulative 1950-1977 set lists Boden, Hilda and refers you to "JUV" which is in the fiction volume (vol. 11) of the set. Or, since you knew you were dealing with fiction, you could have gone directly to vol. 11. Fiction is listed by author, and juvenile fiction is listed separately, following regular or adult fiction. On p. 72 of vol. 11 are listed, under Boden, Hilda, about a dozen titles, and each entry gives complete bibliographic information including publisher, date, paging, etc. This would not necessarily represent a complete listing of all of Hilda Boden's novels for children, but you can assume that it would be most of them, at least for the period covered by this particular source. Again, if you did not have access to the 1950-77 cumulation, you could have searched through the various quinquennial and annual cumulations of BPR (1960-64, 1965-69, etc.).

1b-48: ABPR Cumulative 1950-1977 does include titles which were not listed in the original BPR's. See the answers to #1b-43 and #1b-44. The author index under Pelfrey refers you to vol. 12 (which is the volume for those books for which the original source gave no Dewey Decimal Classification number). Vol. 12 is arranged alphabetically by author, or main entry. The entry for the Pelfrey book is on p. 947 of vol. 12. The publisher was W. C. Brown, and the collaborator was Steve Owens.

1b-49: The American Book Publishing Record Cumulative 1950-1977 covers this 25 year period, and with a classified arrangement most of the books on this subject published during this period should then be brought together in the classification. The trick is to find the classification number which represents your subject. The subject index (vol. 15) has a long list of possible entries under "Medical care," including a specific entry for "Medical care, cost of--United States" which refers you to a series of Dewey numbers, most of which are in the 300's. You could look up these references, and you might also find it helpful to search out some of the other references as well.

1b-50:   See the Sheehy annotation (2AA57), and the preface to the source itself. Similarly to the 1950-77 set (see #1b-43), this cumulation was compiled from the already existing Library of Congress author catalogs (to be examined in Section 4 of this manual); see p. vii of the Preface of the 1876-1949 set. The scope and arrangement of the 1876-1949 set is also similar to the 1950-77 set.

It is interesting to note that 1876 is given in the title as the beginning date of the set (p. vii, third paragraph of the preface indicates why), and the implication of this is that only 1876+ imprints would be included, but the preface then goes on to state (p. viii, first paragraph) that 63,565 pre-1876 entries are also included. The Sheehy annotation does not note this.

In 1982, the Bowker Company also made available the American Book Publishing Record 1876-1981 Author/Title/ Subject Indexes on Microfiche. This approach interfiles in one alphabetical sequence all the entries in the cumulations published through 1981. Besides the microfiche format, the primary difference is in giving only "substantial brief" entries for every title in each of the three indexes. The subject index is comprised of Library of Congress subject headings.

1b-51:   Starting with the title index of ABPR Cumulative 1876-1949, there are four possible references for Life in America (presumably four different publications with the same title). Since no information is given except the title, it would be necessary to check out all four of these references to find the one you want. However, you do know that your title is on the subject of art, and if you also knew that 759.1 was a Dewey class number for art, you would find that the most logical place to start. Even then, however, it is necessary to search through all of the 759.1 items for your particular title (entry "New York. Metropolitan

Museum of Art"). The citation tells you that 10,000 copies were printed. Although these two major ABPR cumulations pull a lot of information together in one set, and provide a basic subject approach for the citations, they can also be very cumbersome and time-consuming to search in.

1b-52:   Using the author index, five possible "E. Flynn"s are given, and you could search through all of these references. Another approach might be subject. Using the Subject Guide, under "Australia --Descr. & trav.," you find references to the Dewey class number 919.4. You could then go directly to that number in the basic part of the set and, within the 919.4s, go directly to Flynn, E. (Being aware of 919 as a reasonable Dewey class number for Australia would have helped you to eliminate some of the possible E. Flynn's in the author index, also.)

1b-53:   BIP (by author or title), if it is still in print. (According to BIP 1982-83, the publisher is Bethany House.) The same information (plus extensive cataloging information) is found in the BPR Cumulative volume for 1982, p. 615.

1b-54:   The in-print status.

1b-55:   BPR Cumulative 1982 is best--all in one spot, and gives 1982 publications only. BIP will tell you all editions in print, including other than 1982, so it is more confusing.

1b-56:   As noted in the answer to the previous question, BIP will give you those which are in print. You want to know in-print status. Therefore, BIP.

1b-57:   There are several possibilities and which ones you could use would depend to some extent upon the resources you have available in your particular library.

Referring to the publishers' catalogs in PTLA (for each of the entries in BIP, and there are several pages of them) might possibly give more information about the books. Checking out each entry as it is listed in American Book Publishing Record might also help, since those entries usually give full cataloging information and are more thorough than BIP.

Even more helpful would be some sort of a bibliography which annotates or discusses the material listed (and which includes Shakespeare). This is somewhat similar to the problem you had

in finding a complete listing of the editions of Tom Sawyer; see #1a-64 and
#1a-65. Here, as you did with Tom
Sawyer/Mark Twain, you could go to
Sheehy or similar listings of reference
works for some suggestions. (Or you
could go to the card catalog of your
particular library.)

   A bibliography of Shakespeare
might be helpful if it included enough
discussion of the various editions to help
you make a choice regarding authentic-
ity, readability, etc. Selective bibliographies, those which set out to list "best
books" or evaluate available books, might
be even more helpful. Sheehy lists some
of these under General Reference Works
--Bibliography--Selection of Books--
Guides, etc. (p. 30 of the 9th edition).
One which would be helpful in giving
information about various editions of
Shakespeare would be the Reader's Adviser (Sheehy AA339, 1AA68). If you
have a recent edition of this source available to you, look to see what it has to
tell you about Shakespeare, which should
help you to see the usefulness of such
"selection aids' or selective bibliographies
or readers' advisory type sources.

NATIONAL BIBLIOGRAPHIC RECORDS (U.S.)--CURRENT

Questions #1c/1--1c/59

All of the titles you have examined so far are publications of the Bowker Co., so by now you should be aware that the Bowker Company is one of the major publishers of current bibliographic information. The Bowker Company is a commercial publishing firm, but one which is very closely associated with the "book trade" and is well known for publishing materials which are of use to the book trade and to librarians. Sources of national bibliographic records are not necessarily always produced by the library profession; this is especially true in the United States.

H. W. Wilson is another major commercial firm involved in the publishing of current bibliographic sources particularly useful to librarians, and in your future examination of bibliographic and reference sources, you will learn about many of their publications. The next titles to examine, of current sources in the U.S. national bibliographic records, are publications of the Wilson Company:

> Cumulative Book Index (CBI) (AA461, AA468)
> Vertical File Index (AA479)

There are only two sources to examine in this section, but there are many questions in this section which review and compare these sources with the ones you have already examined in Sections 1a and 1b.

1c-1   The first of these two sources is the more important: Cumulative Book Index, or CBI. Your first problem is to determine the scope and arrangement of this source. Judging from your past experience, where might you look for this?

1c-2   Who publishes CBI, when did it begin publication, and how often does it come out?

1c-3   Locate the volumes of the Cumulative Book Index on the shelves, and look at the title page of one of the recent issues or volumes (in the paper-covered recent issues, the cover itself constitutes the title page). What is the full title of CBI, including the sub-title?

1c-4   This full title tells you a great deal about this source, beginning with the first word. What does "cumulative" mean, and where has this concept showed up before?

1c-5   What is the major effect, or advantage, of cumulation?

1c-6   Remembering that CBI goes as far back as 1928, look at all of the bound volumes and paper-covered current issues on the shelf, and see if you can figure out the cumulation pattern. This pattern will be fairly easy to determine for the bound volumes, less easy to determine for the current paper-covered issues. For the current issues, check carefully on the cover for a statement that the issue you have "supersedes" or replaces earlier issues, as this will indicate a cumulation. (And remember that other people may also be using current issues from the shelves so that some may be missing when you look at them.) What does the cumulation pattern appear to be?

1c-7   Does CBI appear to cumulate more often than BPR?

1c-8   So far we have concerned ourselves with sources of bibliographic information on current publica-
        tions--this year, this month, this week. We also need at times to have information on older or
        past publications; in other words, retrospective information. What might some of these retrospec-
        tive bibliographic information needs be?

1c-9   Of course, any current information becomes, eventually, retrospective; any current bibliographic
        record will then become, eventually, a retrospective record. There is no clear-cut point at which
        current becomes retrospective. Usually, one would consider the present year, perhaps also the
        past year, as "current," and anything prior to that as "retrospective." But for the needs of some
        people, last week's information could be considered retrospective.
                Suppose you wanted to find the publisher and the correct publication date for Principles
        of Oral Interpretation, by Dana Burns, which you know to have been published in the United
        States in the 1930's. Of the sources which you have had so far in this unit, which ones could
        you use? CBI? Weekly Record? BPR? BIP? PTLA? (Assume that you are searching specifically
        for the 1930's edition so that you are considering retrospective sources--that is, do not assume the
        title is still in print or has been reprinted. If it happens to be still in print, or if it happens to
        have been reprinted and the reprint is still in print, then of course, it would be listed in the cur-
        rent BIP.

1c-10   Of the yes answers for the preceding questions, which would be the easiest to use and why?

1c-11   So far you have concentrated mainly on the "cumulative" aspect of CBI, and as you have seen,
        this is one of its most effective features. This is part of the arrangement of the set. But there
        is much more to determine about the scope and arrangement. Go back to the full title (#1c-3),
        and consider the sub-title itself. What does this tell you about the scope of this source?

1c-12   Is this any different from the scope of the Bowker publications examined earlier? (BIP, PTLA,
        Weekly Record, BPR, etc.)

1c-13   Does CBI then list all books from all countries?

1c-14   Does CBI list only books in English, regardless of where published?

1c-15   What types of publications are included in the scope of CBI? (The full title gives you a clue; a
        more complete answer is in the preface.)

1c-16   Does CBI include periodicals?

1c-17   The "scope" of CBI, then, is a record of book publication, basically, with some specified excep-
        tions, in the United States, and in English anywhere in the world. How does this differ from
        the record in the Weekly Record (and therefore in BPR)? Is the scope of CBI broader, narrow-
        er, or the same as the Weekly Record?

1c-18 What information is given you in the individual entries in CBI? Is this more, less, or the same as that given you in the Weekly Record entries?

1c-19 Is this more, less or the same as that given you in BPR?

1c-20 Using CBI, what was the publisher and original price for The Causes, Prevention, and Treatment of Sports Injuries, by Hans Kraus, published in 1981?

1c-21 What is the arrangement of CBI? (Actually, you had to figure this out in order to locate The Causes, Prevention, and Treatment of Sports Injuries by Hans Kraus.)

1c-22 In #1c-18, you noted the information found in the individual entries. In these entries, is there any indication of the subject of the book (as you have with the LC or Dewey classification numbers, and the subject heading tracings, in the Weekly Record listings)? Is there anything in CBI which appears to indicate subject?

1c-23 Review: What are the three main kinds of access which we need for bibliographic information? (Refer back to #1a-45.)

1c-24 Does CBI have all of these three accesses, and how are they arranged?

1c-25 Is this the same as the arrangement of the Weekly Record?

1c-26 Did BIP have all of these three accesses? How does CBI compare in arrangement to BIP?

1c-27 Does BPR have all three of these accesses, and is its arrangement similar to CBI?

1c-28 Do the CBI title and subject entries give you all of the bibliographic information found under the author entry, or do they serve more as cross-references to a basic entry? Look up two or three examples and compare them.

1c-29 Can you find a list of women's health care centers or services, published in 1981? What kind of "access" do you need to answer this question?

1c-30 Is the CBI subject access a classified one?

1c-31 What other subject access source which you have examined uses subject headings?

1c-32 In #1a-52, you looked up "data processing" in the Subject Guide to BIP. Refer back to your answer for that problem, and then see how CBI treats it. Is it similar?

1c-33 How is fiction listed in Subject Guide to Books in Print? (See #1a-50 and #1a-58.)

1c-34   How is _fiction_ listed in BPR and BPR Cumulative? (See #1b-28.)

1c-35   How is fiction listed in CBI?

1c-36   Where could you go to find, most easily, some titles (and authors) of recently published science fiction?

1c-37   Since CBI attempts to record all English language publications, would you then expect it to be a fairly good and complete record for Great Britain as well as the U.S.? For any other countries?

1c-38   In examining these sources so far, you have stressed only "scope" and "arrangement" from the general criteria for evaluation of reference sources. Another criterion often mentioned is that of "special features." Does CBI have any other things which might be considered as special features? Can you recall any other special features from previous sources you have examined?

1c-39   Find in CBI the entry for _They Talk and Walk_ by Raymond B. Brown, published in 1966 by the Magna Carta Press. How many pages does it contain?

1c-40   You have the information that _Growing Up in Religion_ by Evelyn Derry was published in London in 1963. Who is the publisher?

1c-41   The second of these sources to examine, the Vertical File Index, is one which provides coverage specifically for pamphlet material. What is a pamphlet? What is a "vertical file?"

1c-42   Of the bibliographic sources you have examined so far, which have incuded pamphlets?

1c-43   Who is the pubisher of the Vertical File Index?

1c-44   What is the arrangement of the Vertical File Index? Is it similar to the other Wilson bibliography you have examined already? Does it have the three primary types of bibliographic access?

1c-45   Looking at one of the recent issues of the Vertical File Index itself, can you tell what its _scope_ is?

1c-46   Look through a few recent issues of the Vertical File Index to see what type of subject heading is used, and to see what type of material is listed. (Many of the items listed in the VFI do not seem to fall clearly into the category of "pamphlet," nor are the items always inexpensive or of a minimum number of pages.) If you were looking through the VFI for inexpensive material for your library collection on the general subject of conservation, what subject headings might you find such material under?

1c-47   Does the Vertical File Index include government publications (for example, titles for which the publisher is some agency or branch of the U.S. federal government)?

1c-48   When did the Vertical File Index begin publication? Was it always known by that title? Why is it useful for you to know that a serial or periodical publication has changed title?

1c-49   Is it possible to use the Vertical File Index to identify specific pamphlets? For example, could you use the VFI to locate the publisher and price for David Milne's Environmental Perception and Behavior? (This is a made-up title so do not try to search it.)

1c-50   A two-page pamphlet listing library materials on acid rain was issued in mid-1983. What is its price and where can it be obtained?

1c-51   Would you expect the above title to be listed in BIP? In Weekly Record/BPR?

1c-52   What do you think would be the primary use or purpose of the Vertical File Index? Why is such a source necessary?

        The next few questions, from #1c-53 to #1c-59, are set up as a short review, covering all the sources you have looked at so far in sections 1a, 1b, and 1c. It is not necessary to go back to the sources themselves and look up all the answers, but you may find it helpful to do so, particularly for those aspects which still may not be clear to you.

1c-53   You want to find the titles of some books on anthropology published in 1955 or 1956. Where would you look?

1c-54   You need the current price of the Penguin edition (paperback) of H. Rider Haggard's King Solomon's Mines. What are three possible sources in which you could search for this?

1c-55   A book entitled Adventuring in Lakeland by Arthur H. Griffin was published in England in 1980. Where would you find the name of the publisher?

1c-56   Where would you look to find if there is a "variorum" edition of Yeats' poems available for purchase?

1c-57   Could you have found the answer to the previous question--a "variorum" edition of Yeats' poems-- by checking in BIP under title?

1c-58   You want some inexpensive but up-to-date information on sex education for your school library. Where might you get the names of some titles to send for?

1c-59   You want to find the titles of books on art published recently, this year and last year. What are at least three different sources you could turn to for this information? Which one would be the easiest to use, and why? (If you can't immediately come up with the answer to this question, then try actually looking up such books in all three sources and see what you find out.)

NATIONAL BIBLIOGRAPHIC RECORDS (U.S.)--CURRENT

Answers #1c/1--1c/59

1c-1: Probably you should look for a preface or introduction. Current issues of CBI contain only a short prefatory note; recent cumulative volumes contain approximately the same note. A somewhat fuller statement can be found in some of the earlier (1965/66) cumulations.

    The annotation in Sheehy may also be of help; in this case it is quite full, but somewhat confusing, since CBI appears in Sheehy twice; AA468 refers to the currently-appearing monthly issues; AA461 gives fuller information on the current issues, plus referring to the earlier volumes in the series, including the United States Catalog which will not be discussed in this manual until Section 2a.

    Use Sheehy, plus a recent preface in CBI itself, and a careful examination of the source itself in comparison to the information you get from Sheehy and the preface.

1c-2: The publisher is the Wilson Company. It began publication in 1928, or 1893 if you consider the United States Catalog as part of CBI; see the annotation in Sheehy. It comes out monthly (except August), as of 1983.

1c-3: Cumulative Book Index; a World List of Books in the English Language.

1c-4: Cumulative is a combining or an adding together (check a dictionary or the ALA Glossary for a fuller explanation), and you have already seen it at work with the Weekly Record/BPR/BPR Cumulative sequence.

1c-5: Basically, it reduces the number of places in which you have to search. You have seen it, for example, cumulate weekly issues into monthly issues, and then into annual volumes, reducing the possible search places from 52 to 1.

1c-6: The cumulation pattern for the early volumes is every five years: 1928-32,

1933-37, 1938-42. Then a six-year cumulation (1943-48), followed by two four-year cumulations (1949-52; 1953-56). The pattern was then two-year cumulations: 1957-58, 1959-60, 1961-62, 1963-64 (the 1963-64 cumulation was so large that it was necessary to bind it in two volumes, but it is still only one cumulation for that period, as the volumes are divided alphabetically), 1965-66, 1967-68. From 1969 on, the pattern has been annual volumes. The current monthly issues cumulate quarterly, and then annually.

1c-7: Yes. BPR cumulates annually (from monthly issues), then every five years. CBI cumulates quarterly as well as annually. Frequent cumulation is one of the basic principles behind the Wilson Company publications.

1c-8: Identification of older published materials--determination of correct author, correct title, etc.; further information on older publications--such as the edition, the series (if any) in which published, the publisher, etc., the date of publication; selecting and ordering older publications to fill in a library's collections (last week's publications on a particular subject are not always the best, just because they are the newest; there are "classics" in subject areas as well as in literature); identifying and locating older publications for research purposes; compiling bibliographies.

1c-9: CBI: yes, it goes back to 1928 (or 1893);
Weekly Record: yes, it began in 1876;
BPR Cumulative (annual): no, it goes back only to 1960;
BPR Cumulative 1950-1977: no, it goes back only to 1950;
BPR Cumulative 1876-1949: yes, it goes back to 1876 or earlier;
BIP: no, it began in 1948;
PTLA: no, although it does go back far enough (1873), you don't know

the name of the publisher; if you did know the name of the publisher, you could presumably go back and check through each of the 10 PTLA volumes covering the 1930's, but in fact most libraries would not still have these old editions since they are meant to be used primarily for the year for which they are current.

1c-10:   Probably CBI. You would have to search through three of the five-year cumulations (1928-32, 1933-37, 1938-42) to cover the 1930's, and you could look directly under the author's name.

ABPR Cumulative 1876-1949 has only the one alphabet in which to search, rather than three; however in ABPR Cumulatives, you often have to refer back from the author's name through many complex Dewey numbers to find the specific item you want, and that might end up being more time-consuming than the CBI search. In this particular case, you do have a title as well, and that might be more direct.

In Weekly Record, you would have to go through each weekly issue (52) for each year (10), a possible total of 520 places--and in fact, you would probably not bother unless you were desperate.

1c-11:   "A World list of books in the English Language." It tells you that it includes books publshed in the English language, published anywhere in the world. The prefatory note also tells you this: "an international author, subject, and title bibliography of books published in the English language."

1c-12:   Yes, it is. Those covered only American (or U.S.) publications, none from other countries unless distributed by a U.S. firm. CBI covers all countries.

1c-13:   No, only those in English.

1c-14:   You might well assume that it does, and the current prefatory note (1983) states that "works which are wholly in a foreign language are not listed" although some materials (such as dictionaries) containing some English are included. In the past, CBI has included foreign language publications if published in the U.S. (see for example, in the 1965-66 cumulation under Miller, S. H. and Jacobs, C.: Michel et la pieuvre). However, it is safest to assume that foreign language materials will not be included in CBI.

1c-15:   Cumulative Book Index; a World List of Books.... Books primarily, excluding government documents, most pamphlets, maps, music and other items as listed in the preface (1983).

1c-16:   Basically, no. Nowhere is this specifically stated, but the fact that it is called a "Book Index" or list indicates this to some extent, and the fact that you won't find any periodicals as such listed in its pages should cinch it. (You may find "annuals" listed in CBI, however.)

1c-17:   The types of publication covered are basically similar; CBI also includes English publications from other countries. The scope of CBI is broader than Weekly Record.

1c-18:   Author, title, series, edition, paging, price, publisher, and date of publication. It also gives ISBN if available, and the LC card order number if available. It does not give the cataloging information (Dewey Classification number, LC Classification number, subject headings and added entry tracings) which you got from the Weekly Record. Nor does it give you as full a statement of the size and the binding, usually. The information in CBI is therefore somewhat less than in the Weekly Record. (Note that although CBI sometimes gives the LC catalog card order number, it does not give the LC Classification number.)

1c-19:   Your answer should be the same as in the preceding question, since the BPR entries are the same as those from the Weekly Record.

1c-20:   In the 1981 annual cumulation of CBI, p. 1387, under Kraus, Hans (author). Within the entry, following the title, you are given the paging (147 p.), the fact that it contains illustrations (il), the price ($11.95), the publisher (Playboy Press), the ISBN number (0-87223-674-9), and the Library of Congress card order number (LC 80-54526). Note that this last item is not the LC Classification number (call number) but rather the order number for the LC catalog card. This book will also be found in CBI listed under the title, and under the subject ("Sports--accidents and injuries"). The fullest entry is that found under author.

1c-21:   Basically, it is alphabetical, with all

entries (author, title, subject) in one single alphabet. See the prefatory note.

1c-22: No subject indication in the entry itself unless you can tell or guess from the title. However, there are some entries which have a subject or "subject heading" above the entry. Check in a recent issue to find an example of this, then double check the entry under the author to see if it is entered under author and subject. There is no reference from author entry to the subject entry.

1c-23: Author, title, subject.

1c-24: Yes, it has author/title/subject entries, and all are in a single alphabet.

1c-25: No, CBI includes author, and title, and subject entries, in one alphabet. Weekly Record lists, in one alphabet, only the author or main entry. No titles (unless used as a main entry). No subjects.

1c-26: BIP itself has two accesses: author and title. The third access, subject, is in Subject Guide to BIP. CBI differs in arrangement from BIP because CBI has authors/titles/subjects in one alphabet. BIP has them in two separate alphabets (actually in separate volumes). The arrangement of author/title/subject in one alphabetical list is often called a "dictionary" arrangement (see "dictionary catalog" in the ALA Glossary), and is very typical of Wilson Company publications. Keep it in mind as it will come up again.

1c-27: Yes, BPR has author, title, and subject access. The basic arrangement is by subject (classified rather than alphabetical), and authors and titles are in separate alphabetical indexes, so again they are separate rather than in one alphabetical list as in CBI.

1c-28: Usually the fullest information is found under the author entry, or the main entry. The title entries and the subject entries give enough information to refer to the main entry for more information.

1c-29: You need subject access to answer this. In the 1981 annual cumulation of CBI, under "Women's health services--directories," you find Womancare by Madaras and others.

1c-30: No. BPR is an example of a classified

subject listing. CBI uses "subject headings."

1c-31: Subject Guide to Books in Print.

1c-32: In CBI, in the 1981 annual cumulation, there is a reference from "data processing" to see "Electronic data processing," which is the heading used in CBI. Under "electronic data processing," there is about a page of listings, plus some see also references to other possible headings, such as "analog-to-digital converters," etc.

The heading and the references will only be included in CBI if the volume or issues contain titles on that subject, so recent monthly issues may not show it. This is similar to what you found in Subject Guide to BIP (which also uses subject headings), which had a cross-reference from "data processing" to "electronic data processing," plus two other references.

1c-33: Basically, fiction is excluded from Subject Guide to BIP, except for collections and in some few cases where the background of the fiction is of major historical interest (see the "How to Use...." section of the introductory material in Subject Guide to BIP).

1c-34: In a separate section at the end of the classification scheme.

1c-35: By author and title in the regular alphabetical listing. Also, according to the Sheehy annotation, under subject where appropriate.

1c-36: Most easily and directly, to CBI, checking under the heading "science fiction" (see the answer to #1c-35; this is an example of "subject where appropriate"). You could also look in the fiction section in BPR, but in recent years, BPR has made no attempt to distinguish between science fiction and other fiction, except rarely in the subject heading tracings within the entry, so it would be very time-consuming to find what you want.

1c-37: Yes, you would, and it is, although the information from other countries may be somewhat slower in being listed than that from the U.S. It is also useful as a basic source for Australia, New Zealand, and Canada--other English-speaking countries.

1c-38: The list of publishers with addresses,

included in most of the bound volumes of CBI, is a good example of a special feature, and the same feature is included in BIP. (Lists of abbreviations should not properly be considered as "special features" since an explanation for abbreviations used should be a mandatory feature of any reference source if it is to be most useful.)

1c-39:   It contains 242 pages. The entry for this item is not in the 1965-66 CBI. It is in the 1967-68 cumulation. You should expect that it will appear in the year of publication, or if it is published at the end of the year, it may of course appear in an early issue or cumulation of the following year. But if you do not find it as expected, you should then expect to keep searching forward (to the present date) on the assumption that it may have been listed late. (You might also think in terms of searching backward, in earlier years, in case your given date is incorrect.)

1c-40:   The only source you have so far covering British publications is CBI, and 1963 would be covered in the cumulative volumes for 1963-64. This title is not listed in that cumulative volume. You could then, as you did with #1c-39, work your way forward to the present date, but you would still not find it. In fact, in this case the date was wrong--the publication date should have been 1962, not 1963, and you will find the publication listed in CBI 1961-62. The publisher is the Christian Community Press. When you check in what appears to be a correct source and you don't find the item you are looking for with reasonable searching, you should ALWAYS suspect your information as well as the source itself. And in bibliographic searching, it would not hurt to check a few years back from the date you have, as well as forward.

1c-41:   See the ALA Glossary or a dictionary on both.

1c-42:   BIP excludes free books, unbound materials, pamphlets, among other things. Weekly Record and BPR exclude pamphlets under 49 pages (although the preface to the BPR Cumulative for 1982 indicates that such pamphlets may be included if the subject matter merits public interest....).

1c-43:   Wilson Company, publisher of CBI.

1c-44:   No, the Vertical File Index is not similar

to CBI. It is not a dictionary (one alphabet) arrangement. The basic arrangement is by subject (using subject headings as do Subject Guide to BIP and CBI) with a title index. It has no author access. It is issued monthly. As of 1983, there is no annual cumulation, although the Sheehy annotation shows that it did at one time cumulate annually. (As of 1983, the subject headings cumulate quarterly; the titles do not cumulate at all.)

1c-45:   See sub-title: "A subject and title index to selected pamphlet materials." The scope is limited to pamphlets, and it is selective. Beyond an additional statement in the "Prefatory Note" that "inclusion does not constitute a recommendation," the source itself gives no further indication of the policy or guidelines for selection.
          The Sheehy annotation says: "free and inexpensive pamphlets, booklets, leaflets and mimeographed material considered to be of interest to general libraries. Subjects range from those suitable for school libraries to specialized technical reports."

1c-46:   Conservation, energy, environment, nature, water-pollution, land use, land reform, etc.

1c-47:   You can tell this only by looking through it at the entries. Yes, it does. (See under "land reform" in the June 1983 issue, for example.)

1c-48:   It began publication in 1935, and was previously (to 1955) called the Vertical File Service Catalog. (See Sheehy.)
          If you are searching in back issues and you find that you are looking at something called Vertical File Service Catalog, you won't be confused. Also if you find a reference to it in a source published prior to 1955, it would be useful to recognize it as the currently titled Vertical File Index.

1c-49:   Assuming that the title indicated is a pamphlet, it may or may not be listed in the Vertical File Index. You have no date, and since VFI does not cumulate even annually, you would have to search through potentially many issues, under the title, until you found it, and even then you might not find it because it might not be listed. You can use the VFI for such a purpose but it may not be worth the effort.

1c-50:   See the May 1983 VFI under "acid rain --bibliography" (subject approach). The title is "Acid Rain Materials Every Library Should Have," it is free with a stamped self-addressed envelope, and it is available from the Acid Rain Foundation in St. Paul, Minnesota.

1c-51:   Since it is free, it would not have been in BIP, and since it is under 49 pages, it would not have been in Weekly Record/BPR.

1c-52:   Its main use is suggestions (along with specific ordering information) of available free and inexpensive material suitable for a pamphlet file or vertical file, from a subject point of view. (It can be used for identification of specific materials, but has great limitations in this respect--it is only a selective list and it has no author access or cumulations.) A source such as the Vertical File Index is necessary because much of the material it lists is not included in the major bibliographic sources.

1c-53:   You need a source with subject access which covers that period. Either CBI or ABPR Cumulative 1950-1977 would do. CBI would probably be easier since you could look in the one cumulation covering only 1953-1956 to find those titles from 1955-1956. In ABPR Cumulative 1950-77, you would have to look through many, many titles published over three decades, to find those specifically from 1955 and 1956.
         Subject Guide to BIP did not exist in 1955-56. If you used the SBIP for the present year, you would find only those titles from 1955-56 which happened to be still in print in the present year.

1c--54: BIP (under author or title), PTLA (under Penguin, the publisher), and Paperbound Books in Print (under author or subject): all from Section 1a. CBI does not include "cheap" paperbound books, so probably the Penguin edition would not be listed. Anyway, if it were in CBI, it would be there at the time of its first Penguin publication, and you have (from the question) no idea of the date for this, so you might have to do a lot of hunting to find it. And when you found it, you still wouldn't know the current price or in-print status.

1c-55:   This is an English or British publication (in English, but also in the sense of published in England). The only source you have so far which gives you information on English or British publications is CBI.

1c-56:   "Available for purchase" presumably would mean "in-print," so you would want BIP, the author volume, under Yeats. One of the confusing elements in this problem might have been the use of the word "variorum," if you were not already familiar with it. But by now you should realize that you can clear up most such problems by checking in either a dictionary or in the ALA Glossary.

1c-57:   In the first place, you do not know what the title is--presumably it would be something like "Poems," "Poetry of....," "Collected Poems," "Complete Poems," etc.--and you do know the author's name (Yeats), so it would make more sense to check under author directly. You might be able to find it also in the title volume, with some hunting around.

1c-58:   Inexpensive and current: probably pamphlet material, therefore the Vertical File Index would be useful. CBI might also be helpful. You need a subject approach.

1c-59:   You have to look in those sources which have subject access, so you could use: Subject Guide to BIP (considering that books published last year and this year would probably still be in print); CBI; BPR (monthly issues and annual cumulative). BPR would probably be the easiest to use because of its classified arrangement--"art" is a very broad subject heading, and it would probably be broken up into several more narrowly defined headings in the CBI and Subject BIP, which would mean you would have to look in all of those places; whereas in BPR all the art books would be together in the 700 classification.

NATIONAL BIBLIOGRAPHIC RECORDS (U.S.)--RETROSPECTIVE

Questions #2a/1--2a/44

2a-1   You have examined the major _current_ sources of bibliographic information for the U.S., and you can move on to those sources which are primarily _retrospective_. What is meant by "retrospective"?

Keeping in mind that current sources become retrospective, or that sources which are now retrospective, may have been current at the time of their publication, you should now go on to examine the next group of titles:

    United States Catalog (AA460, see also AA461)
    American Catalogue of Books (AA459)
    Kelly: American Catalogue of Books (AA457)
    Roorbach: Bibliotheca Americana (AA456)

2a-2   All four of these sources were current, at the time of their publication, as CBI is now current. Now, however, they serve us as retrospective sources. The United States Catalog is in fact the forerunner of what current publication?

2a-3   Who was the publisher of the United States Catalog? Who publishes CBI?

2a-4   When actually was the US catalog published? Go to Sheehy for this.

2a-5   Look at the full title, including sub-title, of the US Catalog for 1928. What _was_ it similar to, of the current sources you have already examined?

2a-6   Where would you look to determine the _scope_ of the US Catalog (4th edition, 1928)?

2a-7   Of the two possibilities in the preceding answer, which would be the best?

2a-8   In this case, the preface itself (to the 4th edition, 1928, of the US Catalog) is a very interesting statement of the history of such bibliographic records during the nineteenth and early twentieth century, and you may want to read it entirely as well as looking through it for information on the scope. What _is_ the scope of the US Catalog?

2a-9   Is the scope of the US Catalog then the same as the current CBI?

2a-10   What information is given in the citations in the US Catalog?

2a-11 What is the arrangement of the US Catalog?

2a-12 A book on correlation coefficients by Odell was published by the University of Illinois Press in
       1926. Was this book published as part of a series? What is its correct title?

2a-13 What is the correct title of a Spanish American cookbook by Pauline Kleemann, published in the
       late 1920's?

2a-14 The US Catalog, after the 4th edition, was supplemented, or kept up to date, by CBI. You
       have then with those two sets an unbroken record of US book production from about 1899 through
       the present date. What years are covered by the next set, the American Catalogue of Books?

2a-15 Who is the publisher of the American Catalogue, and what is the publication date?

2a-16 Can you think of any reason why it would have been necessary, or desirable, for a reprint to be
       made of the American Catalogue?

2a-17 Who is the publisher of a book by Lumholtz, titled Among Cannibals: An Account of Four Years'
       Travels in Australia and Queensland, published in 1889?

2a-18 How many volumes are there in the complete set of the American Catalogue, and how are these
       volumes arranged? You can get this answer very directly simply by looking at the spines of the
       volumes as they sit in their correct order on the shelf.

2a-19 What are the three basic accesses which we need for bibliographic sources, and does the Amer-
       ican Catalogue have all of these?

2a-20 Does it have all three accesses for the entire scope of the set?

2a-21 Are these three accesses listed in a "dictionary" type arrangement? (Refer back to #1c-26 or
       to the ALA Glossary for a definition of "dictionary" type arrangement.)

2a-22 In the volumes for the American Catalogue, is each year of the scope (1876-1910) covered by a
       separate volume or separate list? That is, is the material listed for 1906 in a volume or list by
       itself, or cumulated (as in CBI) with other years?

       If you did not fully understand the answer to #2a-18, then questions #2a/19-2a/22 are the types
       of questions which you must ask yourself in order to understand completely the arrangement of
       such bibliographies. If you had difficulties earlier (#2a-17) in locating the publisher of Lum-
       holtz' Among Cannibals (1889), try it again now and see if you find it easier.
            There is a great deal of introductory material in the various volumes of the American Cata-
       logue; if you have time to read them, these prefaces will give you an interesting picture of the
       historical development of U.S. bibliographic control. The prefaces also show that the listings
       in the American Catalogue, from 1876 on, were compiled from the weekly record listings called
       "Annual Catalogues," which were then cumulated--with some additions--into the larger cumula-
       tions as indicated in question #2a-22.

2a-23   Who is the publisher (that is, the original publisher; not the reprint publisher) of the American Catalogue series? (See #2a-15).

2a-24   When you examined the Bowker Company publications in sections 1a and 1b, as part of the current sources, you found that the Weekly Record (as published in Publishers Weekly) and PTLA, although they began publication in the late 1800's (1872 and 1873 respectively), did not serve as effective retrospective records because they did not really cumulate in any reasonable way. Now you find that the records from the early issues of the Weekly Record in Publishers Weekly did in fact cumulate, in a sense, to form the retrospective record of the American Catalogue, which you are now examining. The Bowker Company (or its predecessor, Mr. Leypoldt) is then responsible for an annual record of book production from 1876-1910, and again from the 1960's (with the American Book Publishing Record) to the present. What company moved in to pick up this record during the years 1910 to approximately the 1960's?

2a-25   Preceding the American Catalogue in coverage are Roorbach's Bibliotheca Americana and Kelly's American Catalogue of Books. These are separate publications but are so similar that they are often considered or cited together as Roorbach and Kelly.
        What is the scope of Roorbach? That is, what years are covered by this record? What types of publications are included? Are these publications limited in any way by language or by country of publication?

2a-26   What years are covered by Roorbach, bibliographically? When was Roorbach published, originally?

2a-27   Note then that the years covered and the years published are not necessarily similar. With Roorbach, the first cumulative volume was not published until 1852, but its coverage goes back to 1820. What are the years covered by Kelly, bibliographically?

2a-28   When was Kelly published originally? Is this the same as the "years covered"?

2a-29   Otherwise, is the scope of Kelly similar to that of Roorbach?

2a-30   What information is given in the entries for Roorbach and Kelly? How does this compare with more current sources, such as CBI, BPR, etc.?

2a-31   What is the publisher and original price of Durrie's A Genealogical History of the Holt Family, published in 1864?

2a-32   Can you find in Roorbach or Kelly the first name of the author of Scampavias from Gibel Tarek to Stamboul published in 1857?

2a-33   Who is the author of France and England in North America, a Series of Historical Narratives published in 1865?

2a-34   If you were able to find answers to the last three questions, you have probably then already figured out the arrangement of Roorbach and Kelly. It is, in fact, quite similar to that of the American Catalogue, with one exception. What is the difference? Are Roorbach and Kelly lacking any of the basic accesses?

2a-35   However, is it possible to find in Roorbach and Kelly, the bibliographic information (author, title, imprint) of a book on Arctic expeditions, published in the U.S. in the latter half of the 19th century?

2a-36   Therefore you do have a kind of subject access, through the title. It is limited, however. Could you have found the titles given in the answer to #2a-35 if you had looked under "explorations" or "adventures"? Why or why not?

2a-37   What then is the basic limitation to using titles as a subject index?

2a-38   What is the arrangement of Roorbach and Kelly? Use your experience with the last several questions as the basis for this.

2a-39   What is the cautionary comment made about Roorbach and Kelly in Sheehy?

2a-40   In #2a-35, you found under the title entry, a book by Sargent on Arctic expeditions, titled <u>Arctic Adventures by Sea and Land</u> published by Phillip in 1857. Look in the same source (Roorbach, 1855-1858) under the author (Sargent, Epes). Is the information you find there similar to the title entries?

The next four questions are REVIEW.

2a-41   Where would you look to find the publisher and price for the book <u>Teacher</u> by Sylvia Ashton Warner?

2a-42   Where would you go to find out who is the author of a biography of William C. Macready, published in 1894?

2a-43   James Reeves is the editor of a recently published book of Emily Dickinson's poetry. Where would you go to find the publisher and price?

2a-44   So far, what are the years for which you have a bibliographic coverage? What are the sources which cover these years?

NATIONAL BIBLIOGRAPHIC RECORDS (U.S.)--RETROSPECTIVE

Answers #2a/1--2a/44

2a-1: Older, past, or earlier publications. Not necessarily beginning or ending at any specific date, simply those which are "not current." Probably earlier than the past year or two.

2a-2: CBI. (See Sheehy annotation for AA460 and AA461.)

2a-3: Wilson Company.

2a-4: The last edition was the 4th, in 1928. Three earlier editions were in 1899, 1902, 1912, with some supplementary publications in between. The US Catalog then was published from 1899 through 1928.

2a-5: The sub-title on the title page (of the 4th ed., 1928) is given as "Books in Print, January 1, 1928," so it was at the time of its publication, therefore, similar to the current BIP.

2a-6: You would go to Sheehy, which gives a very full statement of the scope of the US Catalog in the annotation for CBI; or you would go to the preface of the source itself.

2a-7: The preface is usually the more complete statement and in a sense the more accurate, but the annotation in Sheehy is usually more concise, and easier and quicker to read.

2a-8: Basically, American publications--primarily books, excluding most documents, music, pamphlets--plus Canadian publications and importations of American firms. This information is from the preface; the statement in the preface (first page, fourth and fifth paragraphs) on the inclusion of state and then of federal documents is one which will be very interesting to keep in mind when you examine sources for government publications later.

2a-9: Somewhat, but not quite. The scope of the US Catalog is not as broad as CBI

because it does not include publications (in English) from other countries. It is worth noting that the US Catalog did attempt to include some government documents, but later volumes of CBI specifically exclude such publications.

2a-10: Basically, the same information--and in the same form--as in CBI; in fact, the US Catalog sometimes includes some additional information.

2a-11: Like CBI.

2a-12: Although published in 1926, it was still in print in 1928, and is found in the US Catalog, 4th ed., 1928, p. 2076. It is part of a series (Bulletin no. 32 of the Bureau of Educational Research of the College of Education) and the correct title is Interpretation of the Probable Error and the Coefficient of Correlation.

2a-13: You have the subject and the author; the author is probably easier, at least more direct, to search under. You would probably check first in the US Catalog covering 1928. It is not there, so go on to the next in the series, CBI five-year cumulation for 1928-32, where you find, under Kleemann: Ramona's Spanish Mexican Cookery, the first, complete and authentic Spanish Mexican Cookbook in English ... published in Los Angeles in 1928.

2a-14: 1876-1910 (a slight overlapping with the US Catalog). You could, of course, turn to Sheehy for this answer, or you could get it from the spines of the volumes on the shelves.

2a-15: The original publisher was the R.R. Bowker Co.; a reprint was made in 1941 by the Peter Smith firm in New York. The original publisher and publication dates are given on the verso of the title pages of the reprint edition. These bibliographic records were originally published currently with the years they cover (1876-1910), and the cumulated volumes were published from 1880-1911. This can be determined from the annotation in Sheehy, or the title pages of the volumes themselves.

2a-16: As a basic bibliographic record, it would be much in demand by American libraries, especially new libraries just building up their collections, and the demand would probably far exceed the supply of the original publication.

2a-17: Scribner's Sons. First you had to refer to the volumes in the American Catalogue covering the year 1889. These are the volumes for 1884-1890. Then you had to look in the volume covering authors (you could have also looked under the title, but remember that it is usually more direct to look under the author when you have that information), and find Lumholtz. The name of the publisher is given in Italic type at the right of the entry. If you had difficulty finding this answer, go on to the next question for a discussion of the basic arrangement of the set, and then return to look up this problem again. By now, you should find that you can figure out the basic arrangement of these bibliographies, more or less automatically, as soon as you begin to look for some specific item.

2a-18: 13 volumes altogether (in the 1941 reprint). The date groupings (as indicated on the spines of the volumes) are: 1876, 1876-1884, 1884-1890, 1890-1895, 1895-1900, 1900-05, 1905-07, 1908-10. From 1876-1900, each date grouping (such as 1884-1890) has two volumes, one covering authors and titles (in one alphabet), one covering subjects. From 1900-1910, author and title and subject are all in the same volume. If you feel sure that you fully understand this answer, and that you fully understand the arrangement of the American Catalogue, you could probably then skip over the next few questions, #2a-19 to 2a-22. If you do not understand this answer, then these questions should help to make it clear to you.

2a-19: Author, title, subject; yes, the American Catalogue has all three.

2a-20: Yes. From 1876-1900, the subject access is listed separately--in separate volumes, in fact, from the author/title access. From 1900-1910, the author/title/subject access is listed in the same volume.

2a-21: From 1876-1900, they are not, as the subject access is listed separately. From 1900-1920, they are, as all three accesses are listed in one alphabet. CBI is also representative of a "dictionary" arrangement.

2a-22: The years are grouped together approximately every few years. Earlier volumes are grouped together nearly every 10 years; as the set proceeds, the cumulations come more often.

2a-23: Frederick Leypoldt and "The Publishers Weekly" (forerunners of the R. R. Bowker Co.). (See the verso of the title-page of the reprint volumes.)

2a-24: The Wilson Company with the US Catalog and then CBI.
       In Section 1b, you found that in the early 1980's, the Bowker Company published two major cumulative sets of the American Book Publishing Record covering 1876-1949, and 1950-1977. As noted in #1b-43 and #1b-50, most of the pre-1960 publications listed in these sets have been taken from the Library of Congress and National Union Catalog sets which will be covered in Section 4 of this manual. The first of these two ABPR sets thus provides retrospective coverage for the years also covered by the American Catalogue and the US Catalog which you have examined so far in this section. One would assume that most of the publications listed in the American Catalogue and the US Catalog would also appear in the ABPR Cumulative 1876-1949 and, since the ABPR listings are more complete, that the ABPR Cumulative 1876-1949 would therefore supplant the American Catalogue/US Catalog/CBI series. However, since the ABPR Cumulation has some difficulties in use (see #1b-51 and #1b-52), and since all the sets will have some errors and omissions, as well as overlaps, most libraries will probably continue to make some use of all of these bibliographic records where they are available.

2a-25: The years covered are 1820-1860 (and January of 1861). The types of publications included are not clear, but are basically books, with some documents, some pamphlets, even some periodicals (listed separately). The publications included are limited, presumably, to those published in America. Sources for this information: the preface of Roorbach, and Sheehy.

2a-26:   The years covered--as indicated in the scope--are 1820-1860 (and January of 1861); the volumes of Roorbach as you now see them were originally published from 1852-1861. (As with the American Catalogue, there is also a Peter Smith reprint, 1939, and you have to go to the verso of the title page for the original publication and copyright information.)

2a-27:   1861-1870 (and January of 1871).

2a-28:   Kelly was originally published from 1866-1871 (and again, in a 1938 Peter Smith reprint). Again, the publication dates are not the same as the years covered. The first cumulative volume of Kelly was published in 1866, but the years covered go back to 1861.

2a-29:   Yes, except for the years covered, the scope of Kelly and Roorbach are similar --regarding types of publications included, and the limitations by language or country. See the answer to #2a-25.

2a-30:   The information is very brief--author, title, publisher, size, price. In Kelly, the date of publication is given. In Roorbach, the date is not always given. The information is usually not nearly as complete as in current sources.

2a-31:   J. Munsell (of Albany), at $3.00. In Kelly, the volume covering 1861-66, p. 58, under Durrie, D.S.

2a-32:   Roorbach, the volumes for 1855-58, covers this date. The title entry (under Scampavias) lists "Lieut. Wise" as the author, and a reference to the author entry (under Wise) does not give you any further information, so you can't answer this question from Roorbach.

2a-33:   F. Parkman. In Kelly 1861-66, p. 71, under France ... (title). Again, the author entry does not give you any further information.

2a-34:   Roorbach and Kelly have no subject access. The American Catalogue does (see #2a-20).

2a-35:   Yes, it is, but only when the title of the book is the same as or very similar to the "subject heading" you are using. For example, see in Roorbach, volume for 1855-1858, under the title entry Arctic Explorations and Discoveries during the Nineteenth Century.... compiled by Samuel Smucker, and one

above this titled Arctic Adventures.... by Epes Sargent.

2a-36:   No, you could not have found them, because the entries were under the first (real) word of the title: Arctic.

2a-37:   The subject for which you are searching must be the same as the first word of the title, or you will not find it listed. You may find a few books on your subject, if the title is helpful, but you will not find all of them.

2a-38:   The volumes themselves are arranged chronologically, by cumulations of years, as with the American Catalogue and with CBI. Within each volume, covering specified years, the arrangement is by author and title in one alphabet, with no subject access, and no other indexes. A few items, such as some periodicals, law books, etc. are listed separately in appendices. In Roorbach and Kelly, each cumulation is published in only one volume. In the early years of the American Catalogue, the cumulations were published in two volumes--one for authors and titles, one for subject. The cumulation pattern for Roorbach and Kelly is rather erratic, as it is with the American Catalogue, but it is clearly indicated on the spine of the volumes themselves, so there is no reason to remember it.

2a-39:   In the annotation: "Both Roorbach and Kelly are unsatisfactory...."

2a-40:   No. As a matter of fact, the title listed under the author's name, the 1857 Phillips publication, is titled Arctic Expeditions... rather than Arctic Adventures. How do you know which is right, or in fact if either of them is right? This is just one example of the "unsatisfactory" aspect of Roorbach and Kelly.

         As noted in the answer to #1b-50, the American Book Publishing Record Cumulative 1876-1949--despite its title--includes some 60,000+ pre-1876 imprints, and thus one would expect that many of the publications cited in Roorbach and Kelly would also be in the ABPR set. So you could then try to verify this particular title in ABPR Cumulative 1876-1949.

2a-41:   You have no date, and not even an indication of the date. (You may be aware, however, that this is a comparatively recent publication, which will help you considerably.) In any

case, the fact that you are looking for
the price indicates that the inquirer
suspects that the book is still in print.
BIP is always a good place to start a
search, and is your first source of information on current or recent books.

2a-42:   Since the date you have is 1894, you
          could go to either the American Cata-
          logue, or the American Book Publishing
          Record Cumulative 1876-1949. Since
          you do not have either the author or
          the title, you need a subject approach,
          which both sources have. The subject
          in this case is the name of the biographee
          --Macready, W. C. In this case, the
          American Catalogue is somewhat easier to
          use; you can go directly to the volume
          covering 1894, look up Macready in the
          subject list, and find the book you are
          searching for. In ABPR, under Macready
          in the subject list, you are given only
          two Dewey numbers, 917 and 927, and
          you must then search through all the
          entries under those numbers to find
          what you are looking for.

2a-43:   Your main key here is that you are af-
          ter information on a "recently published"
          book. (Don't be misled here by the
          fact that Emily Dickinson lived during
          the time covered by Roorbach and Kelly;
          new editions of well-known writers are
          always being published currently--and
          in fact, none of Miss Dickinson's poems
          were published during her lifetime.)
          Since it is a recent book and you want
          to know the publisher and price, BIP
          would be your most direct source. You
          do not have the title, so you would look
          in the author volume under the author
          (which is Dickinson not Reeves). It
          might also be in the author volume un-
          der Reeves as editor.

2a-44:   1820-61 Roorbach
          1861-71 Kelly
          1876-1910 American Catalogue
          1899-1928 US Catalog

          1928 "to date" (meaning, "to the current
             time") CBI
          1872-date PW/Weekly Record
          1873-date PTLA
          1948-date BIP
          1957-date SBIP

          1876 (or earlier, see #1b-50 and #2a-40)
             -date ABPR

NATIONAL BIBLIOGRAPHIC RECORDS (U.S.)--RETROSPECTIVE

Questions #2b/1--2b/90

All of the sources examined so far are listings compiled more or less at the time of publication of those titles which they list or include--therefore, current or contemporary sources which have now become retrospective. The next group of sources to examine for this unit are retrospective sources which were compiled retrospectively. They are:

Sabin: Dictionary of Books Relating to America (AA451)
Evans: American Bibliography (AA445)
Shaw & Shoemaker: American Bibliography (AA453)
Checklist of American Imprints (AA454, AA455, 2AA60)

2b-1 Taking Sabin's Dictionary of Books first, and looking at it on the shelf, as usual, the first thing you should be aware of is its general physical aspect--and in this case probably the first thing which should occur to you is that Sabin is a set of many volumes, rather than a work in a single volume. By now, you should be quite used to seeing the bibliographic sources as multi-volumed sets. Like many similar undertakings, the set of Sabin was not published all at once, but in fact was published "in parts" over a very long period of time. What is the publication date of Sabin?

2b-2 In examining Sabin for use, what are the two major criteria which you should determine? (You've been over these criteria with previous sources.)

2b-3 In the past you have been examining for scope first, then arrangement. With Sabin, for a change, take the arrangement first, as it is far easier to determine. Sabin, as you found in #2b-1, is a multi-volumed set. You have seen other bibliographic sources which contained several volumes, such as CBI, or the American Catalogue. Are the volumes of Sabin arranged, within the set itself, in the same way as those of CBI or American Catalogue? What is the relationship among the volumes of Sabin? Is this the same as the relationship among the volumes of the American Catalogue, or CBI?

2b-4 Who is the publisher of Electron: a telegraphic epic for the times by W.C. Richards, which was published in 1858?

2b-5 Could you have found the publisher of Electron if you had not known that the author was W. C. Richards? (If you are unsure of how to answer this, look up Electron in Sabin and see what you find, or don't find.)

2b-6 If Electron: a telegraphic epic for the times had been published in 1956, and you had not known the author, could you have found the information?

2b-7 Sabin lists--according to the Sheehy annotation--"some title entries for anonymous works," meaning that when the work or publication cited has been published anonymously, it will be listed in Sabin under its title. What does "anonymous" or "anonymously" mean?

2b-8   How does an "anonymous" work differ from a "pseudonymous" (see #1a-63) work?

2b-9   Can you determine, so far, any general rule for the ways in which bibliographies treat anonymous and/or pseudonymous works?

2b-10   The main arrangement of Sabin is then alphabetical. It is basically an author list, with anonymous works entered by title, and some entries under place-name. Is there anything in the full title of the Sabin bibliography which would have indicated this arrangement?

2b-11   You have had the use of "dictionary" arrangement before, with CBI (see #1c-26), meaning author/ title/subject in one alphabet. Is this therefore the use of the term as it appears in the title to Sabin? Does Sabin have author/title/subject access?

2b-12   Taking scope next, there will be four specific items which you will want to determine--that is, there will be four specific questions which you should ask regarding this particular source. What are these four questions? (If you have trouble, go back to #21-25 on Roorbach, #2a-29 on Kelly, and #2a-30 on both of them.)

2b-13   For Sabin, the scope is not nearly as clear-cut as it might be. It is, in fact, quite difficult to determine. Take your four questions, then, one at a time, beginning with: the years or dates covered by Sabin. First, think where, from past experience, would you go to find this?

2b-14   What is the full title of Sabin? And what does this tell you about the years covered by this source?

2b-15   What then is the beginning date covered by Sabin?

2b-16   What is the closing or ending date covered by Sabin?

2b-17   This seems to be very straightforward. It is, in fact, very misleading. Does the annotation in Sheehy give a clear statement regarding the years covered?

2b-18   The title page of the source, and the Sheehy annotation having failed you here, your only other recourse is to go to the preface or introductory material in the source itself. The only preface in vol. 1 of Sabin is an introduction entitled "Prospectus," published in 1868 in the first part issued. Remember that the actual publication of the Sabin bibliography took place from 1868 through 1936-- a period of 72 years. Sabin himself died long before it was completed, and the work was continued and completed by other bibliographers; under these circumstances, one might expect that the scope of inclusion might have changed somewhat. It is necessary to look further into the set for additional statements of scope and procedure.
        These consist of a "Statement" in vol. 20 (1928), and a Preface, Introduction, Final Statement, and "Bibliographia Americana, 1866 and 1936" in vol. 29 (1936). These statements, telling as they do the story of one of the most monumental and magnificent achievements of American bibliography, give you a very good picture of the frustrations and problems of the compilation of such a bibliog- raphy. You should at least read p. ix-xi of the "introduction" of vol. 29: "The scope of Sabin," for a clearer statement of the changing scope of the bibliography until the time of its completion. Having read this statement, what do you think is the closing or ending date of the Sabin entries?

2b-19 Probably the closest you can come to a statement of the years covered by Sabin is: 1492 to 1800/
       1870.   Admittedly, this is somewhat vague. It is simplest to think of Sabin as covering, more or
       less, through the 19th century; in other words, when in doubt check Sabin.
              If you are trying to locate information on a title published in the U.S. in the 18th century,
       and you do not find it in Sabin, is this then an indication that the title did not exist?

2b-20 The next aspect of the scope is simpler: What types of publications are included?

2b-21 Are the publications listed in Sabin limited in any way by language or country of publication? Go
       back to the full title on this one for a clue.

2b-22 Would you expect to find in Sabin a book by Edouard Auger, titled Voyage en Californie, published
       in Paris in the 1850's?

2b-23 What is the correct date, the publisher, and the number of pages of the book by Auger cited above?

2b-24 In the entry for Auger, a notation "H 2376" is given at the right side of the page. What does this
       stand for? How would you expect to find out?

2b-25 Still referring to the scope of this bibliography, what kind of information is given to you in the in-
       dividual citations?

2b-26 Why might it be important or useful to include, in bibliographies, such location symbols as you had
       with the Auger item (#2b-22)?

2b-27 Writings describing the voyages of Amerigo Vespucci were printed in Europe in 1503 and 1504.
       Where might you expect to find listings of such early books?

2b-28 Would you expect to find in Sabin any information about a book titled References for Literary Writers
       by H. Matson published in 1892?

2b-29 Where would you be able to find such information?

2b-30 Could you find through Sabin the names of some books on witchcraft, published in the early 1800's?

2b-31 You may remember, however, from #2a-35 (Arctic expeditions) that sometimes title entries can give
       you a kind of subject access. Is this helpful for #2b-30, books on witchcraft, in Sabin?

2b-32 Would you expect to be able to find in Sabin any books relating to the state of New Jersey (for
       example: surveyors' lists, public documents, statistics, laws, etc.) even if you did not have the
       author or exact title?

2b-33   Would you then expect to be able to find in Sabin any books on or about the Hawaiian Islands? Can you?

2b-34   Why do you think this is? What's another name by which the Hawaiian Islands have been known, particularly in the 19th century?

2b-35   You have the information that a book by Wharton titled A Treatise on Theism was published in 1859 (in the U.S.). You need to verify and complete this bibliographic information. Would you expect to find this in Sabin?

2b-36   Where then can you look to verify and complete the bibliographic information? What can you find?

2b-37   In the answer to #2b-19, it was stated that one of the reasons you might not locate a title in a given bibliography would be that either the information you had was incorrect, or the information in the bibliography was incorrect. You have already seen (notably with Roorbach and Kelly, as in #2a-40) that some of the bibliographies do list incorrect, inconsistent, and/or confusing information. Aside from careful checking and proofreading, how could the compiler of a bibliography guard against such errors? (See the last page of Sabin's Prospectus in volume 1 of the Sabin Bibliography.)

2b-38   What was the price of "Hughey Dougherty's Staggering-Home-to-Bed Songster" when it was published in New York in 1870?

2b-39   Sabin's bibliography is generally considered as the achievement of one man, although it was in fact completed, eventually, with the help of an organization. It is a retrospective bibliography; and unlike such lists as CBI, American Catalogue, Roorbach and Kelly, it was compiled retrospectively --after the publications of the books, rather than at the time of the publication of the books--by searching library collections, book dealer lists, catalogs, other bibliographies, etc.
        Another such retrospective bibliographic compilation is that of Charles Evans: The American Bibliography. How many volumes comprise the entire set of Evans?

2b-40   If you turn to the title page of volume 1 of Evans, you should be able to get a very clear statement on the scope and the arrangement of this bibliography. What is the scope?

2b-41   And the arrangement of Evans?

2b-42   Like Sabin, the Evans bibliography was compiled and published retrospectively. When was it published?

2b-43   The scope of Evans is indicated on the title page of vol. 1 as from 1639 through 1820. Did Evans in fact complete the bibliography to that date (1820)? Did anyone?

2b-44   The scope of Evans, then, is actually 1639 through 1800. Why do you think Mr. Evans set 1820 as his original closing date?

2b-45 Would you expect to find in Evans, Voyage en Californie by Auger, from #2b-22?

2b-46 Would you expect to find the early printings of the Voyages of Amerigo Vespucci (#2b-27) in Evans?

2b-47 Is the scope of Evans the same as that of Sabin?

2b-48 Does Evans, like Sabin, include location symbols for libraries holding copies of the items listed?

2b-49 In general, do you think that the information given in the entries in Evans is similar to that in Sabin?

2b-50 Is the arrangement of Evans similar to that of Sabin?

2b-51 The arrangement of Evans is chronological, and vol. 1 covers 1639-1729. Is this similar to the chronological arrangement of Roorbach, in which vol. 1 covered 1820-52?

2b-52 Locate in Evans a sermon by Enoch Huntington, called Political Wisdom, or Honesty the Best Policy, printed in 1786. When was it actually delivered, how many pages does it consist of, and what library has (or had in 1903) a copy of it?

2b-53 How do you find out what AAS stands for in the preceding entry?

2b-54 Evans is arranged chronologically. Do you have author or title access?

2b-55 Do you have subject access?

2b-56 Did you have subject access in Sabin?

2b-57 The years covered by the Sabin bibliography overlap Evans, but the arrangement of the two bibliographies is basically quite different. Can you think of any reasons why Evans chose to arrange his bibliography chronologically? Can you think of any advantages of this over an alphabetical arrangement?

2b-58 Thomas Foxcroft (1679-1769) wrote Character of Anna, the Prophetess, consider'd and Apply'd which was published in Boston in the early 18th century. Locate this in Evans. What is the actual date on which it was published?

2b-59 The date in the citation for Foxcroft (see the preceding question, #2b-58) is given as MDCCXXIII, in Roman numerals. How do you translate this into Arabic numerals, and what is the date then in Arabic numerals?

2b-60 Would you expect to find the Foxcroft item (#2b-58) in Sabin?

2b-61 The Foxcroft item <u>is</u> in Sabin, but is not easy to find.   Where is it?

2b-62 What was the first publication printed in America?

2b-63 Which do you think is the easiest to use--the chronological arrangement in Evans, or the alphabetical arrangement in Sabin?

2b-64 What are two basic differences between Sabin and Evans?

2b-65 Did Evans, like Sabin, try to examine copies of the books he described?   Remember #2b-37.

2b-66 All of the major bibliographies you have examined so far have been an attempt at a comprehensive recording of American publications.   In bibliography, comprehensiveness is an aim; completeness is rarely an achievement.   Some bibliographies have achieved more than others.   Evans is considered as a very comprehensive record, but even Evans is not complete.   Have there been any attempts to supplement Evans, to fill in gaps, and make additions and corrections to the record?   (Think: assuming that such a thing has been done and that it then exists as a published record, where would you best look to find out about it?)

2b-67 Another title listed in Sheehy (AA448) is more than just a supplement or index to Evans; it is "an important bibliographic source in its own right" (Sheehy annotation).   This is the National Index of American Imprints through 1800; the Short-title Evans, by Shipton and Mooney (1969).   It lists alphabetically (rather than chronologically) the titles in Evans, plus many additions found since, and clarifies problems.   If you have access to Shipton and Mooney, try checking in it for the Foxcroft item from #2b-58, as a comparison to using Evans itself.   What are the advantages?

2b-68 When he began publication of his bibliography in 1903, Evans intended to take it from the beginning of printing in the United States up to 1820, to the beginning of Roorbach, Kelly, etc., to form an unbroken chronological record of publication in the United States.   In fact, the Evans bibliography was completed only through 1800, leaving a gap of some 19 years before the beginning of Roorbach. Has anything been done to fill in this gap?   (Don't consider Sabin here.)   Look ahead.

2b-69 What are the publication dates of the Shaw/Shoemaker bibliography?   (Dates of publication, not dates of coverage.)

2b-70 This, then, is a comparatively recent addition to our retrospective bibliographic coverage.   The preface in vol. 1 of this set is, like those mentioned earlier, well worth reading for its picture of the processes of bibliographic compilation--in this case providing a comparison of twentieth century procedures with those used by earlier bibliographers such as Sabin and Evans.   What is the scope of the Shaw/Shoemaker American Bibliography?

2b-71 What about the information given in the citations themselves?   Is this also similar to Evans?

2b-72 A short publication entitled "A Few observations on the government of R.I." (Rhode Island) was published in 1807.   The author was Benjamin Cowell.   Find a citation or entry which will give you the number of pages in this publication.   Where would you look?

2b-73   The entry you found in the preceding question shows the author's name in square brackets ([]).
What does this mean? What would you guess it would mean?

2b-74   Could you have found the information on these 1807 observations on the government of R.I. if
you did not already possess the information that the author was, in fact, Mr. Benjamin Cowell?

2b-75   What is the arrangement of Shaw/Shoemaker?

2b-76   Is there a cumulated author and/or title access, as in Evans?

2b-77   Is there a subject access?

2b-78   The sub-title of the Shaw/Shoemaker American Bibliography is "A Preliminary Checklist," and the
preface begins "This bibliography has been gathered entirely from secondary sources." What is
meant by these statements?

2b-79   Were the Sabin and Evans bibliographies compiled from secondary sources?

2b-80   What are "ghosts," bibliographically-speaking, as referred to in the Shaw/Shoemaker preface (p.
ix)?

2b-81   The preface to the Shaw/Shoemaker American Bibliography has indicated that any list--even a
preliminary checklist compiled entirely from secondary sources--of publications of the period for
1801-1819 is better than no record at all. A similar statement has been made about the Roorbach
and Kelly lists. Is any attempt being made, or has any attempt been made, along the lines of
any of the previous sources you have examined, to complete, supplement, fill in, etc., the Roorbach and Kelly records?

2b-82   What is the purpose of the Checklist of American Imprints?

2b-83   What then would you expect the scope of the Checklist to be?

2b-84   You would expect the scope to be the same as Shaw/Shoemaker, but in fact, is it entirely the same?
For instance, does the Shaw/Shoemaker list include periodicals? Does the Checklist include periodicals?

2b-85   What is the arrangement of the Checklist?

2b-86   The Checklist of American Imprints is listed in Sheehy as being compiled by Richard Shoemaker, for
1820-1829.   There is a title index for these years (and also an author index which is not listed in
Sheehy, although published in 1973). The Checklist for 1830- is listed in Sheehy as being compiled
by Gayle Cooper and as being "in progress." How would you find out about publication dates of
future volumes, and how would you find out when--and if--it is completed?

2b-87   A great many of the items listed in the Checklist are of a religious nature (sermons, tracts, etc.)
or of local importance (laws, acts of legislatures, etc.). Joseph Merrill delivered what was prob-

ably a sermon, in Boston, on New Year's Eve, 1826. Was this published, by whom, and how long was it?

2b-88 The Gospel of St. Matthew was translated into the Mohawk language by a man named Hill and published or printed in the early 1830's. What is the title in Mohawk and where could you see a copy of it?

2b-89 Are there any variations in procedures of methods used, and in information given, between the Shaw/Shoemaker and the Checklist?

2b-90 In #2a-44, you listed the years for which you had, at that point, bibliographic coverage, and the names of the sources which covered those years. Do the sources from Section 2b give you any additional years of coverage?

NATIONAL BIBLIOGRAPHIC RECORDS (U.S.)--RETROSPECTIVE

Answers #2b/1--2b/90

2b-1: 1868-1936. You want the publication date, not the coverage (although you will find that the two are not entirely unrelated). As with Roorbach and Kelly, you will need to check the publication date on the title page of the first volume, for the beginning date, and then refer to the publication date on the title page of the last part of the last volume for the closing date (1936).

2b-2: Scope and arrangement.

2b-3: The entire set of Sabin is arranged alphabetically. The entire set of CBI or the American Catalogue is arranged chronologically, that is by year or by date. Volume 1 of Sabin contains "A-Bedford." Volumes 1-2 of the American Catalogue contain the years 1876-1884; within these volumes of the American Catalogue, the arrangement is alphabetical. For CBI and the American Catalogue (as with Roorbach and Kelly), the arrangement is first chronological then alphabetical. The arrangement of Sabin is only alphabetical.

2b-4: The publisher is D. Appleton and Company--found in Sabin by looking in vol. 17, covering "Remarks to Ross," under the author Richards (vol. 17, p. 224).

2b-5: No. Sabin contains, basically, no title entries--primarily author entries, with title entries when the author is anonymous, and some entries under name of place. (See the Sheehy annotation.) An Author-Title Index to Joseph Sabin's Dictionary, compiled by John Molnar, was published in 1974 (Sheehy 1AA96). It gives title access, plus access to information in notes, plus many types of cross-references.

2b-6: Yes, for that publication date you would have had CBI to check in, and you could have checked under title, because CBI gives title entries as well as author entries. Similarly, you could have checked in ABPR Cumulative 1950-1977 under title

2b-7: Use the dictionary or the ALA Glossary.

2b-8: There is considerable similarity, and it might be necessary for you to get into library cataloging rules in some depth in order to clarify the exact difference. Bibliographically speaking, in both cases the author is presumably unknown, and both are therefore published anonymously. Many pseudonyms are very well known, however--such as Mark Twain. Although a book published with Mark Twain given as the author is published "under a pseudonym," it can hardly be said to be published anonymously.

2b-9: Probably not. The rules vary from bibliography to bibliography, which is one of the reasons why it is so important to READ A PREFACE. Frequently, the prefaces or introductions will tell you what the specific bibliography in question does. Sheehy annotations may also tell you. In the case of a book published under a pseudonym, in which a pseudonym (Mark Twain) is used in place of the author's correct name (Samuel Clemens), it is not always understood or known that the name used is a pseudonym. You may find the work entered under the pseudonymous name, or under the correct name if the correct name is known; and if the work is fully cross-referenced, you would find a reference from the pseudonym to the correct name, or vice-versa. If a book is published with no author's name in it at all, or completely anonymously, then it would probably be entered under the title, or in some bibliographies, under the general heading of "Anonymous." If a book is published anonymously, but the correct author is known (or surmised) by the bibliographer, then the book may be entered under the correct name, or it may be entered under the title but indicate the correct name in an annotation or note. Adequate cross-references are enormously important in this whole problem. Bibliographies do not always have such adequate cross-

references. Therefore, in using bibliographies it behooves you to be aware
of all possibilities.

2b-10:   It is called a "dictionary of books"--
          which would certainly imply (although
          not assure) an alphabetical arrangement.

2b-11:   No, not really. Sabin does not have
          complete title access nor, really, any
          subject access at all. Sabin only has,
          basically, author access, but that is
          alphabetical, and the use of the word
          "dictionary" here undoubtedly implies
          only the basically alphabetical arrange-
          ment.

2b-12:   1. What are the years or dates covered?
          2. What types of publications are in-
              cluded?
          3. Are the publications included limited
              in any way by language or country
              of publication?
          4. What bibliographic information is
              given in the entries or citations
              about the individual publications
              cited?

2b-13:   The places you could look for this answer
          are:
                the title page of the source;
                the preface or introduction to the
                    source;
                Sheehy.

2b-14:   A Dictionary of Books Relating to Amer-
          ica, from Its Discovery to the Present
          Time (as shown on the title-page and
          in Sheehy). It tells you that the years
          covered are: "From its discovery to the
          present time."

2b-15:   "From its discovery." The discovery of
          what? America. Which was discovered
          in what year? 1492. Therefore, the
          beginning date for Sabin's coverage is:
          1492, the discovery of America.

2b-16:   "To the present time." What is "the
          present time?" Presumably, the time at
          which the bibliography was being com-
          piled or published, and the date of
          original publication of Sabin was (see
          #2b-1) 1868-1936. The closing or end-
          ing date covered by Sabin would pre-
          sumably be, then, about 1868 for those
          items in volume one, and proceed to
          later and later years as the compilation
          of the bibliography itself proceeded on
          toward the publication of the last volume
          in 1936.

2b-17:   No. As regards "years covered" by

Sabin, the annotation in Sheehy simply
avoids the issue. This is a very good
example of the fact that you cannot always rely on some published source such
as Sheehy, and you must learn to determine these factors on your own.

2b-18:   In general, the closing dates of the ear-
          ly volumes (vol. 1-20) will be approxi-
          mately the 1860's; from vol. 21 on, the
          ending date is progressively moved back
          to the 1800's, growing more and more
          restrictive as it became more imperative
          to finish the task. The closing dates
          of Sabin could be considered then as
          1800-1870, more or less.

2b-19:   Not at all. It merely means that it is
          not listed in Sabin, either because it
          was unknown to the compilers, or be-
          cause it fell outside of the increasingly
          restrictive scope. It may also mean that
          it is listed in Sabin but you did not find
          it there--either because you looked in-
          correctly, or not thoroughly enough,
          or because your information was faulty,
          or because the compilers' information
          was faulty, or because it was entered
          in the bibliography in some unsuspected
          fashion.

2b-20:   The Sheehy annotation tells you "books,
          pamphlets, and periodicals," and by
          glancing through several of the volumes
          and looking at the types of materials
          listed, you can see that the scope of
          Sabin is very broad, in this aspect.
          All types of publications appear to be
          included.

2b-21:   The full title tells you "... Books Re-
          lating to America....," which implies
          at least a broader scope than simply
          U.S. publications or English language
          publications, and again you can con-
          firm this by glancing through the vol-
          umes themselves and looking at the en-
          tries, and by referring to the Sheehy
          annotation ("printed in the Western
          Hemisphere, and works about the re-
          gion printed elsewhere").

2b-22:   Yes, because the date falls within the
          scope of Sabin (it would be in the ear-
          ly volumes, under A-), and it relates
          to America, even though published in
          Paris.

2b-23:   The date is 1854, the publisher is
          Hachette et Cie, the number of pages
          is 238.

2b-24:   In such cases, always look in the in-

troductory pages for a list of abbreviations, or in the preface for an explanation. The preface ("Prospectus") of
vol. 1 does not give any information
here, but there is a page entitled "Explanatory" which indicates what the
"initials which precede the numbers at
the end of the description" stand for.
H stands for Harvard College Library
and is therefore a "location symbol,"
indicating that (at least in Mr. Sabin's
day) the Harvard College Library pos-
sessed a copy of the book or publication cited. The number following the H
is not explained, but a glance up and
down the page on which it appears
should show you that each item listed
is followed by such a number, and that
the numbers follow one another consecu-
tively through the listing; therefore the
number can be surmised to be an "item
number"--or an inventory number within
the bibliogrpahy itself. If further reference should be made to the Auger title, it can be referred to as item #2376,
without repeating the entire citation, and
the location of the citation can quickly
be found.

2b-25:   The usual basic bibliographic information of author, title, publisher, date,
paging, etc., and often the names, or
abbreviations or symbols for the names
of libraries having copies. Furthermore,
you often get lists of contents, bibliographic notes, references to reviews,
descriptions, etc.--the Sheehy annotation
tells you this, and you could see it for
yourself by glancing through the entries.

2b-26:   In this way the person who uses the bibliography, and who finds a title of interest cited there, then has at least
one source he can go to, to look at or
use the material itself. An important
aspect of bibliographic control is the
location of copies (both provision of
copies to be used, and indication of the
location of such copies). This is very
useful for interlibrary loan (although
the location indications as given in Sabin
may be just a bit outdated by now).
This whole question will be of great importance later in examination of "union
catalogs" and "union lists."

2b-27:   First of all, you should realize that
Vespucci was one of the first discover-
ers of America, and these writings would
therefore be included in Sabin as "relating to America." They are listed, under Vespucci. The bibliographic descriptions of these books, in Sabin, are good

examples of analytic bibliography. Note
the very careful, very full, very complete physical description of the volumes,
the leaves, the way the text is set on
the page, etc. This also is an example
of the unexpected treasures of information to be found in Sabin.

2b-28:   No, since it was published in 1892--
this date falls outside the scope covered
by Sabin.

2b-29:   In the American Catalogue (1890-95, authors, p. 284. The publisher was Mc-
Clurg). Also, presumably, in the
American Book Publishing Record Cumulative 1876-1949.

2b-30:   Basically, no, since Sabin does not have
a subject approach.

2b-31:   Not much. Sabin lists no titles beginning
with "witchcraft," and only two--both
apparently novels of some sort--begin-
ning with "witch." Remember, however,
that Roorbach and Kelly had both author
and title access for all entries; Sabin
has only author access (except for some
anonymous titles). No doubt there would
be other books in Sabin whose titles begin with the word "witchcraft" but they
would be listed under their authors only,
so you could not locate them by title.
The title index by Molnar (see #2b-5)
might help.

2b-32:   Yes. In #2b-5, you found that the entries, although basically by author only,
did include some place names, and you
will in fact find quite a bit in Sabin under the general entry of New Jersey.

2b-33:   Yes, you would expect to, since that
is a place name. But there is nothing
in Sabin under Hawaii or Hawaiian Islands.

2b-34:   You might surmise that in the 1860's,
the Hawaiian Islands were not considered a part of America, or of the
Western Hemisphere. There is a better
reason, though.
Try the Sandwich Islands and see
what you find. This is an example of
the way in which some change in usage
--place names, subject headings, etc.--
can throw you off the track in your
search if you do not keep this factor
of change constantly in mind. One of
the best clues to the effective use of
older reference books, whether bibliographies or any other type of reference
source, is to try as much as possible

to think in terms of the time the source itself was published. One of the things librarians can be most grateful for in modern reference book publishing is the concept of extensive cross-references.

2b-35: No, not really. The early volumes of Sabin did go through 1860 or later, more or less, but "W" would be very far along in the compilation of the set, after the scope had been restricted to the early part of the 1800's. Just to make sure, you can check in Sabin to see, but this publication is not there.

2b-36: You can look in the source covering that period, Roorbach for 1858-60 (p. 155), under Wharton. You find that the author's initial is F., but you cannot find his first name. You can verify the title, and find that the rest of the title is "and on modern skeptical theories." You can find that the publisher was Lippincott. But, as is frequently the case in Roorbach, no date is given, so you cannot verify that.
        As noted in #1b-43 and #1b-50, the American Book Publishing Record Cumulative 1876-1949 includes some pre-1876 imprints so that would also be worth checking.

2b-37: It would certainly help to reduce such errors if the compiler or compilers worked directly from the books--that is, if they actually saw, and examined, the books which they were listing and describing. Often it is necessary for compilers to "content" themselves with secondary sources, such as library catalogs, bookdealer catalogs, and other lists. As Mr. Sabin points out, if he were to strive to examine in detail every item listed, he would never complete this task (nor would anyone else).

2b-38: Here again you are on doubtful ground as regards the date of publication--this title might or might not be in Sabin. But in any case, you have been asked to find the original price, and Sabin does not list prices, so you must go to a source which does, and the source which covers that date and which also lists prices is Kelly, 1866-71, p. 197. This item is listed simply as if it were a title entry (which it is) under the first word of the title, Hughey. If you considered Hughey Dougherty as the author, and looked under Dougherty, you would not find an entry. The price of the item, by the way, was ten cents.

2b-39: There are 14 volumes.

2b-40: Years covered "From the genesis of printing in 1639 down to and including the year 1820." Types of publications included: "Books, pamphlets, and periodical publications." Limitations of publications: "Printed in the United States of America." Information given in citations: "Bibliographical and bibliographical notes." Some of these answers will need to be further clarified.

2b-41: "Chronological dictionary"--that is, chronological, by year (as with American Catalogue, Roorbach and Kelly, etc.), and within the year, alphabetically by author.

2b-42: The original publication dates (verso of title page of the 1941 reprint) were 1903-34, for vols. 1-12, 1955 for vol. 13, 1959 for vol. 14.

2b-43: By checking Sheehy and/or the last volumes of the bibliography itself, you will see that Evans completed the bibliography through the letter M of 1799 (in vol. 12). The bibliography was completed later (1955) through 1800, in vol. 13.

2b-44: This would bring his compilation up to the beginning of Roorbach, which--having been published in 1852-61--was therefore already in existence when Evans began the publication of his retrospective compilation in 1903. (Presumably, of course, Evans began compilation of the information long before he began actual publication of it. The preface to vol. 13 tells you that he began recording information as early as 1880. Roorbach was in existence even then.)

2b-45: No, for two reasons: first of all because it was published in 1854, and Evans goes only to 1800; secondly, because it was published in Paris, and Evans does not include non-American publications.

2b-46: No, for two reasons: first of all because they were published in 1503, 1504, before printing in the United States, and because they were published in Europe.

2b-47: The dates overlap but Sabin begins earlier (1492) and ends, more or less, later at least in the early part of the alphabet. The types of publications included are similar. Evans is limited to items printed in America, Sabin includes those items relating to American regardless of where published.

2b-48:   Yes, to the right of the entries; in capital letters.

2b-49:   The information given in Evans is quite full, and similar to that in Sabin, but Sabin often gives a tremendous amount of additional information.

2b-50:   No. Sabin is strictly alphabetical. Evans is chronological.

2b-51:   In Evans, each year is listed separately, and vol. 1 includes separate lists for 1639, 1640, 1641, 1642, etc. In Roorbach all entries for 1820-52 were cumulated together into the volume covering those years.

2b-52:   It was delivered on the 10th of April, 1786, in Middletown (presumably Connecticut); consists of 20 pages, and the AAS (American Antiquarian Society) has a copy. Found in vol. 7, under 1786, then alphabetically under the author's name.

2b-53:   On p. xi of the Preface to vol. 1, the statement is made that such abbreviations would be sufficiently well-known not to need further identification. However, a list of identification is given in vol. 13.

2b-54:   Yes. Each volume has an author index (although no title index). Volume 14 has a cumulated author/title index.

2b-55:   Each volume has a "Classified Subject Index" which is some help, but is not as usable as, for example, the subject access in more modern bibliographies. There is no cumulation of these subject indices.

2b-56:   No.

2b-57:   In the preface in vol. 1 of Evans, on p. xi, are stated some of the advantages to the chronological arrangement, at least from Evans' point of view.

2b-58:   In order to locate this in Evans, you have to go first to volume 14 and look under either the author or the title (if under the author, then to the correct title listed under Foxcroft), which gives you the "item number," which tells you where, in the main bibliogra-

phy, you will find the entry. A location guide for the item numbers is given in the lower corner of each set of facing pages, in vol. 14. In Evans, the item numbers for each title are given on the left side of the page, rather than following the entry as in Sabin. The item number for Foxcroft is #2431, and the date on which the book was published was MDCCXXIII.

2b-59:   The ALA Glossary does not seem to be much help here, but any common dictionary should tell you about the formation of Roman numerals if you do not know it already. For example, Webster's New World Dictionary of the American Language (c1963) gives a short explanation in the definition for "roman numerals," and a fuller explanation under "Special Signs and Symbols" in the back. The date, for Foxcroft, is 1723, (M=1000+D=500+CC=200+XX=20+III=3).

2b-60:   Since it is the early part of the 18th century (you had that information to begin with) you would reasonably expect to find it there.

2b-61:   You have to go through all of the Foxcrofts listed, since their first names are not indicated clearly in the author entries, and they do not seem to be alphabetized according to the first name. You also have to look at all of the small print (this is important in Sabin), and you will find the Character of Anna listed, along with many other titles, in the note to the last Foxcroft entry. This is typical of Sabin. Remember the annotation in Sheehy: "... does not count the added editions and titles mentioned in the various notes."

2b-62:   This is where Evans' arrangement can be very helpful. Presumably the first item listed in his bibliography is the first publication in America: The "Oath of a Free-Man," printed in 1638.

2b-63:   It depends primarily on the information you have to work with. Ordinarily, in identifying a specific item, you would have the author's name, and it is certainly easier to go directly to that name in one alphabetical list and find your information, than to check through year after year of names, or to refer from names in an index back to the fuller information under the year.

2b-64:   One is the arrangement; the second is the coverage or scope--Sabin is broader.

2b-65:   Like Sabin, he tried to, but could not always. This is noted in his own preface to vol. 1, the middle of p. xi. But an even more revealing statement on this problem is in Mr. Shipton's preface to vol. 13, p. vii and the top of p. viii.

2b-66:   If such supplements, additions, further records exist in published form, one of the places where you would expect to find them listed is, of course, in Sheehy --along with the rest of the bibliographic sources. And in fact Sheehy does list several such supplementary publications (AA446, AA447, AA449, AA450).

2b-67:   In Shipton and Mooney, Foxcroft's Character of Anna is listed directly under the author (vol. 1, p. 278); it is not necessary to go through an index as in Evans. The date is given as 1723, rather than in Roman numerals.

2b-68:   The next title on your list--Shaw and Shoemaker's American Bibliography--was compiled and published precisely to fill that gap. (Sabin is so erratic on its inclusion of publications from 1800-1820 in the later part of the alphabet, that it cannot be said to form a real record for this period; furthermore Sabin does not show a chronological record because of its arrangement.)

2b-69:   1958-1983.
         (1801-1819 pub. 1958-1963; Addenda/list of sources/Library Symbols: 1965; Title Index; 1965; Corrections/author Index: 1966; Printer, Publishers and Booksellers Index, Geographical Index: 1983.)

2b-70:   It covers 1801-1819, and like Evans, is intended as a listing of "American publications"--including those published or printed in the United States, and including a rather broad range of type of publications. It is necessary to go to the preface of the work, to see specifically its variations from Evans' methods (see p. ix of the preface).

2b-71:   See p. vii of the Preface; information given is that available, and is "uneven in quality." Library location symbols are given when location is known.

2b-72:   The year 1807 is covered by the Shaw/ Shoemaker American Bibliography, the citation is found in the volume for 1807, under Cowell, and the number of pages is 18.

2b-73:   The ALA Glossary is no help here, but

generally style manuals will suggest the use of square brackets to indicate that the enclosed information has "been supplied." Therefore, in this case, it means that the author's name does not appear in the publication itself. The item was therefore published anonymously. (See #2b-7 on "anonymous.")

2b-74:   Yes, since you have a title index which would (and does) refer you to the entry under Cowell, by means of an item number as in Sabin and Evans.

2b-75:   Like Evans, chronological, each year separately (in this publication, each year is in a separate volume, so it is easy to see at a glance that there has been no cumulation). Within the year, alphabetical by author or main entry.

2b-76:   Yes, in the final volumes (titles in vol. 21, authors in vol. 22). See answer to #2b-69, and the Sheehy annotation.

2b-77:   No.

2b-78:   It is necessary to go to the preface to find out. (Sheehy only repeats the information.) The preface tells you, in essence, that any kind of a checklist at all was better than none, and that this one is admittedly incomplete and uneven--hence "preliminary" (presumably, to be used as the basis for a more comprehensive and reliable bibliography--perfecting citations, laying ghosts, and filling gaps--see p. ix). The use of secondary sources means that the compilers worked from lists, catalogs, other bibliographies--and not from the books themselves.

2b-79:   Refer to #2b-37 and 2b-65. Both used secondary sources; both attempted as much as possible, however, to examine and check the publications.

2b-80:   See the ALA Glossary (under "bibliographical ghost").

2b-81:   Again you might go to Sheehy for this one, and the answer happens also to be the next title on your list: Checklist of American Imprints.

2b-82:   "Designed as a continuation of Shaw/ Shoemaker to provide fuller coverage than those in Roorbach." (Sheehy.) Similar information is given in the Preface to vol. 1 (1820).

2b-83:   Since it is a continuation of Shaw/Shoe-
maker, you would expect the scope to
be approximately the same as that record, beginning however with the year
1820.

2b-84:   This is a good example of why it is important to read the prefaces and not
take too much for granted. The Preface to vol. 1 (1820) of the Checklist tells
you that periodicals are not to be included
in the scope of this bibliography, although
they were included in the Shaw/Shoemaker
list.

2b-85:   Basically, the same as the Shaw/Shoe-
maker bibliography.

2b-86:   Since this is a current publication (although a retrospective bibliography)
each new volume as it appears would
presumably be listed in the Weekly Record.
The completion of the bibliography would
be noted in future editions of or supplements to Sheehy, or in similar listings
of reference and bibliographic sources.
(The volume of the Checklist covering
1834 was compiled by Carol Rinder-
knecht and Scott Bruntjen and published in 1982.)

2b-87:   Delivered on New Year's Eve (Dec. 31),
1826 means it is unlikely to have been
published until 1827. It is in the Checklist volume for 1827, p. 164, under
Merrill. It was published (actually,
printed) by T. R. Marvin, and was 31
pages long.

2b-88:   This is in the Checklist for 1831, p.
153, under Hill, A. The title in Mohawk
is given and a library location symbol is
given.

2b-89:   This is the kind of information you would
expect to find in the Preface. The Preface to vol. 1 (1820) does not indicate
any significant variations in method, but
going on to the Preface in vol. 2 (1821),
p. iii, you will find that: the compiler
is now attempting to check the publications listed somewhat more carefully than
in previous lists, resulting in more accurate and fuller descriptions for the titles
listed. Cross references for pseudonyms, and for anonymous titles, are
given.

2b-90:   1492-1800/1870 Sabin
1639-1800 Evans
1801-1819 Shaw and Shoemaker
1820-[1834+] Checklist of American Im-
     prints

1820-61 Roorbach
1861-71 Kelly
1876-1910 American Catalogue
1899-1928 US Catalog

1928-date CBI
1872-date PW/Weekly Record
1873-date PTLA
1948-date BIP
1957-date SBIP

1876 (or earlier)-date   ABPR

Section 3

NATIONAL BIBLIOGRAPHIC RECORDS (U.S.)--SEARCH STRATEGY AND REVIEW

Questions #3/1--3/18

You have now examined the major bibliographic records, current and retrospective, for American or U.S. publications. The next several questions will refer you, randomly, to all those sources you have so far examined. Before going on to these questions, it might be useful to make a rough chart of the coverage (or scope) and access (or arrangement) of these bibliographic sources, so that you can tell quickly which ones would be the best sources to use in answering the questions. Making the chart and answering the search questions in this set will serve you as a review of the material.

To begin with, you should indicate which sources cover which specific years. Most of the retrospective coverage will be sources from Sections 2a-2b. (Refer back to the answers to #2a-44 and #2b-90.)

3-1   After having listed the sources and the years covered, do you notice any obvious gaps so far? Are there any years which do not appear to be covered, or for which the coverage which exists may be unsatisfactory to use?

3-2   Consider the three major accesses we need to bibliographic sources--author, title, subject. Are any of the sources so far lacking author access?

3-3   What about title access?

3-4   What about subject access?

3-5   Subject access is often considered our weakest area of bibliographic control. Do you think our present subject coverage is an improvement over earlier subject coverage? In other words, do we appear to be making progress?

3-6   If you wanted to compile a list of books published in the United States on witchcraft, what sources could you refer to? Which would be "easiest" to use?

3-7   In searching for bibliographic information, what kinds of information--what elements or pieces of information--could you either have or need?

3-8   One of the most important elements to determine, at least approximately, in searching for biblio- graphic information, is the date, or the general time period. Why is this? (If this is not imme- diately clear, then think about the overall, basic organization and structure of the bibliographic sources.)

To answer the following questions, then, you will need to make a choice from the various biblio- graphic sources of information which you now have available. You could of course search aim- lessly through all of the sources until you found an answer, somewhere. But a more effective approach, which you should be learning, is to search <u>systematically</u> through the sources available, choosing first those sources and that procedure most likely to give you the information you need. You have already been doing this, to some extent. But now your choice of sources begins to widen, so your thinking must be more careful.

In order to choose your source--in other words, in order to set up your strategy--you must first examine your problem or question, to decide what kind of information you <u>need</u>, and what kind of information you already <u>have</u>. Here you are confined to bibliographic sources and bibliographic information.

For the following <u>review</u> questions, as you have done with previous questions, you can either search out the specific answers in the sources, or simplify the process and save some time by just deciding where (and why) you would be most likely to find the answer. Searching in the sources is excellent practice and helps you to get the feel of using them and to remember them in more detail. Searching may also clarify your understanding of the sources. You will need to judge for yourself how much review and practice and clarification you may need at this point.

3-9   Suppose then that you need to find out who is the author of a book called <u>Free at Last!</u> about the Americans held hostage in Iran. How would you go about it?

3-10   Why would you choose to go to BIP as your first search stop in #3-9, instead of directly to CBI or BPR?

3-11   Who is the publisher of Henry Frost's <u>The Communion of Saints</u>, published in 1821? What library or libraries have copies? (Does this mean that these are the only libraries having copies?)

3-12   You have a note about a book by Humphrey Desmond, called <u>Does God Love the Irish</u>, which you believe to have been published in the early 1900's. Can you find a citation for it, with the correct date?

3-13   What is the publisher and date of <u>Miscelanea Americana, Escritos Publicados en la prensa Americana</u> by Luis Ricardo Fors, published in Paris in the 1800's?

3-14   Josephine Blackstock's <u>Songs for Sixpence, a Story about John Newbery</u> was published by Follett in 1955. Is this still in print, and what is the price?

3-15   What is the date of publication of a book by S.P. Godwin, titled <u>Heart Breathings, or, The Soul's Desire Expressed in Earnestness</u>?

3-16   Is Ray Bradbury's science fiction novel <u>Fahrenheit 451</u> available in paperback?

3-17   Richard Simmons is a popular figure on TV these days, as the "star" of a diet and physical fitness program. He is the author of some cookbooks and diet books currently in print, but you might well expect (and, if you are a fan, you might hope) that he would have another book in the offing. How would you find out if Richard Simmons does have another book scheduled for publication in the near future?

3-18   You have in your library a broadside which contains seven four-line verses called "Fellow Craft Hymn, for the use of Holland Lodge, composed by Brother Low." In one corner someone has penciled "NY, 1790." You need to find Brother Low's first name or complete name; you need to verify the date, if possible. Where would you look, and what <u>is</u> Brother Low's first name?

What you have been doing in working with these questions in this review section is a type of elementary search strategy--not just going aimlessly or frantically from one source to another until you find an answer, but rather analyzing the problem, deciding what information you have and what information you need to have, and figuring out a systematic approach to getting the information you need. Search strategy soon becomes so automatic and instinctive that you are not always aware that you are doing it. Remember that problems which seem simple and straightforward may turn out to be difficult and complex, and require a revision of strategy in midstream. Keep an open mind and keep your imagination working.

NATIONAL BIBLIOGRAPHIC RECORDS (U.S.)--SEARCH STRATEGY AND REVIEW

Answers #3/1--3/18

3-1: There is a gap between Kelly (which ends in Jan. 1871) and the American Catalogue (which begins in 1876): 1871-1875. This period is filled in to some extent by the Weekly Record, which began in 1872, and PTLA, which began in 1873.· Neither of these sources is satisfactory to use for retrospective searching, however. Weekly Record for that period means searching main entry only, through 52 non-cumulating issues a year; PTLA means searching annual volumes, but has publisher access only.

The newer American Book Publishing Record Cumulative, which covers 1876-1949, does not, according to its title, cover this period but the preface to this source (see answer to #1b-50) notes that thousands of pre-1876 entries are included in the set, so this set then does provide some coverage for the 1871-1875 period.

3-2: Only PTLA prior to 1948 (BIP) which is of course what makes it basically so unsatisfactory as an answer to #3-1.

3-3: Again, PTLA does not have any prior to 1948. Sabin now has title access through the Molnar index. The Checklist of American Imprints has title access for 1820-29 (and will eventually have a title index for 1830+ when those volumes are completed). Otherwise all the sources have title access, more or less completely.

3-4: Of those sources which are essentially for retrospective searching: Sabin has none, Evans is spotty, Shaw/Shoemaker and the Checklist have none. Roorbach and Kelly have none. American Catalogue, US Catalog, and CBI are the only ones of these retrospective sources which do have subject access. However, the new American Book Publishing Record Cumulative 1876-1949 and 1950-1977 sets, published in 1979-1980, provide subject access through the Dewey classification arrangement and the subject index for materials included in the sets as far back as 1876 and earlier.

Of the sources which are essential-ly for current searching: PTLA does not have subject coverage (in the sense of subject access for individual titles); Subject BIP does provide subject coverage (since 1957) for BIP; CBI has always had subject coverage.

3-5: Certainly yes. As noted in the answer to the previous question, most of the retrospective sources had very poor subject coverage. The ABPR Cumulative 1876-1949 and 1950-1977 sets, however complex they may be for searching index references, do provide badly needed subject coverage for the years back to 1876 or earlier.

3-6: The sources with subject access (see #3-4) would, of course, be the ones you would search in. For retrospective searching, for older publications, the American Catalogue, US Catalog, and CBI all use subject headings and "witchcraft" is used in all three; you also have to be careful to consider other similar terms such as occult/occultism, occult sciences, magic, spiritualism, etc. In the American Book Publishing Record Cumulative 1876-1949 and 1950-1977, you need to check under "witchcraft" in the subject indices to see what the possible Dewey classification numbers would be (133, 398, 610, etc.), and then search through several dozen pages in the appropriate Dewey classifications in both sets to find the relevant citations. The subject heading or subject term approach would seem to be more efficient to use here, since titles on "witchcraft" are scattered a bit through the Dewey classification, but searching in ABPR, though more time-consuming, yields more citations.

3-7: Author, title, subject, date of publication, publisher--primarily. You could be searching for any of these or a combination of any of these. You could already have any of these or a combination of any of these; more likely you would have a combination of elements rather than a single element, however.

(You should also keep in mind that the information you have, for any of these elements, could be either approximate or inaccurate.)

3-8:   As a group, the bibliographic sources you have examined tend to be organized chronologically (by date). For example, in the broadest possible grouping: current and retrospective. (Individually, bibliographic sources tend to be organized either by author or by subject.) In order to determine where to begin your search, you should know or at least make an educated guess at the date, at the general time period, at whether or not it is likely to be current or retrospective. This is why it is important for you to think about these sources both as individual, specific sources, and also as a group, in relation to each other.

3-9:   First you would figure out the elements which you have, and the elements which you need, and you would consider the date or general time period of major importance. You need to find out the author. You have the title (Free at Last!), and the subject (American hostages in Iran). You do not have the date or any indication of the general time period, but you can certainly figure it out from the subject. The subject is relatively recent (since 1980), so you would begin with recent or current sources. Recency combined with popular subject matter would lead you to think that the book would still be in print (BIP), or very recently published (Weekly Record, BPR, CBI). BIP does have a title access, so you might as well begin there. If the book is not listed in BIP, it is likely to be either o.p. (in which case you can then try going backwards in CBI or BPR to locate it), or not yet published (in which case you can try looking in Forthcoming Books). (You could also get this information from your library's card catalog, of course, by checking for a title added entry, but this sort of thing works only if your library has the book in question.)

3-10:   BIP is a one-stop source, and if you find it there, you will have solved your problem by checking in only one place. If you had gone directly to CBI or BPR, since you had only the vaguest idea of the date, you would probably have had to look through several issues or volumes of either one before

you located the title, and therefore your answer. Also by locating it in BIP, you have at the same time established its in-print status.

3-11:   You have most of your basic bibliographic information--author, title, date. The date (1821) is covered by Roorbach and by the Checklist, and probably by the ABPR Cumulative 1876-1949. Since you need an indication of what libraries might have copies, you can find this particular information only in the Checklist. (This title is not in Roorbach anyway.) The publisher (printer) is James Hughes. Libraries having copies are CSmH (Huntington Library in California) and Ms-Ar (probably the Missouri or Mississippi state archives). (The symbols used in the Checklist to identify libraries holding copies are, according to the Preface of vol. 1, those used in the National Union Catalog; you will find out in the next group of sources what this refers to, so do not bother to look it up now.) The location symbols given in the Checklist (as with Sabin, Evans, and the Shaw/Shoemaker) do not list all libraries having copies, only those libraries known to have copies, or those which have reported copies. It is therefore quite possible that libraries other than the two listed would have copies of The Communion of Saints.

3-12:   This book was published in 1918, and its correct title is Why God Loves the Irish. You can assume this is the book you are looking for, since there is nothing else similar to it published at that time. You can find it in the United States Catalog, 1928 volume, or in the ABPR Cumulative 1876-1949 under Geography and History (914).

    To find it, you could have begun with the American Catalogue in 1900 and worked forward to the US Catalog 1928. Or you could have started with the U.S. Catalog 1928 as it contains all books still in print at that date and therefore might include publications from the early 1900's. In ABPR Cumulative 1876-1949, you would have been tempted to go to the title index first, but would likely not have found what you were searching for, since your title was incorrect. The author index in ABPR refers you to several different Dewey classification numbers, each of which you must search out before you find this particular title.

3-13:   This was published in Paris and the only source you have studied so far likely to include such publications is Sabin; the publication is about or "relating to" America, and the date would be covered by Sabin, and you have the author's name. (Even if you do not read Spanish, you should be able to get the general drift of this title.) Sabin does have the book listed; the publisher is E. Denne Schmitz, and the date of publication is 1872. The author's name is listed under Fors; remember that if you are uncertain about what part of the name to search under, you should probably search under all parts.

3-14:   In order to establish its in-print status, and to determine its current price if it is in print, you <u>must</u> first check BIP. If it is not in BIP (and it was not, as of 1983), you can assume that it is out of print. The only way to be sure is to inquire of the publisher.

3-15:   Here you have author and title, but no date, not even approximately, so you can begin either with very current sources (WR, BPR, CBI, BIP) and work back, or with the very old sources (Sabin, Evans, etc.) and work forward. If you have no clue to the date of the book, it is probably six of one and half a dozen of the other which end you start at. However, the title of this book has a peculiarly non-current air, so proceeding on this "feeling," you might decide to start with the earlier sources. In this case, you could begin with Sabin, Evans, Shaw/Shoemaker, etc., working through until you find your publication listed. (It is listed in Kelly, 1867, p. 288; the publisher is Lippincott and the date of publication is 1867.) You could also have gone to one of the two major ABPR Cumulations, under either author or title; the ease of your search would depend upon how many references were given.

      You should also get in the habit of noting where you have searched, and what you searched under, and what results you did or did not find, so that if you have to backtrack, you do not have to repeat all your steps.

3-16:   "Available," again, meaning "in print," meaning BIP (or Paperbound Books in Print) is your first source. (It is listed in BIP and in Paperbound BIP, 1983, in two paperback editions from Ballantine.)

3-17:   You might find it out from reading Publishers Weekly, but a more direct source would be Forthcoming Books (checking under Simmons), or Subject Guide to Forthcoming Books (checking under cookbooks, diet and exercise, etc.).

3-18:   You have the title, the author approximately, and the date approximately. The date is covered by Sabin and Evans. You can check Sabin under Low, as author, but it is not listed. In Evans, you can go directly to the volume for 1790 and check alphabetically under Low for that year, and you will find a citation for your broadside, which tells you that Brother Low's first name is Samuel. The fact that the imprint information, in Evans, appears in square brackets, is an indication that this information did not appear on the publication itself but in fact was "supplied" by the bibliographer. On your copy, remember, it was only written in pencil, presumably at a later time. (If you didn't know what a broadside was, you could have looked it up in the ALA Glossary.)

Section 4

NATIONAL LIBRARY CATALOG AND UNION LIST

Questions #4/1--4/62

One of the purposes of this self-study manual is to instruct you in the method or technique of examining reference sources; so far you have been given a great deal of specific guidance in what to look for and where to look for it. Now, you should find that you are growing more and more independent of such specific guidance. You should have a fairly clear idea of the type of information which you must look for in each of these bibliographic sources, and where you are likely to find it. When you are examining a new or unfamiliar source, you should look for similarities and make comparisons with what you already know.

4-1   Before you begin with the next set of sources, review how you are to proceed. If necessary, go back to the questions on the other sources you have already examined. What do you need to find out or determine about each source, in your examination of it?

Often you will find that there is considerable overlapping of this information. For example, you can frequently tell a great deal about the scope and arrangement of a source from its title, or from its publication dates. Sometimes it is necessary to determine the publication dates of a source before you can make a clear statement of its scope. Sometimes you will need to determine the basic arrangement of the source before its publication dates, or therefore its scope, will be clear to you.

The next set of sources from the bibliographic records of the United States are:

Library of Congress/National Union Catalog "author lists" 1942-1957 (AA92/93/94)
National Union Catalog "author lists" 1958[1956]-1982 (AA94/95)
National Union Catalog Pre-1956 Imprints (Mansell) (AA96, 1AA22, 2AA9)
Subject Catalog (Library of Congress catalogs) (AA99, 2AA11)
National Union Catalog. Books (Washington, D.C., Library of Congress, 1983+; on microfiche)

The LC/NUC catalogs are particularly complex in their scope and arrangement. It helps to understand some of this complexity if you can work through the history of the publication, cumulations, and changes in scope of these catalogs over the years since they first began appearing in 1942. The early sets published prior to 1956 have now been superseded by a later portion of the catalogs, so some libraries may have discarded those early sets or relegated them to the stack areas. The first group of questions in this section of the manual (#4/2-#4/41) can be answered directly from Sheehy rather than from the sources themselves. (Following #4-41, are a group of questions which do require you to use the sources to search out the answers.) Before beginning with the series of Sheehy questions, however, it might be useful to locate the actual LC/NUC sets in your library and look them over in a general way, both inside and out. Keep in mind that the LC/NUC catalogs consist of several series or sets of volumes; they take up a great deal of room on library shelves. If you look through some of the volumes, you will see that the entries within them are in the familiar form of a library catalog card entry. Turn then to the Sheehy entry (AA92/93/94/95) for the first of these LC/NUC sets. The lengthy annotation following the bibliographic citation for AA95 refers to all of those sets from AA92-95.

4-2   Note that this particular source is listed in Sheehy first under "Universal bibliography," then under the sub-heading of "Library catalogs," and then under the further sub-heading of "National libraries." What is a national library?

The Library of Congress in Washington, D.C. functions as a national library for the United States. One of its functions has been to make available to other libraries printed catalog cards for most of its own holdings (the items in its collections), and sometimes items from the collections of other

71

libraries in the country. These printed catalog cards are the same as those which you can see in the card catalogs of most large college and university libraries. The LC "printed catalog," as described in Sheehy AA92, etc., is a reproduction in book form, or in bound volumes, of these printed catalog cards.

Using Sheehy, try then to determine the publication pattern of the LC/NUC catalogs--what the various series consist of, what they represent, and how many volumes they contain, what the cumulation pattern is, etc. In the process of doing this, you should also begin to get a general idea of the scope of the work.

4-3   What are the publication dates (not necessarily the dates of coverage) of the first, or the basic, series of the LC set? How many volumes are there in this first set? What is the title?

4-4   According to the annotation in Sheehy, is this LC catalog then a catalog of Library of Congress holdings?

4-5   The publication dates for the basic series are 1942-1946. Does this then include printed catalog cards issued from 1942-1946?

4-6   The next series is the first supplement to the basic set. How many volumes does it consist of? In what year(s) were they published? What are the issuing dates of the cards which they contain?

4-7   Does this mean that you would find in the first supplement only titles published from 1942-1947?

4-8   Does the 1942-1947 supplement supersede the basic set? Would titles in the basic set appear also in the 1942-1947 supplement? If you were searching for a book published in 1937, where would you look (so far)?

In 1947, the Library of Congress began to publish current supplements to its printed catalog (as represented by printed cards) on the basis of nine monthly issues, three quarterly cumulations, and an annual cumulation. (This same publication pattern has been maintained for the history of the printed catalog, see Sheehy AA95.) The issues which came out during 1947 were included in the 1942-47 supplement, the second series. The annual cumulations for 1948, 1949, 1950, 1951, along with the various monthly and quarterly issues for 1952, were further cumulated into a five-year or quinquennial cumulation (1948-52), which is the third series (see Sheehy AA93).

4-9   What are the imprint dates of publications included in this third series? How many volumes are there in the set? Is there anything special about the last volume?

4-10   What is the next (fourth) series? Is there any difference between the title of the fourth series and the title of the earlier series?

4-11   What does this title change represent according to the Sheehy annotation?

4-12   Do you think then that the scope of the printed catalogs has increased, decreased, or remained the same since its change to the National Union Catalog?

4-13   One of the changes in the LC/NUC catalogs at this point was the inclusion of location symbols in the entries. What are location symbols? Of the bibliographies you have already examined, in the previous questions, which ones included library location symbols?

4-14   How would you find out what the library location symbols stand for?

4-15   What is the importance of such location symbols?

4-16   What is a union catalog?

4-17   What would you think--from your experience, your reading, or your imagination--might be the pur-
        pose or usefulness of union catalogs or lists?

4-18   With the fourth series, 1953-57, the title, the scope and function of the catalogs changed, from just
        LC printed cards to that of a union catalog listing. The fourth series was published throughout
        1953-57 and then cumulated into this set. The title and function change came in 1956, and the na-
        tional union catalog listings were included for only 1956+ imprints. Would you expect to find in the
        1953-57 cumulation an entry with NUC location symbols for a book published in 1954?

4-19   Can you make a brief indication or chart of the pattern for these LC/NUC catalogs or "author lists"
        to this point? Show coverage for imprint date of publications included.

4-20   The fifth of the LC/NUC series was another five-year cumulation, 1958-62. This publishing pattern
        continued through 1982. (In 1983, the publication of the NUC changed to a different format and
        arrangement.) Can you make a brief indication or chart of the pattern for the NUC "author lists"
        from the 1958-62 set through 1982? Show coverage for imprint date of publications included.

4-21   In the various parts of this source which you have examined so far, where would you look to find
        information on a book published in 1887? Would you expect to find library locations indicated for
        it?

4-22   Is anything being done to supply library locations for early imprints, such as the 1887 title?

4-23   Does the NUC Pre-1956 Imprints set supersede or replace any of the earlier sets?

4-24   In the parts of the source which you have examined so far, where would you look to find infor-
        mation on a book published in 1887? Would you expect to find library locations indicated for it?
        What about a book published in 1945?

4-25   In the parts of the source which you have examined so far, where would you look to find infor-
        mation on a book published in 1956? For a book published in 1963?

4-26   You have now determined the publication and cumulation pattern of the various series of the LC/
        NUC catalogs through 1982. What is the arrangement of the material within the source? Is it
        alphabetical or classified?

4-27   What does "author and main entry" mean? Do you remember any earlier source which was also
        arranged in this way?

4-28   If you knew the title of a book, but did not know the author, would you be able to locate it in the LC/NUC catalogs?

4-29   If you specifically wanted to locate the entry in the LC/NUC catalogs for a book of which you knew only the title--for example, a novel titled The Nice and the Good--and you did not know the author, how could you go about it?

4-30   Are there any cross-references in the LC/NUC catalogs?

4-31   Is there any subject access for the LC/NUC catalogs? (See Sheehy.)

4-32   A numbered publisher's series titled "Princeton Essays on the Arts" has been published by Princeton University Press. If you wanted to find out the author and title of No. 3 of this series, published in the 1970's, how could you go about it?

4-33   Libraries cooperating in the national union catalog project may report that they have a copy of a specific book after the entry for that book has appeared in the published NUC. Suppose you are trying to get a specific book on interlibrary loan and the NUC lists only two libraries that hold copies and neither can fill your request. Do you have any way of finding out additional libraries holding copies and reporting them later?

The LC/NUC "author lists" were published in this printed format and arrangement, as described in Sheehy, from 1942 (including imprint dates from earliest printed books) through 1982. In 1983, this publication ceased, and the format and arrangement of the NUC publication changed. At that time, the Library of Congress began publishing essentially a new title--National Union Catalog. Books--in microfiche only. (See the ALA Glossary for a definition of microfiche).

This microfiche edition uses an "index-register" arrangement. The master listing for all items included is in the "register." The complete bibliographic citation for each item included in the master listing or register is given a register identification number, as it is added to the register. The entries in the register are in this numerical order, rather than by author or main entry, or title, or some alphabetical arrangement.

This master listing is indexed by name (including author), title, series' title, and subject. This provides title access for the NUC for 1983+, previously lacking. It also provides subject and series' titles access for the NUC for 1983+, previously available only for LC printed cards. The indexes give brief bibliographic information and reference to the register identification number so that the full entry can be found in the register. The register and the indexes are published monthly. Only the indexes cumulate and each index cumulation completely replaces the preceding issue.

4-34   Although the format and arrangement of the new, 1983+ NUC publication is quite different than the pre-1983 publication, the scope remains essentially the same. You have already considered the scope of the LC/NUC catalog to some extent, when you considered its title change and expansion to the National Union Catalog in 1956 (#4-11). The scope of material listed or included in the LC/NUC catalogs is more or less that of the collections of the Library of Congress and of the collections of the libraries reporting to the NUC. Obviously, this is an extremely broad scope. Most of the sources you have examined previously have been much more limited, to materials published in the United States, materials published in England, materials relating to America. Does the material listed in the LC/NUC catalogs have any such limitations?

4-35   Why are the LC/NUC catalogs listed, in Sheehy, under "universal" bibliographies, rather than under "national bibliographies" for the U.S.?

4-36   Why, then, would we be considering the LC/NUC catalogs as part of the bibliographic records of the United States?

4-37   What kind of bibliographic information would you find in the entries themselves, in the LC/NUC catalogs? Is the information extensive? Is it authoritative?

4-38   Is there any kind of information which is not generally given in the LC/NUC entries and which might be very important to librarians?

4-39   Then where do you look for this information, if it is not given and you need to know it?

4-40   Remember that ideal bibliographic control should cover more than just books. Many of the earlier bibliographic sources you examined were quite limited in the types of publications included. For example, they might exclude periodicals, pamphlets, government publications, dissertations, serials, maps, audio-visual materials, etc. By reading the Sheehy annotation, can you tell if the LC/NUC catalogs seem to have any of these types of exclusions?

4-41   How are serials and periodicals included in the NUC?

In addition to New Serial Titles, and another publication called Newspapers in Microform, both of which will be covered in Section 6 of this manual, there are several other publications which supplement and complement the materials included in the basic LC/NUC catalogs, particularly in providing bibliographic control for some of the non-book and non-print or audio-visual materials. These publications are:

    Music, Books on Music, and Sound Recordings (BH54/55)
    National Union Catalog. Audiovisual Materials (in microfiche, 1983+)
    Audiovisual Materials (Library of Congress catalogs) 1953-1982 (BG116/117, 2AA51)
    National Union Catalog. Cartographic Materials (in microfiche, 1983+)
    National Union Catalog of Manuscript Collections (DB39)
    National Register of Microform Masters (AA123, 1AA32)

By reading the Sheehy annotations on these sources, you can determine their scope and therefore how they fit into the bibliographic pattern set by the LC/NUC catalogs you have considered in more detail.

Up to this point, you have been able to work through the questions in this section by using Sheehy. The next series of questions, #4-42 through #4-57, should be answered by going to the various LC/NUC sets and other publications and catalogs and searching out the answers in the sources themselves.

4-42   A book titled The Commission Executed by E.V. Zollars was published in 1912. Is the author of this book the same as Ely V. Zollars who wrote The Great Salvation? Who published The Commission Executed? Where could you see or from whom could you borrow a copy of this book?

4-43   Locate in the LC/NUC catalog the entry for We Bark at Midnight by Van Lane Ferguson, published in Rutland, Vermont in 1958. In what year and volume did you find it? Who is the publisher? How many pages are there in the book?

4-44   In the entry for the Ferguson book (from the preceding question) what is at least one library which is shown as having a copy of the book?

4-45   Look at the entry for the Ferguson book from #4-43. What does the "58-7495," in the lower right corner of the entry, mean? Where would you look to find out?

4-46   Is there anything in the entry for the Ferguson book (from #4-43) which might give you a clue to what the book is about?

4-47   Locate in the LC/NUC catalog the entry for The Living Bread by Thomas Merton, published in 1956. Who is the publisher of the American edition of this title? What is at least one university library which owns a copy of this American edition?

4-48   Locate in the LC/NUC catalog the entry for Unfolding Character: The Impact of Gordonstoun by Adam Arnold Brown, published in London in 1962. In what year and volume did you find it?

4-49   In the entry for Unfolding Character (see #4-48), several libraries are listed--or their symbols are listed--as having copies of this title. Does this indicate that these are the only libraries in the U.S. holding this title?

4-50   In an earlier question in this manual (#2b-35), you tried to locate and verify information on a book by Wharton entitled A Treatise on Theism, published in the U.S. in 1859. This was not in Sabin, and another source for the period, Roorbach, listed the title but did not actually give a date and gave the author's name only as F. Wharton. Can you now verify this information from the LC/ NUC catalogs?

4-51   Also in an earlier question in this manual, #1a-64, while examining Books in Print, you were asked where you would look to find a list of all the editions which had ever been published of Tom Sawyer by Mark Twain (Samuel Langhorne Clemens). In the answer you were referred to a bibliography of the writings of Mark Twain, which you might locate through Sheehy or a similar source. Would looking in the various LC/NUC catalogs answer this question? Could you look in the NUC Pre-1956 Imprints set and find, under the author, entries for all the editions of Tom Sawyer which have ever been published?

4-52   Can you find the author, the title, and other bibliographic information about a book, published in the 1970s, on the history of the Rose Bowl? (The Rose Bowl is a football stadium in Pasadena, California, and an important football game is played there on New Year's Day.)

4-53   Can you find information about some films on the subject of teenage marriages? (Use the 1982 cumulation of Audiovisual Materials.)

4-54   What orchestra performed on the recording of Maurice Ravel's "Daphnis and Chloé" ballet music, recorded by Angel in 1982? (Use the 1982 cumulation of Music, Books on Music, and Sound Recordings.)

4-55   Charles F. Kettering was an engineer and a friend of Wilbur and Orville Wright. Tape-recorded interviews of friends and associates of both Kettering and the Wright Brothers were made in 1976 as part of the Oral History Project. Where are the tapes and transcripts of the tapes located? (Use the NUC of Manuscript Collections.)

4-56   Can you locate a high quality microform copy of Phillis Wheatley's <u>Poems on Various Subjects, Religious and Moral</u>, published in 1802? (Use the 1978 cumulation of the National Register of Microform Masters.)

4-57   A book titled <u>The Monsters and the Critics, and Other Essays</u> was published in 1983. Who is the author, and what is the subject of the book?

        In summary, then, the scope of the LC/NUC catalogs, which you have examined, plus the various supplementary publications you have also considered, is very broad, and the information given in the entries is--in general--very nearly complete and quite accurate. So you can see that this source serves as one of our most useful, most complete, most accurate sources of bibliographic information, not only for publications of the U.S. but for publications from all countries as well. It serves as part of the U.S. national bibliographic records, and as part of a "universal" bibliographic record.

4-58   Can you see any weaknesses or loopholes in the use of the LC/NUC catalogs as a <u>complete</u> national bibliographic record? For example, do you remember that the Sheehy annotations said that all publications (for example, <u>all</u> books) published in the United States would automatically be listed in the LC/NUC catalogs? Is any provision made to require <u>all</u> publications to be deposited in the Library of Congress or any other official source?

4-59   What is copyright and copyright registration?

4-60   Is there any record of publications which have been sent to the U.S. Copyright Office for registration? Is this record then a complete listing of <u>all</u> U.S. publications?

4-61   Can you tell from the annotation in Sheehy how the Catalog of Copyright Entries compares, in a general way, with the LC/NUC catalogs? Consider type of materials covered.

4-62   It would appear that the scope of the CCE is perhaps in a way much broader than the LC/NUC catalogs since it includes all types of written matter sent in to be copyrighted--for example, games, children's coloring books, etc. Can you see any ways in which the CCE is more <u>limited</u> for bibliographic use than the LC/NUC catalogs? It may not be possible to answer this question without actually examining the source itself, by looking at the entries and the information included in them, and the dates of the material as it is included and published, or made available.

NATIONAL LIBRARY CATALOG AND UNION LIST

Answers #4/1--4/62

4-1: In general you will want to determine: the basic bibliographic information about the source itself; the arrangement of the source, its access; the scope of the source (including the amount of information given in the individual citations or entries); any special features you may note about the source. (This is the information outlined in Sheehy, 9th ed., p. xiv-xv.)

4-2: There is a brief definition of "national library" in the ALA Glossary. The few brief comments in Sheehy (9th ed., p. 9) might also be helpful. You could also look up the Library of Congress itself in a general encyclopedia.

4-3: The first or basic series of the LC catalog was published in 1942-46, and consists of 167 volumes, or volumes 1-167. At that time it was called "A Catalog of Books Represented by Library of Congress printed cards...." (This is item AA92 in Sheehy.)

4-4: No, not really--it is a catalog only of the items "for which Library of Congress printed cards were available" (see note under "scope" in Sheehy, p. 10) and in some cases from collections other than those in the LC. The LC printed catalogs do not record all of the LC holdings, and include as well some holdings from other libraries.

4-5: No, according to the title of the source (title page and Sheehy annotation), it includes printed cards issued up to July 31, 1942. In other words, coverage of imprint dates for the publications to be listed in the set would be from the earliest printed books to [August] 1942, or, items with imprint dates prior to 1943 [August 1942].

4-6: The first supplement (also Sheehy AA92) to the basic set consists of 42 volumes (volumes 1-42), published in 1948. They contain cards issued from 1942 through 1947.

4-7: 1942-47 is the date of issue of the cards, not the imprint date of the titles or publications covered. As in the basic set, coverage for imprint dates of the publications to be listed in the set would be from earliest printed books through 1947.

4-8: No, it does not supersede the basic set; it supplements it--adds to it--to be used in addition to the basic set. In theory, titles in the basic set would not appear also in the 1942-47 supplement. If you were trying to find an entry for a book published in 1937, you would look first in the basic set (imprints through [July] 1942) and if you did not find it there, then look also in the 1st supplement (imprints through 1947).

4-9: The third series contains printed cards issued from 1948-52. Imprint dates of publications included would be from the earliest printed books through 1952. The set has 24 volumes. Vol. 24 contains only listings for "films."

4-10: The fourth series (Sheehy AA94) is another five-year cumulation, covering cards issued from 1953-1957. The original catalogs were published from 1953-1957, and the cumulation was published in 1958, in 28 volumes, of which vol. 27 covers "music and phonorecords" and vol. 28 "motion pictures and film-strips." With the fourth series, 1953-57, the title changed to the "National Union Catalog." Earlier titles were some variation of "Library of Congress."

4-11: The change of title from LC to NUC represents an important change in the scope and function of the printed catalog. See the Sheehy annotation, p. 10, under the scope of "1953-1957." The printed catalog now includes titles reported to the LC by some 500 other libraries, and indicates location of these titles as well.

4-12:   Basically, the scope has broadened, or increased, since the catalogs now contain many titles from other libraries.

4-13:   See the ALA Glossary for "location symbols." They were also found in Sabin, Evans, Shaw/Shoemaker, Checklist of American Imprints (all from Sections 2a and 2b).

4-14:   One should assume that all reference and bibliographic sources would clarify, usually in the preface or introductory material, what the various abbreviations and symbols used in the source stand for. So by checking in the preface of the first volume of one of these LC/NUC series, you should be able to find out what the location symbols stand for, or at least where else to look to find that out. (See #2b-24.)

4-15:   In the case of the LC/NUC sets, these location symbols are particularly useful for interlibrary loan. Librarians can find out in this way what libraries own copies of these particular books, and they may then want to borrow these copies on interlibrary loan. Any other person using the bibliography would have access to the same information, of course. (See #2b-26.)

4-16:   See the definition given in the ALA Glossary.

4-17:   Some of the things you might have suggested would be: location of materials (for interlibrary loan, for example); cooperative buying, cataloging, etc., between libraries, on a local/regional/national basis; a further bibliographic source for information.

4-18:   No, because NUC information was included for 1956+ imprints only. You might expect to find an entry--but for an LC printed card, not for the national union catalog information. In 1961 the Library of Congress decided to make available NUC cards for those 1952-1955 imprints which were not included as NUC items in the 1953-57 cumulation. The National Union Catalog 1952-55 Imprints (see Sheehy, AA94, AA95, top of p. 10), a 30-volume set, served temporarily as a supplement to the 1953-1957 cumulation, but was eventually superseded by another publication which will be discussed later.

4-19:   LC 1942 (imprints through 1942)
         LC 1942-47 (imprints through 1947)

LC 1948-52 (imprints through 1952)
LC/NUC 1953-57 (imprints through 1957)
(NUC 1952-55 imprints only)

4-20:   NUC 1958-62 (imprints through 1962)
         NUC 1963-67 (imprints through 1967)
         NUC 1968-72 (imprints through 1972)
         NUC 1973-77 (imprints through 1977)
         NUC 1978, 1979, 1980, 1981, and 1982 in annual cumulations. (At some point these annual cumulations might be further cumulated into a final 1978-82 set.)

4-21:   For a book published in 1887, you would have to go back to the LC basic set, and if you did not find it there, work forward searching through the various series as indicated in the answers to #4-19 and #4-20. Since libraries currently purchase many books with older imprint dates, you could reasonably expect it to appear at any point, depending on when the LC received and cataloged it and made an LC card available. You would not expect to find library locations--i.e., NUC information--since that is included in the LC/NUC (as you have examined it so far) only for 1952+ imprints (including the 1952-55 imprints catalog published to supplement the 1953-57 cumulation, as noted in the answer to #4-18).

4-22:   Yes, the National Union Catalog Pre-1956 Imprints (Sheehy AA96, 1AA22, 2AA9) which makes available bibliographic information and locations on all titles held by cooperating libraries and reported to the national union catalog in the Library of Congress. It was completed in 754 volumes; vols. 686-754 are a supplement, which includes the almost three million cards which had accumulated since publication of the set began in 1967.

4-23:   Yes, it supersedes the LC/NUC "author lists" for 1942-57, or those sets which are listed in the answer to #4-19. Although it is titled "Pre-1956 Imprints" and in fact includes only pre-1956 imprints, it supersedes the 1953-57 cumulation because, as is noted in the Sheehy annotation for the NUC Pre-1956 Imprints, "in anticipation of the present compilation, 1956-57 imprints were repeated in the 1958-62 cumulation of the NUC."

4-24:   For a book published in 1887, you would now look in the NUC Pre-1956 Imprints (which supersedes those series listed in the answer to #4-19), and if you did not find it there you would continue to search in the NUC "author lists" published from 1958-1982, those series listed in the answer to #4-20. You would expect to find library locations indicated since the entire set that you are searching is now a national union catalog. The same answer would be true for a book published in 1945.

4-25:   For a book published in 1956, you could not of course look in the pre-1956 imprints catalog; you would look in the NUC 1958-62 set, since those 1956 and 1957 imprints in the earlier LC/NUC author lists were repeated in the 1958-62 cumulation. If you did not find what you were looking for in the 1958-62 set, you would then continue to search in the NUC from 1963-67 on. For a book published in 1963, you would begin with the NUC 1963-67.

Note that in the early 1970's, the firm of Rowman and Littlefield published a cumulation of the NUC 1958-62 and 1963-67 sets (Sheehy AA97); this is titled NUC 1956-1967 because of the 1956 and 1957 imprints which were repeated in the 1958-62 set. Many libraries which had already purchased the 1958-62 and 1963-67 sets would not necessarily purchase this new cumulation.

4-26:   The Sheehy annotation states (under "scope") that it is an "author and main entry catalog"; these main entries are arranged alphabetically, although that is not made clear in the Sheehy annotation.

4-27:   Think back to the Weekly Record, arranged by "main entry only." This means that you will find only one entry for each item, primarily author entries but in some cases title entries. There will not be any entry under both author and title (as with CBI and BIP).

4-28:   Not unless it happened that the title was the main entry for the book.

4-29:   Look it up in some other source which does give you title access (for example, CBI) to find out the author, and then look it up in LC/NUC under the author.

4-30:   Yes, there are some. The Sheehy annotation tells you this.

4-31:   There is no subject access in the sets discussed so far. There is, however, another Library of Congress catalog

series called Subject Catalog (prior to 1975 called Books: Subjects, Sheehy AA99, 2AA11), which began in 1950, and which does give an alphabetical subject access, through Library of Congress subject headings (see #1a-53/54), to those publications catalogued by the Library of Congress and a few other libraries and represented by LC printed cards. It does not include all NUC contributions. (Additional locations can of course be found by checking in the NUC catalogs, using the main entry as indicated on the cards in the subject catalog.)

At one time the Subject Catalog included only books; in recent years this has changed to include other types of publications as well. At one time the Subject Catalog included only publications printed in 1945 or later; in recent years this also has changed, and some earlier imprint dates may be found. (This information is in the Foreword to the source, not in Sheehy.)

4-32:   Since the LC/NUC catalogs are main entry only with only a few cross-references, you would expect to find this in the LC/NUC catalogs only if the main entry in this case were the series' title. And if you found an entry under the series' title, it is not too likely that the citation would include a listing of all the authors and titles for the series. However, another Library of Congress catalog series titled Monographic Series (Sheehy 1AA21), which began publication in 1974, exists to give such author and title information under series' entries.

4-33:   Yes, in the NUC Register of Additional Locations (Sheehy AA98, 2AA10). These were published in the last eight volumes of the 1963-67 cumulation, then continued on a semi-annual and annual basis. Currently the Register of Additional Locations is available only in a microform edition. The Register is a listing of LC card numbers (given in the original NUC entry) only, plus additional location symbols.

4-34:   No, certainly no more so than the collections of any college or university library, for example. The LC/NUC will include foreign publications, foreign language publications, as well as U.S. or English language publications.

However, in 1983 the Library of Congress also began publishing a more limited version of NUC.Books, titled

National Union Catalog. U.S. Books.
NUC.U.S. Books includes only materials published in the United States.
(The format and arrangement are the
same as NUC.Books; the scope is more
limited.)

4-35:   Because they do not attempt to limit themselves to listings of the publications of
one language or one country, but rather
include publications in all languages from
all countries. The national union catalog which has actually existed on cards
in the LC is "national" in the sense of
being part of the "national" library of
the U.S., and is contributed to by some
600+ libraries in North America, most but
not all of which would be libraries of the
U.S. "nation," but the publications included in the collections of those libraries
and reported to the NUC are universal
in nature.

4-36:   The LC functions as a national library
for the U.S. One of the functions of
a national library is to collect and preserve the literature (in a broad sense)
of that country. The LC does attempt to
fulfill this function. Also, as a basic
research library, its collections of U.S.
publications will be extensive. Most of
these publications--current and retro-
spective--will be represented by LC
printed cards or reports to the NUC,
and will therefore appear in the LC /
NUC catalogs.

4-37:   Since the entries in these catalogs have
represented photographic reproductions
of actual library catalog cards, you would
expect that they would include all the
kinds of information found on a library
catalog card--including notes, LC/Dewey
class numbers, subject heading tracings,
added entry tracings and call numbers.
This information is usually much more
extensive than that which you find in
most bibliographic sources, and--be-
cause it does represent cataloging from
the publication itself--it can generally
be considered as quite authoritative and
accurate. As the Sheehy annotation
says, "information given is detailed and
represents a high degree of accuracy."

4-38:   Yes, the price. However, many of the
entries in the recent issues do include
the price.

4-39:   BIP, PTLA, Weekly Record, BPR, CBI,
etc.

4-40:   In general, the LC /NUC catalogs include

a much broader range of types of materials or publications than any of the
preceding sources. The Sheehy annotation notes books, pamphlets, maps,
atlases, music scores, periodicals and
other serials, motion pictures, and filmstrips as among the types or formats which
have been included in the LC /NUC catalogs
at various times over the years. Some
of these materials which were included
at one time are now being covered by other supplementary Library of Congress
publications. When the materials are included in the LC/NUC catalogs, it is not
always clear whether they are included
as NUC listings, or only as LC printed
cards; the preface or introductions to
the catalogs themselves are more helpful
here. However, at this point all you need
to realize is that some entries for all of
these various types of materials will appear in the LC /NUC catalogs.

4-41:   Periodicals and other serials have been
included in the LC /NUC catalogs but
generally only for the LC printed cards
--that is, serials reported from other libraries would not be included, and library locations would not be given.
Another Library of Congress publication
called New Serial Titles, which will be
discussed in Section 6 of this manual,
does list serial titles from other libraries
and gives library locations.

4-42:   The book was published in 1912, before
1956. You want library locations as well
as the bibliographic information. In the
NUC Pre-1956 Imprints, both books are
found entered under Zollars, Ely Vaughan,
same birth and death dates. Both books
were published by The Standard Publishing Co. in Cincinnati. The Commission Executed is held by the Library of
Congress (DLC) and the Cleveland Public
Library (OCl).

4-43:   The entry is located in the 1958-62
series, vol. 14 (p. 372) under Ferguson. The publisher is Tuttle and the
paging is given (87 pages) in the "body"
of the card, just as it appears on a
regular catalog card which you might
find in a university library card catalog.

4-44:   The entry gives 6 location symbols.
The first is MH, which stands for Harvard (see preface of vol. 1 of the
1958-62 set).

4-45:   Probably you would not know what this
number stands for and would have to
look it up. You should expect that

reference sources will give you some adequate instructions about abbreviations, numbers, symbols, etc., which are used in the source, and usually these explanations will be located in the prefatory or introductory material in the front of the volume. In this case you will need to go back to vol. 1 of the 1958-62 set, as you did with the location symbols in #4-44, and on p. x there is a description and explanation of the various parts of the entries. The number in the lower right corner is the order number for the LC card (of which the entry itself is a reproduction), so that libraries wishing to order copies of the card may do so by using that specific number.

4-46: In this particular entry, the LC classification number or call number is given in the lower left corner (PZ4 F352 We), and if you knew the classification scheme, or where to look it up, you would be able to tell that PZ is the class number for Fiction in English.

4-47: You want library locations for a title published in 1956. Remember (see #4-23) that 1956-1957 imprints with NUC reported locations were repeated in the 1958-62 cumulation. This particular book is found in the NUC 1958-62 cumulation, vol. 30, p. 323. Two editions are listed; the American edition was published by Farrar, Straus & Cudahy in New York. The first library location symbol listed is PBL (Lehigh University in Bethlehem, Pennsylvania).

4-48: The entry is in the 1963-67 set, vol. 3, under Arnold-Brown, not under Brown. There is a cross-reference from Brown to Arnold-Brown. You do not have the option in the LC/NUC catalogs, as you do with for example CBI, of finding the entry also under the title or of finding a cross-reference from the title to the correct author entry. Although the book was published in 1962, the entry does not appear until the 1963-67 cumulation, meaning that the card from the LC/NUC was not issued in time for its appearance in the 1962 volume. As with most of the other bibliographic sources, the appearance of the listing will not necessarily coincide exactly with the publication of the book.

4-49: No, only that these libraries have reported it to the NUC. Not all libraries report to the NUC. Many libraries may have this title but not have reported it to the NUC. Other libraries may report

it but at a later date so that they would not be included in this particular list. Remember the Register of Additional Locations from #4-33.

4-50: Since it was published in 1859, you would expect to find it in the NUC Pre-1956 Imprints (or if your library does not have that set, in the early sets of the LC catalogs). It is in the NUC Pre-1956 Imprints, vol. 658, p. 603 (under Wharton, Francis; it is necessary to go through many many pages of Whartons whose names begin with F to find the one who wrote this title). It is also in the basic (published 1942-46) set of LC. It shows the same information you found in Roorbach, plus the author's full name, plus the number of pages, plus the date of publication (1859).

4-51: If you looked in the NUC Pre-1956 Imprints, under Clemens, you would probably find a great many of the editions of Tom Sawyer, but you would not necessarily find all of those which had ever been published. You would find only those which (a) the Library of Congress has in its collections, has cataloged, and has made cards available for, and (b) the libraries participating in the National Union Catalog have in their collections, have catalogued, and have reported to the NUC. You would need to go to the NUC sets (1958[1956]-1982, as listed in #4-20, and 1983+) following the Pre-1956 Imprints for those editions published after 1955, and for those earlier editions which may not have been reported until after the Pre-1956 Imprints was published. All of this is likely to be a pretty complete listing of editions published in the United States and/or in English, but not necessarily for foreign language publications. A truly complete list might need some further bibliographic detective work.

4-52: Here you have only the subject. In the Subject Catalog, 1978 annual cumulation, vol. 15, p. 903, you can find such a book. The entry is "Rose Bowl Game, Pasadena, Calif.--History."

4-53: Use the subject index first; there are no references under "teenage," but there are several under "adolescent parents--United States." One of these is to a 20-minute film originally shown on television, titled "Teenage Parents." (The full citation is found on p. 517 of the 1982 cumulation.) This particular title would also have been found had you searched in the main listings (by title) under "teenage."

4-54: Look in the set directly under the composer's name, Ravel. Two recordings of the complete ballet music are listed; the Angel recording was performed by the London Symphony Orchestra. (In the 1982 cumulation, p. 58.)

4-55: Look first in the index (1975-79 cumulated index volume) under Kettering, Charles. The number given (78-1112) refers you to the 1978 cumulation, entry number 1112. Entries in the 1978 cumulation are in numerical order. The tapes and the transcripts are located at the University of Dayton Library in Dayton, Ohio. A brief statement of the contents of the tapes/transcripts is given, including names of the interviewees.

4-56: In the 1978 cumulation of the National Register of Microform Masters (vol. 2, p. 654) under Wheatley, Phillis, two entries are given for that particular title. One microform master is held by Readex, microform positive (mp). The other is held by the New York Public Library (NN); the m* tells you that this is a microfilm preservation master, which is the high quality copy you want.

4-57: For 1983+ publications, you have the new NUC.Books on microfiche, with title access. The title index for 1983 gives you the name of the author (J.R.R. Tolkien) and refers you to the complete entry in the register, register item number A-207-807. In this complete entry, subject tracings are given, and these tell you that the book is about English philology and Beowulf.

4-58: There was no indication that all publications would automatically appear in the LC/NUC catalogs nor that any provisions had been made to require all publications to be deposited there. Coverage would still be extensive, however, since the NUC includes entries from the LC itself plus 600 other libraries. In addition, LC is a depository for books sent in to the U.S. Copyright Office for copyright registration.

4-59: See the ALA Glossary or a general dictionary. Essentially, copyright is the exclusive right--granted in some legal or official way--to reproduce a work. Copyright registration is the official registration of this right, accomplished in the United States by sending copies of the work in to the U.S. Copyright Office.

4-60: Yes, the Catalog of Copyright Entries, published continuously by the Copyright Office in the Library of Congress (Sheehy AA478, 2AA63). No, it lists only those publications sent in for copyright registration.

4-61: Materials covered include books, pamphlets, serials, contributions to periodicals, periodicals, dramas, lectures, music, maps and atlases, works of art, reproductions, scientific and technical drawings, photographic works, prints, pictorial illustrations, commercial prints and labels, motion pictures and filmstrips. Also included are books in foreign languages published outside the U.S. if copyrighted in the U.S., books in English first published outside the U.S., business reports and yearbooks, trade catalogs and directories, manuals, instruction books, etc. (See Sheehy.)

4-62: Entries in the CCE, although reasonably full, do not include as much information as the LC/NUC entries (see #4-37). Entries are listed in the CCE according to the date they were copyrighted (which is usually, although not necessarily, the date of publication): however, the gap between the copyright date and the publication of the CCE is considerably more than in the LC/NUC. Sheehy says nearly a year late.

BIBLIOGRAPHIC SOURCES FOR SERIALS--CURRENT LISTS

Questions #5/1--5/63

The sources which you have examined thus far comprise the major bibliographic records of publication in the United States, both current and retrospective. Some of them overlap, particularly
the current ones, but differences in scope and information given are still sufficient to make it necessary to consider using all of them together to provide an adequate record.

However, national bibliographic control must include coverage of all types of publications:
books, serials, periodicals, newspapers, pamphlets, dissertations, maps, music scores, etc. (And
as our needs move more in the direction of the multi-media concept, bibliographic control must
also be extended to include other types of informational and educational materials such as films,
filmstrips, recordings, transparencies, etc.) One of the primary deficiencies of the sources you have
looked at so far is that they tend to limit their coverage mainly to book publication. The sources
you will be examining in this and following sections will deal with publications other than books:
serials (periodicals, newspapers, annuals, etc.), government publications, dissertations, etc.--
those publications which have generally been excluded from the previous sources. The bibliographic
sources in the following sections are not always considered as part of our national bibliography but
in fact they must be in order to give us proper coverage.

This section, then, begins with sources for bibliographic information about serials, and the first
group to examine are specifically sources for current information--bibliographies, lists, directories of the
periodicals themselves:

> Ulrich's International Periodicals Directory (AE10)
> Irregular Serials and Annuals (AE8)
> Standard Periodical Directory (AE29)
> Ayer Directory of Publications.... (AE24)
> International Directory of Little Magazines and Small Presses (AE5, 1AE2)

5-1   What is a serial?

5-2   "Serial," then, is a broad term which covers several types of publications, similar mainly in their
       successive (serially) or continuous form of publication. One type of publication broadly defined as
       a "serial" is a periodical. What is a periodical?

5-3   In laymen's terms, periodicals include magazines and/or journals, whether of general interest or
       specific subject interest, whether of popular, mass-circulation appeal or professional, technical,
       scholarly appeal. (There is a tendency, not clearly defined, to label general interest, popular
       content, mass-circulation, commercial publications as magazines, and the special subject interest,
       professional, technical, scholarly publications as journals.) Thinking in terms of magazines and
       journals, which you have some familiarity with, and of the definitions in #5-2, can you give two
       significant points about periodicals, one dealing with the format, and one dealing with the content?

5-4   Why are periodicals important items in library collections?

5-5   Of the various bibliographic sources which you have examined so far, which ones are themselves
       periodicals? In other words, which ones are published periodically? PTLA? BIP? Subject BIP?
       Weekly Record? BPR? BPR Cumulative? CBI? Vertical File Index? US Catalog? American
       Catalogue? Kelly? Roorbach? Sabin? Evans? Shaw/Shoemaker? Checklist of American Imprints?

5-6   Of the various bibliographic sources which you have examined so far, which of them attempted to include periodicals (or serials) in their listings? Did the Bowker publications (BIP, PTLA, Subject BIP, BPR, etc.)? Did CBI? What about the retrospective records--Sabin, Evans, Roorbach, Kelly, American Catalogue, Shaw/Shoemaker, Checklist?

5-7   Would you say that periodical or serial publications had been adequately covered in the retrospective and current records you have seen so far?

        The next set of sources you will examine deals specifically and only with records of serial (and/or periodical) publication, and even more specifically with the periodicals themselves, as opposed to the separate articles contained in the periodicals. A separate set of sources will cover the separate articles. It is important to keep in mind this distinction.

5-8   Review: What is the basic bibliographic information which you should ascertain about each source as you examine it?

5-9   What then is the basic bibliographic information about the first title, Ulrich's International Periodicals Directory?

5-10   Looking at the title and subtitle only, what can you tell immediately about the scope of this source? What, if any, are its limitations, in terms of: comprehensiveness, type of publication included, time period covered, country of publication?

5-11   Again, looking at the title and subtitle, can you tell immediately anything about the arrangement of this source? If the title page doesn't give you a clue, what else can you do immediately to determine the arrangement?

5-12   The basic arrangement then is by subject, with periodical titles listed under the subject they deal with, using subject headings, or subject classifications, listed alphabetically. Can you find in Ulrich's a list of periodicals (that is, the titles of the periodicals) dealing with the subject of folklore?

5-13   Can you find the title of a periodical dealing specifically with the folklore of New York?

5-14   How often is this periodical, which deals specifically with the folklore of New York, published? (In other words, what is its frequency of publication; how often does it "come out" or "appear?")

5-15   Why would it be important for a library to know the frequency of publication?

5-16   What introductory material is included in Ulrich's?

5-17   What bibliographic information is included in each citation?

5-18   How would you find the title of a periodical on knitting? (If you have trouble with this, go on directly to #5-19 and #5-20; otherwise you can skip to #5-21.)

5-19   Review: If you have a bibliographic source with a basic subject arrangement, what additional access do you need and where would you expect to find it?

5-20   Does Ulrich's have these other accesses?

5-21   Can you find the titles of some periodicals on UFO's (unidentified flying objects)?

5-22   What about periodicals which do not seem to be limited to one subject--e.g. Time, Life, Reader's Digest?

5-23   If you needed to find ordering information (such as price, address of publisher, frequency of publication, etc.) for the OLA Bulletin, would you expect to find it in Ulrich's and how would you go about it?

5-24   What is the meaning of the number in the upper right corner of the entry in Ulrich's for the OLA Bulletin?

5-25   If you wanted to get not only a current subscription to OLA Bulletin but also a complete file or "back volumes" of all that had been published to date (so far), can you tell from the Ulrich's citation how much has been published?

5-26   Does Ulrich's give you any information on the availability of back files or issues?

5-27   If you were searching in Ulrich's for a specific title, such as the OLA Bulletin, or for titles on UFO's, and you did not find listings in Ulrich's could you assume then that such titles did not exist? Why, or why not? (As always, of course, you should keep in mind that you might be searching, or using the source, incorrectly, or that your information might be faulty, but for this question, assume you did search correctly and your information is right.) On what basis are periodicals selected to be included in Ulrich's?

5-28   If you were looking for a specific title which would appear to meet the requirement for inclusion in Ulrich's and it was not there, what else might you suspect? In regard to periodicals, what is meant by the term "current" in the subtitle to Ulrich's?

5-29   Ulrich's is a list of current, or currently appearing, periodicals, giving ordering/acquisitions information (price, publisher, etc.). Is it similar in any way to any other source you have looked at? (Who publishes Ulrich's?)

5-30   BIP appears annually and is kept up to date through BIP Supplement and Forthcoming Books.
       How frequently does Ulrich's appear? How is it kept up to date? Where would you look to find
       all of this information?

5-31   Review: What is a periodical? How are periodicals defined for inclusion in Ulrich's? How often
       does a periodical have to be issued in order to be included in Ulrich's?

5-32   Would you expect PTLA or BIP to be listed in Ulrich's?

5-33   Where would you find them listed?

5-34   Who is the publisher of Irregular Serials and Annuals and what does this tell you?

5-35   Note that the title of this source refers to "serials" rather than periodicals. What are serials and
       how do they differ from periodicals?

5-36   What is the scope and arrangement of this source? Is it similar to Ulrich's? What is the main
       difference between Ulrich's and Irregular Serials?

5-37   Would you expect a title to be included in both Ulrich's and Irregular Serials?

5-38   Even though the scope differs, would you expect to use Irregular Serials in the same way as
       Ulrich's and find generally the same type of information in it?

5-39   Look up the Educators Grade Guide to Free Teaching Aids. How often is it published and what
       does it cost? Are the publisher's name and address given?

5-40   What can you find out about the Publications of the Indiana Historical Society?

5-41   What can you find out about the publication schedule of Irregular Serials? When is a new edition
       expected? How will it be updated? Will it be handled in a similar manner to Ulrich's?

5-42   A source similar to Ulrich's is The Standard Periodical Directory, which can be looked at briefly
       by comparing it to Ulrich's. What do its title page and introductory matter (Preface) tell you about
       its scope, and how does this compare to Ulrich's?

5-43   How does the arrangement of the Standard directory compare with Ulrich's?

5-44   Look up unidentified flying objects in the Standard Directory. How does its location compare with
       Ulrich's? How do the listings themselves compare to what you found in Ulrich's?

5-45   Where would you find information on newspapers?

5-46   What is the full title of the Ayer Directory?

5-47   Is the publisher of this source one that you are familiar with?

5-48   How frequently is the Ayer Directory published? Can you tell this from the title page or any of the introductory material?

5-49   Does the Ayer Directory limit itself to newspapers, or does it overlap Ulrich's in any way? In regard to types of publication included, is its scope broader or narrower than Ulrich's?

5-50   What about place of publication? Does Ayer's cover more or less territory than Ulrich's?

5-51   What is the basic arrangement of Ayer's? Is this similar to any arrangement you have looked at previously?

5-52   Is it possible to locate in Ayer's the information about a publication if you do not know exactly where it is published?

5-53   Is there any subject access to Ayer's? For example, if you wanted to look up publications on UFO's, as you did in Ulrich's and Standard, could you do it? How about knitting and folklore?

5-54   Can you find, in Ayer's, a list of newspapers and periodicals published in the Chinese language in the United States?

5-55   Is there a daily newspaper in Oxford, Nebraska? How big is Oxford, Nebraska, anyway?

5-56   What is the ordering information for the Detroit (Michigan) Free Press? If you did not know that the Free Press was published in Detroit, could you find it in Ayer's?

5-57   How would you find out how many daily newspapers are published in Tennessee?

5-58   Besides bibliographic information on publications listed, what other useful information can you get from Ayer's? Why do you think all of this is included in the source?

5-59   When you examined Ulrich's, you also looked briefly at a similar source, the Standard Periodical Directory. Are there any other sources similar in scope and use to Ayer's? Where would you look to find out?

5-60   The last source to be examined is also found in the same section of Sheehy: The International
        Directory of Little Magazines and Small Presses (AE5, 1AE2). What are "little magazines" and
        "small presses"?

5-61   Look up the entry for Alternative Sources of Energy magazine in the International Directory.
        Where is it published, when did it begin publication, what is its content?

5-62   Are there any "alternative" or "non-establishment" publications in librarianship?

5-63   So far the sources for serial publications which you have examined have been concerned primarily
        with providing bibliographic information on current (i.e., currently-appearing) serials/periodicals/
        newspapers. Such information is useful for selection and ordering (acquisitions) of materials, and
        is also useful for bibliographic identification. Is there anything in the sources which you have
        just examined which might give you retrospective bibliographic information on serials?

BIBLIOGRAPHIC SOURCES FOR SERIALS--CURRENT LISTS

Answers #5/1--5/63

5-1: See ALA Glossary, 1st definition ("A publication in any medium issued in successive parts ... intended to be continued indefinitely...."). The definition also indicates that periodicals, newspapers, annuals, and numbered monographic series are to be included. (Monographic and publishers' series have been referred to in this manual in question #1a-19.) A significant point to keep in mind about serials is the idea of continuous publication, coming out in parts.

5-2: ALA Glossary again: "A serial appearing ... indefinitely at regular or stated intervals...." Newspapers are not included. Periodicals, then, are serials, but all serials are not periodicals. The exact use of these words, by librarians and by publishers, is not always consistent, and this should be kept in mind when dealing with bibliographic sources which purport to include or exclude serials, periodicals, newspapers, etc. When in doubt, double check.

5-3: Format: the fact that the issues appear or are issued at intervals, such as weekly, semi-monthly, monthly, quarterly, etc.
Content: each issue usually contains several different articles by different authors or contributors, sometimes on unrelated subjects, sometimes related by the subject of the periodical or theme of the issue itself.

5-4: There are many reasons, among them: they are sources of current, up-to-date information (for popular subjects, current events, research, etc.): similarly, retrospective periodicals or "back files" are historical sources for contemporary comment and detail not found in book-length or monographic treatises; they are the largest single type of publication of the total publishing output; many people who will not read books, will read periodicals, etc. See also Sheehy, p. 160, under "Periodicals."

5-5: Weekly Record, BPR (monthly), CBI, and Vertical File Index are periodicals, although they are only bibliographic records and do not contain articles, so they are not really journals or magazines, but they do appear in successive parts at stated or regular intervals and are expected to continue indefinitely.
PTLA, BIP, Subject BIP and most of the BPR Cumulatives are annual publications, and might be considered as periodicals by some libraries and as annuals by other libraries, but probably as serials by all libraries.
The US Catalog, American Catalogue, Kelly and Roorbach might have been considered as periodical publications at the time they were published, as at that time they were probably expected to continue indefinitely, but they have since ceased publication, and are not appearing currently, and would most generally now be referred to as "sets."
Sabin, although published in parts periodically over an extensive period, did have a foreseeable end, and would probably not have been correctly thought of as a periodical; in any case, it also has ceased publication; similarly with Evans and Shaw/Shoemaker.
The Checklist is presently being published, but although volumes are appearing at periodic intervals, the intervals are not really regular or clearly stated, and presumably it does have a foreseeable end. It also would probably be defined as a set or a series, currently coming out.

5-6: The Bowker publications and CBI do not say that they specifically exclude serials, but by their nature they are limited to book publication; "books" does sometimes include certain serials --for example, yearbooks and annuals --but generally excludes periodicals.
The retrospective records vary a great deal in what they include. Surprisingly, many periodical and

serial publications are included in these bibliographies; when in doubt, check.

5-7:   No. Most of the bibliographic sources you have looked at so far have excluded serials and/or periodicals, and those which have included them have done so inconsistently.

5-8:   Full title (and subtitle if significant); author, editor, compiler, etc., if significant; imprint (publisher, place of publication, date of publication); number of volumes; specific edition you are looking at.

5-9:   Full title: Ulrich's International Periodicals Directory
Subtitle: A Classified guide to current periodicals, foreign and domestic
Published by: Bowker Company in New York
Edition: 21st, 1982
Number of volumes: two, in 21st edition
Date of publication: 1982 on title page; copyright 1982 on verso of title page.
The 22nd edition was published in 1983. The answers in this manual are keyed to the 21st edition.

5-10:   Title and subtitle: Ulrich's International Periodicals Directory; a classified guide to current periodicals, foreign and domestic.
Type of publication included: periodicals
Time period covered: current
Country of publication: international: United States, foreign
Comprehensiveness: implied

5-11:   Subtitle: A Classified guide.... "Classified" may ring a bell from the examination of American Book Publishing Record (BPR) and the BPR Cumulative. "Classified" is also defined in the ALA Glossary (as part of "classified index": "grouped under broad subjects"). Another approach to determining the arrangement is to flip through the pages of the source itself: subject headings at the top of the pages (e.g., agriculture, archaeology, engineering, etc.) should alert you to a subject arrangement.
        (Note: the use of the word "classified" may seem to connote the use of some specific subject classification scheme, such as the Dewey Decimal Classification scheme which was used in BPR. Here, in Ulrich's, there is no reference to a specific scheme. The subjects are listed alphabetically, as they were in Subject Guide to BIP,

for example. Also, the subjects are narrower than you would expect to find in a true classification scheme. However, there is some grouping of minor subjects under a major heading--see "Biology," for example.)

5-12:   Yes, under the subject heading "folklore" (under "F"), pp. 702-05 (21st ed.).

5-13:   Yes, New York Folklore. After finding the list dealing with folklore in the previous question, you look through that list till you find a title which seems to fit the requirements.

5-14:   Semi-annually (s-a.) If you didn't know what "s-a." meant, you should have looked for and expected to find a list of explanations for the abbreviations used in the sources--this is in the introductory material.

5-15:   Particularly from an acquisitions point of view, to know how often to expect receipt of the issues so that they can be properly checked in or claimed promptly if they don't arrive on time. (In some libraries the reference department is responsible for the handling of current issues of periodicals.) This is also important from a reference point of view because the frequency of publication will give you some clue to the currency of the material in the periodical (i.e., annual or even quarterly publication will not be as "up to date" as weekly, daily, or even monthly).

5-16:   Contents, Preface, User's Guide, Abbreviations, Subjects, and Cross-Index to Subjects.

5-17:   See "Classified List of Periodicals" in User's Guide in the introductory material. Look at this carefully to see how extensive the information given can be.

5-18:   Look in the main body under Knitting, and find nothing. Then, look in the front matter in "Subjects" under Knitting, and find nothing. Then look in the front matter in "Cross-Index to Subjects" under Knitting, and find: Knitting see Hobbies--Needlework, p. 842 (21st ed.). Or, simply assume right away that knitting would be too specific for this particular subject arrangement, and look directly in the Cross-Index. If you had trouble with this answer, then do #5-19 and #5-20; otherwise you can skip them.

5-19:   Author and title; found usually in in-
         dexes. Possibly a more specific sub-
         ject access than is found in the basic
         arrangement; this too is usually found
         in an index form.

5-20:   No author access, since for this type
         of bibliographic record (listing of the
         periodical itself, not the specific arti-
         cles within the periodical) an author
         access would not be significant.
              Title access is in an index in
         the back, and specific subject access
         is in a cross-reference type of list
         (Cross-Index to Subjects) in the front.

5-21:   Look under "unidentified flying ob-
         jects" in Cross-Index to Subjects, which
         tells you to see Aeronautics and Space
         Flight, p. 33 (21st ed.); there are
         several UFO titles listed in this sec-
         tion but you do have to look through
         several pages to find them. Example:
         UFO Investigator.

5-22:   Look under the section "General inter-
         est periodicals" which is then subdivided
         by country of publication. You more or
         less have to figure this out for yourself
         since the introduction does not note it.
         You can look up Time in the Title Index
         and see where it is classified to get at
         the rest.

5-23:   This is the type of information included
         in Ulrich's citations. There is a title
         index in Ulrich's so you can look up
         this particular title there. Look in
         the index under OLA at the beginning
         of the O's, not under Ola. The index
         refers you to a specific page which is
         in the section for "Library and Infor-
         mation Sciences." (If you had known
         that the OLA Bulletin was published
         by the Ohio Library Association, you
         could have gone directly to the sub-
         ject section, as you did for New York
         folklore, but that isn't necessary.)
              The subscription price for the
         OLA Bulletin is $7.50 (21st, 1982 edi-
         tion of Ulrich's) per year. (The User's
         Guide implies that the price given is
         annual (per year) unless otherwise
         noted.) It can be ordered from the
         Ohio Library Association, and the ad-
         dress is given, and it appears/comes
         out/is published quarterly (q). The
         citation also tells you that the OLA
         Bulletin is indexed in Library Litera-
         ture.

5-24:   This is the ISSN, or International
         Standard Serial Number, which is

similar to the ISBN (see #1a-33). Although Ulrich's introductory material
does note the ISSN as appearing in the
entries, it is not helpful in terms of
just what an ISSN is. However, International Standard Serial Number is defined in the ALA Glossary.
     There is an ISSN index in Irreg-
ular Serials and Annuals, the next
title on your list, so that if you wanted
to know what title was represented by
ISSN 0029-7135, you could look there
and find out that it was the OLA Bulletin.

5-25:   Back volumes ("back issue" is the term
         used in the ALA Glossary) are gener-
         ally those volumes of a periodical other
         than the current volume (or issues).
         A retrospective file would be a set of
         back volumes, or past/retrospective
         volumes of the periodical. (See #5-4.)
              The Ulrich's citation gives you
         the beginning date--for the OLA Bul-
         letin, it is 1931. That means that the
         periodical has been published since
         1931. It does not tell you specifically
         how many volumes there would be (you
         can guess at one per year, but this
         is not always true), and it does not
         tell you that the periodical was pub-
         lished continuously during that time.

5-26:   Back files or issues of periodicals are
         sometimes available from the publish-
         ers, and sometimes in reprinted form
         from other publishers. Ulrich's does
         not give information on these kinds of
         availability.
              However, an increasingly common
         way for libraries to "fill in" back files
         of periodicals is by purchasing them in
         microform. (If you are not familiar
         with "microform," look it up in a dic-
         tionary or the ALA Glossary.) Ul-
         rich's does give information on the
         commercial microform availability of
         many titles. According to Ulrich's,
         the OLA Bulletin is available in micro-
         form from UMI. A list of abbrevia-
         tions for micropublishers is in the Abbrevia-
         tions section in the introductory mate-
         rial of Ulrich's. The full name and
         address of UMI is given. (A library
         could, of course, arrange non-
         commercially to have a microform
         made of periodicals having no com-
         mercial microform publisher.)

5-27:   You should not necessarily assume
         that the titles do not exist. If a
         periodical title is not listed in Ul-
         rich's, it may be only because it was

not included, not because it does not exist.

The Preface to the 21st edition of Ulrich's does not give as clear a statement of which is included/excluded as past editions have done. It states only that it includes currently in-print serials which are "issued more frequently than once a year, and usually published at regular intervals over an indefinite period of time." Ulrich's aims at comprehensiveness but, like all such bibliographic sources, can never be considered infallible.

5-28: Current, here, means "currently appearing." Periodicals, although by definition intended to be "continued indefinitely," do have a way of stopping publication-- or "ceasing" publication--for lack of financial support, lack of interest, lack of staff, change of interests, etc. Life Magazine is a well-known example of this. Every year there are hundreds of new periodicals which start publication and similarly hundreds which cease publication; some do not even last out their first year. Periodicals also "merge" with other already existing periodicals-- again for financial or staffing reasons, or they change their titles (Saturday Review of Literature to Saturday Review, for example), or they suspend their publications temporarily (many European periodicals did this during the war periods), or they cease publication for a time and then start up again (as Life did), sometimes continuing the volume numbering before they "ceased," sometimes starting new volume numbering or a new series of numbers, etc. All of which makes bibliographic searching and identification of periodicals quite complex, and which makes library acquisitions/ordering/processing/handling/cataloging/use of periodicals equally complex. (Note the list of "Cessations" in the back of Ulrich's.)

5-29: Ulrich's is a kind of Books in Print for periodicals, or perhaps more accurately BIP and Subject BIP together. The three are published by Bowker.

5-30: Sheehy says that Ulrich's is published biennially (every other year) and that a supplementary service updating it is "promised for publication at irregular intervals." The preface of Ulrich's 21st (1982) edition says that Ulrich's is now published annually, and refers to Ulrich's Quarterly (Sheehy 1AE4) as an up-dating service.

5-31: See #5-2, and #5-27.

5-32: Since these are annual (once a year) publications, you would not expect them to be included in Ulrich's, according to the definition for inclusion. However, BIP is included in the 22nd edition of Ulrich's, presumably because of the mid-year, updating supplement, although this supplement is not noted in the citation for BIP. PTLA is not included

5-33: In the next title on your list: Irregular Serials and Annuals. You would probably also find them listed in the Weekly Record and BPR, and in CBI, since annuals/year-books and other similar publications are often considered to fall into the category of "books," as well as "serials." When in doubt, check.

5-34: The publisher is Bowker Company and this might tell you that the source would have some relation to Ulrich's--the physical format is very similar also.

5-35: See #5-1, and #5-2.

5-36: Scope: "serials currently published throughout the world" (see Preface, 8th, 1983 ed.); therefore, current and international--same as Ulrich's. For frequency of publication of the titles to be included, Irregular Serials states (Preface, 8th ed.) "titles issued annually or less frequently than once a year, or irregularly; serials published at least twice under the same title, and those first publications which plan to have subsequent issues." (Ulrich's criterion was: periodicals issued "more frequently than once a year.")
Arrangement: same as Ulrich's, basically; subjects alphabetically arranged with a specific subject cross-reference listing, and a title index.

The main difference is in definition of the type of publication included, even more specifically in the frequency of publication of those titles to be included.

5-37: No, the defining factor is mutually exclusive. Basically, Irregular Serials includes those serials which have been excluded from Ulrich's on the basis of (1) the irregularity of their publication, and (2) the frequency of their publication--annual, once a year and less often.

5-38: Yes, since it was published as a complementary or companion volume to

Ulrich's, and is arranged in basically the same manner.

5-39:   You cannot tell from the title if this periodical would be in Ulrich's or Irregular Serials, so you might need to check in both sources. In this case, the title is found in Irregular Serials. In the 8th, 1983 edition, it is found under "Education. Teaching Methods and Curriculum"; the title index refers you to p. 355. It comes out annually and costs $36.75 for each annual volume. The publisher's name and address are given.

5-40:   This title is listed in Irregular Serials under "History--History of North and South America," then alphabetically under "I" for Indiana. Or the title is listed under "Indiana...." in the index which refers you to the page number (p. 479, 8th ed.). The series began publication in 1897, is published irregularly, the last part published was vol. 26, no. 2 in 1981 (8th ed.), and the price per part varies. Publisher's name and address are also given.

5-41:   The answer to this question is similar to that for #5-30, on the updating of Ulrich's. Irregular Serials is published annually, as is Ulrich's, and both directories are updated with Ulrich's Quarterly.

          The prefaces to both Ulrich's and Irregular Serials also refer to a directory published by Bowker called Sources of Serials (Sheehy 1AE3). This is simply a list, arranged geographically by country, of the publishers (and/or corporate authors) of the serials listed in both Ulrich's and Irregular Serials. It can serve then as both a geographical or place index and a publisher/corporate author index to Ulrich's and Irregular Serials.

5-42:   Title and subtitle: The Standard Periodical Directory. The largest authoritative guide to United States and Canadian periodicals ... Information on more than 60,000 publications. (8th, 1983-84 ed.).

          Standard is limited to the U.S. & Canada; Ulrich's is international--all countries. The Preface to Standard indicates a broader definition of periodicals: "A frequency of issue of at least once every two years," meaning it will overlap Ulrich's and may include some (annuals and biennials, for example) but not all of Irregular Serials.

5-43:   The arrangement of both is by subject with title index. Subjects (in the 8th,

1983-84 ed.) are quite specific (almanacs, baseball, blind, cats, dogs, etc.). Standard has a kind of a classification number of each subject heading, apparently its own numbering scheme. There is also a "cross index to subjects."

5-44:   In the Standard Directory, UFO is in the Table of Contents with reference to its own classification (2210, 1983-84 ed.) rather than as part of a larger subject heading as in Ulrich's. The listings include some of those in Ulrich's, but not the ones published in Europe. Information in the entries is similar, with perhaps more attention given in Standard to advertising information.

5-45:   Neither Ulrich's nor Standard specifically states that it includes or excludes newspapers. Ulrich's is generally considered to exclude newspapers. Standard does include many more newspapers, and has one section (1520 in the 1983-84 edition) which covers Newspapers. The Ayer Directory, next source to examine, is a more complete list of newspapers.

5-46:   Title page of 1983 edition: The IMS '83 Ayer Directory of Publications; the professional's reference of print media published in the United States, Canada, Puerto Rico, Virgin Islands, (etc.).

5-47:   The publisher is IMS Press in Fort Washington, Pennsylvania, and is not one of the publishers you are familiar with through this manual so far, so this doesn't give you any handy clues to the source as you had with all the Bowker publications.

5-48:   The title page (1983) tells you annually since 1869. Sheehy says since 1880. Sheehy also notes that Ayer's absorbed another publication which had been published since 1869, which is apparently why the publisher of Ayer's considers it to have been going since 1869.

5-49:   See "Qualifications for Listing in the Ayer Directory" (verso of title page, 1983 edition). There is no direct statement of what is included, other than that the frequency of publication must be "four or more editions or issues annually." Some exclusions are noted. Ayer's includes some things which are also in Ulrich's, and some--primarily newspapers--which are not.

5-50:   Ulrich's is international in scope; Ayer's

is basically U.S. and Canada (like the Standard directory). Therefore its scope for place of publication is narrower than Ulrich's.

5-51:   The basic arrangement is geographical --titles are listed under the name of the state and then city in which they are published; the states are listed alphabetically and the cities are listed alphabetically, within the state. You have not previously examined through this manual any source with this type of arrangement.

5-52:   Yes, there is an alphabetical index of all titles in the back.

5-53:   There is some limited subject approach in Ayer's. The Table of Contents shows some subject lists ("Cross Reference Sections") with special groupings such as college, Black, religious publications, etc. There is also an "Index to Classifications" with about 900 subject headings and cross-references; the page references in this Index are to various groupings within the Cross Reference Sections--not extensive but better than nothing. There is no reference for UFO's, but there are cross-references for "knitting" and "folklore."

5-54:   Yes--see the classified list, "Foreign Language Publications."

5-55:   There is no daily newspaper in Oxford, Nebraska. Look under Nebraska, then Oxford, then for a publication which comes out daily. As of 1983, there is one newspaper in Oxford, published only on Thursdays. The subscription price (presumably annually) is $10.00. The population of Oxford is 1,109.

5-56:   In the main part of Ayer's, look first under Michigan, then Detroit, then Free Press. According to the 1983 edition of Ayer's, it is published every morning, and the local subscription price is $49.40/year. The address of the publisher is given. If you look in the title index under Free Press, you find a list of about 20 "Free Presses" with indications of their city of publication; one of these is Detroit, Michigan.

5-57:   You could get this information by counting all the daily newspapers listed under Tennnessee, but a more direct way is to look at the list of "Tennessee newspaper and periodical statistics" following the general information on Tennessee at

the beginning of that section.

5-58:   Ayer's includes descriptions of the states, provinces, cities and towns in which they (i.e., the publications) are published, including substantial statistics and information on population, income, employment, manufacturing, agriculture, marketing, etc. (See entries.) Also maps. All of this information--besides being a bonus to librarians--is of value to potential advertisers, developers, marketing surveys, etc.

5-59:   As in the past, the first place to look for this type of information would be in Sheehy's Guide to Reference Books. Sources similar to Ayer's would be found in the same section in which Ayer's is listed and annotated. Two publications giving extensive coverage of newspapers as well as related general statistical information are Editor and Publisher International Yearbook (AE25) and Working Press of the Nation (AE30).

5-60:   The ALA Glossary has a very brief definition; a dictionary might also be useful. In general small presses tend to be small (often one-person) and more independent than larger, more commercially oriented publishers. They are usually considered to be out of the mainstream of commercial or establishment publishing, usually concerned with literature and the arts, often now also with some specialized or "alternative" current interest such as crafts, ecology, energy, prisons, women, occult, etc.
         "Little magazines" are their more or less regularly issued publications. (Some further information can be gleaned from the annotation to another title in Sheehy, AE21: The Little Magazine by Hoffman and Ulrich.) Because they are out of the mainstream of commercial publishing, and because they are often ephemeral or irregular in appearance, they tend not to be picked up in the more commercial bibliographic nets.

5-61:   Titles are arranged alphabetically in the main body of the directory, with subject and regional indexes. Alternative Sources of Energy magazine has been published in Milaca, Minnesota, since 1971, and the content is discussed at some length in the annotation (18th, 1982-83 ed.).

5-62:   See the International Directory under the subject heading "libraries." Several titles are listed, and further information on them can be obtained by going to the entries in the title list.

5-63:   You have been looking at these sources --Ulrich's, Irregular Serials, Standard, Ayer's--as if they existed only in the most current editions; in fact, both Ulrich's and Ayer's have been published for some time--Ulrich's more or less regularly since 1932; Ayer's annually since 1869. In their earlier editions, they are rich sources for information on periodicals and newspapers no longer published, and many libraries do keep back files of Ulrich's and Ayer's.

BIBLIOGRAPHIC SOURCES FOR SERIALS--UNION LISTS

Questions #6/1--6/45

6-1   Besides basic bibliographic identification both current and retrospective, ordering information for acquisition, and subject control, what other type of information do we need for full bibliographic control? (Think back to the kinds of information provided in other sources you have examined, particularly in the LC/NUC series and to some extent in the retrospective sources for books.)

6-2   This particular type of information (see answer to #6-1) tends to be even more important for serials than for books. Why would this be?

The next set of sources to examine provides both location of copies and bibliographic information, retrospective and current:

Union List of Serials (3rd ed.) (AE133)
New Serial Titles (AE134)
NST, 1950-70, Subject Guide (1AE34)
Gregory: American Newspapers ... A Union List (AF16)
Brigham: History and Bibliography of American Newspapers (AF19)

6-3   With this set it is easiest to begin with a retrospective source. The first title on the list is the Union List of Serials. What is a union list?

6-4   What is the basic bibliographic information about this first source, Union List of Serials (ULS)?

6-5   What introductory material is contained in the first volume of this source?

6-6   What does the title tell you about the scope of this source? Are there any limiting factors indicated in the title?

6-7   Does the phrase "in libraries of the United States and Canada" in the title mean that the ULS would include only those serials published in the U.S. and Canada?

6-8   Would you say then that the scope of the ULS is international?

6-9   Are all serial publications include in ULS? Are there any exceptions or exclusions?

6-10 How does the scope compare with Ulrich's? Think in terms of definitions and policies for types of publications to be included. (Refer back to #5-10 and #5-27 on Ulrich's if necessary.)

6-11   Look through the volumes at several of the entries. What information is given in the entries? Is
        full bibliographic information given? How does this compare to what was given in Ulrich's?

6-12   Look up in ULS the title <u>Biochemical Bulletin</u>. What information can you find out about it?

6-13   What is the arrangement of ULS?

6-14   Is there any subject access to the ULS?

6-15   Look up in ULS the title <u>American Ski Annual</u>. When did this series begin publication? What is
        the frequency of publication? Is it still being published?

6-16   How can you find out if it is still being published?

6-17   When was the Union List of Serials published? (See #6-4.) Is there a limitation by date on the
        publications included? Will there be another edition? How will it be kept up to date?

6-18   Locate New Serial Titles on the shelves. Look carefully at its physical format, keeping in mind
        that the purpose of NST is to serve as a current supplement to ULS. Basically, the source is
        similar in format to other current sources you have examined previously. It has several bound
        cumulated annual volumes, plus current (this year, perhaps still last year) issues. What is the
        basic bibliographic information about New Serial Titles? (Look in one of the recent issues and in
        Sheehy.)

6-19   Can you tell, in a general way, what the cumulation pattern is for NST?

6-20   Did the LC/NUC catalogs ever include library holdings/locations for serials/periodicals? What is
        the relation of New Serial Titles to the National Union Catalog?

6-21   What is the scope of NST? What type of publications are included? What are the limitations, if
        any, for inclusion? What type of bibliographic information is given for each entry?

6-22   A periodical called <u>Karate-Do</u>, put out by the All American Karate Federation, began publication
        in the 1960's. Where was it published, when did it begin publication, and from what library could
        you borrow the first issues? Does this mean that that library is the only library holding copies
        of this periodical?

6-23   What then is the arrangement of NST?

6-24   A periodical called <u>Journal of Fusion Energy</u> began publication, in the U.S., in 1981. Who is the publisher and how frequently is it published? From what libraries could you borrow copies? What is the subject of this periodical?

6-25   Is there any indication of subject given in the individual entries in NST itself?

6-26   Is there any subject <u>access</u> to NST? Is there any subject access to ULS?

6-27   Can you find, in the Bowker NST 1950-70 Subject Guide, some periodical titles on games such as backgammon and go? How is this NST Subject Guide arranged?

6-28   What are at least two sources in which you could find some titles of currently-appearing periodicals on the subject of linguistics?

6-29   What would be the primary usefulness of ULS and NST from a reference point of view?

6-30   Does the Union List of Serials include newspapers? Does New Serial Titles include newspapers?

6-31   Where would you go then for bibliographic information and for library locations on older newspapers (primarily American, since you are basically concerned with <u>U.S.</u> bibliographic records)?

6-32   Locate both Gregory's American Newspapers and Brigham's History and Bibliography and examine both together. How does the scope differ between the two publications?

6-33   Compare the arrangement of Gregory and Brigham. Are they similar? Are they similar in arrangement to ULS and NST?

6-34   Can you locate items in Gregory or Brigham if you know only the <u>titles</u>?

6-35   Would you expect to find listed in Brigham newspapers which might have been published in Hawaii in 1800, or in California in the 1780's?

6-36   Who was the printer of a daily newspaper called <u>Porcupine's Gazette</u>, published in Pennsylvania and New York City at the end of the 18th century?

6-37   Gregory and Brigham provide a union list for newspapers only through 1936. Where would you look to see if more current such bibliographic sources exist? What can you find that might serve the purpose?

6-38   Where could you find a microform of the <u>Monroe Democrat</u>, a newspaper published weekly in Monroe, Michigan from 1880-1915?

6-39   <u>Heraldica; revue d'histoire nobiliaire et de documentation</u> was published in Paris beginning in 1911. Where would you go to find out when it ceased publication and how many volumes make up a complete set?

6-40   Where would you look to find price and publisher for the magazine titled <u>Environment</u>?

6-41   You need to find some specific information about the various editors of <u>The Boston News-Letter</u> which was published until the time of the American Revolution. You are also concerned about possible changes in title, and you would like to examine some of the actual issues, but your library does not have any holdings of it. Where would you look to find all of this information?

6-42   Where would you look to find the beginning date of the periodical <u>Education and Psychology</u>, published in Delhi, India? (You don't know if it's being published currently.)

6-43   If you wanted to find some periodicals on the subject of business administration, where would you look?

6-44   Where would you look to find information about the daily newspaper in Sacramento, California?

6-45   Suppose you wanted to look at, borrow, or in some way get copies of some issues of a newspaper pubished in Sacramento, California, in the early 1900's?

BIBLIOGRAPHIC SOURCES FOR SERIALS--UNION LISTS

Answers #6/1--6/45

6-1:   Location of copies (see #2b-26).

6-2:   Back volumes of serials are often harder to get than out-of-print books, and are in many ways more costly to acquire, process, and handle.

        For libraries serving research needs, periodicals--especially back volumes--are a source of basic research information, frequently more important than books.

6-3:   See #4-16 or see the ALA Glossary.

6-4:   Full title: Union list of serials in libraries of the United States and Canada.
Publisher: Wilson Co. in New York
Edition: 3rd
Publication date: 1965
Number of volumes: 5

6-5:   The title page is preceded by 1) a list of cooperating libraries and their symbols and 2) explanations. Following the title page come 3) Preface, 4) Introduction, and 5) Sample Entries.

6-6:   "Union list" tells you that it will include information on library holdings. One limiting factor indicated in the title is that the type of publication is limited to serials. The only other limiting factor in the title is "in libraries of the United States and Canada."

6-7:   No, it means it includes serials in the collections of/held by/contained in "libraries of the United States and Canada." It would not list serials unless they were held by one of the cooperating libraries. (Furthermore, it does not list serials unless they are reported to ULS by one of the cooperating libraries.) Presumably many libraries in the U.S. and Canada would contain serials published in countries all over the world.

6-8:   In regard to the publications listed in it, yes, it is international in scope. In regard to the libraries whose holdings are indicated, no, it is limited to U.S. and Canada.

6-9:   See Introduction, which gives you a very specific list of "Classes of Serials Generally Excluded."

6-10:   Both are international in scope. Ulrich's includes only periodicals with publication frequency of less than one year; ULS, even with its list of exclusions, still includes a wider range of serial publications than Ulrich's. Ulrich's includes only current periodicals; ULS includes both current (as of the time of its publication) and retrospective or ceased serials.

6-11:   Title is always given, place of publication is usually given, publisher or issuing organization is sometimes given. Beginning date of publication is usually given, and ending date if publication has ceased. Changes of title are usually indicated, as well as whether the periodical merged, suspended, ceased, etc. Location symbols are given for cooperating libraries which report holdings of the title. Current ordering information (price, address of publisher, frequency of publication) is not given. In fact, there is no sure way of telling from ULS whether a publication is still being published. (See "Sample Entries" in the introductory material.)

6-12:   In volume 1, under B. Published by the Biochemical Association of Columbia University. Published in New York. The series ceased publication in 1916 ("/ /" indicates ceased publication, see "Sample Entries"). The entire set consists of volumes 1-5 (parts or issues continuously numbered no. 1-21), published Sept. 1911-May 1916. Part or issue no. 16 was never published. (You can guess from the number of issues indicated and the approximate way they might be spread over the 5-6 years of publication, that it was probably issued quarterly.) Copies are held by Stanford College Libraries, Stanford in California (CST), etc.

6-13:   You already had to figure this out to lo-
        cate the answer to #6-12, and in fact
        you may have done it without being aware
        of it. The arrangement is alphabetical by
        title. That is, under the main entry (see
        #1b-15 on the concept of main entry list-
        ing) which for periodicals will generally
        be the title, but which may also be an
        organization or institution, for example.

6-14:   No, except what you might accidentally
        get through title.

6-15:   American Ski Annual began publication in
        1928. You can guess from the title that
        the frequency of publication is annual.
        The ULS entry does not show that it has
        ceased publication.

6-16:   You can check in a source such as Ul-
        rich's for current information. Since this
        title is presumably an annual, however,
        you should check first or also in Irregular
        Serials. You could try also in Ayer's.
        Since the organization responsible for pub-
        lication (United States Eastern Amateur
        Ski Association; presumably later called
        the National Ski Association?) is given
        in ULS, you could write to that organi-
        zation for information. (Eventually you
        will examine sources which will give you
        addresses, etc., for organizations.)

6-17:   Third edition, 1965 (title page of source).
        Covers publications begun up to Decem-
        ber 1949, i.e., before 1950 (introduction
        and Sheehy annotation). This will be the
        last edition and it will be kept up to date
        by New Serial Titles (see ULS introduc-
        tion and Sheehy annotation), the next
        title on your list.

6-18:   Full title: New Serial Titles; A Union
        List of Serials Held by Libraries in the
        United States and Canada (title page of
        1982 issues; Sheehy shows a somewhat
        different sub-title, noting that these are
        "serials commencing publication after Dec.
        31, 1949").
        Publisher: The Library of Congress,
        Washington (D.C.) (title page of 1983
        issues and Sheehy).
        Date of publication: 1953- (Sheehy).

6-19:   1950-70 cumulation (in 4 volumes, pub-
        lished in 1973, published by Bowker);
        1971-75 cumulation, 1976-80 cumulation,
        1981 cumulation (published by LC).
             The current pattern is 8 monthly
        issues, plus quarterly cumulations, plus
        an annual cumulated volume (similar to
        that of NUC).

6-20:   See the Preface in a recent NST issue.
        LC had previously issued Serial Titles
        Newly Received, a list of periodical ti-
        tles received by the LC, serving as a
        serial supplement to the LC Catalog of
        Printed Cards, and which was eventual-
        ly expanded to include serial listings for
        LC and for cooperating libraries, as a
        supplement to ULS. In 1953, this list
        was superseded by New Serial Titles.
        Prior to 1983, the LC/NUC did include
        catalog cards for those serial titles cata-
        loged by the Library of Congress although
        not library locations/holdings for serials
        in general. From 1983 on, periodicals
        and most serials will be found only in
        NST.

6-21:   Because NST is an ongoing publication,
        you can expect some changes from time
        to time in the scope or arrangement. The
        "Introduction" in recent issues of NST will
        give you the current coverage.

        Prior to 1981, NST was limited to those
        publications that began publication after
        1949, and the information given in the en-
        tries was the same as that in ULS (see
        #6-8, #6-9, #6-11). Since 1981, NST has
        included titles regardless of the initial
        date of publication, and full cataloging
        information for the entries has generally
        been included. Presently (1983) only li-
        brary locations, but not holdings, are
        given. The definition for "serials" is
        given in the "Introduction." Like ULS,
        NST is international in scope.

6-22:   In the NST 1950-70 cumulation, the title
        is shown, published in Los Angeles, be-
        ginning in 1967, and the University of
        Illinois (IU) has copies from no. 1. The
        University of Illinois library is not the
        only library to hold copies--it is the
        only library, at that point, to report
        holdings. (As with NUC, see #4-49.)
        Later reports of holdings may appear
        in later volumes.

6-23:   Alphabetically, by main entry which will
        generally be the title. As with ULS
        (see #6-13), some items may be listed
        under organizations or institutions, and
        very rarely you might find a title listed
        under an author.

6-24:   This is found in the NST 1981 cumula-
        tion, under the title (p. 683). The en-
        try tells you that the publisher is
        Plenum in New York, that it appears
        quarterly, and several library location
        symbols are given to indicate which li-
        braries have some holdings of the title.

The Library of Congress Classification number (TK9001) and Dewey Decimal Classification number (621.48'4) near the bottom of the entry could help you determine that the subject is electrical engineering. There is also a subject heading tracing, just above the classification numbers.

6-25: In earlier issues of NST, the Dewey Decimal classification numbers were given above and to the right of the entries. In current issues (see the 1981 cumulation, for example), since the cataloging information is included (see #6-21), both the Library of Congress and the Dewey Decimal classification numbers are given at the bottom of the entries, as well as the subject tracings. (See #1b-9 to review what these are.)

6-26: There is no current subject access to NST; nor was there to ULS (see #6-14). That is, you cannot look up a subject in an index and find a reference to a title on that subject. The arrangement or the access of NST is only by title, or main entry. At one time, the LC published the list additionally in a classed subject arrangement by Dewey Decimal Classification number (New Serial Titles-- Classed Subject Arrangement, see Sheehy AE135), but this ceased in 1980.

The Bowker Company published (in 1975) a subject guide to their 1950-70 cumulation: New Serial Titles, 1950-70, Subject Guide, in two volumes (Sheehy 1AE34). This gives some subject access to older titles but there is still nothing for new titles.

6-27: Bowker's NST 1950-70 Subject Guide is arranged by Dewey classification (like the NST Classed Subject Arrangement), then by country of publication. There is an index to subject headings in the front. Looking under "backgammon" in the subject heading index, for example, would refer you to the section of Indoor Games and Sports, Dewey number 793, in the second volume. There you would have to look through the entire list under that heading to find titles dealing with backgammon. If you knew that go was a Japanese game, you might guess titles on it would be published in Japan, so you could look under the subheading Japan for those; although several titles are given, only one appears to be actually in English.

6-28: In Ulrich's, Standard Directory, and

Ayer Directory. Titles from the Bowker NST 1950-70 Subject Guide might not still be currently appearing.

6-29: For inter-library loan (locating libraries with copies of back volumes of specific titles), and for general bibliographic identification and history.

6-30: Since newspapers are generally defined as serials, you would expect so. In fact, newspapers were generally excluded from ULS (see Sheehy annotation and ULS introduction and #6-9). In the earlier years, newspapers were also entirely excluded from NST (see introduction in earlier volumes); however, since 1981, titles included in NST have been those meeting the AACR definition of "serials" (see #6-21), and thus include newspapers. Since this definition states "issued in any medium," this would presumably then include audio-visual materials as well.

6-31: To the next two titles on your list, Gregory's American Newspapers, 1821-1936; a Union List...., and Brigham's History and Bibliography of American Newspapers, 1690-1820.

6-32: Basically by date. Brigham covers 1690-1820 and Gregory covers 1821-1936. Both cover newspapers. Both give basic bibliographic information; Brigham gives considerably more historical and bibliographic information. Both give library locations.

6-33: Both Gregory and Brigham are arranged geographically--by state alphabetically, by cities alphabetically within states, by title of the newspaper alphabetically within the city of publication. This is similar to Ayer's. Both ULS and NST were arranged alphabetically by title.

6-34: In Brigham, yes, since there is a title index. In Gregory, no. There is no title index.

6-35: No, Brigham goes to 1820, but includes only American newspapers of that time period--i.e., newspapers which were published in what was then the United States of America. Neither California nor Hawaii were states in 1820.

6-36: The time period is covered by Brigham. Brigham is arranged by place of publication, with title and printer index. You don't know the printer yet so you can't use that. You know the

place but only generally (Pennsylvania
and New York) so it is easier to use the
title index. There are several listings
with that title or a similar one; take any
and look under the place indicated.
(Pennsylvania is in volume 2, as is the
index) so looking there first, you find
under Philadelphia, a listing for the
Porcupine's Gazette and the information
that the printer was William Cobbett).

6-37: Go to Sheehy. (Section AF on Newspapers, look under "Bibliographies and
Union Lists.") In fact, there are no
more current bibliographies or union lists;
the closest approximation to such a source
is Newspapers in Microform (AF25/26,
AF10, 1AF2, 2AF5) referred to in Section 4 of this manual, which is a union
list of microforms of newspapers to be
found in libraries in the U.S. and Canada. The extensive use of microform to
preserve old newspapers, and the growing use of microform in inter-library loan
has made this union list of microforms a
more currently useful source.

6-38: According to Newspapers in Microform,
United States, 1948-72, copies are held by
Bell and Howell Company (McP) and by
the Michigan State Library (Mi). Newspapers in Microform is arranged geographically, so you can look under Michigan,
then under Monroe, then under Monroe
Democrat. Neither Bell and Howell nor
the Michigan State Library seems to have
a complete set on microform. You need
to look in the introductory material of the
source for an explanation of the symbols
used.

6-39: Since it has presumably ceased publication, it would not be in Ulrich's or similar sources. ULS and NST do tell when
serial publications cease, and they are
international in scope, so would include
French (Paris) publications. Because the
initial date of publication for this title is
1911, it would be more likely to be in
ULS than NST, and in any case would
not be in NST from 1950-80 although it
might be there from 1981 on. (There is
nothing in this question as stated to indicate to you that this title is a periodical except that the French word "revue"
means "magazine.")

6-40: Ulrich's (or Standard). You want ordering information; this is given in Ulrich's.
(It may also be given from time to time
in NST, but even if it is, this is not
necessarily the current ordering information.) The primary purpose of Ulrich's

is to give such current ordering information; the primary purpose of NST is
to list new titles and give library locations. (Here you are assuming, of
course, that the magazine is currently
published.)

6-41: In Brigham. "News-Letter" implies perhaps a newspaper, and Brigham includes
newspapers and covers the time period.
You want library locations, and Brigham
gives this information. You also want
information about editors and title changes,
and this means you would need the kind
of extensive discussion given in Brigham.

6-42: You could check Ulrich's, since beginning
dates are given there, but it would be
listed there only if it is currently published. If it is not listed in Ulrich's,
you could then use ULS and/or NST
(perhaps starting with ULS and working
through NST from 1950 to the current
issue until you found it).

6-43: You need subject access. Ulrich's is
easy and direct to use, and you would
certainly find a large number of periodicals on that subject listed there. You
could also look in the NST 1950-70 Subject Guide, but what you find there
would not necessarily be currently-
appearing publications.

6-44: Newspaper and current--Ayer's. Perhaps Standard, though it is not as consistent with newspapers as Ayer's. Ulrich's basically doesn't cover newspapers,
and daily publication is too frequent for
Irregular Serials whether or not it includes newspapers.

6-45: Since you want to locate copies, you
want a union list. ULS/NST do not
generally include newspapers prior to
1981. Gregory does, and covers this
time period. Newspapers in Microform
would also be a possibility, to get or
locate microform copy.

Section 7

INDEXES TO SERIALS--INDEXING SERVICES

Questions #7/1--7/94

So far the bibliographic sources you have examined for serials/periodicals/newspapers have been lists or directories for only the <u>titles</u> of the serials. One of the distinguishing features about most serials (periodicals and newspapers) is that they consist of a number of different articles, by different authors, which are basically separate entities brought together in one publication (see #5-3). In order to have complete bibliographic control, we need also to have some sort of analytic access to these individual articles or items published within a larger publication.

This brings us to the next set of sources to examine--indexes to serials:

> Readers' Guide to Periodical Literature (AE169)
> Humanities Index (AE172)
> Social Sciences Index (AE173)
> Public Affairs Information Service Bulletin (PAIS) (CA34, 1CA12, 2CA9)
>
> Poole's Index to Periodical Literature (AE164/165/166)
> Nineteenth Century Readers' Guide (AE168)
>
> New York Times Index (AF67/68, 1AF13/14)

7-1   How would you define the word "index"?

We can say that basically we have two types of "indexes" to deal with:

Those which appear <u>within</u> a publication--i.e., an index in the back of a book, or in a set of books such as an encyclopedia, or in an issue or volume of a periodical. These indexes are an integral part of the publication itself and index, or refer to, material only within that specific publication of which they are a part. In a sense, you have been dealing with this type of index all along in the various bibliographic sources--for example, an author/title index to a source which is arranged by subject (BPR, Ulrich's) or chronologically (Evans), or geographically (Brigham).

Those which appear <u>separately from</u> the publication or publications which they index, and which themselves form a specific publication. Generally these indexes are in periodical form, appearing at regular intervals. Those which appear currently and regularly are usually referred to as "indexing services" (or "indexing and abstracting services" if they abstract the material as well as index it).

7-2   Begin by looking at a source with which you may already have some familiarity, the Readers' Guide to Periodical Literature. This is an example of a current indexing service. Therefore, you can expect that, like many of the bibliographic sources you have already examined, it is published on an on-going periodical basis, at regular intervals, and presumably has been coming out for some time; therefore you should be prepared to think in terms of a large number of volumes and parts with possible cumulation patterns, as you have had in so many of the bibliographic sources you have already examined (CBI, LC/NUC, NST, etc.).
    Look first at one of the most recent issues. What is the full title of the source?

7-3   What does this tell you about its scope? What limitations are there to its coverage? Is it limited to a certain type of publication? Is it international or more limited by country of publication? Is it comprehensive or selective?

7-4   Readers' Guide is an index to a "selected" list of U.S. periodicals. What is the basis for selection? Where would you expect to find a full statement of the basis for selection?

7-5   Specifically, by title, what periodicals are indexed in Readers' Guide? Approximately how many?

7-6   Is the periodical Physics Today indexed in the Readers' Guide? What does this tell you about Physics Today?

7-7   Does the Readers' Guide index any periodicals published by the government (federal, state, local, international)?

7-8   Who publishes Readers' Guide and does this fact tell you anything?

7-9   Can you think of two primary distinguishing features of CBI, in regard to its arrangement, which you might also expect to find in Readers' Guide?

7-10   How frequently is the Readers' Guide published, currently? Can you tell quickly what the general cumulation pattern is?

7-11   When did the Readers' Guide begin publication? (Because you are dealing with a long and rather complex set, you might find it easiest to go first to the Sheehy entry and annotation, and then check this against the set you are examining.)

7-12   In the dictionary arrangement of CBI, all authors, titles, and subjects were included in one alphabetical listing. Is this exactly the same in the Readers' Guide? Does Readers' Guide have all three of these accesses?

7-13   Are there any title entries at all in Readers' Guide?

7-14   If, however, you were searching in the index for a specific article, and you did remember only the title and not the author, could you still find it?

7-15   Are there cross-references in the Readers' Guide?

7-16   Are there any indexes within the Readers' Guide? Do you need any? Why or why not?

7-17   Using the March 1982-February 1983 annual cumulation, find a citation for an article on the employment of young people. Where would you find the article itself--that is, in what specific periodical issue would you find the article?

7-18   Why is it important to know the volume number for the periodical, if you have the exact date of the issue?

7-19   Would you expect to find the article cited in #7-17 also in the Readers' Guide under the author?

7-20   If you wanted to subscribe to Change, where would you look for the ordering information? (Price, frequency of publication, name and address of publisher.)

7-21   William F. Buckley wrote an article about Gore Vidal which appeared in Esquire Magazine in the late 1960's. Can you find the title of it, and specific information about the issue in which it appeared? What about an article which Mr. Vidal wrote about Mr. Buckley?

7-22   If you wanted to compile a short list (or bibliography) of the magazine articles written by Mr. Buckley, how would you go about it?

7-23   How far back, retrospectively, would you need to search? Would searching through Readers' Guide give you a list of all the magazine articles Mr. Buckley had written?

7-24   Can you find citations to articles which would give you some information on the problems of poor people living in the city, and specifically what was happening to them because their housing was being torn down and replaced?

7-25   You could have found at least a dozen articles cited in Readers' Guide under the various headings given in the answer to #7-24. How would you know which of these would specifically deal with your topic, or which would be of most use to you?

7-26   Suppose you wanted to find out also how this problem of displacement of the urban poor had been dealt with, if at all, in the 1920's and 1930's. Could you find information on this through Readers' Guide? Would you expect the subject headings to be the same?

7-27   The full title to the Readers' Guide (see #7-2) is the Readers' Guide to Periodical Literature (Unabridged); an index to.... This would lead you to suspect an abridged edition. Is there an abridged Readers' Guide and what is its nature and use? Where would you look to find out?

7-28   The Readers' Guide is relatively limited in the number of periodicals it indexes (170+) but it is still one of the best known and most used of the periodical indexing services because of the general and popular nature of its scope. The next two indexing services to examine--the Humanities Index and the Social Sciences Index--are somewhat more specialized in scope; both are, like RG, published by the Wilson Co. Locate some recent issues of these indexes. How can you tell specifically what periodicals are indexed in the Humanities Index? Who selects the periodicals to be indexed?

7-29   Knowing that the Humanities Index is a Wilson publication you can assume that it will have certain
        similarities to other Wilson publications (CBI, Readers' Guide) which you have already examined.
        The easiest and quickest way to familiarize yourself with the Humanities Index is to compare it with
        the Readers' Guide. Presumably both indexing services would not have the same scope, as they
        are published by the same company. What is the scope of the Humanities Index and how does it
        differ from the Readers' Guide?

7-30   How is the Humanities Index arranged?

7-31   How frequently is the Humanities Index published and how frequently does it cumulate? How does
        this compare to Readers' Guide?

7-32   If you were searching for critical material on the themes, style, sources, etc., of Carson McCullers'
        novels (Ballad of the Sad Cafe, The Heart Is a Lonely Hunter, etc.), where would you look? Can
        you in fact find any such articles?

7-33   The other Wilson index to examine, the Social Sciences Index, is similar to the Humanities Index in
        arrangement, frequency, and cumulation. What is its scope?

7-34   If you were searching for information, based on research data, on the relationship between unem-
        ployment and health, where would you look? Can you in fact find any such articles?

7-35   Both the Humanities Index and the Social Sciences Index began publication in 1974. Were they pre-
        ceded by any similar indexes? (See Sheehy.)

7-36   Was there any difference in the scope or coverage of the International Index and the Social Sciences
        and Humanities Index? Probably the easiest way to answer this is to read the annotation for SSHI
        in Sheehy.

7-37   Where would you expect to find current articles on death and dying indexed?

7-38   The Humanities Index and the Social Sciences Index do not include science and technology in depth
        (although RG does in a popular, non-technical way). Does the Wilson Company publish an indexing
        service which would complement them in covering the sciences in a more specialized way? Where
        would you look to find this out?

7-39   The Wilson Company publishes several other indexing services which are even more specifically
        subject-oriented. These also can be located in Sheehy, under the subjects, or by looking in the
        pamphlet "Cataloging and Indexing Services" put out by the Wilson Company. Some examples are
        Education Index (Sheehy CB83), Art Index (BE31), and Library Literature (AB10) which covers
        librarianship and related subjects. Some of these indexing services have a broader scope than just
        periodicals (as in RG) and also index or list books, pamphlets, parts of books, etc., thus becoming
        true current subject bibliographies. How would you find out if such an indexing service covered
        material other than periodical articles?

7-40   The Wilson Indexing services are sold to libraries on the "service basis" method of charge. What
        is this method of charge?

7-41   An example of an indexing service which does list books, pamphlets, etc., as well as articles in
        periodicals, is the Public Affairs Information Service Bulletin (PAIS). PAIS is limited to the so-
        cial sciences, but is still very broad in its coverage. What is its full title, and what does this
        tell you about its scope?

7-42   What is the arrangement of PAIS?

7-43   Look through one of the recent larger cumulations or current issues at the subject headings. What
        ones do you note that would seem relevant to some of the current problems?

7-44   Some of these headings were also in the Readers' Guide and in the Social Sciences Index. What
        would you expect to find through PAIS that you would not find in the other indexes?

7-45   Who publishes the PAIS Bulletin? What is the P.A.I.S. itself?

7-46   In Section 5 of this manual, you examined a periodical directory titled International Directory of
        Little Magazines and Small Presses, which covered publications of the small presses and material
        considered to be of an "alternative" nature or concerned with social change. Is there any index-
        ing service, or services, which would seem to cover this same area--that is, to index the articles
        which appear in those publications?

        The Readers' Guide has been around for a long time as the only major periodical indexing service
        for general interest, non-specialized, non-scholarly publications, but in fact it covers only a small
        number of those general interest periodicals which are available. In recent years a number of oth-
        er indexing services, such as the Alternative Press Index, have sprung up to cover gaps left by
        the Readers' Guide. Most of these are listed in the first supplement to Sheehy, such as: Access
        (1AE43), New Periodicals Index (1AE49), Popular Periodical Index (1AE50). Another indexing
        service, now titled Index to Periodical Articles By and About Blacks (AE187, 1AE47), has been
        around since the 1960's, but similarly grew out of a need to cover periodicals and subject matter
        not well covered by the existing services. A newer but much more extensive indexing service
        than those just noted is one listed in the second supplement to Sheehy: Magazine Index (2AE23); it
        covers most of the magazines indexed in Readers' Guide plus many others, and is available in
        microfilm format rather than in the standard printed format of those indexes which you have been
        examining. Sheehy also lists a number of indexes specifically for the more literary "little maga-
        zines," such as Index to Little Magazines (AE184) and Index to Commonwealth Little Magazines
        (AE185). All of these indexing services work on the same general principles as the Readers'
        Guide, although the subject headings may vary somewhat from the more standard lists, in order
        to best serve the nature of the material being indexed. If these indexing services are available,
        try to look at at least one or two of them.

7-47   Many other indexing (or indexing and abstracting) services are available for specialized fields,
        and can be located through Sheehy under the appropriate subject. None of the indexing serv-
        ices you have examined so far is an indexing/abstracting service. What is an abstracting serv-
        ice? What is an abstract?

7-48   How can you tell in which one of the several indexing services a periodical will be indexed? If you wanted some articles on the international aspect of librarianship, and you knew that such articles were published in the periodical titled Libri, and you wanted to know which indexing services would cover this periodical, how would you find out?

7-49   Like CBI, the Readers' Guide, the Social Sciences Index, and the Humanities Index are current sources which, in their earlier volumes, also serve as retrospective sources. How far back can you search in them retrospectively?

7-50   You have coverage by the Wilson Company indexing services back to 1900. What do you have as retrospective sources for the 19th century or earlier?

7-51   Look at Poole's Index first. Poole's Index is, now, entirely a retrospective index; it is no longer published. What is the basic bibliographic information about Poole's? What is its full title, how many volumes does it have, when was it published?

7-52   What are the dates of its coverage (as opposed to its publication)? What are the dates of coverage for each volume in the set?

7-53   What is the scope of Poole's Index? You would normally expect to get this information from the preface or introductory material; the Preface to vol. 1 of Poole's is worth reading but is quite time-consuming. As with some of the retrospective bibliographies for books (Sabin, etc.), the prefaces in the various volumes of Poole's Index are in themselves a series of comments on the historical development of this form, on the need for periodical indexes, and on the early concepts of and problems of such indexing. However, as a time-saving device at this point, you might most easily go directly to the Sheehy annotation to find the scope of Poole's Index.

7-54   Is there a list in Poole's Index of the periodicals covered (as there was in Readers' Guide)? What introductory material is given in Poole's?

7-55   Does the arrangement of Poole's Index differ from that of the Readers' Guide? (Consider: does it have all the accesses you have with RG?)

7-56   What kind of subject access does Poole's Index have? Does it appear to be the same as the Readers' Guide? Does it appear to use subject headings as does Readers' Guide?

7-57   Poole's Index is not a title index, but a subject index. Have the titles been modified in any way to create a subject index? Look, for example, at the entries under "Indians" on pages 316-17 of the fifth supplement, 1902-06. (Remember the use of titles as subject access in Roorbach and Kelly, #2a-35, 2a-36, 2a-37.)

7-58   How would you go about using Poole's to find articles written about the Indians in the nineteenth
        century? Would you have to look under other headings? Would you expect to find articles about,
        specifically, the Hopi Indians and the Navajo Indians all in the same place, or under other head-
        ings?

7-59   Look specifically under Hopi Indians on p. 296 of the fifth supplement of Poole's Index, at the
        articles entitled (presumably) "Sky-god personations in worship of Hopi Indians" (or possibly
        "Worship of Hopi Indians in Sky-god Personations" or even "Worship of Sky-god Personations in
        Hopi Indians"). Who is the author and where would you find the article? What is the date of the
        article?

7-60   The information in the front of the fifth supplement to Poole's Index indicated that the Journal
        of American Folk-Lore was published in Boston from 1902-06 in five volumes, which seems un-
        clear if 1902 is vol. 15. If you wanted to get more information about the Journal of American
        Folk-Lore, when it actually did begin publication, etc., where would you look?

7-61   If you wanted to find out if the Journal of American Folk-Lore is still being published, currently,
        where would you look?

7-62   Is there any other way to determine the volume dates in Poole's than checking through the
        "Chronological Conspectus?"

7-63   If you wanted to make a list of the periodical articles written by Andrew Lang during the nine-
        teenth century (as in #7-22 for William F. Buckley), could you do so through Poole's Index?
        What about Lord Macaulay?

7-64   Are there any entries at all in Poole's Index for Lord Macaulay? What are they?

7-65   If you were doing research on Robert Burns, the Scottish poet (1759-1796), would you find
        Poole's Index helpful?

7-66   Look at the next retrospective source on your list, Nineteenth Century Readers' Guide. What period
        does this source cover? Who published it and when was it published?

7-67   The Nineteenth Century Readers' Guide then covers some of the same period as Poole's Index,
        and was in fact published much after Poole's Index was in existence. Why was this? What was
        the point of the duplication? How does the Nineteenth Century Readers' Guide differ from Poole?
        (Read the Preface.)

7-68   Look up the Fewkes article (from #7-59) in the Nineteenth Century Readers' Guide. Look it up by
        subject, not author. How does it contrast to Poole's Index?

7-69   The Nineteenth Century Readers' Guide is a retrospective source which was published more or less
        currently (1944). (According to the Preface, it was intended to continue it back through the entire
        nineteenth century, but this has not yet come to pass.) It was published specifically to correct de-
        fects of an older source covering the same time period. What other bibliographic sources does this
        remind you of?

7-70   Are Poole's Index and the Nineteenth Century Readers' Guide the only periodical indexes we have
       for retrospective general subject coverage?

7-71   Poole's Index, Nineteenth Century Readers' Guide, Social Sciences Index, and Humanities Index
       all cover English-language periodicals, thus including British periodicals as opposed to being limited
       to U.S. periodicals. It is very typical of the periodical indexes and current indexing services to
       cover both the U.S. and Great Britain; this can be seen from the group heading in Sheehy, 9th
       ed., p. 175 (Periodicals--Indexes--United States and Great Britain) for these sources. The sources
       you have looked at so far have been published in the United States. Would you assume that similar
       periodical indexes published in Great Britain would also cover American or U.S. periodicals? Where
       would you look for such British indexes? Are there any other retrospective sources with general
       (i.e., very broad subject) coverage of periodical articles?

7-72   Have the indexes and indexing services you have looked at so far covered newspapers?

7-73   What are newspapers? How do they differ from what has been generally referred to as "periodicals?"

7-74   Think about a possible indexing service for newspapers, in comparison to the ones you have seen
       for periodicals. Would you expect them to differ in any way? Consider all of the basic, possible
       accesses you could have to bibliographic sources. Do you need all of these for newspapers? What
       kind of access would you need for newspapers?

7-75   There are no indexing services for newspapers comparable to those for periodicals. In fact, until
       recently there have been very few newspaper indexes of any kind. The first newspaper index to
       examine is that specifically to one of the best known, major U.S. newspapers, the New York Times.
       Look at the New York Times Index. Is it published continuously as the other indexes are? How
       often? Is it cumulated? How often?

7-76   Is there any introductory or prefatory material in the NY Times Index which tells you how to use
       it, what the abbreviations stand for, etc.?

7-77   Look through some recent issues of the New York Times Index. How does it differ from the other
       indexing services you have seen?

7-78   In the answer to the previous question, it was suggested that you look in the 1981 volume to see
       how much information was given on the attempted assassination of Pope John Paul II, and on the
       wedding of Prince Charles and Lady Diana. How did you find these topics--that is, under what
       heading(s) were they listed?

7-79   Could you find out through the New York Times Index alone (that is, without going to a further
       source to which it leads you) who won the Nobel Peace Prize for the current year? And what it
       was won for?

7-80   In searching for the winner of the Nobel Peace Prize for the current year, you would presumably
       have to look under the appropriate subject heading in each of this year's issues (to a possible

total of 24) until you found the specific item you were searching for. Is there any way you can think of to shorten this search?

7-81   Suppose you want some further information about the awarding of this year's prize but your library does not subscribe to the New York Times so that you can look up the article referred to in the Index. What else can you do?

7-82   Can you tell if the New York Times Index uses standardized subject headings, such as those used in the Wilson indexes? Can you think of any limitations to the use of standardized subject headings in a newspaper index?

7-83   The NY Times Index has subject access only. Are there any names in the subject headings--i.e., names of persons, places, organizations, etc.? What about cross-references?

7-84   Can you find--through the New York Times Index only--the date on which the first "test-tube baby" was born?

7-85   How would you find access to contemporary accounts of the stock market crash preceding the "Great Depression" in 1929/30? Would you expect this to be in the NY Times Index? Would you expect to find it indexed under "Depression," or "Great Depression?"

7-86   What about contemporary accounts of the Civil War? Would you expect to find them indexed under "Civil War?"

7-87   What other newspaper indexes are there in addition to the NY Times Index?

The following series of questions are review questions covering all of the bibliographic sources for serials.

7-88   You plan to subscribe to Science and Children for your school library. Where will you find out how many issues you should expect to receive each year?

7-89   Where would you look to find recent critical articles on the novels of Irish Murdoch (contemporary English novelist)?

7-90   You want to borrow on interlibrary loan some recent issues of the San Francisco Free Press, the Berkeley Barb, and the San Francisco Oracle. How would you find out which libraries have copies?

7-91   Where would you look to find information on the shooting down by the Soviets of a South Korean passenger airliner in the fall of 1983?

7-92   If you wanted "news" type information (details, dates, comments, figures, etc.) on the shooting
        down of the South Korean passenger airliner in 1983, and you were in a library which did not
        have the NY Times Index, where else could you look?

7-93   If you did not already know it, where would you look to find out where <u>Time Magazine</u> is indexed?

7-94   Where would you look to find some recent publications on the formal theory of differentiation in
        organizations?

INDEXES TO SERIALS--INDEXING SERVICES

Answers #7/1--7/94

7-1: See the ALA Glossary or any dictionary. Basically, an index is a list of items (names, subjects, terms, etc.) in a work or works, with reference (usually page numbers) to that work or works.

7-2: Readers' guide to periodical literature (unabridged); an author subject index to selected general interest periodicals of reference value in libraries.

7-3: Limited to periodicals (more specifically, items within periodicals); limited to those published in the U.S. (see Prefatory Note); "selected."

7-4: According to the title, "general interest," "of reference value in libraries." You might expect to find a fuller statement in the prefatory matter of the source itself, or perhaps in Sheehy. Neither Sheehy nor the preface to current volumes or issues give much additional information but older annual bound volumes do go into more detail. The current "Prefatory Note" indicates that the Wilson Company seeks the advice of the American Library Association's Committee on Wilson Indexes.

7-5: A list is given in the front pages or front matter of the RG itself. All issues also contain a list of "Abbreviations of periodicals indexed." Over 170 periodicals.

7-6: Yes, it is indexed in RG. Look in the list of periodicals indexed in an annual cumulation. The fact that it is indexed in RG tells you that the periodical is considered to be of general interest, more or less on a popular level; that is, it is not a highly technical or highly specialized journal in the field of physics.

7-7: Yes. You can tell this by looking through the list of "Periodicals Indexed" included in the front matter of recent issues. You will find, for example, American Education and The Department of State Bulletin published by the United States Government Printing Office, UN Monthly

Chronicle published by the United Nations.

7-8: The publisher is the Wilson Company, which also publishes CBI, so you might therefore expect some similarities to that source.

7-9: The idea of cumulation and the dictionary (author/title/subject in one alphabet) arrangement.

7-10: As of 1983, RG is published semi-monthly (twice a month) in September, October, November, December, March, April, and June, and monthly in January, February, May, July, and August. It cumulates quarterly and annually. Until 1965, it also cumulated every two years, and earlier in a three, four, or five-year pattern. You can find this information by looking at the title page covers of recent issues (dates are given in the upper right corner of the cover) and at the dates of coverage given on the spines of bound volumes; by looking at the list of cumulated volumes given on the page facing the title page of recent annual cumulated volumes; and/or by looking at the masthead on the bottom of the first page of recent issues. Sheehy is also helpful for the earlier cumulations.

7-11: Its coverage begins with 1900 (publication of the first cumulated volume was in 1905). There is also a Nineteenth Century Readers' Guide which will be taken up later.

7-12: No, actually Readers' Guide is only an author/subject list--but it is still in a general dictionary arrangement, since all entries are in the same alphabet.

7-13: Yes, for some items. See "Suggestions for the Use of the RG...." in the front of a recent bound volume. Titles of short stories are listed under the heading "Short Stories" with references to the author's name for the full entry. Titles are also given for ballets, musical comedies and revues, etc., and operas and operettas, etc., when they are re-viewed, with cross-references from the titles to the listings of the reviews. In general, however, there is no real title access to Readers' Guide--probably because in searching for material from periodicals, one is far more apt to be searching by subject, or if searching for a specific item, to know the author rather than the title.

7-14:   Yes, you could find it by looking under the subject--since presumably if you remembered the title, you would also remember the subject.

7-15:   Yes, from various forms of personal names and various forms of subject headings to the form of name or headings used in RG. Also for such titles as noted in #7-13. (See "Suggestions...." in the front of a recent issue.) However, all of these cross-references do not appear in every issue, only in the issues in which they are significant, as in CBI.

7-16:   There are no indexes; you don't need any; you already have the accesses you need (author/subject) in the main arrangement.

7-17:   Searching by subject, you would look first under "youth," then under the sub-heading "employment." There are several citations. The first is:

Berea College's labor program: educating head & hands [excerpt from Berea's first 125 years] E.A. Smith. il Change 14:32-7 N/D '82

The periodical in which this article would be found is Change (had the title been abbreviated, remember that there is a list of abbreviations in the front) on pages 32 through 37 of the November/December 1982 issue, which happens to be in volume 14. The author's name is E.A. Smith, and the title of the article is "Berea College's labor program..." (See the explanation for the sample entry in "Suggestions..." in the front.)

7-18:   Because "back issues" of periodicals in libraries are usually bound and marked by the volume.

7-19:   Yes, you would, and it is. The full name is Emily Ann Smith

7-20:   In Ulrich's International Periodicals Di-

rectory, or in Readers' Guide itself (see List of Periodicals indexed in front).

7-21:   The title of Mr. Buckley's article is "On Experiencing Gore Vidal" and it appeared in the August 1969 issue of Esquire, pages 108-113 and following (volume 72). This is indexed in the 69/70 annual cumulation of Readers' Guide. You could have found it by looking under Buckley as the author or Vidal as the subject. Mr. Vidal's article is "A Distasteful Encounter with William F. Buckley, Jr.," in the September 1969 issue of Esquire, and similarly it would be found under either Buckley as subject or Vidal as author, so that whichever way you looked you should have found both articles together.

7-22:   Search through issues and cumulations of Readers' Guide, under Buckley as author, noting what you found cited, or indexed, there.

7-23:   How far back retrospectively you would need to search would depend on the purpose of your list. If you just wanted recent articles, then you could decide your own cut-off date of 1975 or 1980, etc. If you wanted a comprehensive, complete listing, then you would have to go as far back as Mr. Buckley was presumably capable of writing articles, which would in any case not be earlier than the date of his birth. However, if you wanted a comprehensive list--a list of all the magazine articles Mr. Buckley had written--then you would find in Readers' Guide only the articles in those magazines indexed by Readers' Guide. You would need then to cover other sources as well.

7-24:   The problem here is what subject headings to look under, and there are several possibilities. "City" or "urban" would be a good start. Remember that RG will give some cross-references but not in every issue.
        The 82/83 bound cumulation cites articles under "cities and towns," under "city planning" (with a cross-reference from "urban planning"), under "urban renewal," under "housing" (with a cross-reference from "urban housing"), under "gentrification." Another possibility is "poor" which cites more articles plus referring you to see also entries under the headings "homelessness," "public welfare." Some of the citations will probably be duplicated under some of the headings.

7-25:   You could jot all of the citations down and search them all out in the library's collections (assuming the library had all the periodicals cited), and judge each for itself by looking at it. You could also make an educated guess at their usefulness from the titles of the articles and to some extent from the periodicals in which they appear.

7-26:   You could search back in RG as far as 1900, since RG does go back that far. Subject headings always have a tendency to change as our language changes and as the significance of subjects themselves change. In the January 1929-June 1932 bound cumulation of RG, there are many citations under "housing," nothing under "urban renewal," for example. You would not expect to find anything under the relatively new term "gentrification."

7-27:   One of the most direct places to look is in Sheehy; see item AE170, directly following the annotation for the Readers' Guide itself. The Abridged Readers' Guide is simply what it implies--an abridged edition covering only about one-fourth to one-third of the periodicals indexed in the unabridged edition, issued only once a month, cumulating only once annually, for libraries which cannot afford the larger service or do not need the greater coverage.

7-28:   As in RG, the periodicals indexed are listed in the front (Periodicals Indexed), giving also the ordering information. In the Humanities Index, selection of periodicals is done by subscriber vote (see Prefatory Note in a recent issue), as of 1983.

7-29:   Both are limited to periodicals (i.e., articles within). HI is limited to humanities ("archaeology and classical studies, area studies, folklore, history, language and literature, literary and political criticism, performing arts, philosophy, religion and theology, and related subjects"--see Prefatory Note); RG is very general. HI includes English-language periodicals; RG includes U.S. publications only. HI covers about 290 periodicals; RG covers about 170. See lists of periodicals indexed in each.

    HI indexes periodicals which deal with those subject areas in more depth; more scholarly, more specialized, as compared to the popular level of the periodicals indexed in RG.

7-30:   Like the Readers' Guide: author and subject in one alphabet, some cross-references.

7-31:   HI is published quarterly (every three months) as compared to semi-monthly (twice a month) for the Readers' Guide. See masthead statement in a recent issue. HI cumulates annually (as does RG).

7-32:   Although Carson McCullers is a contemporary and somewhat popular novelist, the material you are searching for seems more of a scholarly nature. Readers' Guide might have something, but Humanities Index seems even more likely. "McCullers, Carson" would be the subject heading; in the June 1983 quarterly issue, for example, there are three likely items listed.

7-33:   Like Humanities Index, it covers periodicals, English-language, but limited to social sciences ("anthropology, economics, environmental sciences, geography, law and criminology, planning and public administration, political science, psychology, social aspects of medicine, sociology and related subjects"--see Prefatory Note, 1983). About 300 titles indexed.

7-34:   There might be something on this topic in Readers' Guide, but since you are looking for research data, a more likely place to search would be the Social Sciences Index. The June 1983 issue has two likely-looking articles, indexed under "Unemployed--Psychology."

7-35:   A previous index, published by Wilson, was titled Social Sciences and Humanities Index (Sheehy AE171); it split into two new titles, with new numbering, in 1974. Social Sciences and Humanities Index itself was formerly titled the International Index which began publication in 1916, changing title to SSHI in 1965.

7-36:   Coverage has varied over the years as titles have been added and dropped. Earlier years of the International Index included some foreign (i.e., non-English) periodicals, and also some scientific periodicals.

7-37:   You might find these in all three of the current indexing services examined so far, depending upon the nature and depth of the material you wish. Some articles of a more popular and general nature might be indexed in RG; Human-

ities Index would include more specialized material relating to such things as
"death in art," "death in literature,"
etc.; Social Sciences Index would have
references to articles on "death--
psychological aspects," "death--social
aspects," etc. And don't forget that
one of the topics included in the scope
of the Social Sciences Index is "social
aspects of medicine" (see #7-33).

7-38:   You would need to look in Sheehy for
this, and you would turn to the section for sciences (E. Pure and Applied
Sciences), then under General Works
(EA, p. 691), then to the section for
"Indexes and Abstract Journals" (p.
698), where you would find the Applied
Science and Technology Index (EA80)
published by the Wilson Company, which
you would expect to use as you have
used the other Wilson indexes so far.
Similarly, in the first Supplement to
Sheehy you would find, on p. 211, the
General Science Index (EA11), also
published by Wilson and which began
in 1978.

7-39:   The simplest way is to look through one
of the issues, if available, to see if entries are included for books, etc. Or
read the prefatory statement or policy
statement in the front of one of the
recent issues. Or read the annotation
in Sheehy (but be sure it is currently
applicable). Or read the annotation for
the service in "Cataloging and Indexing
Services."

7-40:   It means that the library pays according to the indexing it actually uses; for
example, for the Readers' Guide, the
library pays according to how many of
the indexed periodicals it subscribes to.
"Service basis" is defined briefly in the
ALA Glossary. It is also explained in
more detail in the "Cataloging and Indexing Services" pamphlet put out by the
Wilson Company.

7-41:   The full title (from the title page--or
cover page--of recent issues of the
source itself): Public Affairs Information Service Bulletin: a selective subject list of the latest books, pamphlets,
government publications, reports of
public and private agencies and periodical articles, relating to economic
and social conditions, public administration and international relations,
published in English throughout the
world.

7-42:   The current issues have subject access
only (alphabetically by subject headings). Since 1977, there has been an
author index in the annual cumulations.

7-43:   Abortion, city planning, consumer protection, employment, environmental
policy, petroleum industry, women (see
June 15, 1983 issue).

7-44:   PAIS would include books, pamphlets,
and government publications, as well as
periodical articles. For example, in the
June 15, 1983 issue, listed under "Environmental Policy--International aspects," there is a publication on hearings before one of the U.S. House Committee on Foreign Affairs subcommittees,
and under "Environmental Policy--United
States," there is a book by Wesley
Magat titled Reform of Environmental
Regulation.

7-45:   The publisher is the Public Affairs Information Service, Inc., a non-profit
association of libraries (see verso of
title page or cover page).

7-46:   Sheehy, in the same section which includes the Readers' Guide and other
general interest periodical indexes, lists
the Alternative Press Index (AE177),
an index for those publications concerned
with social change, etc., and which, as
Sheehy notes, are not indexed elsewhere.

7-47:   See the ALA Glossary on abstract and
abstracting service, or a dictionary on
abstract. An abstracting service is an
indexing service similar to those you
have looked at, which includes not only
the basic bibiographic information (author, title, periodical, volume number,
paging, date, etc.) for each entry,
but also includes an abstract, or content summary, of the article (or book,
or report, or whatever is being cited).
        Examples of indexing services
which include abstracts in their citations are: Information Science Abstracts (Sheehy AB13), and Library
and Information Science Abstracts
(AB12).

7-48:   You could guess that it would be indexed in Library Literature. You
could look in the front of Library
Literature in the list of periodicals
indexed, and find out for sure. You
could also find out from Ulrich's.
The citations in Ulrich's indicate the
indexes which cover that periodical,
so if a periodical is listed in Ulrich's,

you can find it there.

7-49:   Readers' Guide goes back to 1900. So-
        cial Sciences and Humanities Index, be-
        fore it split, goes back to 1907 (v. 1-
        2 titled Readers' Guide to Periodical
        Literature Supplement, v. 3-52 titled
        International Index, see Sheehy anno-
        tation, AA171).

7-50:   Nineteenth Century Readers' Guide,
        and Poole's Index: the next two titles
        on your list.

7-51:   Full title: Poole's Index to Periodical
        Literature
        Number of volumes: in most editions
        there will be 6 or 7 volumes (the basic
        index in two volumes, plus five sup-
        plements)
        Dates of publication: in most editions,
        1891 through 1908 (the basic index
        originally published in 1882, revised
        edition published 1891). There is also
        a 1938 reprint. (From title pages of
        volumes or from Sheehy.)

7-52:   1802-1906.
        Basic index, 1802-81; 1st sup., 1882-
        86; 2nd sup., 1887-91; 3rd sup., 1892-
        96; 4th sup., 1897-1901; 5th sup.,
        1902-06 (title page says "to Jan. 1,
        1907"). (From title pages of volumes,
        or from spines of volumes, or from
        Sheehy Annotation.)

7-53:   The Sheehy annotation tells you that
        Poole's Index covers 479 periodicals,
        American and English (varying somewhat
        from volume to volume). The dates of
        coverage are given in #7-52. In addi-
        tion, the Preface to vol. 1 of Poole's
        (1891 edition) tells you that, in the be-
        ginning, only those periodicals which
        were likely to be found in libraries
        and private collections were indexed,
        that medical, legal, botanical and other
        purely professional and scientific period-
        icals were omitted, that semi-professional
        periodicals were included if of general
        interest--that the main criterion was the
        wants of general scholars.

7-54:   Volume 1 contains a Prefatory Note (to
        the 1891 edition), a Preface, a list of
        cooperating libraries (like Sabin, Poole's
        started out as the work of one man and
        eventually became the work of a commit-
        tee), abbreviations/titles/imprints (which
        is in effect a list of the periodicals in-
        dexed), and a "Chronological Conspectus
        of the Serials Indexed." Each succeed-
        ing supplement also contains a list of

abbreviations and Chronological Con-
spectus which indicates what specific
periodicals are indexed in that supplement.

7-55:   Poole's has only subject access (RG has
        both subject and author access).

7-56:   Poole's Index does not use the subject
        headings in the same sense that RG does.
        By looking carefully at the way the en-
        tries are constructed, you can see that
        in fact the titles of the articles them-
        selves are used as the entries.

7-57:   The significant indexing word or "catch-
        word" or "keyword" has been pulled out
        of the title for the subject entry or
        alphabetizing word. For example, in the
        first entry under "Indians," the title of
        the article is "The American Indians"
        by C.F. Lummis, published in Land
        of the Sun....). The entry is indexed
        not under the first real word of the title
        (which would be American), but under
        the significant word, "Indians," and the
        title itself within the entry has been in-
        verted (Indians, the American). In some
        cases where the title does not clearly
        contain the significant keyword, it has
        been entered under that keyword any-
        way, much as a regular subject head-
        ing (see "Indians. Cities of the Dead."
        at the top of the right column on p. 316;
        this would appear to be an example; it
        is not always easy to tell).

7-58:   You would look in all the volumes under
        the heading "Indians." You would also
        find it helpful to think of other signifi-
        cant related keywords which might also
        have been used for entries. For exam-
        ple, articles specifically on the Hopi In-
        dians are indexed separately, listed on
        p. 296 of the fifth supplement.

7-59:   The author is J.W. Fewkes. The arti-
        cle is found in Journal of American Folk-
        Lore (see abbreviations in front of the
        volume). "15:14" presumably means
        "vol. 15, page 14." Inclusive paging
        is not given, usually only the first page
        of the article. The date is not given,
        but can be found--more or less--through
        the "Chronological Conspectus" also in
        the front of the volume. The abbrevia-
        tion list tells you that the Journal of
        American Folk-Lore was published in
        Boston, 1902-06, in 5 volumes. It also
        tells you that the number for that title
        in the "Chronological Conspectus" is
        341. You then look in the "Chronolog-
        ical Conspectus" under 341 (p. xiii)

which tells you that 15 is 1902. Presumably then the article is in Journal of American Folk-Lore, vol. 15, p. 41+, 1902.

7-60: Union List of Serials. Which tells you that the Journal of American Folk-Lore began publication with vol. 1 in April 1888 (which would make vol. 15 in 1902) in Boston, N.Y., and Lancaster, Pa., by the American Folklore Society, and that it has been published through at least 48 volumes since library holdings are indicated through 48 volumes. (Since this information is not the same as that which you found in Poole's, it would seem clear then that Poole's gives publishing information only for the dates or years covered by that specific volume.)

7-61: Ulrich's.

7-62: By using Poole's Index Date and Volume Key (by Bell and Bacon), see Sheehy AE166. This is simply titles and dates in one alphabetical tabular form for the entire index. (The Date and Volume Key also contains, p. 5-8, a short and very interesting survey of the origin and development of Poole's Index, and particularly points out the rules for procedure used by the cooperating libraries.)

7-63: There are no author entries in Poole's Index itself. However, there is available a Cumulative Author Index for Poole's Index.... (Sheehy AE165) published in 1971. Entries for Macaulay and Lang can be found here.

7-64: Subject entries--the articles indexed under the subject "Macaulay, Lord" are articles about him, not written by him.

7-65: Yes, you could search Poole's under "Burns, Robert" as a subject entry and find critical, biographical, etc., writings about him.

7-66: 1890-1899 (with some indexing for 1900-1922). (See Preface to source or Sheehy.) It was published by the Wilson Company in 1944 (2 volumes).

7-67: The Nineteenth Century Readers' Guide was undertaken specifically to offer a source which would correct some of the defects of Poole's Index, by using standard subject headings and providing author access.

7-68: The subject heading is still specifically Hopi Indians, with a subhead of Religion

and mythology. The entry itself gives the title correctly and the inclusive paging and the date.

7-69: The Shaw/Shoemaker American Bibliography and the Checklist of American Imprints (both from Section 2b) published relatively recently to re-cover the period of Roorbach and Kelly and to correct defects of those sources and to fill in where the Evans bibliography left off.

7-70: No. Sheehy (same section as Readers' Guide, Poole's Index, etc.) notes other similar sources such as Annual Magazine Subject Index, 1907-49 (AE180/181), Annual Literary Index, 1892-1904 and Annual Library Index, 1905-10 (AE178/179), and the Catholic Periodical Index, 1930-date (AE182/183).

7-71: Yes, you could assume that British indexes would also cover U.S. publications. Reference sources (such as periodical indexes) published in Great Britain are included in Sheehy as well as U.S.-published reference sources. Some of those indexes with retrospective general coverage are listed in the section of Sheehy noted in the question, such as: Subject Index to Periodicals (AE174), retrospective: 1915-1961; British Humanities Index (AE175), current: 1962-date.

7-72: Generally not, considering the general definition of newspapers.

7-73: See ALA Glossary under "newspaper." A newspaper differs from a periodical partly in its physical format, but as regards content, it differs in that its primary purpose is to report, record, describe, discuss daily current news events.

7-74: Basic possible accesses would be: author, title, subject, and chronological (time, period, date of publication....). Do most newspaper articles have titles? (No, although they do have headlines which might possibly be considered as similar.) Do most newspaper articles have authors? (Some have author by-lines, but most do not.) You are left, then, with subject access and chronological access.

7-75: It is published semi-monthly (twice a month). Since 1978, there have also been quarterly cumulations (see Sheehy 1AF13). There are also annual cumulations (now serving as the fourth quarterly cumulation). The annual cumulation is called a "Book of Record."

7-76:   There is a page titled "How to use the New York Times Index" in the back of each issue.

7-77:   Under the subject heading, the date and location of the article or item is cited (for example: Ja 20, 1:8=January 20, page 1, column 8), but in addition, information, content, facts from the article or item are given. In a way these entries are like "abstracts" of the news item--thus the New York Times Index can claim to provide not only a classified index to the news, but a summary, a condensed history of the news itself. Look, for example, in the 1981 cumulated volume to see how much specific information and detail (plus illustrations) can be found in the index alone, on the attempted assassination of Pope John Paul II, or on the wedding of Great Britain's Prince Charles and Lady Diana Spencer.

7-78:   Looking under Pope, John Paul II sends you to see "Roman Catholic Church." Looking under Charles, Prince of Wales, tells you about the wedding.

7-79:   Yes, since that information would be noted in the entry indexed under the subject. For example, in 1982, you would find indexed under Nobel (in the Oct. 1-15 issue of the Index), the fact that Alva Myrdal and Alfonso Garcia Robles were awarded the Peace Prize for their efforts to promote disarmament.

7-80:   You could shorten your search by looking in the last cumulated volume, where you would have to look in only one place under the approximate subject heading, to see from the date of the item approximately what time of year the Nobel Peace Prize was awarded in that year, under the assumption that it would be awarded approximately the same time this year. You could then look in the current issue for this time.

7-81:   On the assumption that your local newspaper, or whatever newspaper(s) your library does have, would have carried a story on the awarding of the prize, and that it would have appeared approximately the same date of the New York Times story, then you could look it up in issues of your local newspaper for that date, or thereabouts.

7-82:   The index itself doesn't indicate whether or not standardized subject headings, such as LC, are used. One of the limitations to using such a list for a newspaper index is that the material to be indexed is basically current events, constantly changing, constantly new. The need is for frequent changes, for new words, for flexibility, for specificity.

7-83:   Yes, there are name entries or headings, although generally with reference to the subject concerned. There are plenty of cross-references in general. See "How to Use the New York Times Index" for a detailed discussion of types of headings used, arrangement of headings (subdivisions, aphabetization, etc.), cross-reference, etc.

7-84:   It would help if you had a general idea of when this event took place, otherwise you would simply have to start from the most recent issue of the Index and work back in time till you found what you were searching for. If you knew that the first baby reproduced from a laboratory fertilization process was born in the late 1970's, this would at least narrow the search somewhat. The significant entry for this is found in the 1978 cumulated volume under "reproduction (biological)." Page references also appear under "test tube babies" but the specific information about the date (July 26, 1978) of the birth is found within the long series of statements about "Dr. Patrick Steptoe...." in the entry on "Reproduction (biological)."

7-85:   Since the NY Times Index goes back basically to the beginning of the newspaper itself in 1851, it therefore would cover events of 1929-1930, the stock market crash, the depression, etc. It would likely not be indexed under "depression," however, since that name for the period did not come into such common use until later. You might need to look under several headings in the indexes for 1929/30. Look, for example, in the Oct-Dec 1929 Index (no annual cumulations then, only quarterly) under "Stocks and Bonds --Prices" for a long series of brief citations giving, in themselves, an interesting and revealing account of the crash. Look also at the volume for 1930 (an annual cumulation)--the arrangement of the entries and the subject headings should remind you of the Wilson indexes.

7-86: These would be covered since the Index goes back to 1851. The annotation in Sheehy shows the index going back to 1913, with earlier volumes from 1851-1905 on microfilm. This earlier period ("Prior Series") has since been published in book form (Sheehy AF68, 1AF14)--some of it in the original handwritten form, some newly prepared, etc. Since some of the indexing for the Civil War period has been more or less currently prepared, then you might expect the headings to reflect a more current view of those times, and entries would be found indexed generally under "Civil War." The Forewords to the volumes of these Prior Series Indexes, especially that to the Sept. 1851-Dec. 1862 volume, and to the July 1905-Dec. 1906 volume, are helpful reading background on the differences between earlier and current indexes, in depth of indexing and in subject headings used.

7-87: Look in Sheehy. In the basic volume of Sheehy, under "Newspapers--Indexes--United States," you can find that there have been current indexes to the Christian Science Monitor (AF64), to the National Observer (AF65), to the Wall Street Journal (AF70). Sheehy also lists the Newspaper Index (AF69, 1AF15/16/17/18) which has provided separate indexes for the Chicago Tribune, the Los Angeles Times, the New Orleans Times-Picayune, and the Washington Post. The second supplement to Sheehy lists the National Newspaper Index (2AF13) which indexes primarily the New York Times, the Christian Science Monitor, and the Wall Street Journal, and like the Magazine Index noted earlier, is available in a microfilm format.

In Sheehy, under "Newspapers--Indexes--Great Britain," you can find that there is also an index to the London Times which goes back to 1790 (AF76/77, 1AF23, 2AF15), as well as indexes to other foreign newspapers.

7-88: Ulrich's. Since you plan to subscribe, it is therefore presumably currently published. Ulrich's gives frequency of publication in its citations.

7-89: Humanities Index. You might also find some indexed in Readers' Guide, but the use of the term "critical" might lead you to the somewhat more scholarly HI.

7-90: Since you want location of copies, you want a union list, and your choice then is ULS and NST. If you recognized the titles given as part of the "underground

press" you would assume that they have probably begun publication since 1949, and therefore check first in NST. (If you weren't aware of the titles sufficiently to make that educated guess, then you would look first in ULS and proceed to NST, or vice versa.) Another problem might be whether or not these publications qualify as newspapers and would therefore be excluded from ULS/NST, or similarly whether as "underground" publications, they would be excluded from ULS/NST. In any case, all three happen to be listed in NST.

7-91: Depending on what type of information you wanted, you could look in the New York Times Index for 1983, which would give you some specific facts and indicate the exact dates of the incident so that you could then search further through the newspaper itself if necessary.

7-92: If your library had the Readers' Guide, you could look in it to find locations of articles in the various current events news magazines (Time, Newsweek, Life, etc.), or for articles on the subject that might have appeared in other periodicals by now.

7-93: Ulrich's. Time is currently published. Ulrich's gives information on indexing in its citations.

7-94: The subject matter is generally social sciences, and it would seem as if a more specialized, scholarly source would be in order. "Some recent publications" could include books, periodical articles, etc.--"recent" combined with a very specific aspect of a topic might lead you to an indexing service for periodical articles in the social sciences, such as Social Sciences Index or others as listed in Sheehy.

Section 8

BIBLIOGRAPHIC SOURCES FOR GOVERNMENT PUBLICATIONS

Questions #8/1--8/61

The bibliographic sources you have examined in the last few sections of this manual have covered serial publications--periodicals, newspapers, annuals, etc. Serial publications are not generally-- or at least not consistently--included in the basic bibliographic records examined in the early sections of this manual. Another type of publication which is not generally or consistently included in these basic bibliographic records is "government publications." The bibliographic sources which cover government publications comprise the next set you will examine:

> Monthly Catalog of U.S. Government Publications (AG25, 1AG10, 2AG9)
>
> Catalog of the Public Documents (Document Catalog) (AG24)
> Poore: Descriptive Catalogue (AG20)
> Ames: Comprehensive Index (AG21)
>
> Index to U.S. Government Periodicals (1AE48)
>
> CIS Index (CJ83/84, 1CJ56, 2CJ48)
>
> Newsome: New Guide to Popular Government Publications (2AG5)
>
> Monthly Checklist of State Publications (AG47)

8-1   What are "government publications?"

Government publications are a good source of information on governmental organization and adminis- tration. They are also a basic source of statistical information. But furthermore--and this is not always as clearly recognized--government publications are available in any field, of both popular and research interest: health, education, agriculture, business, home economics, cooking, child care, social welfare, economics, science and technology, etc.

The U.S. Government Printing Office (G.P.O.) located in Washington, D.C., is generally considered to be the largest publishing and printing plant in the world. Similar materials are al- so published on state and local (county, municipal or city, etc.) levels, although not to the same extent. Other countries also have extensive government publishing programs, such as the HMSO in Great Britain, the Queen's Printer in Canada, etc. Material is also published by international government organizations, such as the United Nations, UNESCO, League of Nations, etc.

Government publications are often considered and treated as a special form or type of publi- cation. In fact, government publications may appear in the same forms (books, periodicals, pam- phlets, etc.) and in the same types (bibliographies, directories, yearbooks, etc.) as the materials available from any of the so-called "trade" publishers. Probably the principal reasons for treating government publications as a separate type or form lies in the fact that the bibliographic control over these materials is in itself quite separate. It does not usually appear in the "trade" bibliog- raphies, but rather in bibliographies especially compiled and published by the government itself. Its "author/title/subject" access may be rather complex.

8-2   How many of the bibliographic sources which you have examined so far have included government publications? Current "trade" bibliographies: BIP, etc., WR/BPR, CBI? Retrospective sources:

123

Sabin, Evans, Roorbach, Kelly, etc.? LC/NUC, etc.? Periodicals and newspaper directories: Ulrich's, Ayer's, etc.? Serial union lists: ULS, NST? Periodical indexing services: Readers' Guide, etc.?

8-3   Some of the bibliographic sources which you have examined are actually government publications themselves. Which ones?

8-4   The specific bibliographic sources covering government publications form a current and retro- spective series. Look first at the basic current source for bibliographic information on federal government publications, the Monthly Catalog of U.S. Government Publications. Who publishes it? How often?

8-5   Is it comprehensive or selective? Does it include publications from all levels of government? Spe- cifically what publications are included? Are any specifically excluded? Does the source itself give you any clear statement of which is included?

8-6   How is it arranged?

8-7   Is there any relationship between access by "issuing agency" and the access by author/title/subject which you have become familiar with in previous sources? Look in a recent issue at the publications listed under one of the issuing agencies, Public Health Service, for example.

8-8   Searching for information by way of "issuing agency" sometimes requires an understanding of the structure of the government. Is there any publication which explains this structure?

8-9   Is there any way you can get, through the Monthly Catalog itself, a very general overall picture of the structure and organization of the issuing agencies?

8-10   If you wanted to find government publications on the general subject of urban problems, what issuing agencies could you search under?

8-11   If you have a broad subject classification on the basis of the issuing agency, do you have any specific subject access? For example, if you wanted to find publications specifically on the Medi- care program, and you did not know which government agency was responsible for the program, how would you go about it? How would you find listings of publications on crime?

8-12   Conservation of energy and resources are two of the major problems faced in the world today. What publications which might offer some help or solutions are available from the U.S. govern- ment? Look through some recent issues of the Monthly Catalog, in the subject indexes, for some possible subject headings which might lead you to publications.

8-13   In cases where a specific <u>person</u> is concerned with the publication, either as author or as subject, do you have any access to the publications through his name? Is there title access?

8-14   The Monthly Catalog is published monthly. Does it cumulate in any way? (Look at the source on shelves and see Sheehy annotation.)

8-15   In 1981 and 1982, hearings were held before a Congressional subcommittee on the Antitrust Equal Enforcement Act. Would you expect to find this material published by the U.S. government? Would you expect to find it listed in the Monthly Catalog? What are two primary ways in which you can locate material in the Monthly Catalog, and which of these approaches can you use with this particular item?

8-16   The hearings on the Antitrust Equal Enforcement Act, from the previous question, were held before the Committee on the Judiciary of the Senate, and the publication of these hearings was listed in the October 1982 issue of the Monthly Catalog. Can you find the listing? How many pages are there in the publication of this particular hearing? Is a price given? How would you obtain the document if you wanted a copy? Could you order the document through the Superintendent of Documents? What is the significance of the letters and numbers immediately above the entry?

8-17   Is there any other way you might locate a copy of the hearings document? What does the black dot in the listing tell you?

8-18   What is a "depository library?"

8-19   In the late fall of 1970, the U.S. Senate voted to return to the Taos Indians (of the Taos Pueblo, in New Mexico) the 48,000 acres of their sacred land surrounding Blue Lake in the Sangre de Cristo Mountains in New Mexico (after a struggle of some 65 years on the part of the Indians). Some hearings on the bill were held in the Senate during the summer of 1970. Locate the entry for these hearings in the Monthly Catalog. What is the number of the Senate bill which was finally passed into law in December 1970? How would you obtain the document of the hearings?

8-20   The government published several bibliographies on American Indians during the 1950's. How would you find citations to these? One of these was a list of books for Indian schools. When was it published?

8-21   What is the annual subscription price and the frequency of publication of the <u>Antarctic Journal of the United States</u> (issued by the National Science Foundation)? (This is a periodical; have any of the Sheehy annotations about the Monthly Catalog mentioned how or if serial or periodical publications are listed?

8-22   Is there a "books in print" type of source for government publications? Does the Monthly Catalog list all government publications in print?

8-23   Is it expensive to subscribe to the Monthly Catalog? Where would you find out the cost of a year's subscription?

8-24   If a library or an individual did not wish to subscribe to the Monthly Catalog, is there any less expensive way of receiving information on current government publications?

8-25   How far back can you search, retrospectively, in the Monthly Catalog?

8-26   What source(s) do you have which give you retrospective coverage prior to 1895?

8-27   What are the dates of coverage for these three sources (Poore, Ames, Document Catalog) plus the Monthly Catalog? Is there any overlapping?

8-28   The Document Catalog (full title: Catalog of the public documents of Congress and of all departments of the government of the United States for the period March 4, 1893-Dec. 31, 1940) overlaps the Monthly Catalog for all but two years of its existence. What is the difference in scope or coverage between the Monthly Catalog and the Document Catalog? Is there any difference in the access? (See Sheehy.)

8-29   Where would you look to find listings of various publications of the U.S. government on the subject of children, published in the 1920's? Look specifically for a pamphlet titled "Campaign against malnutrition" published in 1923. Compare entries in the Document Catalog with those in the Monthly Catalog. Compare subject approach in both sources.

8-30   The Document Catalog was preceded by Ames (1881-1893) and Poore (1774-1881). These bibliographies (like Sabin and Evans, for example) were compiled somewhat retrospectively. Ames was compiled specifically to fill the gap between Poore and the beginning of the Document Catalog. Look at both sources together and comparatively. Are there any differences in scope or arrangement between Poore and Ames?

8-31   Poore is arranged chronologically. Is this the only access you have to the material? Are there any indexes to give you additional access to the basic arrangement?

8-32   How does this compare to the access in Ames? In the Document Catalog? In the Monthly Catalog?

8-33   Have you examined any other sources with a chronological arrangement like Poore's? Is there any advantage to the chronological arrangement? Would there be any special advantage to a chronological arrangement for government publications? Can you find a citation for the Declaration of Independence? Could you find this in Poore's without looking in the Index?

8-34   Another retrospective source listed in Sheehy, with Poore and Ames, is Greely's Public Documents (AG19). Look only at the full title of Greely in Sheehy and compare it to Poore and Ames. What time period is covered by Greely and what does it overlap? What is the difference in scope between Poore and Greely?

8-35   A report was made by the Geographical Survey in 1883 on volcanoes in Hawaii. Where would you find it?

8-36   Could you have used the index in Ames to find the report on volcanoes in Hawaii?

8-37   In what government publication would you find the original publication of John Adams' (not John Quincy Adams) Inaugural Address? What are the general contents of the address?

8-38   Where and how would you look to find what materials--official reports, documents, etc.--about slavery which the government had published during the period preceding the American Civil War?

8-39   What is the "Serial set" (or "Congressional edition")?

8-40   How would you go about finding the report of the volcanoes in Hawaii (from #8-35 and #8-36) in the Serial set? (If you have access to the Checklist of U.S. Public Documents and the Serial set itself, try to find the report.)

8-41   Where and how would you locate an official account or report of Custer's last stand? (On this one, if possible, follow the citation all the way through the Serial set/Congressional Edition to find the actual account.)

8-42   What sources do you have which list and give bibliographic information specifically about government-published serials or periodicals?

8-43   Who publishes the Index to U.S. Government Periodicals? What is the publication (and/or cumulation) pattern? What periodicals are included in it and how are they selected?

8-44   Can you find citations for some recent articles on the subject of inflation, published in government periodicals?

8-45   Another important indexing service covering government publications is the CIS Index (Congressional Information Service Index to Publications of the United States Congress), which began in 1970. The set is somewhat more complex than the other bibliographic sources for government publications which you have been examining, but similar in some ways to those you have already examined in Section 7 on indexing services. Using the Sheehy annotations for this source (CJ83, CJ84, 1CJ56, 2CJ48), what is the publication (or cumulation) pattern for the CIS Index? Who publishes it?

8-46   What types of government publications are indexed by the CIS Index? All of them? Everything covered by the Monthly Catalog, for example?

8-47   The CIS Index not only indexes these publications but also provides <u>abstracts</u>. What are abstracts?
        Does the inclusion of abstracts in the entries give you any special advantage in using this source,
        beyond subject index access to locating particular publications? (How, for example, does it com-
        pare with the use of the New York Times Index?)

8-48   Can you locate in the CIS Index cumulative volume for 1982 the citation and abstract for the par-
        ticular hearing, before a Senate committee, on the extension and revision of the Older Americans
        Act of programs for the elderly? What is the price for this publication? Would it be available in
        a depository library?

8-49   Can you use the CIS Index to locate material on a particular topic without having any specific hear-
        ing or act or report or bill, etc., in mind? How could you, for example, locate listings for publi-
        cations on the particular topic of what has been done in the Congress relating to day care facilities
        or nursing homes for the elderly?

8-50   In question #8-19, you used the Monthly Catalog to locate the citation for the hearings (in the
        Senate, in 1970) regarding the return of the Blue Lake area land to the Taos Indians. Using the
        CIS Index, can you get any further information about what went on at the hearings and who testi-
        fied?

8-51   The bibliographic sources for government publications, which you have examined so far, give you
        to some extent both author (government and personal) and subject access. In dealing with gov-
        ernment publications in general, which of these approaches would seem to be most useful, or most
        important?

        The subject access in the sources you have examined so far is ponderous to use, at best, and re-
        quires searching through numerous volumes and issues to give any kind of collective coverage.
        The next title on your list to examine--Newsome's New Guide to Popular Government Publications
        --is an example of a basic and relatively up-to-date general subject approach to U.S. government
        publications.

8-52   What is the scope of Newsome? Perhaps this can best be answered by thinking in terms of its pur-
        poses or use.

8-53   What are some of the major topics or subjects under which material is arranged in Newsome? Is
        there subject access other than these broad topics?

8-54   Can you find, in Newsome, citations to material which would be useful to a Head Start volunteer
        who is working with Spanish-speaking children?

8-55   Can you locate, through Newsome, more information about a government publication titled "Living
        with Change?"

8-56   If you wanted a list of pamphlets and other material published by the government on the subject
        of energy (as you found through the Monthly Catalog in #8-12), Newsome would be useful; it has

a major subject heading for "energy and related natural resources." Where else might you look for such a list, from those sources you have already examined?

8-57   Are there other similar <u>selective</u> lists to government publications, with a subject approach? Where would you look to find them?

8-58   The Monthly Catalog covers only <u>federal</u> government publications. Where would you look to find publications of the states?

8-59   Who publishes the Monthly Checklist? Are there any limitations to the publications listed there?

8-60   What is the arrangement of the Monthly Checklist?

8-61   What type of publications are issued by state governments? (Look through a recent issue for examples.)

For review, it would be useful to make a chart for the main bibliographic sources examined, showing dates of coverage (see answer to #8-27) and access (see answer to #8-32), plus indications for the serial sources and subject guides.

BIBLIOGRAPHIC SOURCES FOR GOVERNMENT PUBLICATIONS

Answers #8/1--#8/61

8-1: See ALA Glossary. See also Sheehy, 9th ed., p. 191, at the beginning of the section (AG) on government publications. Basically, government publications are those materials published under the authority of or at the expense of the government. These include the state papers, orders, proclamations, speeches, treaties, laws, statutes, codes, bills, session records, proceedings, minutes, hearings, etc., of the government itself: all of these would seem to fall clearly into the category of official papers or documents. The phrase "government documents" (or "public documents") is often used interchangeably with "government publications." "Documents" seems to refer more to such official papers, while the use of the phrase "government publications" gives more indication of the astonishingly broad subject categories of current government publications in the U.S.

8-2: Current trade bibliographies (BIP, WR/BPR, CBI) quite specifically state that they exclude government publications.

The retrospective sources do include some government publications but it is not clear to what extent.

LC/NUC would include some government publications in so far as they are received, cataloged and reported by NUC libraries.

The Catalog of Copyright Entries would not include them (because in general government publications are not copyrighted).

Ulrich's and Irregular Serials do include some government publications, if they fall into the definition of "periodicals" or "irregular serials" in the sources.

ULS and NST include government publications only if they are periodicals or monographic series (therefore excluding government serials which are not periodicals).

Some of the periodical indexing services do, again if the government publication is a periodical. See #7-7 on Readers' Guide, for example.

Other indexing services such as

PAIS which include books, pamphlets, etc., will also include some government publications if they fall within the subject categories indexed. (See #7-41 on PAIS.)

8-3: All of the current sources published by the Library of Congress: the National Union Catalog, LC Subject Catalog, Catalog of Copyright Entries, NST, etc. The older, cumulative volumes of these sources have in many cases been taken over and/or reprinted by commercial publishers (Bowker for NST, Mansell for LC/NUC, etc.).

8-4: Issued by the Superintendent of Documents, U.S. Government Printing Office (GPO), Washington, D.C. Monthly. (See title page.)

8-5: There is no statement in the Monthly Catalog itself about its scope or its comprehensiveness (as of 1983), beyond the title statement that it is limited to U.S., or federal, government publications. The Sheehy annotation indicates that it includes publications issued by all branches of the government, including Congress and departments and bureaus. It is generally assumed to be as comprehensive a listing as possible.

8-6: The basic arrangement is by "issuing agency" or office. Prior to 1976 this was more or less alphabetically by the name of the agency. From 1976 on, it has been alphabetically by the Superintendent of Documents (SuDocs) classification number (example: A 1.9:2148/6) at the head of each item. Since this SuDocs classification scheme has a mnemonic aspect to it (e.g., A=Agriculture Dept., C=Commerce Dept., HE=Health and Human Services Dept., TD=Transportation Dept., etc.), the present arrangement by classification number is somewhat similar to the alphabetical arrangement by issuing agency.

Currently (1983) there are indexes for: author, title, subject, series/report, GPO stock number, and title keyword (see Contents page). (It is important to realize for retrospective use of this source that it was not always this thoroughly indexed. Author and title indexes were not included until 1974; the series/report index was not included until 1976.)

    Also the type of subject indexing has changed over the years. Prior to 1974, the subject index was a specific subject index based largely on keywords from titles; personal author entries (author, editor, compiler, etc.) began to appear in this subject index with increasing frequency during the early 1970's. In 1976, along with some other changes in format, the Monthly Catalog began to use Library of Congress subject headings for its subject index, in place of the title keywords. In 1981, the title keyword index was reinstated, and the subject heading index was maintained.

8-7:   Because the "issuing agency" tends to issue publications in its general subject area (for example, see publication on carcinogens under Public Health Service in the January 1983 issue, p. 91-92), the arrangement by issuing agency/ SuDocs classification also gives a kind of broad subject categorizing or classifying.

    The "author" for most government publications is considered to be the "issuing agency" (Agriculture Department, Commerce Department, etc.); this is almost always true prior to the 1970's when there was little indexing done by author name in the Monthly Catalog.

8-8:   Look in Sheehy, not under bibliographic sources but under subject--i.e., United States government organization, under the very broad category of social sciences (C), then political science (CJ), then government--United States--official registers: item CJ72, United States Government Manual, published annually. Similar information can be found to some extent in the "guides" to government publications listed in the AG section, such as Schmeckebier and Eastin's Government Publications and Their Use (AG13), Morehead's Introduction to United States Public Documents (1AG5), or Boyd and Rips' United States Government Publications (AG9).

8-9:   Look at the "List of Government Authors" in the front, which lists the "issuing agencies" and the SuDocs classification numbers. Not all agency headings will

appear in all issues, only those which are used in that issue.

8-10:   Health and Human Services Department, Housing and Urban Development Department, Urban Mass Transportation Administration, Labor Department, etc. (January 1983 issue.)

8-11:   Currently there is subject access in two ways, through the subject index (which uses Library of Congress subject headings) and the title keyword index. (For example, both "Medicare" and "crime" can be found in the subject heading index and in the title keyword index in the January 1983 issue.)

8-12:   For example, subject headings from the January 1983 issue which might be relevant are: air pollution, conservation of natural resources, energy conservation, energy development, environmental protection, natural resources, etc. Similarly, terms listed in the title keyword index include air, conservation, environment, natural, etc.

8-13:   Yes on both. See the answer to #8-6.

8-14:   The index only cumulates; presently semi-annually and annually. The index has been cumulated again on a 10-year basis (decennial), for 1941-50 and 1951-60 (see Sheehy annotation), and on a five-year basis for 1961-65 (in 2 vols.) and for 1966-70 (in 2 vols.).

    The subject entries from these indexes, plus some original indexing, have been merged into the Cumulative Subject Index to the Monthly Catalog (Sheehy AG26), for 1900-71, published by the Carrollton Press (a commercial, not a government publisher).

    Also, according to the Sheehy annotation for the Monthly Catalog, personal author indexes have been published by Pierian Press, covering 1941-50, 1951-60, 1961-65, 1966-70 (matching the Monthly Catalog's own cumulations). These provide author access for those years prior to 1970 when the Monthly Catalog itself had few if any personal author names indexed (see answer to #8-6).

8-15:   Hearings, bills, documents, reports, etc., as part of the official business of the government, would be printed/ published by the U.S. GPO and should be listed in the Monthly Catalog, although they would not necessarily be offered for sale by the GPO.

The two ways in which you can locate material in the Monthly Catalog are directly under the issuing agency (if you know what it is) in the main part of the catalog, or through the various indexes (author, title, subject, etc.). With this particular item, the name of the issuing agency is not clear, so it would be better to use the index; you have a title (Antitrust Equal Enforcement Act) and a subject (antitrust).

8-16:   House and Senate committee hearings, etc., are found in the SuDocs classification "Y" at the end of the classification, and you could look through all of those till you come to "United States. Congress. House," then "Committee on Education and Labor," then the subcommittee for which you are searching, then the particular hearing for which you are searching.

Or you could go to the indexes. The title index under the name of the Act ("Antitrust....") or the subject index (antitrust) should give you the item number (82-24917, to the right) for the citation which is on p. 300. The document is 681 pages.

No price is given, and there is no "for sale" statement in the entry. See "How to Order Publications" at the front of the issue, which tells you that, if not for sale, Congressional publications may be obtained from the responsible committee, etc. If you wished to get a copy of this item, you could not get it through the Superintendent of Documents. You would have to apply to the Committee on Education and Labor of the U.S. House of Representatives, or perhaps write to your congressman.

The letters and numbers immediately above the entry (Y 4.J 89/2:J-97-60) are the SuDocs classification number (see answer to #8-6).

8-17:   The black dot indicates that the publication has been or will be sent to depository libraries, and can therefore be examined in such a library. (Item 1042 following the black dot is a category number for document librarians requesting from the Superintendent of Documents.)

8-18:   See the ALA Glossary, or the guides to government publications noted in #8-8 (such as Morehead's Introduction to United States Public Documents). See also p. D 1 of the October 1982 issue of the Monthly Catalog ("List of Depository Libraries as of September 1982"

with paragraph of explanation).

8-19:   This document would be listed in the 1970 volume of the Monthly Catalog. Remember that the Monthly Catalog has changed over the years in terms of access, and to some extent in terms of the information in the entries, and you will need to check out some things in the front matter of whatever issue or volume you are using.

The cumulated index for 1970 (under "Taos Indian Blue Lake area land conveyances, hearings") sends you to item 16064 (in the November 1970, issue). The issuing agency is Congress--Senate--Interior and Insular Affairs Committee. The Senate bill was number 750 and the House of Representatives bill was number 471. No price is given, and there is no star to indicate that the item was for sale by the Superintendent of Documents. The dagger at the end of the listing indicates that distribution was made by the issuing agency (Congress, Senate, Interior and Insular Affairs Committee). By now, however, it is probably no longer available. You could, however, locate it in a depository library as the listing has a black dot. See #8-17 and #8-18.

This document could also be found through the Cumulative Subject Index to the Monthly Catalog of U.S. Government Publications 1900-71 (see answer to #8-14). The hearings are listed under "Taos Indians, Blue Lake, hearings." The notation "(70) 16064" refers you to entry or item number 16064 in the 1970 volume of the Monthly Catalog.

8-20:   See the Decennial Cumulative Index to the Monthly Catalog, for 1951-60 (see answer to #8-14), under "Bibliography--Indians--books for Indian schools." The bibliography of books for Indian schools was published in 1953 (item number 11197 of that year). Other references are given under "Indian schools--suggested books," including two more book lists (1955 and 1959).

8-21:   The Sheehy annotation for the Monthly Catalog notes that from 1951-60 a semiannual "directory" of such publications was published; from 1961-, this list was published annually as the February issue of the Monthly Catalog. The updating information about the Monthly Catalog in the Sheehy 1st Supplement (item 1AG10) shows that since 1977, a separate "Serials Supplement" has been published in the spring.

The Serials Supplement is arranged by issuing agency, as is the Monthly Catalog itself, so you need to use the title index or the title keyword index. In the 1983 Serials Supplement, both the title index (under Antarctic Journal...) and the title keyword index (Antarctic) refer you to entry #83-1686 in the citations (p. 243-4) which tells you that the subscription price is $13.00/year, issued quarterly.

8-22:   The Monthly Catalog lists, each month, only those items published during that period--as does CBI, BPR, etc. It does not attempt to list each month all publications available or in print as of that date. There is no published complete list of all "in print" government publications.

See the "General Information" section in the front of a recent Monthly Catalog issue for information on other similar sources. The Government Publications Office now makes available, on microfiche only, the GPO Sales Publications Reference File (PRF), which serves as an "in print" list for those publications sold by the Superintendent of Documents. It gives current prices and availability for all items, and tells what has recently gone out of stock. It has many accesses or approaches to the materials: author, title, subject, keywords and phrases, agency series/report numbers, GPO stock numbers, and SuDocs classification numbers. According to the 1983 Monthly Catalog, the PRF is issued on a bi-monthly subscription basis.

Also noted are the 250+ "subject bibliographies" put out by the GPO (Sheehy 2AG10), of publications available on single subjects or fields of interest. Examples of subjects covered are: Indians, home economics, education, national parks, consumer information, Library of Congress, census, maps, geology, plants, etc. The subject bibliographies and a Subject Bibliography Index are free from the GPO.

8-23:   This information could be found in Ulrich's, or in the GPO's "Serial Supplement" issue (see #8-21). As of 1982, the Monthly Catalog (including annual indexes) costs $90.00/year.

8-24:   Again, see the "General Information" section in the front of a recent issue of the Monthly Catalog for other similar publications. Listed there are two free publications from the Superintendent of Documents: U.S. Government Books (quarterly, with illustrations and annotations; for best-selling publications) and New Books (bi-monthly listing of all new sales publications received by the Superintendent of Documents). Look at sample issues of these lists if possible.

8-25:   See Sheehy. To 1895 (the title varies somewhat over the years, and it has not always been as well indexed as it is now.)

8-26:   Ames, Poore, Document Catalog--the next sources on your list to examine.

8-27:   Poore: 1774-1881
Ames: 1881-1893
Document Catalog: 1893-1940
Monthly Catalog: 1895-date.
The Document Catalog and Monthly Catalog overlap for most of the publication of the Document Catalog.

8-28:   Basically, the Document Catalog is a more detailed, complete, permanent record for that period. According to the Sheehy annotation, it gives "full catalog information" and includes a large amount of "analysis" or specific detail on publications. It is a full dictionary catalog, with author (personal and government), subject and some title access.

The Monthly Catalog for that period was basically an ordering list, without as complete access or information about the publications. The Document Catalog was discontinued in 1947 (with coverage ending with 1940), and the Monthly Catalog was improved and expanded to take on some of the features of the Document Catalog and to become a single permanent record of publications.

8-29:   The Document Catalog and Monthly Catalog both cover the period. Since you want broad coverage on the subject of "Children," the Document Catalog would be the best source, as all entries on this subject are brought together in that source; in the Monthly Catalog (or the Cumulative Subject Index to it) you would have to refer constantly from index references to the entries in monthly issues. The specific pamphlet titled "Campaign against Malnutrition" is in the Document Catalog, vol. 16, 1921-23, p. 380 under "Children"--National Child Health Council; in the Monthly Catalog July 1923-June 1924, p. 267, under Public Health Service. The Monthly Catalog gives price (5¢), which would have been important at the time of publication although it is not now.

8-30: In scope, both attempt to give comprehensive coverage of the government documents or publications of the periods covered. The main difference is in arrangement. Poore is arranged chronologically, Ames by subject. The arrangement of Ames by subject is not so clear from the Sheehy annotation and can better be seen in the source itself --the middle column of entries on each page is the basic arrangement of the source, alphabetically by keyword (see #7-57 on keyword entries).

8-31: The index in Poore generally includes subjects (basically catchword or keyword subjects taken from the titles), some authors, names of people and places, etc. The index appears useful but on experience it is found to be incomplete (see Sheehy annotation, AG20). However, insofar as it goes, the access in Poore is chronological, subject and author.

8-32: The access in Poore is chronological, subject (keyword and therefore possibly title to some extent), and author/name (personal).

The main access in Ames is subject (keyword and therefore possibly title to some extent) with author/name (personal) index.

Document Catalog has author (government and personal), some title, and subject access in one alphabetical (dictionary) arrangement.

Monthly Catalog has had main access by issuing agency (government author), with subject and some personal name indexes (and as of the 1970's, author, title and subject index).

Although the basic arrangements of all of the sources differ, the accesses are generally the same: subject and author. The differences, and the difficulties, are in the extent of the indexing for specific subjects and names. This problem can best be appreciated in continued use of the sources.

8-33: Evans' American Bibliography was also arranged chronologically. See #2b-62 and 2b-63 on the uses of the chronological arrangement. With government publications, dates are the one fact you may know (as opposed to author and title) for a historical document. The citation for the Declaration of Independence is found in Poore, vol. 1, p. 3. You could find it directly under the date, which you would presumably know: July 4, 1776. The citation in Poore shows the document

to be published in Charters and Constitutions, vol. 1, pp. 3-6, and the original draft and document itself to be in the Department of State at Washington, D.C.

8-34: Greely covers 1789-1817, falling within the Poore period. Greely's full title is "Public Documents of the first 14 Congresses, 1789-1817. Papers relating to early Congressional Documents." Greely covers only publications and documents issued by Congress; Poore has a broader scope, including publications from departments and bureaus, etc., as well.

8-35: The date, 1883, would lead you to Ames for the citation, where you would look under Hawaii or under volcanoes as the keyword subject. Ames shows that the information on the volcanoes of Hawaii appears in the Report of the Director of the Geological Survey, and in the Report of the Secretary of the Interior for 1883. The column on the right indicates that these were published as a House Executive Document of the 48th Congress, 1st session, vol. 12; document no. 1, pt. 5, vol. 3, p. 75-219, with 29 plates and 3 figures.

8-36: Only if you knew the personal author (C.E. Dutton) of the report, since the index in Ames is personal author names only.

8-37: It helps to know generally that John Adams lived from 1735-1826 and was the second president of the United States from 1797-1801. This puts the original Inaugural Address within the Poore period. (Otherwise you would simply have to start from, presumably, the beginning with Poore and work forward in time till you found it.) If you knew specifically that Adams was president from 1797, you could go directly to that date in Poore, otherwise you would go to the index under "Adams, John" or "Inaugural addresses and messages-- Adams, John" which would direct you to p. 36. On p. 36, second column, you find that Adams' Inaugural Address was first published in the Journal of the Senate, pp. vii-xvi, and the contents of the address are listed in the citation in Poore's, so it is not necessary to find the address itself to answer that part of the question.

8-38: For slavery preceding the Civil War (1861-65), the material would be listed in Poore which covers that period.

Your approach here would be subject so you would go to the index, which has about three columns of references on the subject "slavery."

8-39:   See ALA Glossary; but better yet see Sheehy, 9th ed., p. 193, comments on "The Serial set" under "Catalogs and Indexes." Sheehy tells you that each bound volume of the set is given a serial number, and it is necessary to use the Checklist of U.S. Public Documents (AG23), for 1789-1909, the Document Catalog (AG24), for 1895-1940, and the Numerical Lists and Schedule of Volumes (AG27), for 1933/34-, to find the serial volume number for specific documents. (A rather expensive "merging" of these various sources with an extensive subject and keyword approach was published in the late 1970's: the CIS U.S. Serial Set Index, see Sheehy 1AG7.)

8-40:   The report on volcanoes in Hawaii was published as House Executive document no. 1 of the 48th Congress, 1st session (see answer to #8-35). You need to find the number of the bound volume of the Serial set in which this is located. Sheehy tells you what sources to use to find this number (see answer to #8-39). The 48th Congress falls within the period of 1789-1909 covered by the Checklist of U.S. Public Documents. (See Sheehy under "The Serial set" or the annotation to the Checklist, AG23.) Look in the Checklist for 48th Congress, 1st session, which appears on p. 70, and then for House Executive Documents, in the middle of the page, then for no. 1, pt. 5, vol. 3; the serial number given in the left column is 2192. Then, if your library has a complete set of the "Congressional edition" of the Serial set, you would look in it for volume number 2192, in which (p. 75-219) you should find the report on volcanoes in Hawaii.

8-41:   You could begin by finding the date of Custer's last stand, which would narrow your search to that general period of time. (American College Dictionary lists Custer, George Armstrong, 1839-76; assuming his last stand to be the date of his death, you could begin with 1876; or you could go on to an encyclopedia for further information--Columbia one-volume encyclopedia lists, under Custer, George Armstrong, that his final battle and death was in 1876 at Little Bighorn river in Montana.)
        The date then falls within Poore,

so you can search in the index under Custer, George Armstrong. There are two references, one of which (1084) is to a resolution to tender condolences to his family. The other (1081) leads you to p. 1081 where you have to search carefully through all the citations until you find: "Message on hostilities of the Sioux Indians. President U.S. Grant. Senate Ex. Docs, no. 81, 44th Cong., 1st sess. Transmitting information in regard to the hostile demonstrations of the Sioux Indians and the disaster to the forces under Gen. Custer. July 13, 1876/6p."
        This information tells you that the report was published as a Senate document ("Senate Ex. Doc., no. 81") of the 44th Congress, 1st session, and as such it should be found in the "Serial set" (see #8-39).
        To locate the report in the Serial set, you turn again to the Checklist (see #8-39), under 44th Congress, 1st session (p. 55) to find Senate Executive document no. 81 (S.ex.docs/1-94) which is in volume #1664 of the Serial set. Then, of course, you have to find volume 1664 of the Serial set and look through it for document no. 81 which should be the report on Custer's last stand.

8-42:   See #8-21 for information on how these are handled in the Monthly Catalog. The next source on your list, the Index to U.S. Government Periodicals, also covers periodicals published by the U.S. government; it is an index to the articles contained within them, similar to Readers' Guide.

8-43:   The Index to U.S. Government Periodicals is pubished by Infordata International Inc. (a commercial, not a government publisher). It is published quarterly with an annual cumulation. The list of periodicals included varies somewhat and there is no clear statement of how they are selected, other than being those items which are considered to be of "lasting research and reference value." (See Sheehy 1AE48, or the source itself.)

8-44:   See, for example, in the July-September 1982 issue of the Index to U.S. Government Periodicals, under the subject heading "inflation," there are several articles listed.

8-45:   According to Sheehy, it is published monthly with quarterly cumulations (CJ83) and annual cumulations (CJ84).

The indexes _only_ are cumulated again on a larger basis: 1970-1974 (1CJ56) and 1975-1978 (2CJ48). It is published by the Congressional Information Service, which is a commercial publisher, not a government publisher; this is not made clear in the Sheehy annotation.

8-46:   The full title to the CIS Index indicates that it is actually quite limited in the type of publications it covers: publications of the United States _Congress_ only (these are, as the Sheehy annotation indicates, committee hearings, committee prints, House and Senate documents, House and Senate reports, House and Senate miscellaneous publications, Senate executive reports, Senate executive documents). This is much more limited in scope than the Monthly Catalog, but the extent of the information given for those publications it does cover is much greater than that provided by the Monthly Catalog.

8-47:   On abstracts, see #7-47. The existence of abstracts in the entries means that, in addition to information for locating the publications themselves, you can also get some _information_ from the CIS Index, as you were often able to do through the New York Times Index (see #7-77). See, for example, in the 1982 annual cumulation of CIS (Abstract volume, p. 5), the citation for item #H141-17: Hearings on "Cutting the Minimum Social Security Benefit: Unneeded Savings and Hidden Costs." Specifically given are the dates of the hearings, and lists of names (and titles) of witnesses, with some brief statement of the contents of their testimony.

8-48:   The index has a reference, to the abstract, under "Older Americans Act," then "Extension and Revision." The citation is located on p. 596 of the abstracts volume (1982 cumulation). The CIS "accession number" or item number for this publication is "S141-6." The accession number is explained in the front of the CIS Index volumes. The "S" stands for "Senate," the 14 for the Senate's Special Committee on Aging, and the 1 for "hearings." The title of the publication is given as "Older Americans Act." The item is free. The black dot and the reference "item 1009" signify availability to a depository library (see #8-17). Names of witnesses at the hearing are listed, along with a very brief abstract of the discussion.

8-49:   As in the Monthly Catalog, you can ap-

proach this problem in CIS Index either through the subject index, with specific headings, or through the basic arrangement of the abstracts volume itself. Both the Senate and the House of Representatives have committees dealing with problems of the aged or elderly, and these can be located through an understanding of the CIS accession number system. As noted in the answer to the preceding question, "14" is the number for the Senate Special Committee on Aging, so the section S14 of the abstracts would contain material on this subject. Similarly the section H14 would contain material on this subject, from the House of Representatives. Specific subject headings which you might find in the index would be: aged and aging, older Americans, home health services, day care programs, hospital and nursing homes, etc.

8-50:   The CIS Index began in 1970, so it would cover this. In the 1970-74 cumulated index, under "Indian claims--Taos Pueblo Indians, Blue Lake watershed land claims," you can find two 1970 references: 70 S441-27; 70 S443-92. You must then go to the cumulated volume for 1970, abstracts, and look for the accession number or item number S441-27. ("S44" stands for Senate Interior and Insular Affairs Committee.) Witnesses listed are Walter J. Hickel, Secretary of the Interior, Clinton Anderson, Senator from New Mexico, various members of the Taos Pueblo Indian tribe, etc., and some brief indication is given of their statements. The second reference, 70 S443-92, is for the report (3 in S443 stands for report) recommending passage of the House of Representatives bill (H.R. 471) restoring the land to the Taos Indians. (The CIS 1970-74 cumulated index has a reference under "Blue Lake, New Mexico" to an item from the House of Representatives; there is nothing in the index under "Taos.")

8-51:   Subject access is most generally useful. Personal name or author is not always known. Subject access is similar to title access.

8-52:   It is a highly selective list of government publications, arranged by broad subject categories, attempting to indicate--through selection, categorization, and annotation--some of the wealth of comparatively inexpensive, authoritative information available to the general public through publications of the U.S. government. Newsome is not truly a "guide" in the sense that it guides one through the mass of bibliographic apparatus dealing with government publications, as do Schmeckebier and Eastin, and Morehead, for example (see #8-8), although Newsome does have some helpful introductory information about acquiring government publications.

8-53: Major topics are: Accidents, aging, agriculture, arts ... economics, education, family living, health, housing, etc. There is a more specific subject index.

8-54: See the subject index in Newsome, under "Spanish Americans--bilingual preschool materials" (item #1227, on p. 232), for example.

8-55: Newsome has a title index, through which you can locate the complete citation for "Living with Change," which was published in 1976, is seven pages long, illustrated, and distributed by the Office of Governmental and Public Affairs, U.S. Dept. of Agriculture.

8-56: In one of the Subject Bibliographies from the GPO (see #8-22), such as Air Pollution or Solar Energy.

8-57: You would look in Sheehy, of course, in the section on "Government Publications" (AG), under "United States," then under either "Guides" and/or "Bibliographies." Several are listed. A source very similar in scope and arrangement to Newsome is Leidy's A Popular Guide to Government Publications (AG11, 1AG4), first published in 1956 and since up-dated in several new editions. Another title is Jackson's Subject Guide to Major United States Government Publications (AG10), published in 1968 so somewhat old by now, but because it has concentrated on titles "of permanent importance" it can still be useful. Sheehy lists several other similar subject guides. You could also look in those books which discuss and describe government publications, such as Schmeckebier and Eastin or Morehead (see #8-8), for other guides.

8-58: Monthly Checklist of State Publications (Sheehy AG47), the next title on your list. There are also lists published for individual states, although these are not given in Sheehy. Sheehy does list an annotated bibliography of state publications, Parish's State Government Ref-

erence Publications (1AG14).

8-59: It is published by the Library of Congress. The limitation is that only those publications received by LC are listed, therefore its comprehensiveness is dependent upon the cooperation of various State agencies (see introduction to a recent issue).

8-60: By state, and then by issuing agency.

8-61: For example, reports and bulletins from agriculture experiment stations and extension services. Statistics and surveys. Publications of state universities and colleges.

Section 9

BIBLIOGRAPHIC SOURCES FOR DISSERTATIONS AND THESES

Questions #9/1--9/23

In addition to the major categories of serial publications and government publications, there are several other types or forms of published material for which our bibliographic control has been rather erratic and incomplete. These include pamphlets, dissertations, microfilms, manuscripts, reprints, maps, music scores, and if we want to extend our idea of bibliographic control or coverage beyond printed publications, we can include also materials such as films, filmstrips, slides, transparencies, recordings and tapes. Coverage of some of these materials is given in the supplementary sources for the Library of Congress/National Union Catalogs in Section 4.
    The next set of sources to examine attempts to fill in a gap of bibliographic coverage for a specific type of publication--dissertations and theses:

  Dissertation Abstracts International (AH14/15, 1AH5)
  American Doctoral Dissertations (AH13)
  Comprehensive Dissertation Index (AH10)
  Masters Abstracts (AH18)

9-1   What are dissertations and theses?

9-2   Dissertations and/or theses are rarely listed in trade bibliographies. In fact dissertations and/or theses are rarely actually published. At one time it was considered an important part of a dissertation to have it published and the research it reported therefore available. However, such material is not commercially saleable, and the publication is therefore costly to the student, as well as costly to the libraries which would have to acquire and process hundreds of thousands of dissertations. The first source to examine is Dissertation Abstracts International. What is the full title of this source?

9-3   What are "abstracts?" How does Dissertation Abstracts International attempt to meet the problem of availability of dissertation research?

9-4   What is the scope of Dissertation Abstracts International? Does it list all dissertations? Is it limited to dissertations from U.S. universities? Does it include master's theses?

9-5   What is the arrangement of Dissertation Abstracts International?

9-6   How long has it been published? Does it cumulate?

9-7   Is there any complete listing of doctoral dissertations from U.S. universities?

9-8   American Doctoral Dissertations is also published by University Microfilms International, the same
        company which publishes Dissertation Abstracts International. (For some time it was published as
        the last issue of Dissertation Abstracts International, and for those years would probably be bound
        in with the final or index volume.) How is American Doctoral Dissertations arranged? Is it the
        same as Dissertation Abstracts International?

9-9   How is American Doctoral Dissertations compiled?

9-10   Dissertation Abstracts International and American Doctoral Dissertations have been published on a
        regular basis and cumulated over many years. A comparatively recent bibliographic source, the
        Comprehensive Dissertation Index, also published by University Microfilms, combines in one set
        much of the retrospective information in both DAI and ADD. What is the coverage or scope of the
        Comprehensive Dissertation Index?

9-11   What is the arrangement of the Comprehensive Dissertation Index?

9-12   The coverage of Comprehensive Dissertation Index is more comprehensive than that of Dissertation
        Abstracts International, and the arrangement is similar. Why then would one need to use DAI at
        all? What does DAI have which CDI doesn't?

9-13   Using Comprehensive Dissertation Index, can you locate the title of Margaret Mead's doctoral dis-
        sertation? When and where did she receive her degree? Where did the compilers of the CDI get
        their information?

9-14   Again using the Comprehensive Dissertation Index, how would you go about locating titles of doc-
        toral dissertations which might have been done on the effects of using media with elementary school
        children? (Do not attempt the major search which might be necessary to answer this question; just
        note down how you would go about it. You might try to find one specific example.)

9-15   If you wanted to know what dissertations had been completed and accepted recently (that is, in
        the past year or two) in the field of English literature, how would you go about it?

9-16   If you wanted to know if a dissertation had been completed and accepted recently on the subject of
        Samuel Taylor Coleridge (English poet), how would you find out?

9-17   A dissertation on Coleridge's "animism" was listed in Dissertation Abstracts International in 1980.
        What university granted the degree? In what year? Which particular poems by Coleridge has the
        author used to examine the poet's mysticism and superstition? How do you obtain a copy of the
        dissertation?

9-18   If you wanted to know if any dissertations had ever been done on specific aspects of Coleridge's
        poetry, how would you find out?

9-19   Could you find a citation for a doctoral dissertation by a specific person?

9-20   How would you go about finding a bibliography of dissertations on a particular subject? For example, is there a bibliography of doctoral dissertations on Asian-Americans or Asians in America?

9-21   Does Dissertation Abstracts International include master's theses? Where can you look to find citations for master's theses?

9-22   How does Masters Abstracts compare to Dissertation Abstracts International? (Use Sheehy if the source itself is not available to you.)

9-23   Masters Abstracts is, so far, a highly selective list of master's theses. How can you find a more comprehensive list of master's theses on the subject of library science?

BIBLIOGRAPHIC SOURCES FOR DISSERTATIONS AND THESES

Answers #9/1--9/23

9-1:   Since neither term is found in the 1983 edition of the ALA Glossary, you would need to turn to a dictionary. See also Sheehy, 9th ed., p. 203. Dissertations and theses are presumably based on original investigation and research; they therefore represent much of the current, new research coming out of our universities, and are primarily sources of information on such research.

9-2:   Dissertation Abstracts International; abstracts of dissertations available on microfilm or as xerographic reproductions.

9-3:   Abstracts, see the ALA Glossary or #7-47. DAI allows the user, through reading the abstract, to decide if he actually needs or wants a copy of the dissertation; he or the library can then get a microform copy or a xerographic reproduction from the microfilm. It is a kind of publishing "on demand." (A copy could also be obtained through inter-library loan, of course.)

9-4:   DAI lists those abstracts which are released to University Microfilms International (most of which are available from University Microfilms International on microfilm). It is not, therefore, a complete listing, although more and more universities are participating in the program and coverage is extensive. Since 1969, when the title changed from Dissertation Abstracts to Dissertation Abstracts International, the scope was extended to include in Section C European universities as well as those in the U.S. and Canada. No master's theses are included. (See introductory material in recent issues.)

9-5:   It is published in three sections: A, Humanities and Social Sciences; B, Sciences and Engineering; C, European Abstracts. Each section is divided into subject categories (such as education, genetics, folklore, women's studies, etc.). The entries and abstracts for each dis-

sertation are given under the appropriate subject category. Currently, there is a keyword title index and an author index in each issue.

9-6:   DAI has been published since 1938 (with some title changes; see Sheehy). The abstracts themselves do not cumulate. The type of indexes and the cumulation pattern for them has varied over the years. Currently only the author indexes cumulate, annually. (An annual subject approach is now available through the Comprehensive Dissertation Index which will be examined later.) DAI has a Retrospective Index (Sheehy AH15) for vols. 1-29 (1938-68), with subject and author access.

9-7:   American Doctoral Dissertations (formerly titled Index to American Doctoral Dissertations, and formerly published as part of Dissertation Abstracts).

9-8:   It is arranged by broad subject categories (fine arts, psychology, etc.) with only an author index. It does not have a specific keyword subject index as Dissertation Abstracts International does.

9-9:   It is compiled from commencement programs issued by the universities and is therefore somewhat dependent upon the cooperation of these universities. See Introduction to the source itself.

9-10:   According to Sheehy, the CDI attempts to list all dissertations accepted at U.S. universities, plus some Canadian and foreign. It covers the period 1861-1972 in one set, with annual supplements from 1973+. (There was a five year cumulation for 1973-1977.)

9-11:   By subject with an author index. The subject arrangement is in broad subjects (chemistry, engineering, psychology, education, language and literature, etc.), then alphabetically by keywords from the titles of the dissertations. Full citations are in both the

141

subject volumes and the author index.

9-12:   Abstracts of the dissertations. See #9-3.

9-13:   You have the name of the author. The author index of the basic set of CDI (1861-1972) is in vols. 33-37. Margaret Mead is listed (alphabetically) in vol. 36, p. 2. The title of her dissertation was: "An Inquiry into the Question of Cultural Stability in Polynesia." She received her Ph.D. in 1928 from Columbia University. The code "L1928, p. 77" indicates that the compilers of CDI got their information from the Library of Congress publication, A List of American Doctoral Dissertations Printed in 1912-1932 (Sheehy, AH11). The codes used for CDI sources are explained on p. xviii-xx of vol. 36. All of this information is found in the author index. You could also find this information in vol. 17 (social sciences).

9-14:   This is a subject search, and the broad subject would appear to be education. In the basic set, there are five volumes (v. 20-24) covering education. The keyword "media" appears in vol. 22, listing four pages of fine print of the titles which include the word "media." You must scan all these titles to find those which mention elementary school children. An example (vol. 22, p. 583, lower right corner): "Some Effects of Concentrated Media on Selected Students at the Brookside Elementary School in Springville, Utah" by Edmund Baker Lambert (Ed.D., 1971, Brigham Young University). Another approach would be the keyword "elementary" (55 pages!). And of course you would have to follow the same procedure for the 1973-77 set, and for all the annual volumes since then.

9-15:   Both the Comprehensive Dissertation Index and American Doctoral Dissertations are published only annually, so neither are as current and up-to-date as the Dissertation Abstracts International for "recent" dissertations. (American Doctoral Dissertations is perhaps a year or more behind CDI in coverage.)
          Look in each monthly issue of DAI for the past year, under the general broad heading of "Literature," then "English." This would give you most of the dissertations for that period. You could do the same for DAI for the previous year, or use CDI for that year if available.

9-16.   Again, "monthly" would probably rule out

using the Comprehensive Dissertation Index or American Doctoral Dissertations, so you would need to go to DAI.
          In DAI, use the specific subject (keyword) index, looking under Coleridge, looking through as many issues as necessary to find what you want.

9-17:   In DAI, using the keyword indexes in Section A for each month of 1980 (or a cumulative keyword index for the year if available), check under Coleridge for the title, then refer back to the complete listing. The title (found in DAI, June 1980) is "The Plenitude of Belief: Animism in Coleridge's Notebooks and Poetry," by Patricia Smith Yager. The degree was granted in 1979 at Yale University. The abstract of the dissertation indicates that the author has used Coleridge's "Frost at Midnight," "The Nightingale," "The Wanderings of Cain."
          A microform or xerographic copy could be ordered from University Microfilms International (publishers of DAI). The Demand Copies Price List in the front of the issue tells you the price for those copies in 1980; you would need to refer to a more recent issue for current prices. The order number is 8012512.
          Similar information can be found in the Comprehensive Dissertation Index 1980 annual supplement (vol. 4, "Languages and Literature," under "Coleridge," p. 335), but since that source does not give you the abstract, the information about the poems used by the author cannot be found there. For that information, you must use DAI which has the abstract. CDI 1980 does tell you, however, that the citation and the abstract can be found in DAI 40/12A, p. 6296.

9-18:   Here you would want to use the Comprehensive Dissertation Index. You would look under the subject: Language and Literature, then Coleridge as the keyword, which you would find in vol. 29 of the basic set, covering 1861-1972. There are about 1½ pages of entries to scan. You would also need to look, in the same way, at the five-year cumulation and the annual supplements following the basic set, and possibly the most current issues of Dissertation Abstracts International for the most recent items.
          After you had found the listings in CDI, if you wanted to investigate any of these dissertations further by looking at the abstracts, you would have to refer back to their listings in Dis-

sertation Abstracts International. Not all of the dissertations listed in CDI would also be found in DAI, however.

If you did not have access to CDI in your library, you could use the Retrospective Index of DAI (see answer to #9-6) as a quick way of finding out about at least those dissertations listed in DAI (under Literature, then using Coleridge as a keyword).

9-19:   Yes, by using the Comprehensive Dissertation Index as you did for Margaret Mead in #9-13; or by looking in the Retrospective Index to DAI, author volume; and/or by searching in each annual volume of American Doctoral Dissertations in the author index.

9-20:   Use Sheehy. Sheehy, p. 203, 9th edition, notes: "For lists of dissertations --both completed and in progress--in particular subjects, see under subjects." Looking under "Asian Americans" in the index to Sheehy (basic volume) does not give you a reference to where lists of dissertations on this subject can be found; it does list several specific titles with "Asian" as the keyword or first word, and you could search out all of those on the chance that one might be what you want. Using another subject approach, looking in the Sheehy index under "minorities," you are referred to "race relations and minorities," and this does lead you to the section in Sheehy, under Social Sciences--Sociology, titled "Race Relations and Minorities," then under "Asian-Americans," where the first item listed (CC139) is a bibliography titled Asians in America: A Bibliography of Master's Theses and Doctoral Dissertations, compiled by William Wong Lum. (A major revision of this title is listed in the Sheehy first supplement, 1CC150.) This particular title is one which was listed in the Sheehy index under "Asian" as a title, but you could not know from what is given in the index that it covered dissertations.

Sheehy also lists, in the section covering dissertations in general, a bibliography of bibliographies for dissertations (item 1AH4, A Guide to Theses and Dissertations by Michael Reynolds) which, if available, would be helpful in locating more possible titles.

9-21:   Masters theses are not included in DAI (see #9-4). A source which does list them is Masters Abstracts (Sheehy AH18).

9-22:   The purpose of both sources is the same.

Both are published by University Microfilms International. Masters Abstracts is more selective (see Introduction to source). The arrangement is similar, basically by subject, but without quite as much indexing as there is in DAI.

9-23:   Follow the same procedure as in #9-20. See Sheehy under AH section (Dissertations), which lists Black's Guide to Lists of Masters Theses (AH17). Also see Sheehy under subject: Librarianship and Library Resources (AB)-- General Works--bibliography--dissertations.

BIBLIOGRAPHIC RECORDS FOR OTHER COUNTRIES--GREAT BRITAIN, FRANCE, GERMANY

Questions #10/1--10/88

You have been examining the national bibliographic records for the United States, plus various supplementary sources covering specific types of publications or materials. Presumably, a national bibliography or bibliographic record would include only publications of that nation or country; since it is necessary to look at so many different and varied sources to get coverage for the U.S., the result is a conglomeration of bibliographic publications serving many purposes.

10-1   Of those sources you have looked at so far, which ones include publications other than those published in the United States? Which ones include publications from other countries, foreign language as well as English language?
>   Book trade sources: BIP, WR/BPR, CBI?
>   Retrospective: Sabin, Evans, Shaw/Shoemaker, Checklist, Kelly, Roorbach, American Catalogue?
>   LC/NUC?
>   Serial/periodical lists: Ulrich's, Ayer's?
>   Serial union lists: ULS, NST, Gregory, Brigham?
>   Periodical indexes: Readers' Guide, etc.?
>   Government publications?

This final set of sources will give you an opportunity to experiment with some foreign language bibliographic material and to test your facility at finding your way about new bibliographic territory. Your facility in dealing with the bibliographic sources for a foreign country, especially in a language which you do not know, should be based on your familiarity with the U.S. bibliographic sources. The best organization of the material is surprisingly similar from country to country, and it is easy to feel your way bibliographically through a language you do not know since you are not concerned with textual material but rather in looking for basic guidelines, patterns, etc. Looking at the foreign bibliographies is also a useful way to review the organization of bibliographic control in the United States.

10-2   Think carefully about all the sources you have examined so far (using your review charts, if you made them, from each section). What kinds of organizational patterns appear again and again? What kind of information would you look for in foreign bibliographic sources?

The sources to examine in this section will cover three countries (Great Britain, France and Germany) and two languages besides English (French and German). The first set is from Great Britain, as follows:

Great Britain
>   British Books in Print (AA673)
>   Whitaker's Cumulative Book List (AA668/9)
>   British National Bibliography (AA667, 1AA125)
>   Pollard and Redgrave: Short-title Catalogue (AA647, 1AA123)
>   Wing: Short-title Catalogue (AA660/661)
>   British Library, General Catalogue of Printed Books (AA100/101, 1AA23, 2AA12, 2AA13)

10-3   Beginning with the British sources lets you practice without a language handicap. What was the first specific source or set of sources which you examined for the U.S. bibliographic records? If a similar source existed for British books, would you expect it to have a similar title? Does a similar source exist for British books?

10-4   Is British Books in Print exactly the same as the U.S. BIP? Does it also have access by publisher and by subject as BIP does?

10-5   Who publishes British Books in Print?

10-6   If you wanted to purchase an Urdu dictionary (English-Urdu), published in Great Britain, what could you find?

10-7   One of the sources serving as a supplement to BIP is Paperbound Books in Print, limited to paperback books but serving essentially the same purpose otherwise as BIP. Is there a similar source for British paperbacks?

10-8   British Books in Print, like BIP, is published annually. The second set of sources you examined of the U.S. bibliographic records were weekly/monthly listings (Weekly Record and American Book Publishing Record) giving you more current sources of bibliographic information to supplement the annual publication of BIP. These sources are published by Bowker, which also publishes BIP, and they are specifically noted in the introductory material to BIP. Does the Whitaker company publish sources similar in purpose, scope, arrangement, etc., for British books?

10-9   As noted in the previous question, Whitaker's Cumulative List is issued quarterly and annually. How is it arranged? How long has it been published? See the Sheehy annotation and/or go to the source on the shelves.

10-10   Using Whitaker's Cumulative Book List, can you find the title of a book on the history of the classical guitar, by Summerfield, published in England in 1982? Where else, of the sources you have examined so far in this manual, could you expect to find the same information?

10-11   The various publications of J. Whitaker and Sons Ltd.--Bookseller, Whitaker's Cumulative Book List, etc.--are "trade" (i.e., book trade, see Appendix A) lists, compiled by and for the book trade, although useful to librarians. A second current source is the British National Bibliography. The BNB is a true national bibliography, not quite like any of the U.S. sources you have studied previously, and therefore you should look at it carefully and in some detail. What organization is responsible for the publication of the BNB?

10-12   How often is BNB published? How does it cumulate? How long has it been published? (See Sheehy or the source itself.)

10-13   What can you tell briefly about the scope and arrangement of BNB from the title page of a recent cumulated volume?

10-14   As far as <u>arrangement</u> is concerned, what is the BNB similar to in the U.S. bibliographic records?

10-15   The materials listed in the BNB are those items received by the Copyright Receipt Office of the British Library. Does the U.S. have anything similar to this?

10-16   Are there any exceptions to the publication or the material listed in the BNB? How then does the BNB compare in <u>scope</u> to such current U.S. bibliographic records as Weekly Record and BPR?

10-17   What kind of information is given, in the bibliographic citations, about each item listed? How does this compare with other current sources for British publications? What is the basic difference between the BNB listings and the Bookseller/Whitaker Cumulative Book List listings?

10-18   Using the British National Bibliography, can you find the name of the author of a book on birds of Africa, published by Academic Press, in England, in 1982?

10-19   Where can you look, so far, to find information on some books recently published in Great Britain on the subject of occultism?

10-20   What sources do you have, so far, for retrospective searching for British publications? Are there additional retrospective sources you can use (see Sheehy)?

10-21   Other sources give coverage specifically for the very early printed books. Two of these sources, because they represent a somewhat different approach to retrospective bibliographies, should be looked at carefully: Pollard and Redgrave's Short-title Catalogue, and Wing's Short-title Catalogue. What are the full titles for these two sources? When were they published?

10-22   From the titles, what is the primary difference in scope or coverage between the two works?

10-23   Would you expect to find any books printed in America listed in the Pollard and Redgrave STC? Why or why not? What about the Wing STC?

10-24   Why might you think that 1475 was chosen as the beginning date for the Pollard and Redgrave STC? Why was 1640 chosen as the closing date?

10-25   How are these two sources arranged, and what bibliographic information is given in the citations?

10-26   Why are the Wing and the Pollard and Redgrave bibliographies called "Short-title catalogues?" Where might you go to find the "long titles" if necessary?

10-27   Both the Pollard and Redgrave, and Wing STC's give indication of libraries possessing copies. This information is, in fact, the basic purpose behind both bibliographies. The Sheehy annotation for the Wing STC states that it is not a "census of copies." "Census of copies" is not defined in the ALA

Glossary. What would you guess might be meant by that phrase? What other term used so far is it similar to? Why is the Wing STC not a census of copies? Is the Pollard and Redgrave STC a census of copies?

10-28   What can you find in Sheehy which does claim to be a "census" of early printed books?

10-29   Would you expect to find any "ghosts" (see ALA Glossary or #2b-80) in the Pollard and Redgrave STC? in the Wing STC?

10-30   How many editions of Shakespeare's The Tragedy of King Richard the Third are listed in the Pollard and Redgrave STC? The first is listed as published in 1597. What libraries have (had) copies?

10-31   According to the Wing STC, does the Folger Library have a copy of The Lucky Chance by Mrs. Aphra Behn? Are you sure?

10-32   The last source on the list for Great Britain is the General Catalogue of Printed Books of the British Library, or the Library of the British Museum (British Museum Catalogue). What is the British Library?

10-33   The British Library Catalogue is therefore similar to what U.S. source?

10-34   Is the British Library Catalogue just the same as the LC/NUC? Does it serve the same purpose?

10-35   In what way are they similar in scope?

10-36   In what ways are they similar in arrangement?

10-37   Is the catalog of the British Library published on a current, continuing basis as the LC/NUC is? What is the cumulation pattern for the various parts of the catalog?

10-38   What is there which does give current, continuing, frequent coverage of books which are, in effect, added to the British Library?

10-39   Can you find in the British Library Catalogue the entry for A Danish Gambit, a novel by William Butler, published in the 1960's? What is the name of the publisher? How many pages does it have?

10-40   Can you find in the British Library Catalogue Fraser's Magazine for Town and Country? (It was published in London.) When was it published and in how many volumes? Where else might you find the same information? Look there and see if you find the same or any different information from that given in British Library Catalogue.

10-41   Where can you look to find information on serials or periodicals currently published in Great Britain?

10-42   Are there periodical indexes or indexing services for British periodicals?

10-43   From your experience with U.S. bibliography thus far, would you expect there might be a biblio-
        graphic source dealing with British government publications? If so, what is it, by whom is it pub-
        lished? How is it arranged, and how often does it come out?

10-44   Where would you find current ordering information for Keeping Honeybees by Judy Urquhart, pub-
        lished in 1978 in England?

10-45   Eleanor Farjeon (1881-1965) was an English author of many well-known books for children. When was
        her book titled The Starry Floor (verses) first published?

10-46   Where would you look to find what books are in print in Great Britain on urban problems?

        Now move on to the bibliographic records for France. In dealing with these, your problems are com-
        plicated only by the fact that you may be working with an unfamiliar language. If you read French,
        your problems should be minimal. In either case, it would be helpful to find a French-English/English-
        French dictionary to have handy to look up an occasional word which does not seem clear in context.
        The main sources to be examined here are:

            Les Livres de l'Année--Biblio (AA616/617)
            Biblio (AA611)
            Catalogue Général de la Librairie Francaise (Lorenz) (AA609)
            Bibliothèque Nationale, Catalogue Générale ... Auteurs (AA105/106, AA596, 1AA24)

10-47   Is there a bibliographic source for France similar to Books in Print and British Books in Print?
        (See Sheehy.)

10-48   If you follow the same pattern which you used for the U.S. sources and then for the British sources
        at the beginning of this section, you would next look for a current source to supplement the books-
        in-print type of source--one which would give you weekly and/or monthly listings of currently appear-
        ing publications. In the British sources, you found both an official list (British National Bibliography)
        and a list published more unofficially by the book trade (Bookseller and Whitaker's Books of the Month,
        etc.). Can you find, in Sheehy, anything which appears to be similar to either of these lists?

10-49   According to Sheehy, this official list, the "Bibliographie Officielle," section of the Bibliographie de
        la France, is the list of publications received through the "Dépot Légal" (legal deposit). What is
        "legal deposit?" What is the French legal deposit law?

10-50   How is the list of publications within the Bibliographie de la France arranged? (See Sheehy.) Can
        you tell what kind of information is given in the citations?

10-51   Current French lists, then, are the Bibliographie de la France, the official list appearing more or less bimonthly, and Livres-hebdo which includes a trade list and appears weekly. Are there any cumulations of either of these lists?

10-52   The annual cumulations Les Livres de l'Année are listed separately in Sheehy, AA616 and AA617. How far back does this list go, and what is its arrangement according to Sheehy?

10-53   Using Les Livres de l'Année--Biblio for 1979, can you find the author, title, and publisher of a catalog of an exhibition of Joan Ferra Miró's designs held in Paris in 1978-79? Can you find titles of some books about the Congo?

10-54   Prior to the merger with Bibliographie de la France in 1971, Biblio existed as a separate publication (Sheehy AA611) from 1934-70, appearing monthly with annual cumulations, and arranged as is Cumulative Book Index, with author-title-subject in one alphabet. Biblio now serves as a very easily used retrospective source for that period. Using Biblio annual cumulation for 1969, can you find a citation for Exercises Grammaticaux by Clément Bouillon, published in Nancy (France) in 1969? Was this book published as part of a series?

10-55   What retrospective coverage do you have so far for French publications?

10-56   What other retrospective sources exist for the 18th, 19th, and early 20th centuries? See Sheehy.

10-57   Does France have a national library similar to the Library of Congress and the British Library?

10-58   Does the Bibliothèque Nationale publish a catalog?

10-59   How does the Bibliothèque Nationale catalog compare to that of the Library of Congress and that of the British Library?

10-60   Although the Bibliothèque Nationale catalog is now complete, many of the early volumes are now badly out of date (see Sheehy annotation). What other sources can be used to supplement it for coverage of French publications?

10-61   Does the Bibliothèque Nationale have a subject access? What retrospective subject access is there for French publications?

10-62   What is a characteristic of the Bibliotheque Nationale catalog which limits its use?

10-63   Pontus de Tyard wrote Mantice, ou Discours de la Vérité de divination par astrologie, which was printed anonymously in 1558. What bibliographic information can you find about this title?

10-64   What bibliographic information can you find about <u>Histoire de l'annexion de la Savoie a la France en</u>
        <u>1792</u>, by J. Masse, published in 1891-1898?

10-65   Where would you look to find some recent French publications on librarianship?

10-66   Where would you look to find out if a book titled <u>Nos Amies les Baleines</u> by Jacques-Yves Cousteau,
        published in 1972, is still available for purchase and what its current price is?

        Finally, some bibliographic sources for Germany--again, it would be helpful to locate a German-
        English dictionary to look up an occasional unfamiliar key word. The German bibliographic sources
        are highly organized, and once you get the general overall pattern, can be extremely easy to use.
        The basic problem with current German bibliography comes from the split in Germany after World
        War II, into East (German Democratic Republic) and West (German Federal Republic). German bib-
        liographies beginning before this split were mostly issued from Leipzig, the book trade center, now
        part of East Germany. Bibliographic sources--official and trade--are still published there. After
        the split, Frankfurt became the book trade center for the German Federal Republic, West Germany,
        and bibliographic sources--similar in purpose, scope, arrangement, and format to the East German
        sources--are now issued from Frankfurt. The sources to examine here are:

                Deutsche Bibliographie; Halbjahres-Verzeichnis (AA633, 2AA77)
                Deutsche Bibliographie; Fuenfjahres-Verzeichnis (AA634)
                Heinsius: Allgemeines Buecher-Lexikon (AA622)
                Kayser: Vollstaendiges Buecher-Lexikon (AA623)
                Hinrichs: Fuenfjahres-Katalog (AA624)
                Gesamtverzeichnis des Deutschsprachigen Schrifttums (GV) (1AA119, 2AA79, 2AA80)

10-67   Begin with the West German current bibliography from Frankfurt, the Deutsche Bibliographie
        (Deutsche=German, therefore German bibliography). This source is published in three main parts
        or series (reihe): Reihe A, "Neuerscheinungen des Buchhandels" (publications of the book trade),
        Reihe B, "Neuerscheinungen ausserhalb des Buchhandels" (publications outside the book trade),
        and Reihe C, "Karten" (maps). How often is each series or reihe published? (See Sheehy AA632
        and 1AA121, or the source itself.)

10-68   How are Reihe A and Reihe B arranged? (See Sheehy or the source itself.)

10-69   Are there indexes to this basic arrangement? What kind of indexes are needed? Is there anything
        which looks like an index?

10-70   When did Deutsche Bibliographie begin publication? Does it cumulate? (See Sheehy.)

10-71   How is the Deutsche Bibliographie; Halbjahres-Verzeichnis (half-yearly list) arranged?

10-72   Using the Halbjahres-Verzeichnis for 1982, if it is available to you, can you find the publisher,
        price, and ISBN for a book titled <u>In Schatten des Ringer</u> by Cynthia Felice, published in 1982?

10-73   Does the Deutsche Bibliographie; Halbjahres-Verzeichnis cumulate further?

10-74   How is the five-year cumulation of the Deutsche Bibliographie arranged?

10-75   Using the Deutsche Bibliographie five-year cumulation for 1956-60, can you find the correct title of a book on the Catholic Church, by Alfons Grunwald, published in Stuttgart in 1956?

10-76   Deutsche Nationalbibliographie is the older East German current bibliography from Leipzig. How is it organized? (See Sheehy AA627 and 1AA120, or the source itself.)

10-77   How long has the Deutsche Nationalbibliographie been published? Does it cumulate in any way? For example, you might assume from past experience that it would cumulate annually. (See Sheehy.)

10-78   How is the Deutsches Buecherverzeichnis arranged?

10-79   What is the scope of the Deutsche Bibliographie and the Deutsche Nationalbibliographie? (See Sheehy.)

10-80   Will you find West German publications in the Deutsche Nationalbibliographie? Will you find East German publications in the Deutsche Bibliographie?

10-81   Do the two current sources you have examined so far, Deutsche Bibliographie and Deutsche National-bibliographie, seem to be comparable to the trade bibliographies or trade publications that you examined for the United States, Great Britain, and France?

10-82   What retrospective sources do you have so far for Germany?

10-83   What other retrospective sources are available for German publications?

10-84   If possible, examine at least one of the four retrospective sources noted in the answer to the previous question. Can you tell, simply by looking at the source itself, approximately what the arrangement is? (Think: what general possibilities do you have for arrangement?)

10-85   A book titled Grundzuege eines Systems des Deutschen Staatsrechts by C. Gerber was published in 1869. What edition was this, and is there any difference in the number of pages between this edition and any earlier editions, if they existed?

10-86   Is there a catalog of a national library for Germany, as there is for the United States (LC), Great Britain (BL), and France (BN)?

10-87   Is there a books-in-print type source for Germany?

10-88   In which bibliographies covered so far might you expect to find current Swiss publications?

BIBLIOGRAPHIC RECORDS FOR OTHER COUNTRIES--GREAT BRITAIN, FRANCE, GERMANY

Answers #10/1--10/88

10-1: The book trade sources published by Bow-ker (BIP, etc., WR/BPR) do not include publications from other countries unless available from a U.S. distributor. CBI does, if they are in English.

Of the retrospective sources, most are U.S./American only, except Sabin which includes publications about America published elsewhere.

LC/NUC does list from all countries, all languages (universal).

Ulrich's is international; Ayer's is mostly American, some foreign.

ULS and NST, like LC/NUC, are universal. Gregory and Brigham are American only.

The periodical indexes tend to include English-language material, thus covering some British as well as American (See #7-71).

Government publications sources are U.S. only.

10-2: Retrospective and current.
Frequency of publication (weekly, monthly, etc.), and cumulation patterns.
Arrangement: author, title, subject, chron-ological, geographical; classed subject, al-phabetical subject; standard subject head-ings, keyword in title subject access; neces-sary indexes.
Information in the bibliographic citations (author, title, publisher, date, collation, price, address of publisher or other order-ing information, classification numbers, etc.).
Types of publications included or excluded; trade vs. non-trade, for example.
Sources of bibliographic control: govern-ment, professional (library), commercial (book trade).
National libraries, copyright laws, etc.

10-3: The first set of sources you examined for the U.S. bibliographic records was Books in Print (plus Publishers' Trade List An-nual and Subject Guide to Books in Print). Because the title of the source is virtually self-explanatory, you would expect similar sources--that is, sources serving similar purposes--for other countries, other lan-

guages, to have similar titles. Looking at the list of sources to examine for Great Britain, you find British Books in Print, which seems obviously to be the similar source you want.

10-4: British Books in Print is similar to BIP, although arranged somewhat differently. In the 1983 annual edition, there are two volumes, with all entries (author/title/ subject) in a single alphabet. The bib-liographic information about each entry is approximately the same. British Books in Print is now published annually, although this was not always so (see Sheehy anno-tation). It is also available in monthly up-dates on microfiche.

British Books in Print's subject ac-cess is not quite the same as that achieved by Subject Guide to BIP. Subject Guide to BIP (and CBI also, for example) have spe-cific subject headings under which appro-priate titles are listed. British Books in Print achieves subject access through the first word in the title if significant (see #2a-35, 2a-36, 2a-37 for other examples), or through an inverted title or "keyword" (or "catchword") entry (see #7-57 for another example). Look in a recent edi-tion of British Books in Print under Chem-istry, where you are likely to find exam-ples of both.

British Books in Print has no pub-lisher access such as PTLA (although the Sheehy annotation indicates that it did in earlier volumes). It does have a full list of publishers with addresses.

10-5: British Books in Print is published by J. Whitaker and Sons, Ltd. in London. It is distributed in the United States by Bow-ker. (See title page of source.)

10-6: Since you want to purchase one, you pre-sumably want one in print, and although you do not have an author or title this is a fairly simple one to find through British Books in Print using "Urdu" as a keyword.

10-7: British Paperbacks in Print; a Reference Catalogue, also published by Whitaker, annually, with author-title access.

10-8: Sheehy lists these publications. They can also be found listed in the advertisements for J. Whitaker and Sons Ltd. on the first pages of the printed versions of British Books in Print, and British Paperbacks in Print. Bookseller (Sheehy AA671), is the weekly list; Whitaker's Books of the Month and Books to Come (Sheehy AA670) is the monthly list, with author, title, and subject-through-title access, which cumulates quarterly, then annually, into Whitaker's Cumulative Book List (Sheehy AA668/669).

10-9: It is arranged, quarterly and in the cumulations, as is the monthly issue, with author/title/subject-through-title access in a dictionary arrangement. Formerly (until 1976?) it was arranged by broad subject areas with author/title/subject-through-title access. It has been published since 1924.

10-10: Use the 1982 annual volume of Whitaker's Cumulative Book List. You can approach it either by author or by keyword from the title. If you did not have the author, you would have to approach it only by keyword from the title, and here is where you would have to hope that the title is sufficiently descriptive of the subject, and preferably that it contains the word "guitar." Looking under "guitar" (p. 420), you will find several titles listed and by scanning them you should find what you are looking for: Classical Guitar: Its Evolution and Players Since 1800 (title inverted to "Guitar, Classical: its..."), author given as Summerfield, published by A. Mark. It can also be found under Summerfield, and under "Classical guitar."

You would also expect to find this title listed in Cumulative Book Index, from Section 1c; remember that CBI includes books in English published all over the world, and has author and subject access.

10-11: See title page of any recent cumulated volume or verso of first page of any recent issue: The British Library: Bibliographic Services Division.

10-12: It is published weekly, with the indexes cumulating in the last issue of the last month. It also cumulates every four months, then annually. It has been published since 1950, and at one time also cumulated every three years.

10-13: Scope: new British books received by the Copyright Receipt Office of the British Library;

Arrangement: classified subject according to the Dewey Decimal Classification with author, title, series, and subject index.

10-14: American Book Publishing Record--classed according to Dewey with author, title, specific subject index.

10-15: The Catalog for Copyright Entries comes closest, since that list is based upon books received in the U.S. Copyright Office. American Book Publishing Record is more similar to BNB in scope and arrangement, but the items listed there are not based upon books received as part of the copyright registration procedure.

10-16: Only a few items are excluded--see Preface of an annual volume. As of 1982, the exclusions were periodicals (however, the first issues of new periodicals are listed), music, maps, some government publications, publications without a British imprint, except those published in the Republic of Ireland.

The scope of BNB is much broader than WR/BPR--which excludes all government publications, and serials/periodicals, pamphlets under 49 p., etc.

10-17: BNB citations give full cataloging information (as does American Book Publishing Record), as well as price and other information for ordering. This is fuller information than is given in the other current British sources. Bookseller and the other Whitaker lists are trade lists; BNB is more library-oriented.

10-18: Use the BNB annual cumulation for 1982. Here you have neither the author nor the title, so you must approach it by subject. The subject index is in the second volume of the annual cumulation. Here, under "Birds. Africa" is a reference to the Dewey Decimal Classification number 598.296. By looking under this number in the classified section, in volume 1 of the annual cumulation, you will find listed a book titled The Birds of Africa, by Leslie Brown, published by Academic Press in London, in July 1982.

10-19: You want recent information with subject access. Whitaker's Cumulative Book List, under keywords such as "Occult" and "Occultism," for publications of the past three months or past year; and/or British National Bibliography under Dewey Decimal Classification 133 for past week, month and year. (Whitaker's Books of the Month and the Bookseller would give you even more recent information.) CBI would also give you this information, of course, although perhaps not as quickly as you would find it in the British sources.

10-20: BNB to 1950; Whitaker's to 1924. (You also have CBI to 1928, and LC/NUC all the way back, see #10-1). These sources give coverage, to some extent, for the early 20th century. By looking in Sheehy, you can find other sources giving coverage for the 19th century--English Catalogue of Books (AA666), and earlier--for example, Lowndes' Bibliographers' Manual of English Literature (AA639) and Watt's Bibliotheca Britannica (AA640). These are somewhat similar to the sources for U.S. retrospective bibliography which you examined in Sections 2a-2b (Sabin, Evans, etc.).

10-21: Pollard and Redgrave: A short-title catalogue of books printed in England, Scotland and Ireland, and of English books printed abroad, 1475-1640; Wing: Short-title catalogue of books printed in England, Scotland, Ireland, Wales, and British America and of English books printed in other countries 1641-1700. Pollard and Redgrave was first published in 1926, with a 2nd, revised edition in 1976 (still in progress as of 1983; vol. 2 came out prior to vol. 1). Wing was first published in 1945-51, with a 2nd, revised edition in 1972 (still in progress as of 1983). (It may be better to use the introductory material from the first editions for explanations of scope, etc., until the revisions are completed.) Neither was compiled during the time period that it covers; both were compiled retrospectively.

10-22: The dates covered. Pollard and Redgrave: 1475-1640. Wing: 1640-1700. Both include books published in Great Britain and English (language) books printed elsewhere.

10-23: No, you wouldn't; since the first printing in America was not until 1638 (see #2b-62), and the Pollard and Redgrave STC covers only to 1640. The Wing STC does include books printed in America (see the title).

10-24: 1475 was chosen as the beginning date presumably because the first book in English (The Recuyell of the Histories of Troy, printed by William Caxton in Bruges) was printed at approximately that date. 1640 was chosen as the closing date presumably to match the divid-

ing date of the transcripts of the registers of the London Stationers' Company (see Sheehy AA645 and AA659).

10-25: Both are arranged alphabetically by author (and other main entries if the author is not known or is not used as the main entry). Generally speaking there is no title access (except for some anonymous entries), no subject access, and few cross-references. Citations include brief bibliographic information and indication of libraries possessing copies. (Library location symbols are explained in the introductory material of each source.)

10-26: The titles listed in these bibliographies are "abridged entries" (see introductory material in both sources), meaning that the titles (traditionally lengthy and complex for books of this period) have been shortened or abridged (see, in the first editions, "Memoranda" to Pollard and Redgrave, and "Preface" to Wing, specifically "Method of Abridgement" in both). Other bibliographic sources for the period found through Sheehy, might give fuller entries --such as The Catalogue of Books in the Library of the British Museum ... to the year 1640 (AA643), Evans and Sabin for American books, several sources listed (Sheehy, 9th ed., p. 20-22) as bibliographies of "early and rare books" (Hain, Copinger, Proctor, etc.).

10-27: A "census of copies" would be a listing of all known copies. It is somewhat similar to a "union list" but even union lists do not always aim at listing all known copies. See Wing Preface under "Number of Copies Listed:" "This is not a census of copies, but only a guide to inform scholars where each book may most conveniently be consulted.... Usually only one copy is located in any one city...." (1st edition); "In general only one copy is located in any one city" (2nd edition). The same is true of the Pollard and Redgrave STC (see Preface of 1st edition, p. viii, and "Memoranda," p. xii-xiii), although since books of that period are considerably scarcer, sometimes it does in fact "aim to record all known copies of very rare items" (see Sheehy annotation).

10-28: See Sheehy, 9th edition, p. 20-22, "Early and Rare Books--Union lists": item AA218, Goff's Incunabula in American Libraries; a Third Census....

10-29: Since both STC's aim to list books "copies of which are known to exist--thus a catalogue of the books of which its compilers have been able to locate copies, not a bibliography of books known or believed to have been produced" (see introductory material in both sources), then presumably neither bibliographies would have any ghosts. The "Memoranda" to Pollard and Redgrave, 1st edition, p. xiv, mentions one ghost, of a sort, and the "Preface" to the first edition of Wing, p. vii, indicates that in fact he was able to examine only 90% of the books listed so that some ghosts may exist. Note also the section titled "A Gallery of Ghosts" in the Preface to the Revised Edition of Wing.

10-30:   Pollard and Redgrave, p. 326, vol. 2 of 2nd ed., or p. 519 of 1st ed., under Shakespeare as author, alphabetized as Richard III: 8 editions are listed. The first, item 22314, was published in 1597. Libraries holding copies are British Library, Bodleian, Huntington, Folger, Yale. "4°" means "quarto," signifying the size of the book.

10-31:   Wing, vol. 1, under Behn (p. 146 in 2nd ed.; p. 131 in 1st ed.). WF is the Wing symbol for the Folger Library (see p. xviii of 2nd ed., p. xiii of 1st ed.); it is not listed in Wing as having a copy, but this does not mean that the Folger does not have a copy, since the Wing list is not a census of copies but only a selected list.

10-32:   The national library of Great Britain. See Sheehy, 9th ed., p. 9, under "Library catalogues," for British Museum Library. The British Museum Library has been called the British Library since 1973.

10-33:   LC/NUC.

10-34:   No, not exactly. The British Library Catalogue is a catalog of holdings of the British Library and only of the British Library. The LC/NUC has never been really a catalog of the holdings of the LC. It was, in earlier series, a catalog or listing of LC printed cards; later it listed holdings for other cooperating libraries as well, and became a union catalog. The British Library catalog does not serve to indicate library locations, except that books listed there are presumably available in the collections of the British Library.

10-35:   As catalogues of the national libraries of their countries, one of the functions of which is to collect and preserve the literature of the country, both represent extensive and comparatively complete collections of the publications of their country. In addition, they serve as universal bibliographies because they represent extensive collections of materials from all countries, all languages, all periods of time. Both include most types of publications, books plus periodicals, government publications, etc.

10-36:   Both are arranged basically by main entry (generally author) only, alphabetically, with some but not extensive cross-references; usually no title entry unless the title is the main entry. Both have some subject access through a separate form of publication; for the British Library (Museum) subject coverage, see Sheehy AA101 and 1AA23.

10-37:   No. The British Library catalog is not published in current, monthly, quarterly, annual issues as is the LC/NUC.
          The main or basic set, in 263 volumes, was published from 1959 through 1966, and includes material catalogued through 1955 (therefore imprints through 1955). There is also a first (10-year) supplement for items cataloged 1956-65, in 50 volumes, a second (five-year) supplement for items cataloged 1966-70, in 26 volumes, and a third five-year supplement for 1971-75. Sheehy (2AA13) notes that this third supplement was to be the "last" with further additions to be done through machine-readable records. The fourth supplement, for 1976-82, was issued in 1982 on computer-output-microfiche.
          K.G. Saur is in the process, as of 1983, of publishing the British Library General Catalogue of Printed Books to 1975, which will cumulate into a single alphabetical sequence of 360 volumes the basic set, and the first, second, and third supplements. Saur has also published in regular print form the fourth, 1976-82, supplement.

10-38:   The British National Bibliography, since it is a list of books received by the Copyright Receipt Office of the British Library, does give current, continuing, frequent coverage of some of the materials added to the British Library. The current acquisitions of the British Library are not limited to books received by the Copyright Receipt Office; current acquisitions may include older British publications, or current and retrospective publications from any other country. These will not appear in the BNB. The LC/NUC current issues will include, for example, recent publications from Great Britain; the BNB current issues will not include recent

U.S. publications.

10-39: A Danish Gambit was published in 1966. The publisher is Peter Owen. It has 167 pages. In order to locate the entry for this book you would have to check the first two supplements (1956-65 and 1966-70) to the main set, since you only know it was published sometime in the 1960's. The entry is in the second supplement, vol. 4, column 653. (This item can also be found in the Saur cumulative edition, see #10-37, in v. 49, p. 296; the author is listed as "Butler (William) novelist.")

10-40: It is located in the basic or main set of the British Library Catalogue in vol. 185, p. 338, under Periodical Publications-- London. There is a cross-reference from Fraser's Magazine at the beginning of all the entries for Fraser, vol. 78, column 696. It was published from 1830-69 in 80 volumes and from 1870-82 in 26 volumes. (As of the end of 1983, the Saur cumulative edition had not yet reached the P's.)
    You could also find this in Union List of Serials (Section 6), where it is listed under Fraser's Magazine; dates and volumes numbering are the same as in the British Library Catalogue, although months are given in ULS. ULS gives clearer information on title changes and indicates what titles superseded it.

10-41: Ulrich's, in Section 5, is international in scope and should therefore include British serials and periodicals. First issues of new periodicals are listed in the British National Bibliography (see #10-16) but that does not give current order information.

10-42: Yes, many of which are the same ones as for U.S. periodicals. See answer to #7-71.

10-43: Yes, you would expect one. See Sheehy under Government Publications (AG)-- Great Britain (9th ed., p. 199+)--19th and 20th centuries: items AG87, 88, 89: Great Britain. Stationery Office. Catalogue of Government Publications, 1922+. It is published by the Stationery Office, equivalent of the U.S. GPO. It comes out monthly and annually and is arranged basically by issuing agency.

10-44: BNB, Whitaker's, CBI, and British Books in Print would presumably all include the listing, but only British Books in Print would tell you current price and in-print status.

10-45: Since you don't have a date, your first choice should be a source which would bring together in one place as much as possible by this author--here, the British Library Catalogue. In the basic set through 1966, and in the Saur cumulative edition through 1975, this is listed as being published in 1949, and since no earlier publication is listed, it is reasonable to assume that this was the first edition. In Whitaker's, BNB, and CBI, you would have to search either from beginning to date, or from current volumes back (it could have been a posthumous publication) through many volumes. (LC/NUC might also be a possible source, although you would have to be sure there that you did not find the first U.S. publication which may have been later than the first British publication.) If the title is listed in British Books in Print, the date given would not necessarily be that of the first publication.

10-46: Since you want books in print, you would go to the latest British Books in Print which has no full subject access, so you would be limited to finding only those titles which have "urban" in the title; you could also look under related words (housing, poverty, city, slums, welfare, etc.; see #7-24).
    You could also look in current issues and cumulations of BNB under appropriate subject classification, and Whitaker's Cumulative Book List under similar keywords. (Once you found the authors and titles, you could then check against BBIP for in-print status.)

10-47: Sheehy shows (in the main volume, under "Bibliography--National and Trade--France --Current," p. 53+) two possibilities (you have to read through the annotations, though, to find them): AA614, Le Catalogue de l'Edition Française, and AA618, Répertoire des Livres de Langue Française Disponibles. In the first Supplement, Sheehy shows that the first of these has been superseded by Les Livres Disponibles (1AA118). All of these in general seem to follow the same approach as Books in Print, etc.: there is both author and title access, subject access is sometimes included, the bibliographic information given may be somewhat limited, but the price is given, and usually publishers' addresses are given.

10-48. The current French list which appears in the Sheehy basic volume is the Bibliographie de la France (AA612, AA613, 1AA117). This publication has been appearing in some format since 1811. From 1972-1979, it was called Bibliographie de la France--Biblio (Sheehy AA613, 1AA117). The Sheehy second supplement notes that in 1979, it was superseded by a publication called Livres-hebdo (2AA74). Actually, although the new publication Livres-hebdo does include a weekly list of new publications and does include the publishing news and articles and advertising which had previously appeared in the Bibliographie de la France (see the annotation for AA612, "2.pt." and "3.pt."), the "Bibliographie Officielle" section of Bibliographie de la France (see "1.pt." of the Sheehy annotation for AA612) has continued to appear under the original title of Bibliographie de la France. Livres-hebdo, then, continues as the book trade list.

10-49:   Legal deposit is defined in the ALA Glossary. The current legal deposit law in France is given on the first page of the Bibliographie Officielle section of Bibliographie de la France, the note at the bottom, second paragraph which translates roughly as: It is recalled that by the terms of the law of June 21, 1943, amended by the decree of November 21, 1960, deposit must be made first, by the publishers, not later than 48 hours after first being put on sale (deposits made directly to the Administration) and three days before being put on sale (if sent by post) for books, immediately before being put on sale for periodicals; second by printers of finished drawings for books and periodicals.

         In this sense, the Bibliographie de la France is similar to the British National Bibliography, in that it represents a list of publications officially received (see #10-13 and #10-15).

10-50:   The list of books (livres) is "classed," arranged by broad subjects (e.g., general works, philosophy, religion, social sciences, linguistics, pure sciences, etc.) using the Universal Decimal Classification, with author (auteur) and title (titre) indexes. As of 1983, these indexes cumulate quarterly. Although the list of books originally appeared on a weekly basis, as of 1983, it appears approximately every other week, or twice a month. There are several supplements, published at various intervals, covering other types of publications (serials, official or governmental publications, music, maps). Sheehy indicates that "full cataloging information" is given in the citations.

10-51:   Sheehy indicates that, in the past, the

Bibliographie de la France included a trade list, "Les livres de la semaine," which cumulated monthly (mois), then quarterly (trimestre and semestre), and then annually into Les Livres de l'année. The annual cumulations, Les Livres de l'année and later Les Livres de l'Année --Biblio, are also listed separately in Sheehy, items AA616 and AA617. It would appear from the Sheehy annotation for Livres-hebdo that these monthly, and then presumably annual, cumulations have continued as part of the Livres-hebdo publication.

10-52:   From 1953-70, it was titled Les Livres de l'Année (Sheehy AA616) and arranged, as are the weekly and monthly lists, in a broad subject classification with various indexes. This further cumulated into Librairie Française, Catalogue Général .... (Sheehy AA615), which is shown as going back to 1930.

         In 1971, Bibliographie de la France merged with another non-official list called Biblio (see Sheehy annotations for AA612 and AA613) and the annual cumulation was then titled Les Livres de l'Année--Biblio (Sheehy AA617). This annual list then took over the dictionary catalog arrangement of Biblio: author-title-subject in one alphabet, similar to the U.S.'s Cumulative Book Index.

10-53:   Both are subject approaches. Les Livres de l'Année--Biblio is arranged like the Cumulative Book Index, with authors, titles, subjects all in one alphabetical list. The book about Miró is found on p. 709 of the 1979 volume, under "Miró Ferra, Joan" as the subject. A fuller entry will be found under the author. Some titles of books about the Congo are found under "Congo," on p. 235, with a note to see also "Brazzaville."

10-54:   In Biblio annual cumulated volume for 1969, you can find the full citation under the author, Bouillon, Clément. The series note is given in parentheses following the complete title, and you find that this book publication was indeed published as a part of a series, apparently an unnumbered series: Publications of the Group de Recherches et d'Applications Pédagogiques of the Institute d'Anglais of the University of Nancy. It is possible that this title might appear in a library card catalog only under the series, rather than under author. It is also possible that a library might place a standing order to receive all of the publications of this particular institute or organization, rather than ordering each separately by author and title. In either case, to locate or to order, it could be vital to know the series information.

10-55: Biblio back to 1934 (Sheehy AA611); Bibliographie de la France back to 1811, with annual and 10-year cumulations back to 1930 as Librairie Française (Sheehy AA615) and Les Livres de l'Année (Sheehy AA616 and AA617).

10-56: Quérard: La France littéraire ... XVIII et XIX siècles (AA606)
        Quérard: La littérature française ... 1827-49 (AA607)
        Catalogue général de la librairie française 1840-1925 (Lorenz) (AA609)
        Vicaire: Manuel de l'amateur de livres ... 1801-1893 (AA610)

10-57: Yes, the Bibliothèque Nationale, see Sheehy, 9th ed., p. 12.

10-58: Yes, see Sheehy, items AA105 and AA106.

10-59: The Bibliothèque Nationale catalog, like that of the British Library, is not published on a current monthly basis as is the LC/NUC. The basic set of the BN was in progress of publication from 1900 through 1981. A supplement covering 1960-69 has been published. The Sheehy annotation indicates that it is likely there will be supplements every five years or so.
        Like the British Library catalog and unlike the LC/NUC, the Bibliothèque Nationale catalog is a catalog of the holdings of the Bibliothèque Nationale.
        Like the British Library catalog and like the LC/NUC, because it collects publications from all countries, all times, as well as the national literature, it serves as a universal bibliography.
        Like the LC/NUC and the British Library catalog, full bibliographic information and notes are given.
        Unlike the LC/NUC and the British Library catalog, the BN has entries under personal author names only (no titles, no periodicals, no corporate authors, no government authors, etc.).

10-60: All current and retrospective sources, see answers to #10-55 and #10-56. Also the LC/NUC and the British Library catalog.

10-61: No, there is no subject access to the BN catalog. There is some subject access through Biblio (Sheehy AA611) for 1934-70, through Les Livres de l'Année (Sheehy

AA615/616/617) back to about 1930, and some through Lorenz or the Catalogue général de la librairie française (Sheehy AA609) from 1840-1925.

10-62: The fact that it has only personal author entries, with no title entries for anonymous works, no corporate author entries, no government author entries, etc.

10-63: Although it was published anonymously, you do know the author (or presumed author), and you may therefore expect to find it in the Bibliothèque Nationale catalog. It is in vol. 196, p. 526, under author, Tyard (Pontus de). The author's name is given in square brackets in the citation, indicating that it does not appear on the publication. It was printed in Lion by J. de Tournes, in 98 pages; other information is also given, about the title page, etc. Similarly, a citation for this title (with less information) is given in the British Library catalog (basic set, vol. 242, under Tyard).

10-64: Period is late 19th century, which is covered by Lorenz' Catalogue Général, partially by Vicaire's Manuel, and Bibliothèque Nationale catalog. This title is located in Lorenz, vol. 15 covering 1891-1899 I-Z, under author Masse, Jules. The title was published in 3 volumes from 1891-1898, the publisher was Allier in Grenoble (France), and it is extracted (taken) from the Bulletin de l'Academie delphinale.
        This title is also listed in the Bibliothèque Nationale catalog, vol. 109, p. 241--the author's name is given as Mases, Jules, but this appears to be a misprint since it is filed as if it were Masse. The same information is given with the addition of the series and volume numbering for the periodical (Bulletin de...).

10-65: You need a currently published source with subject access: as of 1983, there is the Bibliographie de la France, and Livres-hebdo. Both have a classed subject arrangement like the American Book Publishing Record. Librarianship is usually found under "O. Généralities."

10-66: You would want to look in an "in-print" source: see your answer to #10-47.

10-67: Reihe A is published weekly, Reihe B semimonthly, Reihe C quarterly, according to Sheehy AA632.

10-68: Both are arranged basically in classed

or broad subject groups, which are listed on the title pages of each series, such as: religion (religion), philosophie (philosophy), politik (political science), schoene literatur (literature), musik (music), medizin (medicine), etc.

10-69: Author and title indexes plus possibly specific subject indexes are needed for a broad subject grouping or classed arrangement. In each issue of both Reihe A and B there is an index in the back, now titled "verfasser- [author], titel- [title], u. stichwort [catch or keyword] register [index]," which gives author, title, and specific subject access. The indexes cumulate quarterly.

10-70: It began in 1947. The index to Reihe A, the weekly list of in-trade publications, cumulates monthly (monatregister) and quarterly (vierteljahrregister). Reihe B has an annual index. Reihe A and some B and C titles further cumulate into a half-yearly or semi-annual list: Deutsche Bibliographie; Halbjahres-Verzeichnis (Sheehy AA633), since 1951.

10-71: More or less the same as the yearly cumulations of the Deutsche Nationalbibliographie: the first part, in two volumes, is the Titelverzeichnis (really an author list) and the second part, in two volumes, is the Stich- und Schlagwortregister (catchword title and subject index).

10-72: It is listed in the Halbjahres-Verzeichnis 1982/II, covering July-December 1982, in the Alphabetisches Titelverzeichnis (author listing), volume covering A-K, on p. 756. The publisher is Moenig, the price is 7.80 DM, the ISBN is 3-8118-3577-7.

10-73: Yes, it cumulates into Deutsche Bibliographie; Fuenfjahres-Verzeichnis (five-year list), published since 1945-50 (Sheehy AA634).

10-74: Same as the half-yearly cumulation of the Deutsche Bibliographie (see #10-71): an author listing and a subject index.

10-75: The main part (or Teil I, Alphabetisches Titelverzeichnis) of the Deutsch Bibliographie five-year cumulation for 1956-60 is in five volumes, from A-Z. Using Teil I, vol. 1, A-E, on p. 2432, you will find under the author (Grunwald, Alfons--the only title by this author) a listing for a book titled Die Naturrechtliche Staatsanschauung der Katholischen Kirche, published in Stuttgart by Klett in 1956, in a 2nd edition. This appears to be the title

you want.

10-76: Basically, the Deutsche Nationalbibliographie is organized just like the Deutsche Bibliographie. There are three series/reihe: A (trade, issued weekly), B (non-trade, issued semimonthly), C (dissertations, issued monthly). A and B are arranged in the same large subject groups as the Deutsche Bibliographie with author (verfasser), title (titel), subject (schlagwort), and catchword (stichwort) indexes.

10-77: It has been published since 1931. It has cumulated (since 1945) annually into the Jahresverzeichnis [yearly list] der Verlagsschriften, formerly titled the Jahresverzeichnis des Deutschen Schrifttums (see Sheehy AA630 and AA6239), and then every five years into Deutsches Buecherverzeichnis (Sheehy AA631, 2AA77). According to the Sheehy second supplement annotation, the Jahresverzeichnis did not appear in 1971-80. Although Sheehy notes that it was expected to resume in 1981, it has not appeared as of 1983.

10-78: Deutsches Buecherverzeichnis is arranged, as was the Jahresverzeichnis, in two parts: Titelverzeichnis (which is essentially an author list), and Stich- und Schlagwortregister (catchword title and subject index).

10-79: All materials published in Germany, and German materials published elsewhere.

10-80: Yes to both.

10-81: These two sources are really official national bibliographies, rather than trade lists, similar to the British National Bibliography, or the "Bibliographie Officielle" section of the Bibliographie de la France. They are similar in arrangement to American Book Publishing Record but broader in scope, as they list many non-trade (Reihe B) publications usually not listed in BPR or other trade sources.

10-82: Deutsche Nationalbibliographie back to 1931 (its five-year cumulation Deutsches Buecherverzeichnis actually goes back to 1911), and Deutsche Bibliographie back to 1947.

10-83: Those listed in Sheehy, under Germany --early, 18th and 19th centuries, such as Heinsius: Allgemeines Buecher-Lexikon, covering 1700-1892 (AA622), Kayser: Vollstaendiges Buecher-Lexikon, covering 1750-1910 (AA623), and Hin-

richs: Fuenfjahres-Katalog, covering
1851-1912 (AA624). Sheehy also notes
the Gesamtverzeichnis des Deutschsprachigen Schrifttums (GV) covering
1911-1965 (1AA119 and 2AA79), and in
the second supplement, the GV covering
1700-1910 (2AA78). Note in the Sheehy
annotations that the GV series are compiled from sets such as the Heinsius,
Kayser, and Hinrichs lists, above, and
the Deutsches Buecherverzeichnis and
Deutsche Bibliographie lists from earlier
questions, but that these lists are not
entirely superseded by the GV lists.
You can also use LC/NUC, British Library catalog, and the Bibliothèque Nationale catalog (all are universal bibliographies).

10-84:   Heinsius, Kayser, and Hinrichs are arranged by chronological periods, which
you can tell from the dates on the spines.
Heinsius has author and catchword titles
in one alphabet. Kayser has author and
catchword titles in one alphabet, with
some separate subject (sach- and schlagwort) indexes. Hinrichs has an author-
title list with subject index. The GV
sets are arranged alphabetically by main
entry but no subject access.

10-85:   This title is found in Kayser, vol. 17/18
covering 1865-1870 A-Z, p. 348. The
edition published in 1869 (869) is shown
as having 254 pages (254 S.; s=seiten).
It is the 2nd edition (aufl.=edition). A
previous edition, 1865, is shown, in the
same entry, as having 208 pages.
        The title is also found in Hinrichs,
in the volume for 1869, p. 95, under
Gerber, C.F.; this shows a 2nd ed. with
254 pages, does not give information here
on the earlier editions. (Some of Hinrichs is in Gothic script but not all of
it, so it is not impossible to use, and the
entry for Gerber is not in Gothic.)
        The title is also found in Heinsius,
in the volume which covers 1868-74 (XI. .I),
A-K, p. 556, under Gerber, C.F. Here
the 2nd ed., with 254 pages, is shown as
being published in 1863, which is probably
an error. (As with Hinrichs, some but
not all of Heinsius is in Gothic script.)
        The title is also found in the GV
set covering 1700-1910, in vol. 45 (Gel-
Ger), see p. 241-42. The entry, for
"Gerber, C.F. v.," is filed as if it were
"Gerber, Karl Friedrich," however, with
no cross-reference.

10-86:   Sheehy, under Library Catalogs--National
Libraries (9th ed., p. 9+), lists three
items (AA102, AA103, AA104), all pub-

lished by the Preussichen Staatsbiblio-
thek (Prussian State Library) in Berlin,
but none really up-to-date or currently
active. Coverage from these sources is
therefore rather sporadic and not really
comparable to that obtained through the
LC, BL, and BN. Current national library bibliographic activity in Germany
is seen in the publications Deutsche
Bibliographie and Deutsche Nationalbibliographie.

10-87:   Sheehy lists one (item AA636) titled
Verzeichnis Lieferbarer Buecher; the
annotation shows it as having author
and title access, which is what you
would expect. It now also has subject
(schlagwort) access.

10-88:   CBI if in English; Deutsche Bibliographie
and Deutsche Nationalbibliographie if in
German; Bibliographie de la France or
Livres-hebdo if in French.

Section 11

REVIEW OF PART I

Questions #11/1--11/60

This section is a review of Sections 1-10 of Part I: Basic Bibliographic Sources, covering the basic sources for the U.S. and selected sources from other countries.

In this review, you should follow the same procedure used in Section 3 (Search Strategy and Review): you can either search out the specific answers in the source, or simplify the process by deciding which source(s) you would use to answer the question, or use a combination of both methods. What you do should depend on how much time you have and how much practice and review you think you need.

Even if you do actually search out the answers, you should still begin by deciding which source or sources to use. Think in terms of the scope of the question (i.e., type of publication, time period covered, etc.) and the scope of the sources available. Think in terms of what information you have, what information you need, what access there is to the various sources available, what information is given in the various sources available. If you find that you are not really sure which source(s) you should choose, and why, then it may be that you need more practice in and use of the sources to clarify your understanding of them. Try searching out the answer to the question in various likely sources, and see if this procedure helps you to compare the usefulness and scope of the sources.

For many of the questions, there may be several possible sources in which you could find the answer. You should try to think of as many possibilities as you can, because you may not be working in a library which will have all of the sources studied in this manual. Remember also that none of the sources are infallible, and a source which seems for every good reason to be the obvious source may, in actual use, not give you the desired information, and you may have to go on to search in other sources.

However, one of the objectives here is to learn to search systematically through the available sources, as opposed to searching aimlessly or frantically. Therefore, in this review section, you should assume that you have available all of the sources studied in the manual, and you should then think in terms of which would be the best or the most likely source to use and why. Think of the basic organization and structure of the bibliographic sources and of bibliographic control as it now exists.

If you have made the various charts as suggested, you have them to use as an aid. Try to become independent of using the charts as crutches, however. To get away from the feeling that you must memorize the charts, try this approach: first, review the charts (or whatever notes you have) for the overall view, then put the charts to one side and try to answer the questions without referring back to them. Guess, even if you guess wrong. If you are always or frequently guessing wrong, then you may need more review of the charts, or you may, as suggested above, need more use and practice with the sources. Do some of your reviewing in the reference collection, if possible. Just looking at the sources themselves will jog your memory, as it would in an actual working situation. There are intentionally plenty of review questions, and many repeat the same type of problems at intervals, so that you can use them for review as you feel you need them.

11-1   Is the novel Tree of Man by Patrick White still in print?

11-2   What is the title of a recently published biography of author Virginia Woolf?

11-3   The U.S. Congress voted to authorize loan guarantees to the Chrysler Corporation in late 1979/ early 1980. Where could you find information about the publication of the Chrysler Corporation Loan Guarantee Act?

11-4   Where would you find a list of all the books currently available from the University of Missouri Press?

11-5   Where would you look to find citations for various articles about Senator Gary Hart which have appeared in Time, Life, Newsweek, National Review, etc., during the past few years?

11-6   What is the subscription price for Sunset Magazine?

11-7   Where would you find listings of recent pamphlet-type material on summer employment opportunities for high school students?

11-8   Who is the author of a book titled The Value of a Child; or, Motives to the Good Education of Children, published in Philadelphia in 1753?

11-9   Where would you find the Library of Congress classification number for a book by Charles Grout titled The War Game, published recently? (This is a made-up title; do not try to search it out.)

11-10   What German language newspapers are published in Chicago?

11-11   What doctoral dissertations, if any, have been written in the past few years in the field of medieval art?

11-12   Who was the publisher of François Mauriac's novel La Sagoiun, published in Paris in 1951?

11-13   Can you find the address of Four Winds Press, a U.S. publisher?

11-14   Where would you look to find some information on the current death rate from drug abuse?

11-15   Where would you find a listing giving a descriptive annotation for the 1977 Yearbook of Agriculture (published by the U.S. Dept. of Agriculture) titled Gardening for Food and Fun? Where would you find ordering information?

11-16   Where would you find the name of the author of a recently published book titled Vietnam's Will to Live? (This is a made-up title; do not try to search it out.)

11-17   Can you find the authors and titles of some books about education published in the 18th century?

11-18   Is there a current paperback edition available of Time Probe; the Sciences in Science Fiction by Arthur Clarke?

11-19   Can you find ordering information for a magazine titled Aging, published by the U.S. Department of Health and Human Services?

11-20   Where would you find population statistics on Sacramento, California?

11-21   Where would you find a list of available editions of the poetry of John Donne (English poet, 1573-1631)?

11-22   Where could you borrow back volumes of the series Studies in American Literature, published in The Hague (Netherlands) since 1964?

11-23   Can you find the subject of a book titled The Nightmare of History by Ralph S. Morgan, published in the 1970's?

11-24   Lud is the name of a periodical published by the Polish Society of Ethnology. When did it begin publication? Is it still being published, as far as you can tell?

11-25   Can you find the address of Faber and Faber, a British publisher?

11-26   Where would you find a list of government publications on maps and map reading?

11-27   Where and how would you find the citation (date, paging, volume number, etc.) for an article titled "The Future of Solar Power," which appeared in Atlas in late 1979?

11-28   Are there any books to be published soon on the general subject of ecology, the protection of the environment, air and water pollution, pesticides, etc.?

11-29   Where would you look to find recent articles of criticism dealing with the poetry of Edmund Spenser (English poet, 1552-1599)?

11-30   Can you find listings for some recent (this year, last year?) phonograph recordings of any of Bruckner's symphonies?

11-31   Can you find a citation to the text of President John F. Kennedy's proclamation in the 1960's on the removal of Soviet weapons from Cuba?

11-32   What mystery novels written by Agatha Christie are still in print?

11-33   A filmstrip titled "Odyssey, the Birth of a New Work" was issued in 1982 by Educational Audio
          Visual. Where would you find information about it such as how long, whether in color, subject
          matter?

11-34   Who is the publisher of the most recent novel by John D. MacDonald?

11-35   What is the subscription price of Elle, a woman's magazine published in Paris?

11-36   Who was the publisher of Vengeance of Private Booley by Cyril Jolly, published in England in
          the 1950's?

11-37   What is the annual subscription rate of the Washington (D.C.) Post?

11-38   Does the book Glass Candlesticks by Margaret and Douglas Archer contain any full color illustra-
          tions?

11-39   Where would you look to find information on what bibliographies (in English) of Flaubert (a French
          novelist) are currently available?

11-40   At what university did Frances A. Spurrell complete study for a doctoral degree during the year
          1955-56?

11-41   How would you locate some recently published material on racial attitudes?

11-42   Is Beginning Spanish, published by Houghton Mifflin, designed for elementary schools, secondary
          schools, or for colleges?

11-43   From what libraries could you borrow on interlibrary loan a copy of Psychosomatic Music by Alvin
          Langdon, published in 1960?

11-44   Where would you find titles and information about motion pictures and films (8mm, etc.) on the sub-
          ject of "communication," issued in the past five years?

11-45   What are the titles of some books published in the 1950's about archaeology?

11-46   What is the organization responsible for publishing the current quarterly journal called Daedalus?

11-47   What was the publisher and original price for <u>Economic Aspects of the Welfare State in India</u> by R. Agarwal, published in India in 1967?

11-48   C.E. Lovejoy's <u>The Story of the Thirty-Eighth</u> is a regimental history. With what war is it concerned?

11-49   How would you check to find out if Gloria Steinem (feminist) has published anything recently in popular women's magazines such as <u>McCall's</u>, <u>Vogue</u>, <u>Ladies' Home Journal</u>, <u>Mademoiselle</u>, <u>Good Housekeeping</u>, etc.?

11-50   What was the publisher and original price of <u>Was ist Kybernetik?</u> by Felix von Cube, published in Munich in 1972?

11-51   What libraries on the east coast have copies of a book by Henry Wilson Lockette titled <u>An Inaugural Dissertation on the Warm Bath</u>, published in 1801?

11-52   How would you find out if <u>Red-Wing; or, the Weird Cruiser of Van Dieman's Land</u> by G. S. Raymond, published in 1853, was published in the U.S. or Great Britain?

11-53   How would you find the titles of some books published in the 1960's on the subject of music--including opera, vocal music, musical comedies and reviews, church music, choral music, composers, etc.?

11-54   Can you find the citation for an interview with G. Gordon Liddy published in <u>USA Today</u> in 1981?

11-55   How would you go about finding as much bibliographic information as possible about a series of religious tracts written by the Reverend Thomas Boston, published in the 1800's?

11-56   Can you find information on the director, screen writers, photographers, film editors, etc. of the television production "Roots," released in 1977 (Wolper Productions)?

11-57   <u>Guide for Musées Suisses</u> by C. La Mer was published in Paris in early 1980. Where would you look to find out if this is a new edition or just a reprinting of an earlier edition? (This is a made-up title; do not try to search it out.)

11-58   Can you find the birth and death dates of Stewart Culin, the author of a pamphlet titled <u>Chinese Games with Dice and Dominoes</u>, published by the U.S. GPO in Washington, D.C., in 1895?

11-59   If you were searching for periodical articles written <u>in</u> the nineteenth century <u>about</u> education, where would you look?

11-60   Does Sweden have a national bibliography?

11-1: Books in Print. The only source which will tell you if a book is in print, except PTLA and you can't use PTLA because you don't know the publisher. You have no reason to think this title is anything but a U.S. publication. However, if you checked in BIP and did not find it listed, you might consider also checking British Books in Print to see if it is still in print in Great Britain.

11-2: A recent source with subject access (Woolf as subject): Subject Guide to Books in Print and Subject Guide to Forthcoming Books; BPR; CBI. Subject Guide to Forthcoming Books is probably the most likely.

11-3: Since this would appear to be a government publication, the Monthly Catalog of Government Publications for that time period would give you detailed information about the publication itself. Whatever order information is given there would not necessarily be currently correct, however.

11-4: PTLA.

11-5: Periodical indexing service, in this case it should be fairly obvious that these would be in the Readers' Guide. Use Hart as the subject.

11-6: Ulrich's.

11-7: Vertical File Index (pamphlet materials with a subject approach).

11-8: Evans--covers the period and has title access. Sabin also covers the period and has title access through the Molnar index. LC/NUC does not have title access for that period.

11-9: Weekly Record/BPR give full cataloging information and include LC classification number, and are current. LC/NUC also gives this information--whether or not it would be listed there yet depends on how recently the title was published.

11-10: Ayer's--see separate language listings, or see under Illinois, Chicago.

11-11: Dissertation Abstracts International under specific subject heading in keyword index. Comprehensive Dissertation Index and American Doctoral Dissertations can also be used but may not yet be available for the most recent years.

11-12: French publication in French, therefore Biblio or Les Livres de l'Année which cover the period. Biblio would probably be easier. Remember that it may be necessary to check in the source beyond the date given; i.e., check in 1952 if not found in 1951 volume, etc.

11-13: BIP, PTLA (publisher's catalog), CBI.

11-14: Current events--New York Times Index. This source would probably give you some information directly. Current periodical articles might also be a source of information, so the Readers' Guide could be used, but you would then have to look up the articles cited there to get the information required.

11-15: For the descriptive annotation, try Newsome's New Guide to Popular Government Publications; title access through index or subject access ("agriculture"). You could also find information in the 1977 Monthly Catalog of U.S. Government Publications (title or subject access through the annual index), but no annotation. Both Newsome and the 1977 Monthly Catalog would also give order information but it would no longer be current. For that, you would need to check the GPO's Publications Reference File.

11-16: Recent sources with title access: Books in Print and Forthcoming Books; BPR; CBI. Forthcoming Books is probably the most likely, depending on the time of year. Subject access is also a possible way to search but since the sources are the same in either case (see #11-2), title is probably easier.

11-17: Sabin and Evans and LC/NUC cover this period. Only Evans has subject access. Sabin has title access through the Molnar index, so you might get some subject-through-title access there. LC/NUC has neither subject nor title access.

11-18: Paperbound Books in Print or BIP. "Available" meaning in print in this case.

11-19: A government publication, thus in Monthly Catalog of U.S. Government Publications, in the separate "Serials Supplement" published in the spring.

11-20: Ayer's.

11-21: Since you want available editions, you want currently in print (not therefore retrospective sources for his lifetime): BIP for those published in the U.S., and British Books in Print for those published in Great Britain.

11-22: Union list for serial or periodical publications; NST since that includes titles beginning after 1950.

11-23: You have author and title and are trying to find the subject, so you are not interested here in sources which have subject access, only those which are likely to give you in the citation some subject indication.

LC/NUC is probably the best source; listings there give full cataloging information, and you can find the subject from subject tracings on the bottom of the card or from the classification number, just as you can from a card in a library's card catalog. And the source cumulates sufficiently so that you would not have to look in several places to cover the 1970's, as you have the date only generally. BPR Cumulative similarly gives full cataloging information; this source only works, of course, for titles published in the U.S.

Sources such as CBI which have subject access are not really useful for this problem because you cannot find the subject entry for a title unless you already know the subject. Author/title entries do not give the subject unless it is somehow indicated in the title itself. For example, if you wanted to know the subject of The Ample Proposition by John Lehmann, published in 1966, the CBI author entry (CBI, 1966-68 cumulation) gives the full title as The Ample Proposition: autobiography 3.

PTLA (by using BIP first to deter-

mine publisher) might work, if the publisher's catalog gives some sort of annotation showing subject matter for each item, and if the book is still in print (unless you can go back to out-dated PTLA's).

11-24: Ulrich's (if it is currently published and if it is listed there, the beginning date should be given). If not in Ulrich's, then check ULS and NST; those sources will not tell you if it is still being published, but if they include it, they should include the beginning date.

11-25: British Books in Print or CBI.

11-26: Newsome's New Guide to Popular Government Publications has a short section on maps and mapping. There would probably be a Subject Bibliography from the U.S. GPO on this subject, or something broader which would include it. Or you could go through several issues or years of the Monthly Catalog of U.S. Government Publications, checking under the relevant subjects in the indexes, and compile your own list.

11-27: Periodical indexing service. (Atlas is a periodical.) This is indexed in Readers' Guide, which you could guess at if you were familiar with the periodical, or find from Ulrich's, or check in the list in the front of Readers' Guide. You have no author, and RG has no title entries, so you would have to look under the subject (solar energy).

11-28: Subject Guide to Forthcoming Books, check under all relevant subject headings.

11-29: Probably Humanities Index; sounds too scholarly for Readers' Guide. "Article" would indicate you want a periodical index.

11-30: Music, Books on Music, and Sound Recordings (LC Catalogs).

11-31: The Monthly Catalog of U.S. Government Publications would lead you to whatever has been published by the government. Actually, this might more easily be located through the New York Times Index, since the New York Times is noted for publication of the complete text of such speeches, documents, etc. In either case, it would help to pin the date down to a year for ease in searching.

11-32: BIP, and since she was British, also in British Books in Print. You could also check Paperbound Books in Print, and British Paperbacks in Print.

You would also probably want to check the latest Forthcoming Books, to see if any new reprints or re-issues have been added to what is listed in BIP.

11-33: Audiovisual Materials (LC Catalogs).

11-34: BIP, or if too recent for that, then Forthcoming Books.

11-35: Ulrich's (international in scope).

11-36: British Books in Print only if it is still in print or has been reprinted. Otherwise: CBI, BNB, English Catalogue, Whitaker's Cumulative Book List, British Library Catalogue, LC/NUC.

11-37: Ayer's (newspaper).

11-38: You want a source which gives as full bibliographic information as possible and you do not have a date.

LC/NUC would probably be the best source since it will/should give that information in the citation, and there are probably fewer places to search for the entire time span. CBI might also give the information. If it happened to have been published since 1876, BPR Cumulative might give the information.

11-39: Subject Guide to Books in Print followed by Subject Guide to Forthcoming Books-- looking under Flaubert as the subject. You want "currently available" which has been taken to mean "in print." You need a subject access since you do not know author or title. You could also look in CBI and BPR, both of which are current and have subject access, going back perhaps five years to cover "current," but then you would have to recheck in BIP the titles which you found in CBI and BPR to find if they were still in print.

11-40: Dissertation Abstracts International, Comprehensive Dissertation Index, and/or American Doctoral Dissertations.

11-41: Vague, but sounds like periodical articles. Therefore a periodical indexing service: Readers' Guide, Social Sciences Index, and Humanities Index would all do. Also PAIS which would include books, pamphlets, documents, etc. Subject heading(s) might vary, such as "race relations."

Possibly also New York Times Index

for information.

11-42: Publisher's catalog in PTLA sometimes gives this type of information. El-Hi Textbooks in Print (under Spanish) is another source, much more likely to give this information.

11-43: You need a union catalog for books: LC/NUC.

11-44: Audiovisual Materials (LC Catalogs).

11-45: BPR Cumulative, now that it goes back to 1950, would probably be the best source, because of its classed subject arrangement, bringing most of the books on archaeology together in one place. CBI also has subject access and covers the time period, but might require more searching in subject headings. Subject Guide to BIP, current volume, will contain only those 1950 publications which are still in print. (Retrospective volumes of Subject BIP, for the late 1950's, could be used, of course, but that seems very cumbersome when you have other easier alternatives.)

11-46: Ulrich's.

11-47: CBI includes books from other countries if in English. LC/NUC might also have it, might not be so likely to have the price.

11-48: This is similar to #11-23; you actually need some subject information but through a source which will give you sufficient information in the citation--such as LC/ NUC and WR/BPR which give full cataloging information; you can get the information from the subject tracings, possibly from the classification number, possibly from a fuller title if there is one. Here you have no date, so you have to begin from the earliest possible time and work forward or from current dates back. In either case, LC/NUC is probably more likely to yield the title than WR/BPR.

11-49: Check Readers' Guide under Steinem as author.

11-50: German current bibliographies: Deutsche Nationalbibliographie (and cumulations), Deutsche Bibliographie (and cumulations).

11-51: You want a union catalog, showing library holdings, for books, for an 1001 publication. NUC Pre-1956 Imprints would probably be the best source.

Shaw/Shoemaker and Sabin also cover the period and give library locations.

11-52:   The simplest first source to go to is one which will cover both U.S. and British publications: LC/NUC and/or British Library Catalog. If it is not listed in either of these, then you could check U.S. bibliographies for the period (Kelly), then British bibliographies for the period (English Catalogue), or vice versa.

11-53:   Sources with subject access which cover the 1960's: BPR Cumulative, CBI, Subject Guide to Books in Print. BPR Cumulative is probably the best for this topic since it will bring all material on music together in the Dewey 780 section, whereas CBI and Subject Guide to BIP, with subject headings, will scatter the material alphabetically (i.e., under music, church music, opera, etc.).

11-54:   Periodical indexing service, again you can guess Readers' Guide as the most likely. Search Liddy as subject.

11-55:   Search all the sources covering the period, under author, cumulating and collating your information as you go. LC/NUC, possibly Sabin, Shaw/Shoemaker, etc.; possibly American Book Publishing Record 1876-1949 cumulative.

11-56:   Audiovisual Materials (LC Catalogs).

11-57:   You need a current bibliographic source for French publications: Bibliographie de la France or Livres-hebdo. The French in-print source might also help if the book is in print.

11-58:   Although this is a government publication, the major bibliographic sources for government publications are not likely to give information such as birth and death dates. Many government publications are listed in the LC/NUC if received and cataloged by either LC or an NUC library, and LC citations, being cataloging cards, do give birth and death dates for authors, especially in early years. Try the NUC Pre-1956 Imprints.

11-59:   Poole's Index and Nineteenth Century Readers' Guide.

11-60:   See Sheehy.

Part II

BASIC REFERENCE SOURCES

Section 12

DICTIONARIES

Questions #12/1--12/76

You have examined and used a great many sources so far, but they have all been variations on one type of source: bibliographies. Bibliographic sources are basic to library work, in technical services (materials selection, acquisition, and cataloging) as well as in public services (reference/information and advisory work). For librarians, particularly, but also for library users, they answer many questions directly (for example, going to Books in Print to find out the price and availability of a specific title). They are also indirect sources (for example, looking under the subject headings in CBI to find out what books have been published on the subject of coin collecting so that one may try to locate and use those books to find out more about coin collecting). Bibliographic sources are probably less well understood and used by library users than the more direct and familiar sources we are used to finding in reference collections.

In the second half of this self-study manual, you will examine several other types of reference sources: dictionaries, encyclopedias, yearbooks, handbooks, etc. The technique of examination and evaluation of a source that you have used with bibliographies is applicable to these other reference/information sources as well.

The first type of source to be taken up in Part II is dictionaries. Everyone is familiar with dictionaries, but perhaps not sufficiently so to use them as well as possible. The best way to approach dictionaries is to examine one in great detail and then more briefly consider a variety of others in comparison/contrast to the first.

Webster's Third New International Dictionary (AD10)
Webster's New International (2nd ed.) (AD9)
Funk and Wagnalls New Standard Dictionary (AD7)
Random House Dictionary (AD8)
Oxford English Dictionary (AD25/26/27, 1AD5)
Craigie: Dictionary of American English (AD105)

12-1   Dictionaries are a type of reference source with which you have had some experience in the past. Based on this experience, and any reading which you might have done on this topic, how would you define what a dictionary is? In your own words--that is, do not look up a definition; make up one. Then look up a definition in a dictionary (any). Does it differ substantially from your own definition?

12-2   One of the elements which appears to be basic to any dictionary is the aspect of alphabetical order --its arrangement. How are dictionaries arranged? Would it be safe to say that all dictionaries are arranged in this way?

12-3   If a book or reference source uses the word "dictionary" as part of its title, what is this likely to mean? Can you think of any examples from the sections on bibliographies?

12-4   A basic way to evaluate a reference source is to know how well it fulfills its functions, and to do this, you must first know what its functions are, or should be. Again, based on your past work with dictionaries and/or any preliminary reading you have done, what are some of the functions of dictionaries? What are dictionaries used for?

12-5   Begin your examination of specific dictionaries with the largest unabridged, English, adult, general
        dictionary--Webster's Third New International Dictionary of the English Language. First, look at
        the publication as a physical entity; get a quick overall idea of its general format: size, shape,
        color; number of volumes (i.e., more than one, more than five, etc.), number of pages (i.e., a
        lot or a few), type of binding, typography, layout, printing: type-set, mimeographed, etc.; easy
        to read, illustrated, etc. This quick physical orientation with a publication should soon become
        an automatic part of your examination and first use of any reference source.
                What is the general format of Webster's Third New International Dictionary?

12-6   What is the full title of Webster's 3rd? Does the title tell you anything about the scope?

12-7   What information about the imprint is given on the title page? Is a publication or copyright date
        given? Is there an edition statement on the title page of Webster's Third? What does Sheehy tell
        you about the edition of Webster's Third? What is the publication date for Webster's Third, as
        given in Sheehy?

12-8   Why do the publication dates and copyright dates vary? Why aren't they consistently given as
        1961?

12-9   What is the importance of the publication date or copyright date?

12-10   What introductory or explanatory material is given in Webster's Third? It is useful to look spe-
        cifically at each part of the introductory material, rather than simply noting it from the Table of
        Contents.

12-11   Who are the person or persons responsible for the content of Webster's Third? Who made the
        decisions about what was included, what definitions were used, what pronunciation is given, etc.?

12-12   What connection, if any, does Webster's Third or the Merriam-Webster Company have with Noah
        Webster and his 19th century dictionary?

12-13   Look up the word "orator" in Webster's Third. Seven meanings are listed. How do you distin-
        guish between them? What do the bold face numbers and letters mean?

12-14   Of the two major meanings or senses given for "orator," which seems more currently relevant to
        you? Is there any indication that the other sense may no longer be relevant?

12-15   How is the word "orator" pronounced? Is the stress (accent) on the first syllable or second
        syllable?

12-16   What is the historical derivation (etymology) of the word "orator"?

12-17   Does the entry in Webster's 3rd give any synonyms for the word "orator"?

12-18   Can you find out who George Eastman is through Webster's 3rd?

12-19   Can you find out where the Styr River is through Webster's 3rd?

12-20   Can you find out anything about the goddess Venus or about the planet Venus through Webster's 3rd?

12-21   What does "zip" in "zip code" stand for?

12-22   How would you address a judge in Great Britain?

12-23   Webster's New International Dictionary, 2nd edition, which would appear to be superseded by the Third, is still listed as a major item in Sheehy. Why is this? (See Sheehy annotation to Third.)

12-24   When was Webster's 2nd edition first published? (See Sheehy.)

12-25   What are the major differences between Webster's 2nd and 3rd editions? (Use Sheehy annotation.)

12-26   Look at the entry for "orator" in Webster's 2nd. How does it differ from that in Webster's 3rd?

12-27   Can you find information on George Eastman, the Styr River, the goddess Venus, and the planet Venus through Webster's 2nd? If so, where?

12-28   Can you find what "zip" in "zip code" stands for in Webster's 2nd? Why or why not?

12-29   Another major full-sized or comprehensive dictionary, which compares in size to Webster's 2nd and 3rd, is Funk and Wagnalls New Standard Dictionary. How current is the Funk and Wagnalls New Standard Dictionary? (See the Sheehy annotation. See also the copyright date on the title page or verso of title page of the specific copy you are able to examine.)

12-30   Does the arrangement of the Funk and Wagnalls dictionary differ from Webster's 2nd? Does the arrangement and scope of the Funk and Wagnalls dictionary differ from Webster's 3rd?

12-31   Does the arrangement of the definitions in the entries of the Funk and Wagnalls dictionary differ from the Merriam-Webster (Webster's 2nd and 3rd editions) dictionaries? Does the pronunciation guide differ? Look up the entry for "orator" and compare with what you found in #12-13, #12-14, #12-15, and #12-26.

12-32   The Webster's New International Dictionaries published by the Merriam-Webster Company and the Funk and Wagnalls New Standard Dictionary have long publishing histories. A much newer work is the Random House Dictionary. When was it first published? How would you know if it is being revised or changed from time to time since this first publication date?

12-33   Is the Random House Dictionary comparable in size to those you have already examined?

12-34 What material is included in the Random House Dictionary which is not included in the other comprehensive, unabridged dictionaries you have examined?

12-35 Of the four dictionaries examined so far (Webster's 2nd, Webster's 3rd, Funk and Wagnalls, and Random House) which one would seem most likely to contain a definition for the current usage of the word "quadraphonic"? Which one does?

12-36 Is the Webster's 2nd edition still available for purchase? How would you find out?

12-37 Of the three major dictionaries examined which are still available for purchase--Webster's 3rd, Funk and Wagnalls, Random House--which would seem to be most useful for home purchase (as opposed to library purchase)? Why?

12-38 What does the word "obsolete" mean specifically as used in dictionaries?

12-39 Would you expect to find obsolete words in the major comprehensive dictionaries that you have examined? Why or why not?

12-40 What sources are there which would cover older, obsolete words now no longer listed in the currently published dictionaries?

12-41 Another of the major English dictionaries listed in Sheehy is no longer published--The Century Dictionary and Cyclopedia. When was it published? How does it differ from the other major dictionaries you have examined? (See Sheehy or see title page of source.)

12-42 The Century Dictionary was published in the United States. Another older dictionary of historical use was published in England: the New English Dictionary or Oxford English Dictionary, edited by Sir James Murray. What is the difference between the New English Dictionary (N.E.D.) and the Oxford English Dictionary (O.E.D.)? (See Sheehy annotation.)

12-43 Does the OED claim to be a complete listing of all known words?

12-44 What would be the principal use of the OED in comparison to the major unabridged dictionaries you have examined?

12-45 Can you find, in the OED, the meaning of the word "alderdom?" What is the exact reference or citation for the first quotation listed for this word?

12-46 Since the OED does not claim to be complete, are there other sources which can be used to supplement it? For example, what about a dictionary on historical principles for American English?

12-47 Craigie's Dictionary of American English is a good example of one of the "regional" dictionaries that
       have a purpose similar to OED but supplement it by including words that could not be included in
       the OED. What is the major criterion for including words in Craigie?

12-48 What is the meaning of the word "ash-pone"? Try both Craigie and the OED.

12-49 Check "almanac-maker" in both Craigie and the OED. Do both definitions give the same date for
       the earliest known use of the word in England?

       The dictionaries you have examined so far tend to be large and unwieldy. The new group of dic-
       tionaries, commonly called "desk" dictionaries or "college" dictionaries, are of a more portable type.
       The major examples of these dictionaries are:

           American College Dictionary (AD11)
           American Heritage Dictionary, standard or 2nd college ed. (AD12)
           Doubleday Dictionary (1AD2)
           Funk and Wagnalls Standard College Dictionary (AD13)
           Random House College Dictionary (AD14, 1AD3)
           Scribner-Bantam English Dictionary (1AD4)
           Thorndike-Barnhart Comprehensive Desk Dictionary (AD15)
           Webster's New Collegiate Dictionary (9th ed.) (AD16)
           Webster's New World Dictionary, 2nd college edition (AD17)

12-50 It is not necessary to examine all of these, but at least a few should be looked at. Look at the
       entries and annotations for these dictionaries in Sheehy. Can you get any clues for quick identi-
       fication of the differences or variations in these "desk-sized" dictionaries?

12-51 Webster's Ninth New Collegiate Dictionary is published by the Merriam Company and based on Web-
       ster's Third New International. Is there any way in which the desk dictionary varies from the un-
       abridged?

12-52 Is the Webster's New World Dictionary of the American Language related to Webster's 3rd New In-
       ternational, or to the original Noah Webster's dictionary?

12-53 Although not related to the Merriam-Webster Company, the Webster's New World Dictionary is a
       very reputable dictionary. How is it arranged? What is the order of the definitions? Does it in-
       clude proper names, etc.? (Use Sheehy.)

12-54 Do you think it is necessary to remember which dictionaries give historical meanings first and which
       give common meanings first?

12-55 Is the American College Dictionary related to any of the major unabridged dictionaries?

12-56 Are there "portable" versions available of the two major "retrospective" or historical dictionaries
       you have considered (the Century Dictionary and Cyclopedia, and the Oxford English Dictionary)?
       (Use Sheehy.)

12-57 Most of the dictionaries you have looked at are specifically of American origin, as opposed to Brit-
       ish, although of course the English language is common to both countries with some variations.
       Which of those dictionaries you have examined are of British origin, if any?

12-58 Presumably there are dictionaries of the English language published in Great Britain, comparable
       in size and scope to those American dictionaries you have examined. Where would you look to find
       information on them? What are the titles of some British dictionaries?

12-59 In addition to Sheehy, another useful guide to dictionaries is Kister's Dictionary Buying Guide
       (1AD1). What types of dictionaries does Kister review?

12-60 Does Kister evaluate any other kinds of dictionaries?

12-61 The dictionaries that you have examined so far are for use by adults. Are there any dictionaries
       that are intended for use by children? Where would you look to learn about such dictionaries?

12-62 The dictionaries covered so far have been English-language dictionaries. Where would you look
       for information on foreign-language dictionaries?

       The following questions to the end of this section are search-type questions covering all of the
       dictionaries you have examined so far. It is not as easy with these sources as it was with the
       bibliographic records to decide clearly which specific source/title will best answer the question,
       or be most likely to contain the answer.
             Therefore, your best use of these questions is probably to search out the actual answers
       in the sources, using a variety of the dictionaries available to you--both unabridged/comprehen-
       sive and desk/college sizes. For example, in the few brief questions covering the desk/college
       dictionaries, you did not really look carefully or in detail at any of them; this is an opportunity
       to use them comparatively. For most of the questions, try to find the answer in at least two
       sources, or more if you have time, and compare ease of search and information given. The more
       sources you can check in for comparison, the more feeling you will get for differences and vari-
       ations in the dictionaries.

12-63 What is the preferred spelling of the word "judgement"?

12-64 Does the adjective "simon-pure" have anything to do with Simon Peter in the Bible?

12-65 What is a seismograph?

12-66 What is the correct pronunciation of the word "Hegira"? For this one, especially if you are one of
       those who is confused by the pronunciation scheme used in dictionaries and further confused by the
       presumable variations in such schemes, you might find it most helpful to use this word to check the
       pronunciations in several dictionaries. Copy down, one under the other, the full phonetic spellings
       given in each dictionary; then you can easily look at them in comparison. Try Webster's 3rd un-
       abridged, Funk and Wagnalls' unabridged, and Random House. Then you might go further to try
       Webster's New World, American College Dictionary, and American Heritage of the desk size. Note
       also where you have to look in each dictionary to find the meaning of the various phonetic symbols
       used.

12-67   Can you find a use of the word "librarianess"?

12-68   In what dictionaries can you find the meaning of the word "robotics"?

12-69   What is another more common word for "anaphylaxis"?

12-70   What is the first recorded usage of the word "lazy-bones" in the English language? (Give full citation of author and title.)

12-71   Where is the island of Nauru? What country has administrative control over it? Would you expect to find this information in all of the dictionaries? (If possible, compare the entries in the Random House and the ACD.)

12-72   What is a manticore, and can you find a picture of one?

12-73   Can you find out who wrote the novel From Here to Eternity through the dictionaries?

12-74   What is the origin of the word "kaput" (as in finished, destroyed, kaput)?

12-75   Can you find a definition of "quadraphonic" in the "desk" or "college" size dictionaries?

12-76   Can you find a definition of "off the wall" in any of the dictionaries that you have covered thus far?

12-1:   Your definition should probably be something along the line of: a list of words in alphabetical order giving definitions, etc. One of the simplest definitions of a dictionary is: a wordbook. See also, for example, "dictionary" as defined in Webster's Third New International Dictionary.

12-2:   In a single alphabetical list. Yes, probably.

12-3:   Arranged in a single alphabetical list. Sabin's Dictionary of Books Relating to America.... (a list of books alphabetically arranged). (See Section 2b.)

12-4:   Definitions (meanings, synonyms, antonyms, homonyms); specifically for foreign words, abbreviations, signs, symbols, names, places;
   Usage (slang, dialect, colloquial, idiom, substandard, nonstandard);
   Etymology (derivation);
   Orthography (spelling), syllabification;
   Pronunciation;
   Morphology, syntax, grammar.
   (If you do not know the meaning of any of the above terms, look them up in any dictionary.)

12-5:   In one very large and unwieldy volume, therefore unlikely to be standing on a shelf; more likely to be on a table or stand. It has regular binding, regular printing, some scattered illustrations.

12-6:   Webster's Third New International Dictionary of the English Language, unabridged. (See title page.) It tells you mainly that it is a dictionary of the English language. Third, new, international, and unabridged should all have some significance but it is not clear yet just what they are.

12-7:   Publisher (G. and C. Merriam Company, Publishers) and place (Springfield, Mass., U.S.A.).
   Copyright date(s) are given on the verso of the title page (date varies).
   Publication date is sometimes given on the title page (date varies). The copyright and publication dates will vary according to the date of purchase of the specific copy you are looking at.
   The edition is indicated only in the word "Third" in the title. See Sheehy annotation, first paragraph, about the edition. Actually, the "Third" is not really a new edition, based on the "Second," but rather an entirely new publication. The date for the Third given in Sheehy is 1961.

12-8:   1961 is the date of the first publication/ printing of the Third. Later publication and/or copyright dates are for later printings. Presumably whenever new or changed material is added to the publication, it is newly copyrighted. A copyright date later than 1961 (first publication of the Third) shows that some new material has, presumably, been added since 1961. See Sheehy annotation under Webster's 2nd (AD9), first paragraph, for comment on this.

12-9:   It tells you, to some degree, how up-to-date or how current this source is. You can't assume that a source with a 1972 copyright date is current to that time, but you can assume that one with a copyright date of 1950 is not going to include information from the 1960's.

12-10: The Table of Contents follows the title page, and lists all introductory material, including an explanatory chart and notes, pronunciation guide, list of abbreviations, etc. All of this material is basic in using and understanding the dictionary. At least look briefly at each section to know what it includes.

12-11: Editor in chief Philip Babcock Gove and the Merriam-Webster Editorial Staff (see title page). Also see Merriam-Webster Editorial Staff listed and Outside Consultants listed.

12-12: See first paragraph of the Preface.

12-13: Bold face numbers and letters are "sense numbers" and "sense letters" --see "Explanatory Chart," which indicates you should look under item 12 in "Explanatory Notes" for fuller explanation. For "orator," there are then two major senses, the first of which has three coordinated or related subsenses, and the second of which has three coordinated or related subsenses.

12-14: The second: a public speaker, etc. The first sense, advocate or pleader, is labeled obs. (obsolete, see abbreviations).

12-15: Pronunciation is given at the beginning of the entry between "reversed virgules" (reversed slashes). Symbols are explained in the introductory material (Merriam-Webster Pronunciation Symbols). The basic pronunciation is given, with what would appear to be four variations, none of which indicate the major or primary stress on the second syllable. Make the effort now to try to figure out the pronunciation using the symbols as given; you may have to do it some day with an impatient user hovering near.

12-16: Etymology is given following the pronunciation and preceding the definition, in square brackets (from a Middle English word which is from Middle French or Latin).

12-17: No, it doesn't. Synonyms would be specifically indicated by the use of the abbreviation "syn" followed by a see reference (as an example of this, look at the entry for "comatose") or by a "synonymy," a brief paragraph discriminating between synonymous words (as an example of this, look at the entry for "abjure"). See section 18 of the Explanatory Notes, or under "synonymous cross-reference," etc., in right hand column of Explanatory Chart.

12-18: No, there are no biographical entries in Webster's 3rd, either directly in the main list or in a separate appendix.

12-19: No, there are no geographical place entries in Webster's 3rd, either directly in the main list or in a separate appendix. (There is a form of geographical place name information available through W3, circuitously, via the adjectival route: see the entry for "danube green," for example, which does give,

in a very general way, the location of the Danube River. A similar approach can be used for biographical name identification. This only works if the names can be used adjectivally, however. It does not work for the Styr River.)

12-20: Not directly, as there is no entry for Venus, the goddess. However, you can find out through the etymology under the noun "venus" that the word derives from the Roman goddess of love, or from the 2nd planet from the sun. This is the same kind of circuitous approach described in the answer to #12-19; these examples show that it is perhaps not strictly correct to say that no proper names, geographical or biographical, can be identified through Webster's 3rd, but it is neither a very dependable nor very efficient route. As the Sheehy annotation for Webster's 3rd (AD10) puts it: "all proper nouns have been excluded, although proper adjectives remain, all in the lower case."

12-21: See entry for zip code in Webster's 3rd (© 1971, 1976, 1981) Addenda Section. (The "Addenda" section was published separately by Merriam in 1976 as 6,000 Words, Sheehy 1AD16.)

12-22: See "Forms of Address" in introductory material, p. 51a-54a (Webster's 3rd, © 1971). As you can see from this and the previous question, there is a great deal of information in Webster's 3rd which is not found in the main alphabetical section.

12-23: As the Sheehy annotation to Webster's Third indicates, there have been varying opinions on the 3rd edition of Webster's, and libraries have often chosen to retain and use the older editions as well as (sometimes in preference to) the new one.

12-24: 1934 (see Sheehy annotation; publication date in the Sheehy citation is given as 1961, which is the same as the first publication date for Webster's 3rd).

12-25: Scope: word total reduced from 2nd to 3rd meaning that since new words were added, many older words have been dropped; gazetteer and biographical information dropped; proper nouns dropped; etymologies and pronunciations expanded.
        Arrangement: abbreviations, etc., included in main alphabet in 3rd rather than separate appendices.

W3 stresses current usage (as does W2, but 1961 is considerably more current than 1934) and has dropped most of the qualifying labels (colloquial, vulgar, etc.) which users of W2 had come to rely on for indication of acceptability or correctness.

12-26:   Typography and arrangement of entry is somewhat different; W2 may seem clearer. Pronunciation: W2 gives only one variation, as opposed to several variations in W3. Oldest meaning is still given first, but other meanings are specially labeled as "law" or "Eng. Univ." Etymology similar but expanded in W3.

12-27:   Yes to all. Eastman in A Pronouncing Biographical Dictionary in appendices; Styr River in A Pronouncing Gazetteer in appendices; Venus in main alphabetical list under Venus (capitalized), goddess meaning no. 1, planet meaning no. 7.

12-28:   No. The word is too recent to appear in a dictionary published prior to 1961.

12-29:   Thorough revision published in 1913 and changed periodically with new issues or reprints (Sheehy). Copyright dates on verso of title page reflect revisions or changes.

12-30:   In F&W, all entries, including proper names are in a major alphabetical list rather than in appendices in back as in W2. F&W includes proper names (biographical, geographical) which W3 does not, but the arrangement is similar to W3, since all entries are included in the major alphabetical list.

12-31:   The arrangement differs in that F&W lists the most recent or common meaning first. Merriam-Webster dictionaries list historical or oldest meaning first.
         F&W gives two pronunciation guides; no. 1 is called the "Revised Scientific (or National Education Association) Alphabet"; no. 2 is the "text book key" (use of diacritical marks, similar to that used by Merriam-Webster).

12-32:   1966 (see Sheehy entry). Later copyright dates in individual copies would indicate changes or revisions of material.

12-33:   Random House, 260,000+ entries. It is approximately half the size of the other so-called "unabridged," or comprehensive dictionaries you have looked at.

12-34:   See Table of Contents or Sheehy annotation. Foreign word lists, atlas, list of reference books; various lists of dates, presidents, continents, ocean deeps, states, parks, air distances, lakes, waterfalls, islands, deserts, volcanoes, etc.

12-35:   Probably the most recently published or most recently up-dated would be most likely to include a word of relatively recent usage. As of the 1973 copyright for Funk and Wagnalls and the 1967 copyright for Random House, neither includes it. The 1976 and 1981 copyright printings of Webster's 3rd do list it in the Addenda.

12-36:   Available meaning "in print"; therefore look it up in BIP, or in the Merriam Company catalog if it is in PTLA. It is no longer listed, therefore not available new (although secondhand or used copies may be found).

12-37:   Probably Random House, for all its additional "encyclopedic" type information. (See answer to #12-34 and note in Sheehy.)

12-38:   Generally, it means no longer current, no longer used, out of date. Specifically, see Webster's 3rd, Explanatory Notes, Section 8 on "Status Labels": obs. or obsolete means no evidence of standard use since 1755. (See #12-14.)

12-39:   In general, these dictionaries reflect current word usage. Although they are comprehensive, they are still limited in size, and do not claim to include all words ever used. When new words are included, older or obsolete words must be dropped. (See #12-25.)

12-40:   Older editions of the current dictionaries. For example, many obsolete words not listed in Webster's 3rd would be listed in Webster's 2nd. Also in the older dictionaries no longer published.

12-41:   The latest edition listed in Sheehy is that revised and enlarged in 1911, in 12 volumes. (Earlier editions may be found in some libraries.) It differs in size (much larger), date of publication (older), many quotations, full etymologies, encyclopedic type information. If possible, see entries under "pearl" or under "Cuckoo," for example.

12-42:   The Oxford English Dictionary was originally published, under the name of New English Dictionary, in 10 volumes plus a supplement, from 1888 through 1933. A reprint in somewhat different size (12 volumes plus supplement) was made in 1933, and called the Oxford English Dictionary. The more common name for the set is now Oxford English Dictionary or OED. (See Sheehy annotations for AD25 and AD26.)

The OED is now also available in a "compact edition," the entire 1933 13-volume set reduced photographically to two volumes.

A Supplement to the OED (Sheehy AD27, 1AD5), which will eventually replace the 1933 supplement in the older sets, was begun in 1972. Three volumes (A-Scz) have been published and the final, fourth volume is scheduled for publication. This adds to the basic OED words which have come into the language since 1933.

12-43: See Sheehy annotation for NED/OED. No, it is still somewhat selective.

12-44: Historical background, etymologies, derivations fuller than in other dictionaries; older obsolete words excluded from current dictionaries; some colloquial or slang words with full historical background when included, etc.

12-45: Found in OED directly under "alderdom," indicating obsolete, meaning "lordship, chief authority." The first quotation listed is c950 (the date), Lindisf. Gosp., Luke XIX. 20. To find the exact reference or citation for "Lindisf. Gosp.," you look in the last volume of the set (vol. 13 of the 1933 set and 1961 reprint, or vol. 12 of the 1970 reprint) in the "List of Books Quoted in OED."

12-46: The annotation for NED/OED in Sheehy lists other similar dictionaries, including the Dictionary of American English edited by Craigie and Hulbert, which is also listed and annotated in Sheehy under "regional dictionaries" (AD105).

12-47: See the preface to Craigie or the Sheehy annotation (AD105). Includes words or phrases which are clearly or apparently of American origin, have greater currency in America, or denote something which has a real connection with the history of America.

12-48: "Ash-pone" is found in Craigie, vol. 1, p. 85, and is defined as "a pone of cornbread baked in the ashes." An 1816 reference indicated that it was baked by American slaves. The definition for "pone" (vol. 3, p. 1788) indicates that pone may be a version of an American Indian word meaning bread.

There is no definition of "ash-pone" in the OED in spite of the fact that it seems to fall within the OED's scope. "Ash-cake," a word with a similar meaning, is given in the OED supplement.

12-49: Yes, they both give 1611 as the date.

12-50: Several are based on the larger unabridged dictionaries, and will therefore follow the "parent" dictionary in style, arrangement, etc.

12-51: The Webster's [9th] New Collegiate lists abbreviations, signs, symbols, etc., in separate lists rather than in the main list as in W3. Webster's 9th includes separate lists of biographical names and geographical names, which W3 does not include at all.

Definition order, pronunciation symbols, etymologies, and general standards for inclusion and usage will be the same as in the unabridged.

12-52: No, it is published by World Publishing Company, and the Foreword makes no mention of its being related to other Webster dictionaries. Any dictionary can be called a "Webster's" and many are. The word does not always indicate a connection with the original Webster's or with the company which currently publishes the unabridged Webster's 3rd.

12-53: All entries in one alphabet, including proper names and places. Definitions give earliest meaning first, as do the Merriam-Webster dictionaries.

12-54: It is helpful but not necessary to remember which dictionaries do which. What you must remember is that they do not all do the same thing.

12-55: No, not really. However, the entry in Sheehy under the Random House Dictionary indicates that that dictionary, a later work than the ACD, has many characteristics similar to the ACD.

12-56: Yes, see New Century Dictionary of the English Language (Sheehy AD6) and Shorter Oxford English Dictionary (AD28). Both entries for the shorter versions follow, in Sheehy, the entries for the large sets.

12-57: OED.

12-58:   Look in Sheehy under "Language Dictionaries--English Language--English" (see also Sheehy's comments, 9th ed., p. 109 under "English Language" on comparisons between American-English and British-English dictionaries). Some titles: Cassell's English Dictionary (AD29); Concise Oxford Dictionary (AD30, 1AD6), etc.

12-59:   According to the preface of the Dictionary Buying Guide (© 1977), it reviews 58 general adult English-language dictionaries, ranging from large unabridged works to small pocket dictionaries. It also evaluates approximately 60 school and children's dictionaries.

12-60:   Yes, the Dictionary Buying Guide also covers 225 special-purpose dictionaries and word-books which complement or supplement general dictionaries (such as etymological, usage, slang, synonym, and pronunciation dictionaries).

12-61:   Sheehy: under General Reference Works--Language Dictionaries--English Language--Juvenile Dictionaries, p. 112. You might also look in Kister's Dictionary Buying Guide or the Subject Guide to BIP, but remember that the information given in Subject Guide to BIP is less descriptive and is not evaluative.

12-62:   Again, Sheehy: under General Reference Works--Language Dictionaries--Foreign Languages, p. 121-160. See also the introduction to foreign language dictionaries on p. 121 of Sheehy. Kister doesn't cover foreign language dictionaries.

12-63:   Most dictionaries list "judgment" first with "judgement" second or at the end of the entry or not at all. (See W3 and F&W unabridged, Random House, Webster's New World, for example.)

12-64:   No, it is from a character in a play. See W3, Webster's New World, etc.

12-65:   Most dictionaries have definitions. American Heritage has a definition and illustration of one.

12-66:   W3, F&W, RH all list two pronunciations, the first with the stress on the second syllable, the second with the stress on the first syllable. The dictionaries have different phonetic respellings to indicate the pronunciation, and their phonetic keys are found in different places. For example, in W3, you must turn to the end-

paper for the phonetic key, but you find there all the vowel and consonant sounds plus explanations of stress signs, etc.; RH gives at the bottom of the right page the symbols for the vowels but you must turn to the end-paper or the introduction for the full key including consonants.

12-67:   OED, under "Librarian." (1862 Trollope quote given.) The word as quoted is actually "librarianesses."

12-68:   American Heritage. Random House. Webster's 3rd (© 1971 and 1981 in Addenda). You should recognize this as a word of relatively recent origin, therefore more likely to be contained in the dictionaries most recently revised, or in those dictionaries which claim to be most "with it."

12-69:   W3, RH, ACD, W New World all give definitions but do not give another more common word. F&W gives the definition for anaphylaxis as part of the definition for its opposite word, prophylaxis, with a cross-reference from anaphylaxis. American Heritage (standard edition) gives a similar definition to the others and further gives "allergy" as part of the definition.

12-70:   OED, under "lazy-bones"; date 1592, author G. Harvey, title Pierce's Super. (See last volume for full citation.) Other dictionaries would probably include the word "lazy-bones" and might give a quotation showing usage, but you want the first recorded usage, and this is a piece of information which you know specifically you should find in the OED, therefore you might as well go directly there (assuming that you have access to the OED).

12-71:   You would generally expect to find it in all of them except W3 which does not include people--or place-names. W3 does list it as an adjective, however (see #12-19). It is not listed in Funk and Wagnalls unabridged (© 1963). It is included in W2, and in the separate list in the back. Random House includes it. ACD and Webster's New World also include it. All definitions indicate that it is in the Pacific, some give more specific locations than others (e.g., RH: "near equator"; W2: "26 m. S. of the equator"). All indicate that the former name was Pleasant Island, and W2 in addition says that it has phosphate deposits. W2 says that it is a jointly held trust territory of Britain,

New Zealand, and Australia; RH says it
is administered by Australia. RH should
be more up-to-date than W2 but, in fact,
Nauru has been an independent republic
since 1968, which is not reflected in any
of these dictionaries. (RH College Dictionary, © 1982, which is more current
than W2 or RH, says it is "an island republic ... administered by Australia before 1968."

12-72:   W3, W2, F&W unabridged have definitions
          but no picture. Random House doesn't
          have (© 1967). American Heritage has
          with an illustration.

12-73:   Yes, in Random House, 1966, under From
          Here...; the College edition does not in-
          clude it.

12-74:   A brief indication of the origin/deriva-
          tion/etymology is given in the diction-
          aries which include the word: W3 indi-
          cates it is German, from the French;
          Webster's New World indicates it is Ger-
          man and came into English through
          slang; American Heritage (standard edi-
          tion) indicates it is German (see full
          etymology in the Appendix). It is in
          the OED Supplement (1972), vol. 2,
          which also indicates that it is German
          from the French.

12-75:   We have already seen (in #12-35) that of
          the four unabridged dictionaries covered
          earlier, only the 1976 and 1981 printings
          of Webster's 3rd give a definition. Of
          the "desk" or "college" dictionaries, it
          can be found in American Heritage (1982),
          Doubleday (1975), Random House college
          (1982), Scribner-Bantam (1977), and
          Webster's New Collegiate, 9th ed. (1983).

12-76:   Possibly, but it is probably too recent
          in origin to be picked up by any but
          those having recent editions. (For ex-
          ample, it is in the "addenda" section of
          W3 © 1981, and in Random House college
          edition, © 1982.) More likely sources
          would be the slang dictionaries to be dis-
          cussed in Section 13.

Section 13

SUPPLEMENTARY LANGUAGE SOURCES

Questions #13/1--13/88

13-1   In the previous section you examined and compared the major unabridged/comprehensive English language dictionaries, plus to some extent the "desk-size" versions, in regard to their scope and arrangement, and specifically in regard to the way each dictionary handled or treated the various types of information commonly found in dictionaries. What types or kinds of information do you expect to find in dictionaries?

The next set of sources to be examined also cover some of these same kinds of information. These next sources, however, are limited to some specific aspect of word study--such as synonyms, slang, usage, abbreviations, etc.--and for that particular aspect, they can usually be expected to provide additional and more thorough information than can be found in even the major dictionaries. Most of these sources are self-explanatory in scope and arrangement and can be looked at quickly for general comparison and for the basic purpose of getting an overall picture of the available sources. However, all will repay more thorough study and use than they will be given in this manual. If time is available, it would be both useful and revealing to read the prefaces to these sources.

       Fowler: Dictionary of Modern English Usage (AD58)
       Evans: Dictionary of Contemporary American Usage (AD56)
       Follett: Modern American Usage: A Guide (AD57)

       Webster's New Dictionary of Synonyms (AD102)
       Roget's International Thesaurus (AD100 or AD99)
       Roget's II: The New Thesaurus

       Wentworth and Flexner: Dictionary of American Slang (AD93, 1AD18)
       Berrey and Van den Bark: American Thesaurus of Slang (AD87)
       Partridge: Dictionary of Slang and Unconventional English (AD91)

       Mathews: Dictionary of Americanisms (AD106)

       De Sola: Abbreviations Dictionary (AD34, 1AD7)
       Acronyms, Initialisms, & Abbreviations Dictionary (AD36, 1AD8)
       Bernstein's Reverse Dictionary (1AD19)

       NBC Handbook of Pronunciation (AD73)

       Wood's Unabridged Rhyming Dictionary (AD84)

13-2   Of all the kinds of information found in dictionaries, which do you think is most likely to prove controversial? For which type of information are you more likely to need to refer further for additional information or to other "authorities"? Think of this particularly as it relates to the Webster's Third and Webster's Second controversy (see questions #12-23 and #12-25 and any reading you have done).

13-3   The first examples of the supplementary sources to be considered deal with this problem area of usage, the way in which words are used. There are several of these: see Sheehy's section on "Idioms and Usage" (9th ed., p. 115) following American and English dictionaries. Part of the problem with usage is whether it is defined as "the way words are used" or "the way words should be used." These books may reflect to a great extent the personality and views of their authors,

186

and may come to have almost a personality themselves. Getting the flavor of this "personality" is one of the best ways to distinguish between the various usage books available. One of the oldest, most well known, and perhaps most personified is Fowler's Dictionary of Modern English Usage. The edition cited in Sheehy is the second edition, published in 1965. Was Fowler himself responsible for the second edition? When was the first edition published?

13-4   What is the basic arrangement of Fowler? Is it similar in arrangement to the dictionaries?

13-5   Does Fowler cover <u>only</u> usage? Are other areas of word study covered as well?

13-6   Is Fowler more concerned with British English than with American English? How would you find out?

13-7   If time permits, read the preface to the Revised Edition (p. iii-x) of Fowler which will give you some feeling for Fowler himself as a person as well as the place his book has assumed in this field. In addition and/or otherwise, reading some of the entries themselves is revealing. For some shorter Fowlerisms, see for example: I.Q.; iron out; hiccup; subtopia; Santa Claus; battered ornaments; fissionable; foreign danger; the various entries under "female" through "feminineness...."
       Another usage book which might be compared to Fowler is Evans' A Dictionary of Contemporary American Usage. What is one major way in which Evans is obviously dissimilar to Fowler?

13-8   How does the arrangement of Evans compare with Fowler?

13-9   Would you expect Evans to include the same entries as Fowler does? That is, can you find everything in Evans that you can find in Fowler, and vice versa?

13-10 To get some of the personal "flavor" of Evans, see such entries as: live audience; dog's life, lead a; ruination; square; flash in the pan; profession.
       How would you find out where Evans stands on the usage controversy--whether his comments are apt to be more or less "permissible" than Fowler?

13-11 What is the difference between infer and imply? Can they be used interchangeably? Compare Fowler and Evans.

13-12 Another usage source listed in Sheehy (AD62) is Nicholson's A Dictionary of American-English Usage. How does it relate to the two sources you have just looked at?

13-13 Is there a reference book which explains American English to Britishers? How would a Britisher find out that "gas" in American means "petrol"?

13-14 Modern American Usage; A Guide, by Follett, is listed in Sheehy also. How can this be compared quickly to the other sources you have seen?

13-15 Another kind of purpose for which dictionaries are frequently used is to find synonyms, antonyms, homonyms. What is meant by synonym, antonym, homonym?

13-16   Again, there are several sources which list and discuss synonyms; see in Sheehy under "Synonyms and antonyms." Two of these--Webster's and Roget's--can be looked at comparatively. Look at Webster's New Dictionary of Synonyms first. Does the use of the word "Webster's" have any particular significance? What else can you look for which might be more significant?

13-17   What is the arrangement of Webster's synonym dictionary?

13-18   Does Webster's simply give a list of synonymous words for each entry? For example, see under "discrimination" and under "discuss." Where would you look to find an exact indication of the use of the word "acumen" as compared to "discrimination?"

13-19   What are "analogous words" as used in the Webster dictionary of synonyms?

13-20   What are some words which can be used in place of "luxurious?"

13-21   Another well-known synonym book which can be compared to Webster's is Roget's International Thesaurus. Actually, there are several synonym books which use Roget in the title somewhat as Webster is used for dictionaries. If possible, look specifically at the one titled Roget's International Thesaurus, published by Crowell, 4th ed., 1977 (see item AD100 in Sheehy for a description of the 3rd ed., 1962). The Original Roget's Thesaurus of English Words and Phrases published by St. Martin's Press in 1965 (Sheehy AD99), could also be used for these questions. What is the most basic, most obvious way in which the Roget differs from the Webster's?

13-22   What is the basic arrangement of Roget's? Is it similar to the dictionaries? Is it similar to anything you have examined in the bibliographies?

13-23   Who is responsible for the classed arrangement of words found in Roget's? What is the idea behind it? Can you see any advantages of it in use over the strict alphabetical arrangement of Webster's?

13-24   How does the Roget arrangement deal with antonyms?

13-25   What does "thesaurus" (as used in the title of Roget) mean?

13-26   Can you use Roget's to find simple synonyms, such as "other words for luxurious" as in #13-20?

13-27   If you wanted to know if the word "babel" could be used as exactly synonymous with the word "hullabaloo," would it be better to look in Webster's or Roget's? Try both if in doubt.

13-28   If you were looking for a list of various noun words used for demons or evil spirits, would you find Webster's or Roget's more helpful? If in doubt, try both.

13-29 If you were trying to remember a word similar to "derogatory," which you couldn't quite recall but needed only to see it to jog your memory, would it be better to look in Webster's or Roget's?

13-30 What type of person might find Roget's more easily used, perhaps even more useful, than Webster's?

13-31 Yet another thesaurus with Roget in the title is Roget's II: The New Thesaurus. When was it published, who is the publisher, and how is it arranged?

13-32 Would you expect to find synonym discrimination in the usage books?

13-33 Sheehy lists another source entitled Webster's Collegiate Thesaurus (1AD21). Is it similar in arrangement to Roget's International Thesaurus? (See Sheehy.)

13-34 Another popular type of supplementary word source is concerned with slang, and again there are many sources to choose from. Two of these--Berrey and Van den Bark's American Thesaurus of Slang (2nd ed., 1953) and Wentworth and Flexner's Dictionary of American Slang (2nd supplemented ed., 1975)--can be compared much as the Webster's and Roget's synonym books were. Looking at the titles alone, what can you immediately say about the probable difference in the two sources? Look quickly at both sources and see if your supposition is true.

13-35 What is slang? What is the difference between slang, colloquialisms, dialects, jargon, and argot?

13-36 On what basis were the slang terms included in Wentworth and Flexner?

13-37 What is a lounge lizard?

13-38 What does "off the wall" mean?

13-39 How is the American Thesaurus of Slang (Berrey and Van den Bark) best used? What are the advantages and disadvantages arising from its arrangement?

13-40 What are some slang terms having to do with writing and publishing?

13-41 If you were reading, or perhaps even writing, a story about boxing, which included lots of slang words, which of these two sources might be the best approach to clarify the terms? What, for example, is meant by the phrase "cutting out paper dolls?"

13-42 Can you find definitions for "soul," "soul food," "soul brother"? What about "right on," "ego trip," "fast food," and "pig out"?

13-43   Both the American Thesaurus of Slang and the Dictionary of American Slang are specifically related to American usage.   A Dictionary of Slang and Unconventional English by Eric Partridge is a good one for basically British slang usage.   How recently has it been up-dated, and how?

13-44   Does Partridge include anything except slang terms?   Does he restrict himself to British slang terms?

13-45   Do the entries in Partridge seem to give any different type of or fuller information than that given in Wentworth and Flexner?   See entry for "grit," for example.

13-46   Does the Oxford English Dictionary (OED) include slang terms?   Is there an overlapping between the OED and Partridge?   Would you expect to find in OED everything that is in Partridge?

13-47   Specialized word information sources somewhat similar to the slang sources are lists or dictionaries of regional and dialect variations in languages.   What is meant by regional and dialect variations?

13-48   What sources have you looked at previously which would include this information?

13-49   Apparently in the sense that American English can be considered a regional variation of English, Sheehy has listed Craigie's Dictionary of American English (first noted in this manual in Section 12) under "Regional and dialect" sources (9th ed., p. 119).   Another major source also listed there is A Dictionary of Americanisms on Historical Principles by Mitford Mathews.   What is the difference in scope between Craigie and Mathews?   What is meant by "Americanisms" as used in the Mathews' title?

13-50   How does Mathews differ from Craigie other than being more limited in scope?   Does Mathews simply "abridge" Craigie, in a way, or does it add new material specifically to its own scope?

13-51   What is the purpose of Mathews' Dictionary of Americanisms?   See preface.

13-52   According to Mathews, what is the origin of the word "filibuster?"   How long ago was it first used?   Does the fact that it appears in Mathews mean that the word is unknown in British English?   How would you find out if it is or has been used in British English?

13-53   Next are two examples of sources specifically devoted to abbreviations.   The first one, De Sola's Abbreviations Dictionary, was published in 1981 in an Expanded International sixth edition.   Is currency important for abbreviations?

13-54   What is the scope and arrangement of the De Sola Abbreviations Dictionary?

13-55   What are acronyms?

13-56   What is "id." (in footnotes) an abbreviation for, and what specifically does it mean?

13-57   What do the words "Patience and Fortitude" refer to?

13-58   A second example of an abbreviation source is the Acronyms, Initialisms, & Abbreviations Diction-
        ary, 8th ed., 1983-84, published by Gale Research Company. What fields does it attempt to cover?

13-59   Does the Gale Research Company's Acronyms, Initialisms, & Abbreviations Dictionary differ in scope
        from the De Sola dictionary?

13-60   Does it differ in arrangement from De Sola?

13-61   What is ALA an abbreviation for besides American Library Association?

13-62   What does "flak" stand for?

13-63   Does CARE stand for any organization that has changed its name? What was the earlier name?

13-64   Using vol. 3 of the 7th edition, The Reverse Acronyms, Initialisms, and Abbreviations Dictionary,
        can you find the acronym for Library and Information Science Abstracts?

13-65   What if you knew the synonym or definition for a word, rather than an acronym, but couldn't re-
        member the word itself? For example, what might be the term for "atmosphere of a place or situ-
        ation" or the synonym for "surroundings?"

13-66   Pronunciation of words--whether standard, slang, regional, etc.--is usually given in the sources in
        which they are listed (the major exception being the synonym books). There are also a few spe-
        cialized sources for pronunciation. Of those listed in Sheehy, look specifically at the NBC Hand-
        book of Pronunciation (3rd ed., 1964). What does NBC stand for in the title and what does that
        tell you?

13-67   Does the NBC Handbook attempt to list a variety of pronunciations for every word listed, showing
        regional variations, etc.? What is the standard used for the pronunciation listed?

13-68   The NBC Handbook lists 20,000 words--obviously a limited number. How were these words chosen?

13-69   Look up the pronunciation of the word "Hegira" (see #12-66) in the NBC Handbook of Pronuncia-
        tion. How does it differ from that which you found in the dictionaries?

13-70   Of the other pronunciation sources listed in Sheehy, do any attempt to give U.S. regional varia-
        tions?

13-71   Another type of supplementary word source is the rhyming dictionary. The information found in
        these sources cannot easily be found in dictionaries. There are several rhyming dictionaries or
        handbooks listed in Sheehy (9th ed., p. 117, under "Rhymes"). Look at the Sheehy annotations

or at one or two of the books themselves. In what way do these rhyming dictionaries vary in arrangement from regular dictionaries?

13-72 If you wanted to find a rhyme for the word "librarian," in Wood's Unabridged Rhyming Dictionary, how would you locate it?

13-73 What other information besides lists of rhyming words is often found in such sources?

The next several questions to the end of the section cover the supplementary sources examined in this section, and the dictionaries from the previous section. You can use these questions as review, deciding which of the possible sources would best answer the question. Or you can use them as additional opportunities to use and compare the sources you have examined. As you did with the dictionary questions, try to look up some of the questions in more than one source, and compare answers.

13-74 You are writing a report and you need a word which is similar to "ensuing" but that isn't quite the word you want to use. What other possibilities are there?

13-75 What is the correct abbreviation for kilogram?

13-76 Who is Theodore Roethke?

13-77 What does the Australian slang phrase "put the nips into" mean?

13-78 What is a word which means the opposite of "reprehend"?

13-79 If someone offered to sell you a hand of herrings, how many fish would you expect to receive?

13-80 If someone complained to you that the word "finalize" is in Webster's Third but he or she still didn't understand when it should be used, how could you help him or her?

13-81 Can you find some words which are used to express the idea of color, particularly yellowness and orangeness?

13-82 A line from Chaucer (English poet, 1340?-1400) reads: "Buy thynne, it lay, by colpons oon and oon." What does "colpons" mean?

13-83 Who or what is Barnaby Rudge?

13-84 Anapests, iambs, and spondees are metrical patterns for scanning poetry. What do they mean; how
       are they used?

13-85 Can you find definitions for laser, quasar, and/or pulsar?

13-86 What is the origin of the term "Podunk," as in "Oh, I don't know, he comes from Podunk some-
       where..."?

13-87 Why is "squirrel" sometimes used as a slang word for psychiatrist?

13-88 Is it really considered bad grammar to use "like" in place of "as" ("like" as a conjunction, as in
       "like a cigarette should")?

Section 13

SUPPLEMENTARY LANGUAGE SOURCES

Answers #13/1-13/88

13-1:   This is the same answer as that to question #12-4, what are dictionaries <u>used for</u>.

13-2:   Probably the area of usage ("usage" as defined by W3: "habitual or customary practice or use ... the way in which words or phrases are actually used ... generally or among a community of persons...").

13-3:   2nd ed., 1965, revised by Sir Ernest Gowers (Fowler died in 1933); first edition published in 1926 (see Sheehy citation and annotation, or see title page and verso of title page of source). The second edition was reprinted, with corrections, in 1983 by Oxford University Press.

13-4:   The arrangement is alphabetical by word entries; this is similar to dictionaries, of course, but the individual entries are generally much longer and more discursive than dictionary entries; some in fact are almost essay length (see "elegant variation").

13-5:   See "Classified Guide to the Dictionary," p. xv-xx, which appears in the 2nd edition only, and which indicates that most of the articles fall under "usage" but there are also some on pronunciation, punctuation, word formation, spelling, etc.

13-6:   The Sheehy annotation doesn't really say, and probably the easiest way to decide without reading the entire preface is by the fact that it is a British publication (publisher: Oxford University Press in Oxford, England, with offices also in New York, etc.).

13-7:   Evans is American usage (see title, Sheehy annotation, preface to source) and Fowler is British (see #13-6). Evans is published by an American publisher (Random House, New York, © 1957).

13-8:   The same, basically: alphabetically by word entry with entries themselves being often discursive.

13-9:   Not really, since both are basically personal compilations; although it is surprising that so many comparable entries are found.

13-10: The Sheehy annotation doesn't really give any clues. Reading the preface should be of some help. Looking up controversial problems in both sources and comparing results should give even further clues. Kister, in his Dictionary Buying Guide, does indicate that Fowler is very proper.

13-11: Fowler (entry: infer) would maintain the distinciton; Evans (entry: imply) is more permissive to the loss of distinction between the two words.

13-12: From the full title alone, as given in Sheehy or on the title page of the source, it should be clear that Nicholson is an American version of Fowler.

13-13: To a certain extent, these things can be found out through the sources you have already examined--the dictionaries themselves often give the British equivalent for an American term (see W3 under "gas"), and the usage books often give such distinctions (see Evans under "gas"). A somewhat dated source which exists to serve this specific purpose is item AD61 in Sheehy, included with the "idioms and usage" books: Horwill's Dictionary of Modern American Usage.

13-14: Like Evans, it is <u>American usage</u>. Evans was published in 1957; Follett, having been published in 1966, should reflect somewhat <u>more current</u> usage than Evans. Also, having seen the personal quality of Evans and Fowler, one can expect Follett to reflect some of the opinions and idiosyncracies of

194

its author (in this case, authors); comparing entries, as in #13-11, may show some differences. Compare what Follett has to say on the infer/imply question.

All the usage books so far are published in the 1960's or earlier so they do not truly reflect current usage. A similar source published in 1975 is the Harper Dictionary of Contemporary Usage, by Morris and Morris (Sheehy 1AD14). As well as being more up-to-date, Morris and Morris differs from the other usage books in that it includes a panel of "authorities," giving a variety of opinions, thus showing more clearly than the other books that many of these matters of usage are often a personal and/or arbitrary decision. See the entry in Morris and Morris for "infer/imply" (#13-11), for example. See also "irregardless," "could care less," and "sexism in language."

13-15: See any dictionary.
        Synonym: meaning the same
        Antonym: meaning the opposite
        Homonym: having the same pronunciation, but different meaning.

13-16: The use of the word Webster's, used by itself, does not have any significance (see #12-52); however, you can look for the name of the publisher which might be more significant--in this case it is Merriam Company which also publishes Webster's Third unabridged.

13-17: Again, from the title itself, you can assume that it would be alphabetical, and a quick glance through the source itself confirms this.

13-18: Under "discrimination," three groups of words are listed: synonyms; analogous words; contrasted words. In some entries antonyms ("ant") are also given. In each group, the starred word should be referred to for a fuller discussion (i.e., discrimination) of the exact use of the words. To find the more exact use of "acumen" as compared to "discrimination," see under "discernment." The entry for "discuss," following that for "discrimination," is an example of a discriminated article or entry. These are similar to but generally longer than the synonymies found in Webster's Third unabridged (see #12-17). See the subtitle of Webster's New Dictionary of Synonyms; a Dictionary of Discriminated Synonyms.... See also the Sheehy annotation, to some extent. The fullest and best explanation of the way the

source works would of course be found in the preface and other introductory matter; for this, the "Explanatory Notes" on p. 32a (© 1978) are sufficient. The Introduction is more detailed. If time permits, reading the "Introductory Matter" (p. 5a-31a) of this source is an excellent way to get background on the use and importance of synonyms, etc. Another somewhat shorter approach is to read what Evans and Fowler have to say on the subject of synonyms (entry: synonyms).

13-19: See "Introductory Matter" under "Analogous and Contrasted Words," p. 30a-31a.

13-20: In Webster's (1978 ed.) under luxurious, are listed sumptuous, opulent, etc.

13-21: Basically, in arrangement.

13-22: The basic arrangement of Roget's is not alphabetical as in the dictionaries but rather a classified arrangement, similar to the classed or classified subject arrangement in such bibliographies as American Book Publishing Record. It is not exactly similar; that is, the classification scheme does not follow Dewey, for example, but the principle of arrangement is the same.

13-23: The classed arrangement of Roget's was thought up by Roget himself, the purpose being to show what words could be used to convey an idea, thus the arrangement of words classed according to the idea they express. He based it on the general system of classification used in natural history. (See "Peter Roget's Preface to the First Edition" in the Crowell, 4th, 1977 edition; or the Introduction in the St. Martin's 1965 edition. See also p. 14a-15a of the Introductory Matter of Webster's New Dictionary of Synonyms.) An advantage of Roget's arrangement is that, like any classed arrangement, it brings together in one place all related words rather than scattering them alphabetically. See, for example, category "825. Thief" in the Crowell, 4th, 1977 edition ("789" in St. Martin's 1965 edition). Listed in that section are many similar although not necessarily synonymous words related to "thief," including slang terms, foreign words, literary allusions (although with no explanations), names, etc.

13-24: See, for example, category 548, intelligibility, followed by category 549, somewhat antonymous words under unintelligibility. (Comparable entries are given in the St. Martin's edition under categories 516 and 517.)

13-25: Treasury or storehouse, hence a book containing a store of words, a dictionary; or especially a book of classified synonyms (from Webster's New World Dictionary). Thus, the use of "thesaurus" in a title can often mean a basic classed arrangement of words like Roget's.

13-26: Yes, by looking in the alphabetical list in the back, which refers you, under luxurious, to the various categories or sections in which similar/related words will be found. It necessitates more looking back and forth than Webster's, but can be done.

13-27: Roget's only lists the words, does not try to distinguish or discriminate between them. Webster's under "din" (both babel and hullabaloo indicate the discriminatory discussion will be found under "din"), discusses the exact differences. In this case Webster's might be more useful. A dictionary would also probably be more useful than Roget's.

13-28: Here is where Roget's is useful. Demon, in the alphabetical index, refers you to several categories, each of which gives useful lists of related words; the Crowell 4th ed. lists "evil spirit" which gives you specifically the list you want. The St. Martin's edition lists "devil" but not "evil spirit" under "demon." Demon is not listed in Webster's but demonic and demonaic are.

13-29: Since this isn't a case of needing careful discrimination between words, either Webster's or Roget's would do the job. A dictionary might also do it. Since Roget's tends, by virtue of its arrangement, to list more related words than either Webster's or a dictionary, it might be more likely to be helpful--depending how close in meaning your elusive word comes to "derogatory." Roget's lists more "analogous" (see #13-19) than strictly synonymous words.

13-30: Roget's lists lots of synonymous and analogous and related words, with no clear distinction between them. Writers or others who use words frequently and are already basically knowledgeable about them can use Roget's more easily because in most cases they are searching

for a word which they are already familiar with but can't quite remember (as in #13-29) and they do not need to be so dependent upon the discriminatory articles which are an important part of Webster's. Those who are less certain, less knowledgeable about words would generally find Webster's more helpful and Roget's somewhat confusing.

13-31: It was published in 1980 by Houghton Mifflin. In spite of Roget being in the title, Roget's II is alphabetically arranged in dictionary form. Each page is in two columns with the left alphabetically arranged by main entry word followed by a definition adopted from the American Heritage Dictionary. The right column lists appropriate synonyms and idioms, but no antonyms.

13-32: Yes, since this often is in fact a problem of correct or common usage. See Fowler on "foam; froth" and "flurried; flustered; fluttered." See Evans on "reticent, secretive, taciturn, laconic."

13-33: Webster's Collegiate Thesaurus is arranged alphabetically, as is Webster's New Dictionary of Synonyms and Roget's II, in contrast to the Roget thesaurus. It has been advertised as "easy to use as a dictionary," and "without complicated cross-indexes." The fact that it is called a thesaurus further blurs the useful distinction between a dictionary-type arrangement and a thesaurus- (or related words together) type arrangement.

13-34: One is called a "thesaurus," the other a "dictionary"; presumably the main difference will be in arrangement--the thesaurus classed like Roget (see #13-25) and the dictionary alphabetical. The sources themselves bear out this difference.

13-35: See definitions in Webster's Third unabridged, or in Preface of Wentworth and Flexner Dictionary of American Slang. (The entire preface is good reading, if time permits.)

13-36: See first paragraph of "Explanatory Notes."

13-37: See Wentworth and Flexner: a ladies' man, etc.

13-38: See the Supplement to Wentworth and Flexner. Note that this is the term you were unable to define using the standard dictionaries (#12-76), with the exceptions of the Addenda section in the 1981 printing of Webster's 3rd, and the Random House college edition, 1982.

13-39: Berrey and Van den Bark is based generally on the Roget classed arrangement of words (see "Explanation" in front matter). As such, it has most of the same advantages and disadvantages of the Roget arrangement. Slang terms are only listed, not always clearly defined. Individual words or phrases can be found through the index with reference to the classed arrangement. Similar and related terms are brought together in broad and often useful groupings.

13-40: Basically, this can be found only through the Berrey and Van den Bark thesaurus approach--see various categories 518-526: Journalism, writing, publishing.

13-41: The thesaurus (Berrey and Van den Bark) has a long list of related slang words about boxing. This would bring all the terms together in one place. Many of the terms could be found, alphabetically, in the dictionary (Wentworth and Flexner), and a clearer statement of meaning might be given. In this case, you might find it useful to use both sources together. The phrase "cutting out paper dolls" is listed in Wentworth but with no meaning given that relates to boxing. If you looked in Berrey under the category of boxing, you would have to check through all the many lists of words till you found "Cutting out paper dolls" under "punch-drunk," dazed. You could also look it up alphabetically in the index which refers you to the specific section on Boxing--Punch-drunk.

13-42: All of them are listed in the supplement of the Wentworth and Flexner 2nd supplemented edition, with the exception of "pig out," which is apparently too recent to be included.

13-43: 7th edition, 1970; the supplement or second volume of the work has been revised, the first part left unchanged. See verso of title page or Sheehy annotation. This is similar to the updating done on Wentworth and Flexner.

13-44: He includes colloquialisms, catch-phrases, solecisms, catachreses, nicknames, vulgarisms, and such Americanisms as have been naturalized (see sub-title or Sheehy annotation). Australian and

New Zealand slang is also included, although not so clearly noted in the prefatory matter.

13-45: Perhaps more etymology, derivation, quotes, historical and now obsolete terms. In general, Partridge seems to have more of the historical aspect of slang than Wentworth and Flexner.

13-46: The OED does include some slang terms. Actually, Partridge is more inclusive, broader in scope, for slang, than even the great OED. See Preface to 1936 edition (reprinted in 1970, 7th edition) in which he compares relevant terms and claims to include all slang, etc., terms from the OED plus about 35% more.

13-47: See Webster's Third unabridged, or check your answer to #13-35.

13-48: The OED for basically British English. Also Craigie's Dictionary of American English for American English. To some extent it is also included in any dictionary.

13-49: "Americanisms" is used to mean "a word or expression that originated in the United States...." (see Sheehy annotation or preface of source). The Craigie dictionary is less limited in scope than Mathews, including "not only words ... of American origin ... but also every word denoting something which has a real connection with the development of the country and the history of its people." (See Sheehy annotation or preface of source.)

13-50: In the first place, Mathews was published in 1951 including material up to the time of publication (see Sheehy annotation), and Craigie, published 1936-44, covers only to the end of the 19th century (see Sheehy annotations). Mathews also attempted to refine and build upon the material in Craigie, in some cases with new evidence leading to new conclusions.

13-51: The purpose is to treat such words historically. Note that the OED, Craigie's Dictionary of American English, and Mathews are all built on "historical principles."

13-52: The origin is from the Spanish; quotes are given as early as 1850's. Its appearance in Mathews does not limit its use to America; it means that it first came into use, in that specific sense, in America. It may since have been used in Great Britain; it may have come into British English via some other route or with some other meaning. Checking in the OED or any of the British dictionaries should indicate if it is commonly known in Great Britain.

13-53: Probably more so than in any other aspect of word study except possibly slang. New abbreviations come into use every day, and keeping up with them and identifying them are often almost impossible.

13-54: Arrangement is alphabetical; scope is "abbreviations, acronyms, anonyms," etc., as listed on the title page. Note also the special lists indicated in the table of contents.

13-55: Words formed from the initial letters of other words, such as "radar" from Radio Detection and Ranging.

13-56: Abbreviation for idem, which is Latin and means "the same." (De Sola, p. 406, 6th ed.) It would probably also be in any standard dictionary.

13-57: De Sola, 6th ed., p. 626: Mayor La Guardia's nickname for the couchant lions flanking the steps of the New York Public Library. This example illustrates the rather wide scope of De Sola.

13-58: See list on title page: aerospace, associations, etc.

13-59: In recent editions both the Acronyms, Initialisms, and Abbreviations Dictionary and the De Sola Abbreviations Dictionary have extended their scope considerably. This increased scope is reflected in the Acronyms ... Dictionary title changes over the years (see Sheehy and preface). Both are now similar in scope. The preface to the Acronyms ... Dictionary has a short discussion of the distinctions among the terms acronyms, initialisms, and abbreviations. Part of the reason both sources have expanded in coverage to include abbreviations as well as acronyms, and acronyms as well as abbreviations, is because it isn't easy to define these terms for inclusion/exclusion. The Acronyms ... Dictionary has some continuous updating (see volume 2), and a reverse approach (see volume 3).

13-60: Volume 1 and 2 don't differ from De Sola, but volume 3, the reverse dictionary,

is in reverse form--that is, the definition or term is given and then its acronym or abbreviation. (Volume 3 of the 8th edition is expected to be essentially the same as that of the 7th edition.)

13-61: American Latvian Association and American Legion Auxiliary, among others. (See both De Sola and Acronyms.)

13-62: Fliegerabwehrkanone, etc.--the German word for antiaircraft gun, used for antiaircraft fire (also Fondest Love and Kisses, according to Acronyms). The Acronyms Dictionary gives somewhat more information here.

13-63: Cooperative for American Relief Everywhere is listed in both De Sola and the Acronyms Dictionary. The Acronyms Dictionary (8th ed.) lists two former names, for which the letters remain the same.

13-64: The terms are arranged alphabetically by translation or meaning rather than by acronym, initialism, or abbreviation. So by simply looking up Library and Information Science Abstracts in the alphabetical listing, you find that its acronym is LISA.

13-65: A reverse dictionary such as Bernstein's Reverse Dictionary (1AD19) would be a likely source to which to turn. Under each of those two headings, as well as others, one would be given "ambience" as the target word.

13-66: NBC stands for National Broadcasting Company, and indicates that the pronunciations given therein are likely to be in some way approved by or used by NBC announcers; it should also indicate an attempt to cover material--such as names and places--which might frequently appear in the news.

13-67: See "Standards of American Pronunciation" in the introductory matter. It attempts to record the pronunciations used by educated persons in the greater part of the U.S.--that is "General American" pronunciation. Only one pronunciation is given and that is chosen more or less arbitrarily.

13-68: See "Standards of American Pronunciation," bottom of p. ix.

13-69: NBC Handbook gives two pronunciations! one in "respelling" and one in the International Phonetic Alphabet (IPA). The "respelling" (hi JIGH ruh) pronunciation is probably much easier to use than the dictionary diacritical markings, unless you are very familiar with those. It might be helpful regarding pronunciation notations in general to read the section titled "Ways of Noting Pronunciation" in the "Standards of American Pronunciation" in the front matter of the NBC Handbook.

13-70: Kenyon and Knott: A Pronouncing Dictionary of American English (Sheehy AD76) does, for example.

13-71: The arrangement is not alphabetical by the first letter of the word as in dictionaries. In fact the approach is almost backwards. Words are grouped by the rhyming syllables--the last, last two, last three, etc., syllables of the words. Sometimes they are arranged alphabetically within these groupings. Wood's Unabridged Rhyming Dictionary (Sheehy AD84), for example, is grouped in single, double, triple rhymes and arranged within those groups strictly by phonetics or sound, rather than spelling.

13-72: If you wanted to rhyme the last three syllables, you would look in the "triple rhymes" section, words accented on the second syllable from the last (beginning p. 809 of © 1943 edition); then under the phonetic equivalent of the last three syllables of "librarian"--ar-i-an--under which you find such possibilities as antiquarian, grammarian, barbarian, humanitarian....

13-73: General information on poetry, forms, definitions, mechanics, etc.

13-74: A synonym book (Webster's or Roget's) would be useful; or any dictionary might also be helpful, depending on how extensively it lists synonyms for the specific word. In all you would start under "ensuing," following up other possibilities which are mentioned under that word. In both Webster's Third unabridged and Webster's New Dictionary of Synonyms you would have to look under "ensue"; in Roget's you can actually look under "ensuing." Suppose that the actual word which you vaguely had in mind was "resultant," even though that may not be strictly synonymous with ensuing. In this case Roget's would have given you your word immediately, just in the index alone.

13-75: This is a somewhat different approach to the abbreviation problem that can be solved with the abbreviation dictionaries. It would be easiest to go to a dictionary and look under "kilograms" to find the abbreviation. You could also guess that the abbreviation might be "kg" and look in an abbreviation list to see if you were correct, but this is essentially a backwards approach, and not really necessary.

13-76: An American poet who died in 1963, and whose importance is apparently too recent to get him into either the Funk and Wagnall unabridged (© 1963) or Webster's 2nd unabridged (did you check in the Third? why?), but Random House Dictionary (© 1967) lists him, in the regular alphabetical order.

13-77: Slang, and specifically Australian, which leaves out the Dictionary of American Slang and the Thesaurus of American Slang, and therefore leaves Partridge's Dictionary of Slang. Partridge lists it under "nips in(to), put the." You might also try the OED; the Supplement, vol. 2 lists it (and cites Partridge as the reference).

13-78: You want an antonym. Antonyms are sometimes given in the dictionaries, and perhaps more often in the synonym books. Webster's Third, Funk and Wagnalls, Random House give synonyms, no antonyms for reprehend. Webster's New Dictionary of Synonyms gives synonyms but no antonyms for reprehend. Roget's (Crowell, 4th ed.) index leads you to the category of "Disapproval" (969), preceded by the generally opposite category of "Approval" under which you find sanction, accept, etc., which will probably suit your needs.

13-79: Webster's Third unabridged (and Second) both list under definitions for "hand"; five articles of the same kind sold together. Not listed in Funk and Wagnalls unabridged (© 1963) or in Random House (© 1967).

13-80: Probably the best thing to do is to go to a usage book. Finalize is listed in Webster's Third (but not in the Second) with no usage label to indicate its acceptance in formal writing, etc. Neither Evans nor Follett deals with the word; Fowler, rather surprisingly, says that there are a "few occasions when it is an improvement on completed or finished."

13-81:   This is a case where Roget's thesaurus-type arrangement is probably the most helpful source, looking directly under the category for Color, and the various more specific categories (i.e., orangeness) following. Webster's New Dictionary of Synonyms and Webster's Third unabridged are no help.

13-82:   OED. (You could of course also check unabridged dictionaries, since you don't know for sure that the word is not in current usage, but it seems more reasonable to go directly to the historical source.) Under "colpon," you find that the word is a variant of "culpon," being obsolete, meaning "cut, piece." Further information is given in the main entry under "culpon," including the quote from Chaucer. Century Dictionary lists only under "culpons" with no cross-reference from "colpons."

13-83:   Webster's Third would not have it as it is a name; Funk and Wagnalls unabridged (© 1963) and Random House (© 1967) do not have it. It is listed in Webster's Second Unabridged under Barnaby (not Rudge, although there is a cross-reference from Rudge, Barnaby to Barnaby Rudge at the bottom of the page--underneath the line--on which Rudge would appear).

13-84:   You could look each up separately in any dictionary. A better way would be to turn to one of the rhyming dictionaries (Wood's, for example) which includes discussion of versification and scansion to find more detailed and comparative information.

13-85:   All are relatively recent terms. Webster's Third unabridged lists laser in the main section; as of the 1981 printing, quasar and pulsar are in the Addenda. Random House (© 1967) lists laser and quasar. American Heritage lists all three. Another source which might not immediately occur to you as a possibility is abbreviation books, on the assumption that these words are acronyms of some sort (like radar). De Sola (6th ed., 1981) lists all three, and the Acronyms, Initialisms, & Abbreviations Dictionary (8th ed., 1983-84) lists all three, but does not attempt definitions.

13-86:   Webster's Third unabridged lists it as from a village of that name in Massachusetts or Connecticut. Dictionary of American English (Craigie) and Mathews' Dictionary of Americanisms further identify it as of Algonquian Indian origin. Not in OED.

13-87:   Wentworth and Flexner (2d sup. ed., 1975), under squirrel, noun, meaning 2: that is, one who examines "nuts."

13-88:   Webster's Third lists the use of like as a conjunction as acceptable. If you prefer not to take the word of Webster's Third, President Eisenhower, Art Linkletter, and the Winston Company, you can go on to the usage books for further discussion. Fowler says it is generally condemned as vulgar, and has colloquial use in the U.S.; Follett says it cannot be used in place of "as." Evans is more permissive, says it is an established function, and points out historical and literary precedent (quotes from Keats being, presumably, more acceptable to the prescriptive grammarians than quotes from Art Linkletter).

ENCYCLOPEDIAS

Questions #14/1--14/110

14-1   If you wanted to find the definition of "communism," you would look it up in a dictionary. If you wanted to find out the historical development of Communism, would you expect to find this in a dictionary? What type of reference source would give you this information?

14-2   What is an encyclopedia? How would you define the term?

The next set of sources to be examined are:

Encyclopedia Americana (AC1)
New Encyclopaedia Britannica, 15th ed. (AC3)
Collier's Encyclopedia (AC5)
Academic American Encyclopedia (2AC1)

New Columbia Encyclopedia (AC6, 1AC2)
Lincoln Library (AC7)

Compton's Pictured Encyclopedia (AC17)
World Book Encyclopedia (AC20)

Chambers's Encyclopaedia (AC4)

Encyclopedia Buying Guide (1AC4)

14-3   The first few encyclopedias to examine are the major well-known American adult encyclopedias: Americana, Britannica and Collier's. All are listed in Sheehy's section on encyclopedias under "American and English." It is probably easiest to examine all of them together and comparatively, checking against the Sheehy annotations and remembering that any of the specific comments in Sheehy may now be outdated. Look first at the Americana. What is the full title, and what is the name of the publisher?

Just as an encyclopedia itself is a vast undertaking, so is the examination and evaluation of any specific encyclopedia. For real evaluation, one must rely on the published reviews and comments of experts. A feeling for the general usefulness of encyclopedias, perhaps more so than for any other type of reference source, must come from continued and daily use in a reference or research situation. However, there are several specific points on which you can compare and contrast the encyclopedias and which may help you get a general idea of the types of information which can be found through encyclopedias, and the most efficient ways of using them.
    As with other reference sources, you should look first at the basic physical bibliographic facts about the source: full title, publisher, copyright date or edition of the set you are examining, number of volumes, etc.
    Then, as with the other reference sources, you can go on to determine general scope and arrangement, and you can check for specific types or kinds of information included (illustrations, maps, bibliographic references, etc.).

14-4   Be sure to note the date of the edition or set of the specific set which you are examining.   Where would you expect to find this date?   What does the date indicate to you?

14-5   Do the encyclopedia publishing companies come out with completely new and revised editions every year?   How do they make provisions for revising or up-dating the material in the encyclopedias?   (See Sheehy.)

14-6   Does the Encyclopedia Americana use the "continuous revision" policy?   How can you tell?

14-7   Can you tell what material is changed or revised each year?

14-8   What introductory or prefatory matter is included?

14-9   Is there anything in the introductory matter which tells you how to use the encyclopedia?

14-10   What is the publishing history of the Americana?   When was it first published?   When was the last major revision?

14-11   How many volumes are there to the set?

14-12   What is the basic arrangement of the set?   What can you tell from the spines of the volumes?

14-13   With encyclopedias, it is not really sufficient to say that the arrangement is alphabetical.   So much information is included that it is also necessary to know how it can be found alphabetically and to what depth it is discussed.   Considering the type and depth of information found in encyclopedias, what are the possibilities for arrangement of material?   Look, for example, in vol. 1 of the Americana under Alaska and Adak.

14-14   Are the articles or entries in the Americana mostly short or long?

14-15   The arrangement of the Americana is alphabetical, with a mixture of long and short articles.   If you wanted to locate in the Americana information on The Maid's Tragedy, a 17th-century English play by Beaumont and Fletcher, would you look under Maid's Tragedy, under Beaumont, under Fletcher, under English literature, English drama, drama, seventeenth-century drama?

14-16   Does the Americana have a separate article on German Shepherd dogs?

14-17   If you were looking in the Americana for information on education, for which there is a separate article, how could you be sure that all the pertinent information you might find helpful would be included in that article?   How could you find out where else in the set you might find pertinent information?

14-18   Is there any way in which you can judge the relative authority and accuracy of the articles in the

Americana? For example, who wrote the article on Air Pollution and what are his/her qualifications for doing so?

14-19   Are all articles signed?

14-20   There is a list of contributors in the introductory matter of vol. 1. Does this give you additional information to that found at the end of the articles? The list of contributors may seem impressive. Can you actually tell to what specific topic they made some contribution?

14-21   Would you expect to find maps in the encyclopedia? Where are they found in the Americana? What company is responsible for the maps in the Americana? Can you tell how recent the maps are?

14-22   What other kinds of illustrations or graphic material do you find in the Americana? Do you think this illustrative material is important?

14-23   Do the encyclopedias give you access to any further information, beyond the scope of their contents? For example, if you had read the article on air traffic control in the Americana, and wanted further information on the subject, what could you find in the Americana to help you?

14-24   These "bibliographies" (lists of further references is perhaps a more accurate term than bibliographies) are very important in the proper use of encyclopedias. It is too easy to think that all information is contained in the encyclopedia, or that the encyclopedia is really the only source you need to refer to for information. Does the Americana have bibliographies for all articles? Is the information given in the bibliographies complete? Do the bibliographies list foreign works, or only English language materials? How do you tell if the bibliographies are up to date?

14-25   If you looked in the Americana to find further information on Hegira, could you also find out how to pronounce it at the same time?

14-26   In checking the article on Air Pollution in the Americana (see #14-18), did the entry for that article precede or follow the article on aircraft?

14-27   So far, the questions you have been answering about the Americana have dealt with specific items for which there are reasonably clear answers. You have considered the basic arrangement of the encyclopedia, the general authority of its contributors, and the general way in which it is revised or kept up to date. The only way in which you have dealt with the problem of "scope" is by looking for specific kinds of information or features such as bibliographies, maps, illustrations, pronunciations, etc. In a very general and obvious sense, what is the "scope" of an encyclopedia?

14-28   Considering the scope of an encyclopedia to be "all knowledge" is pretty overwhelming. Can this be narrowed down in any way? What is the purpose of a modern encyclopedia? Is the purpose of an encyclopedia to provide highly technical, specialized information to a person already an expert in the field? Should an encyclopedia article on nuclear physics be written in such a way that it can be understood only by a nuclear physicist? Should it be written in such a way that it can be understood by an eighth-grade student? Should an article on musical harmony be written in such a way that it can be understood only by a musicologist? Should it be written in such a way that it can be understood by a nuclear physicist? At what audience or level is an encyclopedia aimed?

14-29   What is the audience at which the Americana is aimed? Where would you expect to find this information?

14-30   From young students through adults is still a very broad range. In general, do you think that young students would understand the material in the Americana? What is one way in which you could try to test this (short of finding a young student and asking him/her)?

14-31   Is there any other way in which the scope of an encyclopedia can be narrowed? Consider the country (and/or language) of publication.

14-32   Is the Americana noted for any special aspects or strong points? (See Sheehy.)

14-33   The next major encyclopedia to be examined is the Encyclopaedia Britannica. In 1974 the publisher, Encyclopaedia Britannica, Inc., published the 15th edition which is quite different in format from its 14th edition and from other major adult encyclopedias. Due to the significantly different format of the 15th edition, many libraries keep older editions, such as the 14th, as well. Note that both the 14th and 15th editions are treated by Sheehy (as were the 2nd and 3rd editions of Webster's New International Dictionary). The 15th edition of the Britannica is entitled The New Encyclopaedia Britannica. How is the New Britannica organized? How many volumes are there?

14-34   What are the purposes of the Propaedia, Micropaedia, and Macropaedia? (See Sheehy.)

14-35   As the Macropaedia is arranged alphabetically, why should one first locate an entry in the Micropaedia before turning to the Macropaedia?

14-36   What about maps, and other illustrations in the New Britannica?

14-37   What is the revision policy for the New Britannica?

14-38   What is the intended audience of the New Britannica?

14-39   The Britannica has long had a reputation as the most scholarly, most technical, most advanced of the encyclopedias, but the trend with revisions has been more to the popular level, more in competition with the nonspecialist level of the Americana. What could you do to test this?

14-40   How does the Britannica's article on Alaska compare with that in the Americana? Can you find any information on Adak in the Britannica?

14-41   Does the Britannica have an article on air pollution? Can you find any information on air pollution?

14-42   Who is the author of the article on "aluminum products and production" in the Britannica?

14-43   Look at some of the bibliographies in the Britannica. How do they differ from those in the Americana?

14-44   The next major encyclopedia is Collier's. Who is the publisher? How many volumes? What is the revision policy? Note date of the set.

14-45   How does Collier's differ from the other encyclopedias (Americana, Britannica) in regard to scope, audience or level?

14-46   Does Collier's differ from the Americana in regard to arrangement?

14-47   Can you find through Collier's a list of further readings on the subject of air pollution?

14-48   Why are the bibliographies in Collier's arranged in this fashion, rather than following the articles as in the other encyclopedias? What are the advantages and disadvantages of such an arrangement?

14-49   The items in the bibliographies--see History: The Ancient World, for example--are not listed alphabetically following the subject heading. On what basis are they listed?

14-50   How are the bibliographies in Collier's arranged, and how do you find one on air pollution?

14-51   How do the maps and other illustrative matter in Collier's compare to the other encyclopedias?

14-52   Who wrote the article on Africa in Collier's and what are his qualifications for doing so?

14-53   You have examined and compared, briefly, three major adult encyclopedias. In general, how did they differ? What kinds of comparative statements can you make about their scope, arrangement, special features, etc.?

14-54   Look specifically at the articles on libraries in all three encyclopedias and compare them. Is the access similar for all (direct or through the index)? Is the length similar? Is the structure similar? What about illustrations? Which of them discuss librarianship itself? Which give information about education, certification, degree requirements, etc.? Which give the most information about foreign libraries and library systems? Do any of them give basic information to help someone use the library (the card catalog, the reference sources, etc.)?

14-55   Using these three encyclopedias, can you find a picture of Canterbury Cathedral (in England)? How did you go about searching for it? How did you locate it?

14-56   Using the indexes only, can you find out who Jean Arp was? Can you find out when he lived and what he was noted for? Compare all three encyclopedias.

14-57   When and how is St. Nicholas' Day celebrated in various countries? What is its historical signifi-
         cance? Try all three encyclopedias and compare results.

14-58   How do you read the symbols on a weather map? Try all three and compare. What is your best
         approach to this? If you looked directly for an article on "weather" or "weather maps," what
         would you find?

14-59   In which of these three encyclopedias could you find the titles of some books on chemistry suitable
         for high school students?

14-60   A new encyclopedia aimed at a relatively wide audience is the Academic American Encyclopedia.
         Who is the publisher? How many volumes does it contain? What is the revision policy? What is
         its audience or level?

14-61   How is the Academic American arranged? Where is the index? What about its scope?

14-62   How does the Academic American deal with "libraries" (see #14-54)? How long is the article?
         What is the access point? Can it be located through the index? How about a bibliography? Is
         the article signed?

14-63   Using the index only, can you determine who Jean Arp was? (See #14-56.)

14-64   Does the Academic American have any information about St. Nicholas' Day? (See #14-57.)

14-65   If you wanted to "get some background information" on various North American Indian tribes, where
         they were originally located, something about their languages, their customs, the relationships be-
         tween the tribes, their current status, etc., to what type of source would you go? How would you
         use this source?

14-66   Why is it useful (or necessary) for a library to have more than one encyclopedia?

14-67   What is the importance of the index in using encyclopedias?

14-68   The best use of an encyclopedia is probably for general information or background questions, such
         as those on the celebration of St. Nicholas' Day, the symbols on a weather map, the background
         information on American Indian tribes. However, encyclopedias are also used extensively for locat-
         ing "facts" or illustrations, for quick answers to specific questions, etc. For these uses, the in-
         dex of an encyclopedia is indispensable, since it is generally the only access you have to specific
         information.
              How does the use of an encyclopedia differ from the use of a dictionary in regard to arrange-
         ment? Both are arranged alphabetically, but the dictionary does not need to have an index. Why
         not? Does it have anything to do with the kind of information they give?

14-69   Does the information given in encyclopedias overlap that in dictionaries? How? Could you find
         out who Jean Arp was through the dictionary? Could you find out when St. Nicholas' Day is
         celebrated through the dictionary?

14-70   The next three encyclopedias on the list represent a form which seems to fall half-way between
         the dictionary and the encyclopedia: the "one-volume" encyclopedia. Look at the Preface to the
         New Columbia Encyclopedia. What is the purpose of such a single-volume encyclopedia? What is
         it trying to do? How does it differ from a dictionary? from a regular encyclopedia?

14-71   What does the Preface tell you about the scope of the work? Any special aspects covered?

14-72   What is the arrangement of the New Columbia Encyclopedia? Is there an index? Is an index
         needed?

14-73   Does the New Columbia Encyclopedia contain such special features as maps, illustrations, bibliog-
         raphies, pronunciation guides, etc., as the regular encyclopedias do?

14-74   What is the major obvious way in which the Lincoln Library differs from the New Columbia En-
         cyclopedia?

14-75   How does this compare to other sources you have examined previously? What are the advantages
         and disadvantages to these two types of arrangements?

14-76   Did Roget's Thesaurus and the slang thesaurus have indexes? Does the Lincoln Library have an
         index? Why is an index needed?

14-77   Using either of these two compact encyclopedias (New Columbia and Lincoln Library), can you find
         out what Jean Arp is noted for? Can you find the location of Adak, Alaska?

14-78   In which of these two encyclopedias would you expect to find a "background" type article on
         mineralogy, discussing its relationship to geology, with lists and descriptions of various rocks and
         stones, possibly with illustrations? Could you find the definitions, etc., of the various rocks and
         stones through the other encyclopedia?

14-79   Can you find some background material on American Indians in these two encyclopedias?

14-80   How do the revision policies for the New Columbia Encyclopedia and The Lincoln Library compare?

14-81   A new "compact" encyclopedia, the Random House Encyclopedia, was published in 1977. What is
         its intended audience? (See Sheehy, 1AC3.)

14-82   How is The Random House Encyclopedia arranged? (See Sheehy.) Does this seem similar to the
         arrangement of any of the major encyclopedias?

14-83   One of the ways in which encyclopedias differ is in level: reading level, level of understandabil-
         ity, etc. (See #14-29, 14-38, 14-45, 14-53.) All of the encyclopedias you have examined so far
         have been basically adult level, with one exception. Which of the encyclopedias that you have
         looked at seems to be aimed at a younger audience?

14-84   Look first at Compton's Pictured Encyclopedia. What is the basic information you need to know
         about it: publisher, number of volumes, revision policy, date of set you are looking at?

14-85   According to the preface of the set itself, what is the general grade level or reading level aimed
         at by Compton's?

14-86   What is the basic arrangement of Compton's? Does it differ in any way from the adult encyclopedias
         you examined?

14-87   Can you find, through Compton's, who Jean Arp was and what he was noted for? How about
         Adak, Alaska?

14-88   How does the Compton's article on libraries compare with those in the adult encyclopedias (see
         #14-54 and #14-62)?

14-89   The other children's or juvenile encyclopedia to be examined is the World Book Encyclopedia. Note
         the publisher, the number of volumes, revision policy, and date of the set you are examining.
         What is the general grade level or reading level aimed at by this set?

14-90   Does the arrangement of the World Book differ in any way from the other sets you have examined?
         Can you find anything about Adak, Alaska or Jean Arp through the World Book? Can you find
         anything about the location of the Aran Islands?

14-91   Can you find, in the World Book, broad general background information on the American Indian?

14-92   Since Compton's and World Book are encyclopedias designed primarily for children, what would
         this lead you to assume about the illustrations, maps, other graphic material? Is your assumption
         borne out by examination?

14-93   What can you determine about the authority behind the articles in Compton's and World Book?
         Would you expect the same authority as with the adult encyclopedias?

14-94   Where could you find a short list of books on chemistry for a junior high school student?

14-95   If you had no background at all in science, and you wanted to know in a general way what lasers
         are and how they work, where might you go for an introductory article?

14-96   Should the use of the children's or juvenile level encyclopedias be limited to school libraries or children's collections? Would it be useful for an adult reference collection to have a juvenile level encyclopedia as well as the adult level?

14-97   Besides the obvious one of reading level, does the approach of the children's encyclopedias differ from the adult encyclopedias in any major way?

All of the encyclopedias listed in this section thus far have been American publications. If, for example, you desired more of a British perspective you could turn to one of the British encyclopedias. The largest British encyclopedia (though now discontinued) is Chambers's Encyclopaedia (Sheehy item AC4).

14-98   Can you find a list or a map or something which shows the location of the present day estates of the Duchy of Lancaster? Where or what is Lancaster?

14-99   The encyclopedias you have examined in this section have been only the major and well-known titles. There are others listed in Sheehy such as Britannica Junior (AC16) and Merit Students Encyclopedia (AC19). How would you judge the relative worth of other, perhaps lesser-known encyclopedias, or a newly published encyclopedia?

14-100 What are "subscription books?"

14-101 Another published source which gives some information about all of the available encyclopedias is the Encyclopedia Buying Guide edited by Kenneth Kister (Sheehy 1AC4). What kind of information is given in this work?

The following questions are to be used for review, drawing on sources from the dictionary, supplementary language and encyclopedia sections. For some, where it is not clear what source would give the best answer, a check in more than one source, or in more than one type of source, will help you gain familiarity with using the sources to best advantage.

14-102 Who is John Rolfe? When did he live?

14-103 What are the names of the various figures in figure skating?

14-104 In the section on dictionaries, you found a definition of "seismograph". If you wanted help in understanding how a seismograph actually worked, where would you look?

14-105 What can you find out about the word "hello"? Is it mainly an American usage? Is it also used in Great Britain? How did it originate? What other forms does it have?

14-106 What is the art of falconry? Is a falcon the same as a hawk? Is there any current interest in falconry? Where? How do you train the falcon?

14-107   What time is "five bells", ship's time?

14-108   Where would you look to find some general information on folk music, how it got started, some of the well-known singers, names of some of the songs, something about folk music in other countries?

14-109   Specifically, what does a student mean when he refers to a class or an assignment as "mickey mouse"?

14-110   Can you locate Hainan on a map?   Where is it?   What is it?

ENCYCLOPEDIAS

Answers #14/1--14/110

14-1: This is highly unlikely to be given in a comparatively brief dictionary definition. The type of reference source which would probably give you the information is an encyclopedia.

14-2: See Webster's Third Unabridged or the ALA Glossary.

14-3: Full title: The Encyclopedia Americana, International Edition. Publisher is listed on the title page as Grolier Inc. (© 1983 printing).

14-4: The date would appear probably on the verso of the title page, as a copyright date (e.g., "copyright © 1983 by Grolier Incorporated"). There will probably be a series of dates; the latest date given is the last date on which any new or revised material has been added to the set. This date will vary according to the time at which your set was purchased. (A new set purchased in 1983 should have a copyright date of 1982 or 1983.) See #12-8 and 12-9 for the same situation in regard to dictionaries.

14-5: Sheehy, 9th ed., p. 97, under "Encyclopedias," discusses the "continuous revision" policy for bringing encyclopedia sets up to date.

14-6: Yes, it does. Check the preface or the Sheehy annotation. Also the yearly copyright dates on the verso of the title page indicate that new material was added or changed each year, which is a fairly safe indication of a continuous revision policy.

14-7: No, you can't (except by tedious, detailed checking of dates, statistics, etc., from one year's printing to the next). That is, there is no way in which new or revised material is clearly designated or separated from other older unchanged material.

14-8: See volume 1: Preface, Editorial Staff, contributors, key to pronunciation, abbreviations--much the same as in the dictionaries.

14-9: Nothing specifically so titled. However, there is material in the Preface ("arrangement of contents," "special features," etc.) which would be helpful.

14-10: See the Preface and the Sheehy annotation.

14-11: 30 volumes. This seems to remain constant with each year's printing. (Page numbering, however, may be very inconsistent due to the requirements of the revisions--see Preface under "Arrangement of Contents.")

14-12: Basic arrangement is alphabetical. The last volume, vol. 30, is an index.

14-13: The choice is basically between a separate short entry for each specific subject (as in dictionaries) and a long entry or article bringing many smaller subjects together under a more collective entry. Adak is a short entry, for a place name in Alaska, giving more information than would probably be found in a dictionary entry, but still brief, as compared to the longer collective-type article for Alaska.

14-14: There is a mixture. In vol. 1, see the article on Africa which is really a good-sized pamphlet, see also the article on Alaska (shorter than Africa), on adult education (moderate length), and on alkali (fairly short), etc. Americana is generally considered to have more separate articles than the other major encyclopedias.

14-15: Probably the simplest thing to do would be to look in the index under Maid's Tragedy and find that it is on pp. 416-417 of volume 3, which happens to be the article on Beaumont and Fletcher (1983 printing).

14-16: You could look directly under German Shepherd dogs in the volume covering that alphabetical entry, or you could look in the index under the same entry where you would find the words in capital letters, indicating that there is a separate article on it. The index will also give references to other articles in which pertinent information is given; in this case, there is an illustration of a German Shepherd dog in the encyclopedia but it is not in the article on German Shepherd dogs; it is in the article on Dogs, and you could only be sure of finding it by using the index.

14-17: Some of the articles have cross-references within them to other articles in the set. The index also gives references: under the entry Education in the index, you are referred to the main entry plus several other related entries, plus references to other articles.

14-18: The name of the author and his affiliation is given at the end of the article (© 1983: John T. Middleton; University of California, Riverside). It is not clear from this what his qualifications are. However, note that the author of the article on Air Traffic Control--which can be found near that on Air Pollution--is given as Charles F. Blair, Jr.; Captain, Pan American World Airways; Brigadier General, USAF Reserve, Retired. This statement does give some indication of the qualifications of the latter authors. The authors are identified but their particular qualifications may not always be made clear.

14-19: No, most of the smaller ones are not.

14-20: Their full titles are usually given, and this is not always included in the reference at the end of the articles. It is not clear, at least in the © 1981 and 1983 printings, to what topic they have contributed.

14-21: Yes, you would expect to find maps, since the kind of visual information maps give is important to an understanding of many areas or topics. They are found throughout the articles in the Americana, for example, in the articles on Alaska and Africa. The Hammond Company is responsible for some of the maps (see copyright note on the maps themselves, or see the Preface). No dates are indicated on the maps.

14-22: Pictures, photographs, drawings--both color and black and white; maps, charts, technical drawings. Again, this kind of visual information is helpful to an understanding of the material presented--

in illustrating certain points, in clarifying technical material, etc. Also it adds a great deal to the general attractiveness of the presentation.

14-23: A short "bibliography" is at the end of the article on air traffic control, indicating books on the subject which you might read.

14-24: Not all of the articles in the Americana have bibliographies. Author, title, place of publisher and date of publication are given. Publisher and paging are not given. All bibliographies seem to include only English language materials. You can tell to some extent, by the dates of publication, how up-to-date the bibliography is. The list of books following the article on Air Pollution in the 1981 Americana lists nothing more recent than 1969; the 1983 printing includes articles as recent as 1981. Some bibliographies are more up-to-date than others (see Sheehy annotation).

14-25: Americana gives pronunciations for the entry words; the key (diacritical markings) used is given in the front matter of volume 1. In the index under Hegira, you would find a reference to the main entry for it plus other references; the main entry for Hegira indicates the pronunciation.

14-26: Americana arranges articles alphabetically word by word rather than letter by letter. The entry for "air pollution" preceded the one for "aircraft." This will differ from encyclopedia to encyclopedia (and for various other reference sources as well). Note when you examine other encyclopedias such as Colliers and Britannica that they use the letter by letter arrangement (Newark precedes New York, for example).

14-27: For the general encyclopedia, as opposed to subject or special encyclopedias, the scope is "all knowledge" (see definitions from your answer to #14-2).

14-28: A major meaningful distinction between available encyclopedias, and a major problem in using encyclopedias, lies in this area--the audience at which the encyclopedia is aimed, the level at which the material is presented. Both the virtues and sins of encyclopedias lie in their trying to be all things to all people. The major modern encyclopedias seem to have settled for the non-specialist, but even here there are varying levels of education: the elementary school student, the high school student, the high school graduate, the college student, the college graduate, etc.

14-29: You could get it from the Sheehy annotation (which, actually, is no more specific than "for general use"). You could also find it in the Preface. For example, the preface of the 1983 printing states "Americana's articles communicate to a wide range of readers ... young students ... teachers, librarians and adults in other fields...."

14-30: You could try to select a reasonably technical subject on which you had no knowledge whatsoever, read the article for it, and see how well you understand it. For the student, it depends on how young and how bright he/she is, of course.

14-31: Although most of the encyclopedias are regarded as international in scope, it is inevitable that the material included will reflect the country in which it is published. For example, although the Americana has a lengthy article on Africa itself, compare the size of the article on Alaska with the article on Nigeria, one of the countries in Africa.

14-32: See Sheehy annotation--strong on information for American towns and cities, for evaluation of books, operas, works of art, etc.

14-33: See Sheehy (AC3) or the set itself. The New Britannica is organized under three subtitles: Propaedia, 1v.; Micropaedia, 10v.; and Macropaedia, 19v. (1983 printing).

14-34: The Propaedia presents an outline of human knowledge which attempts, according to the introductory material in the set itself, to "set forth in some orderly way the major topical rubrics that must ultimately be dealt with in a general encyclopedia." Sheehy goes on to say that "Its disciplinary overviews can be useful to the beginner in a given subject field, and its references to the Macropaedia can serve as a guide for independent study." The Micropaedia is both the index to the Macropaedia and an independent ready reference source providing short articles. The Macropaedia provides longer, "in-depth," signed articles similar in type to those of the 11th edition.

14-35: See "Helps for the reader" following the Preface of the Propaedia (1983 printing)

and Sheehy: "The use of the Macropaedia without reference first either to ... the Micropaedia or to the ... Propaedia is not to be encouraged," because facts and data presented in the Micropaedia may suffice and because it facilitates determining the proper headings. (Headings in the Macropaedia vary considerably from the 14th ed. and from the direct-entry approach of many other encyclopedias.)

14-36: Maps are scattered throughout, rather than in a separate atlas volume. There appear in general to be more illustrations, and more of those are in color in the 15th edition than in previous editions.

14-37: Sheehy indicates that a continuous revision policy is used, and there is also a yearbook.

14-38: Propaedia (1983 printing) p. xv of the edition's Preface: "... the curious, intelligent layman." This statement is rather vague but note that the preface does say a lot about how a general encyclopedia is to be used and who uses it for what.

14-39: As it was suggested in #14-30, you can find an article on a technical subject of which you have no knowledge, read it, and see how well you understand it. You can then check the same subject in the other major encyclopedias for comparison.

14-40: The article on Alaska seems shorter in the Britannica, certainly with fewer colored illustrations, maps, etc. There is no separate article in the Britannica on Adak, nor is it listed in the index.

14-41: There is no article on air pollution in the Macropaedia; the Micropaedia has a short article on the Air Pollution Control Act with a reference to the "history of health and safety laws."

14-42: K.R.V.H. You have to refer to the back of the Propaedia volume to "Initials of contributors and consultants to the Macropaedia," p. 64 of that section, to find the name (and position) of K.R.V.H. (1983 printing).

14-43: They are frequently quite long; they often include foreign language publications; the citations are briefer, giving author, title, date, but no publisher.

14-44: Macmillan Educational Company, 24 volumes, continuous revision (Sheehy), 1983 printing.

14-45: See Preface under "Scope": "...essential content of the curricula of colleges and secondary schools, as well as the upper grades ... in depth for the non-specialist, but included, too ... desired by the professional in the field." Sheehy annotation indicates that the level is high school and junior college and is not as advanced as Americana and Britannica.

14-46: Very similar: alphabetically with an index in the last volume. Like the other encyclopedias, the index is detailed, showing main entries plus references to other sources of information in the set, and entries for subjects not treated as separate entries. The articles are mostly long, although there are some short entries.

14-47: Bibliographies are not with the article itself, as in Britannica and Americana. In Collier's, the bibliographies are all listed in the Bibliography and Index volume.

14-48: See "How to use the Bibliography" in the last volume.

14-49: See "How to use the Bibliography." They are listed more or less in increasing order of difficulty.

14-50: The bibliographies in the last volume are arranged in a general classed order, with an alphabetical subject guide at the beginning. Air pollution is too specific to be included in that list, but the index includes references to the bibliographies as well as to items in the set itself. The index entry for air pollution lists Bib. in vol. 24, p. 147, item 241. There is one title listed (1983 printing).

14-51: Maps are scattered throughout, as in Americana and the 15th Britannica. Illustrations are similar to Americana (more than in Britannica, more in color).

14-52: In Collier's the full name of the author is given following the article, but not his position. Contributors with their positions are listed in the front of volume 1.

14-53: In general, the encyclopedias differ mainly in special features (i.e., location of maps, extent of illustrations, location of bibliographies, location of names of authors of articles, etc.). In arrangement

they are very similar, with the exception of the New Britannica. All include both long and short articles. All indexes are similar in detail and use with, again, the exception of the New Britannica. They are similar in scope, with the Britannica perhaps retaining some British bent, the Americana being perhaps stronger on American geographical items. In theory, they differ in level, although not always noticeably: the Britannica is still generally considered at the most advanced level, followed by the Americana, with Collier's at a level perhaps not so advanced as the other two, certainly usable at a high school level for most students. In sum: the encyclopedias are strikingly similar, and getting more so each year.

14-54: All three have a major full-length article on libraries. Access is direct but can also be located through the indexes and the indexes also give other references not in the articles themselves. All have bibliographies. (Collier's of course is not with the article but is presumably in the Bibliography volume.)

Americana gives short outlines at the beginning of the articles so that the content and structure are easily seen. Americana seems to have the most information on the profession of librarianship, educational requirements, etc. (None have separate articles on "librarianship.")

The best information on how to use a library is probably given in Collier's article called "Library Research and Reporting," following the articles on Libraries and Library Association.

14-55: All three encyclopedias will indicate illustrations through the index (although it is not clear that they index absolutely all illustrations). Therefore it would seem reasonable to turn to the index first, and follow up all references which indicate an illustration. All three list Canterbury Cathedral in the index. Only Collier's has an article exclusively on Canterbury Cathedral. Not all of the illustrations referred to turn out to be full pictures of the outside of the Cathedral. (The 1981 and 1983 printings of the Americana have a good picture of the outside of the Cathedral, in the article on England and the article on Canterbury.)

14-56: The indexes in all three indicate that he was an artist. Collier's says he was a French artist; Americana says he was an Alsatian artist and poet. The Micropaedia of the New Britannica, which is a ready reference as well as an index, devotes almost one-half of a column to Arp.

14-57: Search in the indexes under St. as if it were spelled "Saint."

Americana lists nothing under St. Nicholas' Day. It does provide a little information under Nicholas, St. (but nothing about how it is celebrated) and a reference to Santa Claus.

Collier's index includes "St. Nicholas' Day" as an entry but refers the reader to the article on "Santa Claus." This article is quite good on when and how celebrated, with some history, and good comparison to the more American custom of Santa Claus.

The New Britannica has a full column article in the Micropaedia under Nicholas, Saint but nothing under St. Nicholas' Day.

14-58: Direct access: None have full articles on "weather maps" as such. Americana has articles on "weather," "meteorology" (the science of or study of the atmosphere or weather) and "weather forecasting." Collier's has articles on "meteorology and climatology" and "climate." Britannica has no articles or cross-references in the Macropaedia on weather or weather maps as such but does have an article on "weather forecasting." Index: All have references under weather maps. Americana refers you to the article on "meteorology and weather forecasting" which contains symbols (1983 printing). Britannica 15th ed. has an entry in the Micropaedia for "weather maps," with a short article with no illustrations or explanation of the symbols, and with a reference to the article on "Atmospheric Sciences," in the Macropaedia, which does not explain the symbols either (1983 printing). Collier's refers you to the article on "meteorology and climatology," which does include a picture of a weather map with some symbols indicated (1983 printing).

14-59: Collier's "Bibliography" in the index volume specifically lists books in order of increasing difficulty, so presumably titles coming first in their list on chemistry might be suitable for high school students. Level of reading/difficulty is not so clear for the bibliographic references in the other two encyclopedias.

14-60: The Academic American Encyclopedia (2AC1) was first published in 1980 by Arête Publishing Company, Inc., in 21

volumes. It is now published by Grolier, Inc. According to the Preface (© 1980), it will apparently use a form of continuous revision and have a yearbook. Again according to the Preface (© 1980), the encyclopedia is intended for students in junior high school, high school, college, and "inquisitive adults."

14-61: The encyclopedia is arranged alphabetically, word-by-word. The index is in vol. 21, and is, like the text, arranged alphabetically word-by-word. The Preface (© 1980) states that the encyclopedia is comprehensive and "is not narrowly focused on the United States and its perspectives."

14-62: There is a three-page article entered under "library" with several illustrations, as noted in the index. (Sheehy, Hern 2AC1, notes that the articles average 500 words.) The article can be accessed directly or through the index. Under the main index heading for "library," are several references to specific libraries, persons, library organizations, etc. There is a short bibliography at the end of this article, as well as many of the others. The article is signed, and the author's name and position can be found in the list of contributors in volume one. (Sheehy indicates that 75 percent of the articles are signed.)

14-63: Jean Arp is listed in the index and references are given to two articles. The index alone does not give any information about Arp.

14-64: Academic American indexes nothing under St. Nicholas except a magazine by that name. The index does refer to an article under "Nicholas, Saint." The article itself is short and only obliquely refers to the saint's day.

14-65: An encyclopedia would probably be the best source for this very general nonspecific background information. Turning directly to the main article on Indians (being aware of the possibilities for variation, such as American Indian, South American Indian, etc.) would probably be satisfactory; however, turning first to the index might give you a general idea of how the material was located--for example, whether there was a major article on Indians, whether material on specific tribes or for specific locations would be located in separate articles, etc. If after or during your reading of the main article you wanted more specific information or facts, you could make use of the index. Finally, the encyclopedia article should give you some additional or further reading through the bibliographic references.

14-66: Information varies from encyclopedia to encyclopedia--in depth, in currency, in level, in access; it also varies factually. The more encyclopedias a library can have available, the more possibilities there are for locating hard-to-find information, and for double-checking information.

14-67: Most of the encyclopedias themselves stress that the index should be the first place you should look. The advantage of the index is to cover all possibilities. Specific information may not always be located in the article in which you think it should be. If you want general information, it is probably sufficient to go directly to the article itself; if you want specific information, it is probably necessary to work through the index.

14-68: The entries in the dictionary are so specific that no index is necessary to get at all the information they offer, although some cross-referencing is necessary in dictionaries. Even though the trend in modern encyclopedias is away from the very broad, all-encompassing survey articles toward more specific shorter articles, the specificity of an encyclopedia can never be as great as that in a dictionary. A dictionary is concerned with words (which can be specific) rather than with ideas (which cannot be so specific).

14-69: The dictionaries contain much factual, quick answer type of information, especially for names of people and places, and some things, events, etc. Information given is usually very brief, but may be sufficient for many needs.

14-70: "Compact and ready for instant reference ... authentic and accurate information in condensed form ... a wide-ranging variety of subjects ... companion of the dictionary and the atlas" (4th ed., 1975).

14-71: "Preoccupation with American interests and American topics" (3rd ed., 1963). The "articles [now] cover a wider variety of people, countries, and cultures than ever before" (4th ed., 1975).

14-72: Alphabetical, very short specific topics. No index needed because of the specific topics (although it may be remembered that facts and details will appear in even these short entries for which there is

no direct access).

14-73: Yes, all these features are included, but obviously to a lesser extent.

14-74: In arrangement: Lincoln Library is "classed," with information on major topics such as government, fine arts, etc., brought together rather than scattered alphabetically (1982 edition).

14-75: For example, this is comparable to the alphabetical arrangement of Webster's New Dictionary of Synonyms, as compared to the classed arrangement of Roget's International Thesaurus. (Or the dictionary of slang, and the thesaurus of slang.) For advantages, etc., see answer to #13-23. Better yet, see the Preface to the Lincoln Library.

14-76: All have indexes. The indexes are needed to provide specific access to names, places, subjects, etc. See the discussion of the index in the preface of the Lincoln Library (1982 edition).

14-77: Both are in New Columbia (under Arp, and Adak--Adak refers the reader to Aleutian Islands); information given is not extensive but is adequate. Only Arp is in the index of the Lincoln Library, with a short biography in the biographical section (p. 1369).

14-78: This would be in the Lincoln Library (in major section on Science, following Geology--see Contents page). Each of the rocks, stones, gems, listed would probably also be listed and described in the New Columbia Encyclopedia, but you would have to know the name of the rock or gem to find it.

14-79: New Columbia has an article on Indians, North American (no cross-reference from American Indians). It also has short articles on specific tribes, such as Hopi.
        Lincoln Library has a moderately long section on American Indians (in the major section on History--Peoples of the World); this is not too clear from the Contents page, but the index under Indians gives enough references to this general area to make you suspect it is a long article, plus other scattered references.

14-80: New Columbia is revised periodically with new editions (see Sheehy annotation); Lincoln Library is revised with each new printing (continuous revision) (see title page and/or Sheehy annotation).

14-81: Sheehy indicates that no particular level is aimed at, although--as a "family" encyclopedia--one would assume then a wide range of readership from child through adult.

14-82: It is divided into two main sections-- Colorpedia and Alphapedia. The Colorpedia provides lengthy articles with color illustrations and is arranged by topics. Every important person, place, or thing mentioned in the Colorpedia has an entry in the Alphapedia, which is intended to provide brief answers to factual questions. As the name suggests, the Alphapedia is arranged alphabetically. It provides cross references to the longer articles in the Colorpedia. This is somewhat similar to the Micropaedia/Macropaedia of the New (15th) Britannica.

14-83: Lincoln Library. (All of the adult level encyclopedias can be used on a high school level, depending on the abilities of the student, etc.) Lincoln Library is not specifically a children's encyclopedia, but it is set up to be useful in schools and with children.

14-84: Publisher: F.E. Compton Co., Division of Encyclopaedia Britannica (title page); number of volumes: 26 (in © 1983 printing; earlier printings may have fewer volumes); continuous (see verso of title page, or Sheehy annotation); date of set you are examining will vary--see verso of title page for last date.

14-85: "Young people." (The Sheehy annotation says "upper elementary and high school.")

14-86: Basic arrangement is alphabetical. Length of article is moderate to long. There is no index in the last volume as with the adult encyclopedias you looked at. Each volume has its own index at the end with the same alphabetical designation. It is called a Fact-Index, and is really more than an index. There are entries for articles in the encyclopedia and references to other articles (in other volumes) in which further information may be found, as in the adult encyclopedias. There are also entries which give a brief definition or description of the item (facts), and these may or may not have references to appearances in the encyclopedia itself. The index thus serves as a ready-reference or quick reference source. What Compton's has done is to take the very short articles which the adult encyclopedias have included in the main body of the arrangement, and move them to the back of the volume interfiled with the index entries. Thus the articles in the main part of the set tend to be longer, broader, bringing related facts together. This arrangement is comparable to that of the New Britannica.

14-87: Neither is listed in the 1983 printing of Compton's.

14-88: Compton's article on libraries in the 1983 printing is long (41 pages). It provides some history, some information about foreign libraries, some pictures. It gives the main classes for the Dewey Decimal Classification with some further subdivisions, and the main classes for the Library of Congress Classification. It devotes about three pages to librarians with some information about their education, etc. A multi-media bibliography is provided. In addition to the article, there is almost a full page in the Fact-Index of references to libraries and librarians.

14-89: Publisher is World Book, Inc. 22 volumes. Continuous revision policy plus a Year Book published each March. Date of set will vary. Age level is in the Preface, under "Aims and Objectives" and "Readability": "students in elementary school, in junior high school, and high school...." Also adults. (1983 printing.)

14-90: The basic arrangement of World Book is alphabetical, with many short specific entries. There are some long articles (see those on the states, such as Alaska, or "astronomy" for example). There are lots of cross-references within the set in the main alphabetical entries. Prior to the 1972 printing, the set had no index as such, relying instead on the specific entries and many cross-references in the set itself. From 1972 on, the last volume in the set is a Research Guide/Index which provides the same sort of separate specific index and cross-references as the major adult encyclopedias; the cross-references and short specific articles have been maintained within the set itself, however. In the 1983 printing, there is a short article on Arp, plus an index reference. Adak is not listed, in the main set or index. The Aran Islands are listed in the index, with a reference to Ireland.

14-91: Contrary to what you might expect from

the World Book stress on short specific articles, there is a long broad background article on Indian, American. The end of the article lists related articles, as well as an outline of the major article itself and a short bibliography. You could also refer to the Research Guide/Index for other references.

14-92:   Most modern educational materials designed for the child are highly illustrated with pictures, maps, graphs, charts--all kinds of visual materials which will interest the child and aid in the learning process. The children's encyclopedias are replete with visual aids of all kinds. See for example the set of illustrations in Compton's article on "anatomy" and in World Book's article on "Human body."

14-93:   Articles are not signed in Compton's but a list of contributors with general subject areas is given in volume 1. Articles are signed in World Book, usually only with names; names and titles and articles are identified in the introductory matter in volume 1. Even though these encyclopedias are designed for children, you would expect the same authority and accuracy behind the information as you would with the adult encyclopedias.

14-94:   Both World Book and Compton's include bibliographies, though neither does as consistently as the adult encyclopedias. For example, World Book provides a six item bibliography with its article on chemistry (1983 printing). Both Compton's and World Book divide their references into books for younger readers and books for older readers.

14-95:   Depending on how ignorant you really are and how much you really want to know, you might find the articles in the major adult encyclopedias helpful; but you might also find that a more simplified version in one of the juvenile encyclopedias would be even more helpful. Compton's (1983) has a two page article with illustrations and a short bibliography. World Book (1983) has a good article with many illustrations, and information on what a laser is, and what they are used for, how they work, and some history.

14-96:   Many adults would find the more simplified material and plentiful illustrations helpful for certain topics.

14-97:   There is some difference in the way the indexes have been constructed and used. As noted in #14-90, prior to 1972, World Book had no index at all but did have specificity available through cross-references and very short articles. Since 1972, World Book has had a regular index (probably in deference to the fact that it is a popular encyclopedia for adults as well as children) but it still retains many cross-references within the set itself, and many short articles. As noted in #14-86, Compton's spreads the index throughout the set and combines it with short, specific fact entries. Claims are made that children find it difficult to use the more traditional index approach. Counter claims are made that the lack of the traditional approach in children's encyclopedias does not prepare or train them to use the adult encyclopedias properly.

14-98:   Checking in Chambers's under Lancaster, you would find an extensive article including a map showing the present day estates of the Duchy (Chambers © 1968). Other highly recommended, British-produced encyclopedias that might answer this question include Everyman's Encyclopedia and the New Caxton Encyclopedia.

14-99:   See comments in Sheehy, 9th ed., p. 97-98. Published reviews are probably the best source of information on new or unknown encyclopedias; Sheehy specifically notes those that appeared in Subscription Books Bulletin Reviews (Sheehy item AA400), and Reference and Subscription Books Reviews (AA401). (The section of Booklist from which such reviews are taken is now called Reference Books Bulletin, and presumably the new cumulations of reviews will be similarly titled.) Look at a recent volume, if possible, of these reviews and read at least one of the reviews of a not-recommended encyclopedia, to get an idea of the usefulness and thoroughness of these reviews (check at the end of the review for the general recommendation). Sheehy also gives a thorough outline for testing and examining an encyclopedia, much of which you have already been doing in the previous questions.

14-100: See ALA Glossary.

14-101: According to the Preface, it "reviews all general English-language encyclopedias published or distributed in the United

States and Canada as of early 1981" (3rd ed., 1981). It provides general information on choosing an encyclopedia, some bibliographic references; specific information on the sets listed includes publisher, size, cost, age level, arrangement, etc., plus references to reviews. Some of the information is comparatively treated.

14-102: Some of the dictionaries will give you brief information. For example, Webster's 2nd unabridged, in its biographical list, and Random House, in its main list, indicate that he was the husband of Pocahontas and an English colonist, and give dates. Webster's 9th Collegiate, in its biographical section, states that he was an English colonist and gives dates. The encyclopedias have more information: World Book, Americana, and Colliers all have articles on Rolfe of varying length.

14-103: Dictionaries don't really get you anywhere in this, which is not surprising because this is really more "background information" than definitions. If you knew the names of the figures and looked up each in the dictionary for a definition, that might prove more successful. Encyclopedias are better; most under "Ice Skating" or "figure skating." World Book and Collier's give some names and illustrations. The New Britannica has short articles on both figure skating and ice-skating in the Micropaedia; the article on ice-skating gives a reference to a related article on winter sports in the Macropaedia and to articles on ice dancing, etc. in the Micropedia.

14-104: Encyclopedias.

14-105: This is more of a "word" problem than an encyclopedia problem. Unabridged dictionaries don't give much on origin and forms. Usage books--Evans and particularly Fowler--are very helpful. OED and Dictionary of American English are other possible sources.

14-106: Dictionaries will define falcons and falconry. Beyond that you have to go to encyclopedias. The Britannica has a short article in the Micropaedia with a reference to a longer article in the Macropaedia.

14-107: Partly a problem in guessing the entry. Webster's 3rd lists under "bells." World Book article on "Ship" gives the information under "Nautical terms" (1983 print-

ing). The DeSola abbreviations dictionary has a special list of ship's bell time signals, as noted in the Contents; one of those odd things found in odd places.

14-108: Encyclopedias--you might have to look in more than one to find all the information you needed.

14-109: Presumably a slang term, therefore a slang dictionary (Wentworth and Flexner lists, in Supplement) or perhaps a regular dictionary (Random House has a slightly different definition).

14-110: Any source with maps detailed enough to show it. Of the dictionaries, Random House has maps in the back with a special index, and it is listed there. Most of the encyclopedias should have it. In the New Britannica there is a short article in the Micropaedia with a reference to a map in the article about China in volume 4 of the Macropaedia; it is not indexed by World Book (1983 printing); in Collier's and Americana you would look in the regular index for a map reference.

Section 14b

SUPPLEMENT: FOREIGN LANGUAGE ENCYCLOPEDIAS

Questions #14/111--14/132

14-111   The encyclopedias you have examined so far in this section have all been in the English language and mostly American publications. Although their scope is certainly universal and international, there is inevitably a stronger coverage of minor American people, places, institutions, arts, events, etc., as compared to those of other countries. Similarly, an encyclopedia published in another country will tend to stress minor topics relating to that country. In addition, some of the foreign encyclopedias are especially noted for superior coverage in certain areas, such as illustrations, literature, etc. Sheehy lists several foreign language encyclopedias following the section for English language encyclopedias. What does Sheehy indicate as the use of such encyclopedias?

Because the foreign language encyclopedias can prove so helpful beyond the American sets which you have the most access to, you should have some experience, even if brief, in using them. The following titles are some of the major French, German, Italian, and Spanish encyclopedias selected from Sheehy.

French	Encyclopaedia Universalis, 1968- (AC34, 1AC8) La Grande Encyclopédia, 1971- (AC38, 1AC7)
German	Brockhaus Enzyklopaedie, 17th ed., 1966- (AC43, 1AC9) Meyers Enzyklopaedisches Lexikon, 9th ed., 1971- (AC47, 1AC10, 2AC4)
Italian	Enciclopedia Italiana di Scienze, Lettere et Arti (AC57)
Spanish	Enciclopedia Universal Illustrada Europeo-Americana (Espasa) (AC82, 2AC11)
Russian	Bol'shaia Sovetskaia Entsiklopediia, 3rd ed. (AC72, 1AC12, 2AC9) Great Soviet Encyclopedia (AC73, 1AC13, 2AC10)

14-112   Rather than going through each of these titles individually, to check scope and arrangement, it will be less time consuming to treat all of them as a group. Just by looking at the titles as listed and looking briefly at the citations and annotations in Sheehy, you should be able to see that there are well-known "names" of foreign encyclopedias, in each country, as there are in the United States with "Britannica," "Americana," etc. What is the name of each of the major encyclopedia publishers in France? in Germany?

14-113   Can you tell, from looking at the Sheehy citations and annotations, anything about the general revision policies for foreign language encyclopedias? Are they similar to American encyclopedias in this respect?

14-114   Some of the foreign language encyclopedias listed in Sheehy are actually quite old: La Grande Encyclopédie, published in the 19th century (AC37), and the Larousse Grand Dictionnaire Universel du XIXe Siecle (AC39), for example. What is the point of considering these encyclopedias at all? Are they not so out-of-date by now as to have lost their basic usefulness?

14-115   Another characteristic of the foreign encyclopedias is that they are not published all at once but rather as each volume is finished, and the publication may go on for an exceedingly long period of time. With some of them, the earlier volumes may be out of date before the final volumes are published. Is there any particular way in which some of these old but basic sets are up-dated? For example, look at the Sheehy annotations for the Enciclopedia Italiana di Scienze, Lettere ed Arti (AC57) and the Enciclopedia Universal Illustrada Europeo-Americana (AC82, 2AC11).

The following questions are to be answered from the foreign language encyclopedias. The first few are to be answered by using the specific encyclopedia noted. The others may be answered from any of the sets, although it is likely from the nature of the material that one of the sets is more apt to have the answers; if you do not have access to all of the encyclopedias listed, use those which you do have. Some practice with the foreign encyclopedias is especially helpful in fixing their existence in your mind and in helping you to overcome any reluctance to use foreign language material. If you have time, checking some of the problems against one or more of the American encyclopedias would also be useful.

14-116   Can you locate the article on Joan of Arc in the Encyclopaedia Universalis (Sheehy AC34, 1AC8)? How did you find it? Who wrote it?

14-117   For comparison, find the article on Joan of Arc in La Grande Encyclopédie (Sheehy AC38, 1AC7). Is it entered in the same way? Is the article signed?

14-118   Can you find in the Enciclopedia Italiana (Sheehy AC57) some pictures of the cathedral in Aix-la-Chappelle?

14-119   Using the Brockhaus Enzyklopaedie, 17th ed. (Sheehy AC43, 1AC9), can you find an article about the contemporary German writer Günther Grass?

14-120   For comparison, try to find Günther Grass in the Meyers Enzyklopaedisches Lexikon (Sheehy AC47, 1AC10, 2AC4). How did you find it? Did it differ in any way from what you found in the Brockhaus Enzyklopaedie?

14-121   Where would you be most likely to find an illustrated article on Alhambra, a palace of the Moorish Kings?

14-122   Where can you find a picture of the Brandenburg Gate in Berlin?

14-123   Where would you find a long article with a lot of illustrations on the city of Rome?

14-124   If you wanted to find an article on the libraries of France, where would you look and how would you go about it?

14-125   Can you find a portrait or picture of Mariano Chacel y Gonzales, Spanish poet and dramatist of the 19th century; also some of the names of his plays?

14-126 Where would you look to find a bibliography of and about George Hegel, a German philosopher (1770-1831)?

14-127 Jean-Pierre Duprey was a French poet who lived from 1930-1959. Where would you find a list of his writings and something about his short life?

14-128 Can you find a colored reproduction of El Greco's painting of San Lorenzo? Where can the painting itself be seen?

14-129 Can you find a picture of the Piazza Garibaldi in Parma?

14-130 If you were looking for a portrait of Stalin, you would probably expect from the previous questions that you might be likely to find it in a Russian encyclopedia (although for someone as well-known as Stalin, it would also be likely to be found in American or other encyclopedias). Is there a Russian encyclopedia (in Russian)? Can you find a picture of Stalin in it?

14-131 Even if you did not know the Cyrillic alphabet, and you absolutely had to find the picture of Stalin in the Soviet encyclopedia (in Russian), how could you set about it?

14-132 Although it is possible to locate things in the Soviet encyclopedia without knowing much more than a transliteration of the Cyrillic alphabet, it is not possible to do much more than that without some reading knowledge of the language. Fortunately we now have an English translation of this encyclopedia, the Great Soviet Encyclopedia (Sheehy AC73, 1AC13, 2AC10). Can you locate the article on "bibliography" in this encyclopedia?

14-111: See Sheehy, 9th ed., p. 102, especially the second paragraph on "three main types of questions." Read all the introductory comments in Sheehy on foreign encyclopedias.

14-112: In France, Larousse is a well-known encyclopedia publisher, Brockhaus or Herder in Germany. Often, these publishers are known for dictionaries as well, as you can see by checking the foreign language dictionaries section in Sheehy.

14-113: Foreign encyclopedias have not yet really taken over the American procedures of continuous revision. They still tend to be published in major new revisions. For example, the Brockhaus Enzyklopaedie (AC43, 1AC9) is a new (17th) edition, with a new title, of Der Grosse Brockhaus (AC42). The Meyers Enzyklopaedisches Lexikon (AC47, 1AC10, 2AC4) is shown as a new edition of a long series of older Meyers encyclopedias represented by AC46. The Encyclopaedia Universalis (AC34) is called a "major new encyclopedia." La Grande Encyclopédie, 1971- (AC38, 1AC7) is also called a "wholly new work" and not a revision of a 19th century encyclopedia by the same name (AC37).

14-114: See Sheehy annotations for both titles. Like the famous scholarly early editions of the Britannica, these sets are still useful for their authority and thoroughness on topics for which currency is not so important. Similar older German encyclopedias are also listed in Sheehy.

14-115: Some of the foreign encyclopedias are updated with supplements. The Enciclopedia Italiana has been up-dated with supplements to the 1960's. The Enciclopedia Universal Illustrada Europeo-Americana (Espasa) has been up-dated to 1980.

14-116: Remember that "Joan of Arc" is an English language version and you are looking in a French encyclopedia (see Sheehy's comments on the use of foreign encyclopedias, p. 102). American dictionaries and encyclopedias tend to enter Joan of Arc under Joan, and if you searched this way in the French encyclopedia, you would have to realize that the French form of Joan is "Jeanne." (If you did not know the French form of Joan, you could look up Joan of Arc in a dictionary giving biographical information, and you would probably find the French form of the name also given. See Random House Dictionary, for example.) The index to Encyclopaedia Universalis is located in the last three volumes and is labelled "Thesaurus-Index." Within the Thesaurus there is an entry for Jeanne D'Arc with a reference to an article (vol. 9, p. 416). There are also references to other articles in which Jeanne D'Arc is mentioned. Short articles are included within the Thesaurus for many of the other entries. In this respect, the index to Encyclopaedia Universalis is comparable to the Micropaedia, or index to the New Encyclopaedia Britannica, 15th edition. The author's initials are given at the end of the article, and there is a list of authors in the first volume with full names and positions.

14-117: The article in La Grande Encyclopédie is also found under Jeanne d'Arc. The index entry refers you to the page numbers of the full article and also gives references to several other articles that include some mention of Jeanne d'Arc. There is also an index entry for the variant, Arc (Jean d') with references to the two pages of the article within which Jean d'Arc is mentioned.

14-118: Look in index under Aix-la-Chapelle which refers you to the article on Aquisgrana (in vol. 3, p. 812e). Aquisgrana is the Italian name for Aix-la-Chapelle which is the French name for Aachen in Germany.

14-119: The Brockhaus Enzyklopaedie does not

223

have an index but the encyclopedia is arranged alphabetically, so you can simply search the encyclopedia directly. There is a short article under GraB [Grass], Günter with short bibliographies of works by and about Grass at the end.

14-120: The treatment of Günther Grass in Meyers is quite similar to that in Brockhaus. Again there is no index, so the contents must be accessed directly. The article in Meyers is under Grass, Günther and is a bit longer, but still relatively short. Both articles include a photograph of Grass. Meyers also has bibliographies of works by and about Grass, but the list of works about Grass is longer in Meyers than in Brockhaus.

14-121: Spanish encyclopedia: Espasa (Sheehy AC82, 2AC11). (If you did not already know, or could not tell from the question, that the palace of Alhambra is located in the city of Granada, Spain, you could have looked it up in another source, such as a dictionary which gives geographical information, or a one-volume encyclopedia, or any encyclopedia through the index.) Located directly under Alhambra. You would probably find information, possibly even full articles, on Alhambra in American encyclopedias. The chances of finding a number of illustrations might be better in a Spanish encyclopedia.

14-122: You may first need to check an English-German dictionary to find that the German word for gate is "tor." There is an article under "Brandenburger Tor" in Meyers with a picture. There is another picture in the article about Berlin. Brockhaus has no entry for "Brandenburger Tor" but does provide a picture of the gate in the article under Berlin.

14-123: The Enciclopedia Italiana (Sheehy AC57), which besides being Italian and therefore a good source of coverage for an Italian city, is also noted for its long articles and many illustrations. The entry would be "Roma," the Italian name.

14-124: If you are going to search in a French encyclopedia, you would want to go first to an English-French dictionary (Sheehy AD279, for example) to find the French word for "library," which is "bibliothèque." Checking under the entry "bibliothèque" in the French encyclopedias, you could find an article devoted, at

least in part, to French libraries in, for example, Encyclopaedia Universalis.

14-125: In Espasa (the Spanish encyclopedia; Sheehy AC82, 2AC11), under Chacel y Gonzalez, Mariano. In the Spanish alphabet, "Ch" is considered as a separate letter following "C," therefore entries beginning with "Ch" will follow those beginning with "Cz." This is noted in Sheehy's comments on foreign encyclopedias, 9th ed., p. 102.

14-126: The articles on Hegel in both Brockhaus (17th ed.) and Meyers provide extensive bibliographies.

14-127: The French bibliographic sources in Section 10 of Part I of this manual might list his publications. The French encyclopedias might be more likely to give information about his life and the titles of his writings as well. See, for example, in the Encyclopaedia Universalis (Sheehy AC34, 1AC8); there is a short article about him in the first of the Thesaurus or index volumes. La Grande Encyclopedie (AC38, 1AC7) index has only a reference to him as a sculptor in a larger article on art.

14-128: El Greco was a Spanish painter, born in Greece (Crete, actually). Espasa encyclopedia (Sheehy AC82, 2AC11) under "Greco (el)" gives a cross reference to see ("v.") the entry Theotocopuli (Domingo), his correct name. If you had known his correct name to begin with, you could have looked directly under that, but it wasn't necessary in this case. If you hadn't known his correct name, and there was no cross-reference from El Greco, you could have looked up the correct name in some other source, such as a dictionary which gives biographical information, or an American encyclopedia. The article on Theotocopuli (Domingo) gives reproductions, both colored and black and white, of several of his paintings, including that of San Lorenzo. The illustration itself notes in the title line that it hangs in the Museo del Prado in Madrid.

14-129: Parma is a city in Italy. The Enciclopedia Italiana (Sheehy AC57) has a picture of the Piazza Garibaldi in the article on Parma, in Appendix III, volume 2.

14-130: The Russian encyclopedia is the Bol'shaia Sovetskaia Entsiklopediia (Sheehy AC72, 1AC12, 2AC9); we will consider

the English translation later). The encyclopedia is in Russian, of course, and
also in the Cyrillic alphabetic, and the
guide-letters on the spines of the volumes
are also in the Cyrillic alphabet. So unless you happen to know the Cyrillic alphabet, you probably cannot even find
the entry for Stalin or even the volume
in which it might be.

14-131: Find some sources which would give the
characters of the Cyrillic alphabet and
their transliteration into roman letters.
Webster's Third unabridged, for example, has an alphabet table (listed under
Index to Tables, on the Contents page)
which includes Russian or Cyrillic. You
could then transliterate (or change) the
roman letters of STALIN to the Russian
or Cyrillic characters of СТАЛИН,
note that the Cyrillic character "С" is
alphabetized between "Р" and "Т," find
the volume of the Russian encyclopedia
covering "С," find the entry for Stalin
as written above, and find the picture.
In the 3rd (1970) edition, the entry is
in vol. 24, part I, on p. 400; the picture is small but recognizable.

14-132: Here it is necessary to begin with the
index. The Russian version has been
translated into English volume by volume
so that the translated material is found
according to the initial letter of its Russian original rather than the English
translation. Thus you look in the index
(to vol. 1-25 so far, © 1981) under
"bibliography" and find that the main
article on this subject is located in vol.
3, p. 250. Several other references are
noted. (Similarly, the index tells you
that the main article on "library science"
is also located in vol. 3, p. 716.) It is
interesting to read the article on bibliography, particularly on its use in capital-
ist countries (last paragraph on p. 250);
there is also information here on the
Soviet legal deposit law (remember section 10): the "obligatory (control) copy."
      The article on Stalin is in vol. 24,
p. 451, of the translation.

Section 15

YEARBOOKS AND ALMANACS

Questions #15/1--15/86

15-1   If you wanted to find the name of the winner of the Nobel Prize in Medicine for last year, would you expect to find it in an encyclopedia? If you wanted to see what the developments were last year in the American Indians' struggle for equal rights, would you expect to find it in an encyclopedia? If you wanted to know what is the longest bridge in the world, would you expect to find it in an encyclopedia?

15-2   What two ways are used to keep encyclopedia sets up to date and current? One way has already been discussed.

There are many annual or yearly publications, including the encyclopedia yearbooks, which give extensive coverage of current information. These yearbooks and almanacs, a special form of yearbook, comprise the next set of sources to be examined, as follows:

      Americana Annual (AC11)
      Britannica Book of the Year (AC12)
      Collier's Year Book (AC14)
      World Book Year Book (see AC20)
      Annual Register of World Events (DA50)
      Facts on File (DA51, 1DA16)
      Keesing's Contemporary Archives (DA52)
      World Almanac (CG75)
      Information Please Almanac (CG66)
      Statesman's Year-Book (CG45)

15-3   One of the first problems is that of terminology. For example, the yearbooks of the three major encyclopedias are titled: Americana Annual, Britannica Book of the Year, and Collier's Year Book. What is a yearbook or an annual?

15-4   The word yearbook, rather than annual, will be used in this manual as a general term. If possible, look at the yearbooks of the Americana, Britannica, and Collier's together and comparatively, and try to compare them all for the same year. Check the date on the spines and on the title pages. Is there any variation in the way the date is designated? Does the date of the volume consistently indicate the date of the events covered?

15-5   Where would be the best place to look to see quickly any variations in the scope and arrangement of the three yearbooks?

15-6   From the Table of Contents of each, does there appear to be any variation in presentation and content among the three yearbooks?

15-7   Look at the Table of Contents for each, and then looking through the books themselves at their general arrangement, do you see any basic similarities in scope and/or arrangement? What items are included in all of them? Are these items presented in the same general way?

15-8   The main section or main body of each of the yearbooks is an alphabetical arrangement of various short articles on events of the year. Would you expect that there would be an article, in the yearbook, to correspond with each of the articles in the main set of the encyclopedia?

15-9   Are the articles in the yearbooks for very specific topics (e.g., New York City Ballet) or more general (e.g., dance)? What access do you have for specific topics such as New York City Ballet?

15-10   Would you expect the articles included in the yearbooks to be exactly the same in each of the three? Do all three have articles on education, libraries, art, etc.? Do all three have articles on some of the major current issues such as crime, consumer affairs, energy, nutrition, pollution, population, poverty?

15-11   1982 was the year of the Falkland Islands conflict. How would you find information on it in the yearbooks?

15-12   What prominent people died during the past year? Are deaths listed separately in some way, or must you check the index?

15-13   How can you determine the authority behind the various articles in the encyclopedia yearbooks?

15-14   Using the encyclopedia yearbooks, can you find who won the Nobel Prize for Medicine last year? Can you find through the recent yearbooks who won the Nobel Prize for Medicine in 1970? Do the yearbooks attempt to include retrospective or historical information? Are the indexes retrospective in any way?

15-15   Look at a recent yearbook from World Book, one of the two children's encyclopedias you examined. Do the yearbooks for the children's encyclopedias appear to differ in any major way from those for the adult encyclopedias?

15-16   Are the encyclopedia yearbooks indexed in the basic sets themselves? If you had a 1983 printing or edition of the Britannica, would the index include references to the 1982 or 1981 yearbooks?

15-17   Would a recent printing or edition of an encyclopedia completely supersede earlier yearbooks? Is there any value to the old yearbooks? Where would you look if you wanted to find out the developments in medicine in 1979?

15-18   Are the encyclopedia yearbooks limited in coverage to the United States?

15-19   If you needed a survey of current events, similar to the encyclopedia yearbooks, which stressed
        events in Great Britain, what would you look for? Where would you look?

15-20   What is the title of the Annual Register, and where is it published? How often is it published?
        Is the date of coverage clear, or is there apt to be some confusion as with the encyclopedia year-
        books?

15-21   Does the Annual Register have any connection with some other publication such as an encyclopedia?
        Is it an annual supplement to something?

15-22   In what section of Sheehy is the Annual Register listed? Is it listed as a general reference work?

15-23   How does the Annual Register differ in scope and arrangement from the encyclopedia yearbooks you
        have examined?

15-24   If you wanted to read about major opera events that occurred in the United Kingdom during 1981
        how would you locate them?

15-25   One of the values of such current surveys as the encyclopedia annuals and the Annual Register is
        that they give statements of contemporary (i.e., of the same date or time) opinion or viewpoint on
        historical events. If you wanted a source which would give you, literally, an 1864 viewpoint of the
        American Civil War, not a 1980's viewpoint, where could you look?

15-26   In the previous question, you wanted contemporary viewpoints of the Civil War. In question #15-
        14 you wanted the name of the winner of the Nobel Prize in Medicine last year and in 1970. What
        other sources have you had previously in which you could also answer both these questions, pos-
        sibly in even more detail than through the annual survey type of sources?

15-27   The New York Times Index was examined earlier as a bibliographic source; that is, basically as
        an access to articles appearing specifically in the New York Times or to some extent in any news-
        paper through the date. It was noted then that the NY Times Index provides not only an index
        to the newspaper but a summary or abstract of the news itself. Could you find, through the New
        York Times Index, a survey of the developments in medicine in 1981 (see #15-17)?

15-28   If you wanted to find out who won the Nobel Prize for Medicine for this year (assuming that it has
        actually been awarded by the time you are at this point), could you find it out through the ency-
        clopedia yearbooks? Where would you have to look?

15-29   Sheehy lists two other sources as "Annual and current surveys" along with the Annual Register
        (see 9th ed., p. 602). Both of these, Facts on File and Keesing's Contemporary Archives, are
        perhaps more similar to the New York Times Index than they are to the Annual Register. What is
        the full title of Facts on File, and where is it published? How often does it appear?

15-30   Is there anything in Facts on File itself which tells you how to use it?

15-31   How does Facts on File differ from the New York Times Index?

15-32   Can you find in Facts on File information about recent activities of Ralph Nader?

15-33   Does the scope of Facts on File differ from the New York Times Index?

15-34   Could you tell, through Facts on File, specifically what The St. Louis Post Dispatch had to say about the 1982 Worlds Fair (in Knoxville, Tennessee)?

15-35   In 1982 several deaths from cyanide-laced Tylenol occurred in the United States. In what city did some of the deaths occur? How many bottles of Extra-Strength Tylenol were recalled as a result of the deaths? Could you answer these questions as easily through the New York Times Index for 1982?

15-36   The New York Times Index is issued twice a month, and until the cumulated annual volume is published, it is necessary to check each issue in a search for information. Is this also true with Facts on File?

15-37   Facts on File seems most valuable as a very current (weekly) source of information on very recent events. Does it also provide a yearly survey of events or activities as the Annual Register or the encyclopedia yearbooks do?

15-38   How far back can Facts on File be used as a retrospective searching source?

15-39   Somewhat comparable to Facts on File is Keesing's Contemporary Archives. Where is it published, how often is it issued, and how far back does it go?

15-40   In use, Keesing's is similar to Facts on File. In coverage or scope, it is somewhat different. What can you assume might be one obvious difference in coverage?

15-41   On February 19, 1982, the DeLorean Motor Company, located in Belfast, Ireland, collapsed. Can you find in Keesing's an account of the event or more information about DeLorean?

15-42   Look up the same topic in Facts on File. How do the information and the access compare to Keesing's?

15-43   Does Keesing's provide the same kind of annual survey as Facts on File does (see #15-37)?

15-44   How do the annual summaries of news events differ from the annual summaries of the encyclopedia yearbooks? Is there any difference in arrangement? Is there any difference in point of view, in perspective, in interpretation of material?

15-45   Do you see any difference in which these two types of annual summaries can or should be used?

15-46   Facts on File and Keesing's, and to some extent the Annual Register, obviously would seem to be of most importance as sources of current information. Why are they listed in Sheehy under "History and Area Studies?"

15-47   Another yearbook-type of source are the almanacs. These have many of the features of the annual surveys you have been examining, with some special aspects. What is an almanac?

15-48   Probably the easiest way to see what an almanac really is is to look at one closely. The first on your list, the World Almanac, is also one of the oldest. When was it first published?

15-49   What is the arrangement of the World Almanac? Is it similar to the encyclopedia yearbooks?

15-50   What kind of specific subject access do you have? How would you find out, for example, that the "Off-Beat News Stories of 1982" are on p. 54 between Mayors and City Managers and Consumer Survival Kit?

15-51   Because of the nature of the material they contain, and because of the indexing, almanacs are very useful for answering factual questions. How many of the following "facts" can you ascertain from the World Almanac:
a.   the number of calories in a bagel?
b.   the name of the inventor of the slide rule?
c.   the zip code of Opp, Alabama?
d.   the address of the U.S. Metric Association?
e.   the birthday of ex-Beatle Paul McCartney?
f.   the 1950 winners of the Stanley Cup (hockey)?
g.   the name of the President whose portrait appears on a $500 bill?
h.   the magazine with the largest circulation in the United States?
i.   the westernmost point of the United States?
j.   the number of people in Calaveras County, California, who voted for Ronald Reagan in the 1980 presidential election?

15-52   The almanacs are useful for other kinds of information also. How many of the following things can you locate in the World Almanac:
a.   how to obtain a passport?
b.   what an IRA is?
c.   how to become an American citizen?
d.   U.S. parcel post rates?
e.   a table of metric weights and measures?
f.   the U.S. federal income tax law?
g.   the copyright law of the U.S.?

15-53   Can you find through the World Almanac, any information on:
        a.   Martial Law declared in Poland in 1982?
        b.   Who won the Nobel Prize for medicine in 1982?
        c.   A list of notable people who died in 1982?

15-54   What is the real key to locating information in the almanacs?

15-55   From questions #15-51, 15-52, and 15-53, how does the scope of the World Almanac differ from the
        encyclopedia yearbooks? Does the almanac include any features found in the encyclopedia year-
        books? Does the almanac include current--i.e., up-to-date--information? Does the almanac include
        retrospective information (which the encyclopedia yearbooks do not)? Does the almanac include
        basic standard information such as you might expect to find in an encyclopedia itself?

15-56   Some of the information included in the almanacs is basic or standard information probably also
        found in other sources--such as citizenship laws, first aid, geographical locations, zip codes, ad-
        dresses, etc. Is there any difference in the information found in the almanacs and that found in
        the encyclopedias? For example, on the question about the IRA--Individual Retirement Account
        (#15-52), would the answer be the same in a 1982 printing of an encyclopedia as it would be in a
        1982 almanac or 1983 almanac?

15-57   How does the Information Please Almanac compare to the World Almanac?

15-58   The Information Please Almanac does not have quite the long history of the World Almanac. When
        was it first published?

15-59   Are there other almanacs similar to the two you have examined?

15-60   There are other, more specialized almanacs which focus, for example, on Blacks or women. Can
        you find more information on these almanacs in Sheehy?

15-61   Is there any way in which you can check the authority of the information given in the almanacs,
        or must you just take it on faith? Are sources given?

15-62   What are the latest population figures you can find for Tokyo? Do these figures represent the
        city-proper or the total urban area? Compare World Almanac and Information Please Almanac.

15-63   Can you find a list of endangered animal species of the world?

15-64   How many Presidential libraries are there in the U.S.? Where are they?

15-65   Has Orville Wright been named to the Aviation Hall of Fame? In what year did the Wright Brothers
        make the first airplane flight? If you wanted a source which would give you some contemporary
        comments on that first airplane flight, where would you look? Can you be sure that such a source
        would actually have information on that first flight?

15-66 Where might you look to find a discussion of current income tax laws and rates in England?

15-67 If you wanted to find a list of the addresses of the Foreign Consuls in Canada, where would you look?

15-68 Where would you check to find the prices for sources such as the World Almanac, Whitaker's Almanack, Britannica Book of the Year? These appear annually; would they be listed in Ulrich's International Periodical Directory? What about Facts on File?

15-69 What do you see as the major uses of the yearbooks as compared to the uses of the encyclopedias?

The yearbooks, including the almanacs, which you have examined so far have been very broad in scope, general in coverage. There are many yearbooks or annual publications which specialize in certain fields, such as science (the Britannica Yearbook of Science and the Future, Sheehy EA43, or Science Year; the World Book science annual, Sheehy EA44) or even more specifically, agriculture (the Yearbook of Agriculture published by the U.S. Government Printing Office, Sheehy EL50).

Others have wider subject coverage but include only certain types of information. The Statesman's Year-Book is an example of a yearbook which might be said to represent subject coverage: e.g., government. However, it is one of the most generally useful sources in any library and the information it includes actually has an extremely broad scope.

15-70 What is the full title of the Statesman's Year-Book, and where is it published?

15-71 The date given on the volume itself is a double one: 1982/83, for example. Does this mean that it is published every other year? How often is it published?

15-72 How is the Statesman's Year-Book arranged?

15-73 Much of the information given in the Statesman's Year-Book may also be found in some form in the almanacs and encyclopedia yearbooks. It is perhaps then the more straightforward arrangement by country which makes the Statesman's Year-Book so generally useful. What information is given in the Statesman's Year-Book? What information can you find out about Denmark, for example?

15-74 What is the present name of the African country of Nyasaland? Is it part of the British Commonwealth? When did it become independent? Where could you find further information on its history?

15-75 Is the population figure for Tokyo given in the Statesman's Year-Book any different than those which you found in the almanacs (question #15-62)?

15-76 Is there an airfield in the country of Sikkim?

15-77 Are there other yearbooks providing similar coverage of world governments? What about information on local and state governments?

These last questions can be used as review for the sources examined so far in sections 12, 13, 14, and 15.

15-78   Can you find what the signal is for the letter "K" in the Morse Code? What is the difference between Morse Code used in the United States and Canada, and International or Continental Morse Code?

15-79   What were some of the major new acts passed by the British Parliament in 1982?

15-80   When is the next Year of the Snake according to the Chinese calendar?

15-81   What does I.Q. mean? What tests are used to determine it?

15-82   What were some of the notable American novels published in 1982?

15-83   How do you pronounce the word "eleemosynary?"

15-84   For what crimes may capital punishment be imposed in the Soviet Union?

15-85   Where would you find information about President Reagan's visit to Brazil in November/December 1982?

15-86   What is the currency used in Austria and what is its exchange rate with U.S. dollars? If you needed absolutely up-to-the-minute information on this question, what could you do?

15-1: Some facts on all these topics would probably be found in any of the encyclopedias. Whether you would find the recent material you desire on the Nobel Prize and the Indians would depend on how recent a printing you had, and how thoroughly it had been brought up to date or revised. The information on bridges may not seem, at first, as such a necessity for current information, but in fact, since bridge building is going on all the time, such statistics will change and current information is necessary.

15-2: Continuous revision (see #14-5), and encyclopedia annuals or yearbooks (see Sheehy, 9th edition, p. 98, section V.B of the outline for examining encyclopedias, and the section "Encyclopedia annuals" following the citations for American and English encyclopedias).

15-3: The ALA Glossary defines both; an annual is defined only by the fact that it is issued once a year, a yearbook by its content. Webster's Third unabridged defines both, and the definitions are similar. The key ideas are that they are published once a year, and that they cover current information, events or developments, either generally or in a special field.

15-4: The date of a yearbook is often the date of the year in which it is issued, not the date of the year which it covers. A yearbook issued in 1983 could not yet cover all the events of 1983; the 1983 volume will therefore in most cases actually cover the year 1982. For example, the Americana yearbook covering the events of 1982 was published in 1983, and is labeled on the spine as "1983 Annual"; the title page states "The Americana Annual 1983, an encyclopedia of the events of 1982." This same problem is relevant to all of the yearbooks, annuals, almanacs, etc.

15-5: The Table of Contents.

15-6: Yes, there is variation, although it is not as much as it may seem. For example, the Table of Contents pages for Britannica may be a bit more detailed than Americana; but Americana has in addition a classified listing of articles.

15-7: All three usually contain a brief chronology (listed in chronological order) of the main events of the year.
    All three usually have some special or feature articles on major events of the year. The number of these varies from year to year.
    All three usually have, as the main body of the book, a selection of moderately short articles, arranged alphabetically, covering in more detail the events of the year (e.g., Americana: The Year in Review; Britannica: Book of the Year).

15-8: The articles in the yearbook do not attempt to correspond with the articles in the main sets, since they are only for current coverage and there may be no current activity in all of the areas covered in the main sets. For example, it is highly unlikely that there would be any reason to have coverage in the yearbooks on St. Nicholas' Day.

15-9: Most of the articles are of a general nature, such as "Dance." Specific items can be found through the indexes. The Britannica 1983 Book of the Year lists New York City Ballet in the index with reference to the article on "dance."

15-10: Common topics such as education, art, music, libraries, sports, etc., are usually consistently covered by all three. The current issues will not be as consistently covered in all three, although this is sometimes more a matter of arrangement than of judgment or choice of material. For example, Americana 1983 has "special reports" on the nuclear freeze movement, cost of education, industrial production, and the national debt.

15-11: Specific item, check index under "Falkland Islands conflict," yearbooks covering 1982. For example, Britannica
has references to the articles on Ar-
gentina and on the United Kingdom.

15-12: All three deal with them separately in
some way, e.g., Americana has a separate article, outside of the alphabetical
section but noted in the Contents, titled "Obituaries," giving such a list.

15-13: The same way as in the basic sets themselves; signed articles and lists of contributors in the source itself.

15-14: The yearbooks list winners of the Nobel
Prize for the previous year, with access
through the indexes. You cannot necessarily find out the 1970 winners through
the yearbooks. Generally, none of the
yearbooks attempt to include retrospective
information unless it is really pertinent in
some way to the material discussed. Basically the indexes are not retrospective
either; that is, they index only the volume of which they are a part, they do
not index past yearbooks. However, the
Britannica indexes do include an indication of the yearbook years (not pages)
in which some of their major articles,
obituaries, and biographies have appeared.

15-15: Other than reading/comprehension level,
no. The children's yearbooks tend to be
lavishly illustrated (see the 1983 World
Book Year Book special report, "The
Video Revolution"). They include a
chronology of events, an alphabetically-
arranged section of articles on various
topics (the to-be-expected areas such as
education, sports, art, etc., and some
of more current interest such as energy),
and special articles or reports.
   Note that the World Book Year Book
is indexed, and that the index is retrospective: The 1983 index covers the 1981,
1982 and 1983 editions of the WBYB.

15-16: No. Actually, the encyclopedia yearbooks
are quite independent of the encyclopedias,
and can be purchased and used quite
satisfactorily as entirely separate publications. Nor is it necessary, in using the
encyclopedias themselves, to have the
yearbooks. It is only necessary to realize that, even with continuous revision,
the encyclopedias would not be and cannot be entirely up-to-date in all respects
and some more current sources must be
referred to for current information.

15-17: Presumably some of the current material appearing in the yearbooks would be
absorbed into the basic set from time to
time with continuous revision. However,
coverage of current topics in the yearbooks is more in depth for that particular year than you would find for it
in the basic set, even at a later date.
Also, coverage of topics in the basic
sets is not usually set up on a year-
by-year basis so it might be quite difficult, even from an entirely up-to-date
article, to determine exactly what the
developments were during a specific
year.

15-18: No, the scope is international. In
fact, many of the articles in the main
alphabetical listings in the yearbooks
are specifically on other countries--
Australia, Canada, China, etc.--giving
surveys of the major important events
of the year in those countries. However, as with the encyclopedias themselves, stronger, more thorough coverage will be given to the United States.

15-19: Conclude that there might be a yearbook for the British encyclopedias and
check Sheehy to find out. Sheehy does
list a yearbook for the Chambers's
Encyclopaedia (AC13a). Another source
which is very similar to the encyclopedia
yearbooks and which does have British
emphasis is the Annual Register of World
Events, the next source on your list to
examine.

15-20: Title page: The Annual Register; A
Record of World Events. Published by
Longman in London (distributed in the
U.S. by Gale). It is published annually. The date of coverage (for example,
World Events in 1981) is clearly indicated
on the spine and on the title page as
part of the title itself. However, the
volume is published in the year following the year it covers (for example, the
1981 volume was published in 1982 as
indicated on the title page, and copyrighted in 1982 as indicated on the verso of the title page).

15-21: No, it is an independent publication.
You would probably have to go to the
Sheehy annotation to find any history
or background of the source.

15-22: It is not listed under "A: General
Reference Works" but rather under
"D: History and Area Studies." This
is the first of the major sources you
have looked at which is classified in

a subject field in Sheehy (except for a few of the subject-oriented periodical indexes noted in Section 7, and some of the non-book bibliographic sources noted in Section 4). From now on, most of the sources you examine will be drawn from the subject areas in Sheehy, although they will be examined here as basic sources for general reference work.

15-23: It is obviously smaller, and not illustrated as heavily as the encyclopedia yearbooks.

In scope, it has broad coverage with a British and British Commonwealth slant. But like the encyclopedia yearbooks, it is limited to current information, not retrospective.

In arrangement, it is quite different. It is arranged by broad general topics, with specific access through the index. The topics themselves are actually quite similar to those in the encyclopedia yearbooks (names of countries, the law, sports, science and technology, art, economics, etc.) but they are not arranged alphabetically. The arrangement can be seen easily through the Table of Contents.

Like the encyclopedia yearbooks, it has a list of deaths (obituaries) and a chronology of major events of the year.

15-24: Annual Register for 1981: see the index under "opera" for references, including one to the general section on The Arts.

15-25: None of the U.S. encyclopedia yearbooks examined date back that far (see Sheehy annotations). The Annual Register began in 1758 so would cover that period; this of course would be a British point of view, which might be interesting in itself. However, Sheehy lists under encyclopedia annuals another American annual source not currently published--Appleton's Annual Cyclopaedia and Register of Important Events (AC10)--which began in 1861 and should therefore give U.S. coverage of the event (see Sheehy annotation).

15-26: New York Times Index (see Section 7). To get any viewpoints on the Civil War, and to get further detail on the Nobel Prize, you would have to refer to the newspaper itself, of course.

15-27: Yes, under the entry "Medicine and Health." It might not seem as clear as it would in the encyclopedia yearbook articles, and it might require more references back and forth, and you might want to refer further to the newspaper articles themselves for details or

clarification, but basically access to the information and much of the information itself is there. The New York Times Index annual cumulated volume (A Book of Record) for 1981 has 8 pages of entries on medicine and health, many for specific countries other than the United States.

15-28: The encyclopedia yearbooks are annual publications only, and therefore they will be at least a year behind in their information all the time. For example, if the Nobel Prize for medicine were awarded in October of 1982, it would not appear in the encyclopedia yearbook until the edition for 1983 (covering 1982), and that particular edition would probably not be published until late in 1983. For very current information you must go to a source which is issued more frequently. The New York Times Index is issued twice a month.

15-29: Facts on File, weekly world news digest with cumulative index. Published by Facts on File, Inc., New York. Appears weekly. See cover page in binder, or Sheehy annotation.

15-30: There are instructions for the index on the separator sheet for the index.

15-31: Facts on File appears weekly; New York Times Index appears twice a month. Facts on File is completely self-contained; it consists of a narrative digest of the news and a specific index to that digest. NY Times Index is itself an index, with references to another publication for fuller information, although it does give some digest of the news as well.

15-32: Check most recently available index under Nader, then follow up all references. The references themselves do give you some information; for example, a reference under Nader in 1983: "Health group charges CAT scan radiation peril 4-20, 291F2." Fuller information can be found on page 291 of the April 20, 1983 issue.

15-33: Both are international in coverage with extensive coverage of United States' national affairs. New York Times Index is limited in scope, however, to that news which appears in the New York Times, while Facts on File draws on more than 50 foreign and U.S. newspapers and magazines.

15-34: No. Facts on File does not quote or cite specifically from its sources.

15-35: Facts on File Index for 1982, under "Tylenol"--see "Medicine-drugs." The New York Times Index for 1982 under "Tylenol (Drug)" and "Pain-Relieving Drugs." The information under the latter heading indicates that several deaths occurred in Chicago and that Extra-Strength Tylenol capsules were recalled but it does not indicate how many. Apparently it would be necessary to go to the newspaper itself to learn that fact.

15-36: No, Facts on File is issued weekly but the index is continuously cumulated, so that it is rarely necessary to check in more than one or two places.

15-37: Yes, since the index eventually cumulates into an annual issue. The index is all that cumulates; the digests of news do not cumulate; it is still necessary to refer from the index to the individual weekly issues. But like the New York Times Index, the information is there, although not as concisely organized as in the Annual Register or the encyclopedia yearbooks. (Furthermore, the index also cumulates every five years.) However, Facts on File also publishes a yearbook-type of source called News Dictionary (not mentioned or listed in Sheehy); it is very similar in size to the Annual Register, and has a dictionary arrangement of short topics, with cross-references and no index.

15-38: 1940 (see Sheehy annotation).

15-39: Published in London since 1931; now is-sued monthly.

15-40: Both Facts on File and Keesing's are international in scope, but Keesing's-- a British (London) publication--is apt to have more stress on British and British Commonwealth activities.

15-41: Keesing's index is arranged by countries with sub-categories for more specific topics. In addition, there is a separate name index. The 1982 Keesing's has two short articles on the collapse of DeLorean Motors.

15-42: Facts on File 1982 has considerably more information than does Keesing's. There is one article indexed under "Great Britain" and seven articles under "De-Lorean, John Z." Facts on File tends to use more specific references than does

Keesing's, but Keesing's generally cites its sources more precisely.

15-43: Yes, because the index cumulates.

15-44: The news summaries, since they are pre-pared and issued weekly or monthly rath-er than annually, are closer to the facts and the situations and allow for very lit-tle perspective; all information pertinent at the moment is given. Basically, they do not attempt to offer judgment or in-terpretation of events.

The annual summaries of the en-cyclopedia yearbooks are prepared at somewhat greater distance from the events themselves, and are more selec-tive; this offers the opportunity for fallible judgment in selection--an event which seems very minor at the time may become of major importance later on, or vice versa.

The arrangement of these sources differs also. In the news summaries, events relating to one topic will be scattered throughout the issues although brought together in the indexing. In the encyclopedia yearbooks, events re-lated to one topic will be brought to-gether.

The 1983 (cover 1982) Americana Annual has an article on the Falklands confict; the facts and events upon which that article is based will probably be found indexed in the New York Times Index or Facts on File, plus more mate-rial, but all of it will require some time to search out in the newspapers or in the news digest of Facts on File.

15-45: The encyclopedia yearbook type of an-nual survey will show trends or develop-ments more clearly.

The news summary type of annual survey will give facts, details, minor in-formation more clearly, plus some primary source material for further research.

For example, it is probably easier to refer to the encyclopedia yearbooks for a general discussion of current trends in consumer affairs activities or current developments in ecology action. For specific facts such as Nader's activities relating to the "CAT scan radiation peril" (see #15-32), the news summaries might be more useful; this information may never find its way into the encyclo-pedia yearbook.

15-46: Anything current becomes retrospective. What is news today is history tomorrow. And for libraries especially, there is very little which is of current value only; all current material, however ephemeral, can be used for historical research on many levels. Not all libraries can afford to keep retrospective files of such sources, of course, but those which do have resources of much value for research.

15-47: See ALA Glossary. This definition is essentially the same as that of a yearbook but does not stress the <u>currency</u> of information. Originally, almanacs were yearly publications containing calendar information such as planting dates, church festivals, weather forecasts, tide tables, etc. The almanacs to be examined here are of a somewhat broader scope, but the idea of being a miscellaneous compendium of information is certainly common to both types of almanacs.

15-48: 1868 (Sheehy annotation, or title page).

15-49: It's not really easy to figure out what the arrangement of the World Almanac is, and unfortunately there is no Table of Contents page which lays out the <u>arrangement</u> for you. The almanac consists of a great many short articles, tables, charts, lists, etc., arranged in a vaguely subject-classed rather than alphabetical order. You get, for example (in the 1983 edition), a section on Economics (p. 113+), followed by a section on Manufactures and Minerals (p. 131+), followed by Energy (p. 140+) followed by Trade and Transportation (p. 149+), etc.

15-50: There is a specific subject <u>index</u>, located in the front. This index is in some ways astonishingly specific. There is also a Quick Reference Index in the back, but it is too general to list such specific topics.

15-51: According to the 1983 World Almanac:
a. p. 100, Consumer Survival Kit-Food Values (index under calories);
b. p. 818, Inventions and Scientific Discoveries (index under inventions);
c. p. 218, U.S. Places of 5000 or more population with zip and area codes (index under zip codes);
d. p. 346, U.S.--Associations and societies (alphabetized under Metric rather than U.S.) (index under associations and societies);
e. p. 394, Noted personalities--entertainers (index under births--notable persons, dates);
f. p. 837, Sports--hockey (index under Stanley cup);
g. p. 121, Economics Bureau of the Mint (index under portraits on U.S. currency);

h. p. 430, Circulation of leading U.S. magazines (index under magazines--circulation);
i. p. 435, U.S. Superlatives (index under superlative statistics, U.S.);
j. p. 268, presidential election returns by county (index under Presidential elections; also under California--presidential elections; shows both 1976 and 1980).

15-52: According to the 1983 World Almanac:
a. p. 590, (index under passport regulations-U.S.);
b. p. 75, (index under Individual Retirement Account);
c. p. 592, (index under citizenship-U.S.);
d. p. 971, (index under parcel post);
e. p. 808, (index under metric measures);
f. p. 55-57, (index under income taxes-Federal);
g. p. 820, (index under copyright law, U.S.).

15-53: According to the 1983 World Almanac:
a. p. 922, located in the Chronology of the Year's Events, beginning p. 918--(index under Poland--Martial Law);
b. p. 36, located under Late News, Addenda, Changes (the lists of Nobel Prize Winners on p. 411 under Awards --Medals--Prizes only covers up to 1981)
c. p. 951-953, located under Deaths, Oct. 31, 1981-Nov. 1, 1982--index under "Obituaries (1981-82)" and "Deaths--Year (1981-82)."

15-54: The index--that is, either the specificity of the index, or your own ingenuity in figuring out the terminology used.

15-55: The almanacs and the encyclopedia yearbooks include, for the past year, chronologies, obituaries, summaries of developments in specific fields. Both include current up-to-date information such as prize winners. <u>In addition</u>, the almanacs include retrospective information (1950 winners of the Stanley Cup, birthday of Paul McCartney, inventor of the slide rule). <u>In addition</u>, the almanacs include standard information (nutritive values in food, first aid, copyright laws, income tax laws, citizenship laws, etc.).

15-56: Some of the so-called standard information does have a way of changing from time to time. This is just the sort of thing which is difficult to up-date in an encyclopedia. For example, all wage earners under the age of 70½ became eligible to set up their own tax-sheltered IRA in 1982. Prior to 1982, only those workers not covered by another plan, such as a company pension or profit sharing program, could set up an Individual Retirement Account. Since this is so current, the older encyclopedias would not contain the necessary information, and it is cheaper to buy a new almanac every year than a new encyclopedia printing every year. The almanacs are extremely useful for up-dating encyclopedia information in this way.

15-57:   Basically it is the same in format and scope. The index is in the back. The table of contents in the front is an alphabetical listing of major categories, similar to the Quick Reference Index in the back of the World Almanac. Information Please includes a chronology and a list of deaths for the past year. It does have three "Special Features" in the 1983 almanac, which are similar to the "special articles or features" appearing in the encyclopedia yearbooks. Much of the information is duplicated in both almanacs, but the Information Please Almanac has some features or sections (e.g., "Where to Find Out More," p. 502+, 1983 edition) not in the World Almanac, and vice versa.

15-58:   1947 (Sheehy).

15-59:   Sheehy, 9th ed., does list similar almanacs in the section under Social Sciences-- Statistics--Compendiums. You may want to take a look at Sheehy's annotations for Reader's Digest Almanac (CG67) and People's Almanac (1CG15, 2CG17), for example.

15-60:   Check in the Sheehy index for the subjects in which you are interested. There are references under both "Afro-Americans" (and "Negroes") and "women," but not for almanacs as such. Both subject headings do list many items in section CC, which is Social Sciences--Sociology--Race Relations and Minorities, and which has sub-headings for both "Afro-Americans" and "women." The Sheehy supplement lists, in this section, The Negro Almanac (1CC142), under "handbooks." There are similar sources for women, such as the Women's Action Almanac: A Complete Resource Guide (2CC168).
          Both of the examples given are not

up-dated annually, as were the other almanacs you examined, but they are collections of miscellaneous facts and information up-dated frequently enough so that the information is reasonably current. There is some overlap between these subject-specific almanacs and the handbook-type sources which will be discussed in Section 17 of this manual.

15-61:   Some sources are given, mostly for the tables, lists, statistics, population figures, etc. For example, the table, Public Debt of the U.S., in the World Almanac, 1983, comes from the U.S. Treasury Department.

15-62:   World, 1983. Indexed under Tokyo, Japan--population. p. 590: "Population of World's Largest Urban Areas." Tokyo is listed as 11,696,373 according to a 1978 estimate.
          p. 535: article on "Japan." Tokyo is listed as 8.2 million (1978 census).

          Information Please, 1983. Indexed under Tokyo, Japan. p. 214: article on "Japan." Lists as 8,350,000 estimated 1980.
          p. 127: "Largest Cities of the World." Same information as in "Japan"; given as a 1980 estimate.

          Both sources use different figures, different years, different bases, and the differences are not always made clear. Presumably, the smaller figure in World and both figures in Information Please are for "Greater" Tokyo, or the city only, and the larger figure in World is for the entire urban area.

15-63:   World Almanac 1983, p. 804 (index under endangered species); also Information Please Almanac 1983, p. 649-50 (index under endangered species).

15-64:   Information Please Almanac, 1983, p. 320-22 (indexed under Libraries, Presidential; Presidential Libraries and Museums; and Presidents--Libraries). This information could also be found in the encyclopedias but it might not be up-to-date.

15-65:   World Almanac, 1983 edition, p. 163, Aviation Hall of Fame (indexed under Aviation Hall of Fame). Year of the first airplane flight by the Wright Brothers, p. 708 in Memorable Dates --indexed under Wright Brothers Flights (1903). For contemporary comments, you have to go to a source covering

1903, and there aren't too many from your list: Annual Register, and the Appleton's Annual Cyclopedia noted in the answer to #15-25. The World Almanac goes back that far, but might not have comments. New York Times Index does exist for 1903 (see Sheehy AF68) and could lead you to newspaper articles on the event. The problem here is that the Wright Brothers flight may not have seemed nearly as significant in 1903 as it does in 1983.

15-66: The American almanacs are world-wide in scope but stress American material. A British publication similar to the American almanacs is more likely: one of the best-known and most useful in American libraries is Whitaker's Almanack (Sheehy CG130).

15-67: You might expect this to be in Whitaker's as Canada is part of the British Commonwealth, but it isn't there (1983 ed.), and it is unlikely to be in the American almanacs, so another possible source is a Canadian almanac if one exists and you have access to it. Check Sheehy, in the same section in which the American almanacs are listed, under the foreign country divisions, under Canada (see item CG98, Canadian Almanac and Directory).

15-68: World Almanac, Whitaker's Almanack, Britannica Book of the Year are all annuals; Ulrich's does not include annuals but Irregular Serials and Annuals (see section 5) does.

Facts on File appears weekly, and should therefore be in Ulrich's as a periodical.

Sources such as CBI, BPR, and BIP do not claim to include annual or yearbook publications but in fact they often do.

15-69: Current up-to-date information not yet in the encyclopedias or other older sources, that which is constantly changing (prize winners, population figures, etc.) and trends in certain fields or areas which would possibly not yet be in the encyclopedias and in any case would not be as clearly set forth (medicine, education, pollution, consumer affairs, etc.). In the older yearbooks, contemporary comments on events (Civil War, Wright Brothers, etc.). In the almanacs particularly, quick answers to factual questions.

15-70: The Statesman's Year-Book: statistical

and historical annual of the states of the world for the year ... published by Macmillan in London (also St. Martin's Press in New York). See title page, also Sheehy.

15-71: It is an annual (see title, and see Sheehy), published once a year. The double date is probably used because it comes out in mid-year; the 1982 publication would therefore be used through part of 1982 and part of 1983. The next issue would be dated 1983/1984, so the date would always overlap.

15-72: See Contents pages. Basically, it is arranged by area: first, international organizations, beginning with the United Nations; then countries of the world in alphabetical order; the United States of America entry includes the states listed alphabetically. There are also "place and international organizations" and "product" indexes.

15-73: Constitution, government, present rulers, flag, national anthem, local governments, area, population, vital statistics, religion, education, number of newspapers, social security, justice, economy (currency, budget), defence, production, agriculture, fisheries, manufacturers, power, tourism, commerce, shipping, roads, railways, aviation, post, banking, weights and measures; also information on the Faroe Islands and Greenland.

15-74: Statesman's Year-Book 1982/83, index under Nyasaland refers you to Malawi. The history section states that Malawi became an independent member of the Commonwealth in 1964 and a republic on July 6, 1966. A short bibliography is at the end of the article, for further information, as is true for most of the articles.

15-75: In the 1982/83 Statesman's Year-Book: under Japan, then under Area and Population, then the list of leading cities: Tokyo is given as 8,349,000 as of October 1980. Compare to the 1983 almanacs in #15-62.

15-76: Look up Sikkim in the index, Statesman's Year-Book 1982/83, p. 664, under "Communications"; states that the nearest airport is at Bagdogra (India).

15-77: See Sheehy. A source comparable to the Statesman's Year-Book is the Europa Year Book (CJ62). It is dis-

tributed in the U.S. by Gale Research
and provides detailed factual information
about every country in the world, as well
as descriptions of principal international
organizations.

      A relatively comprehensive source
of information about local governments of
the U.S. and Canada is the Municipal
Year Book (CJ118a, 1CJ76). It provides
information on local government operations
and municipal organizations, as well as
governmental trends. A comparable yearbook for U.S. states is the Book of the
States (CJ118).

15-78:   This sounds like the kind of thing to
turn up in the almanacs, but it isn't
there. The Morse code itself is given
in most of the dictionaries (for example,
Webster's Third unabridged, American
Heritage, Funk and Wagnall's unabridged).
It should also be given in the encyclopedias; check in the indexes or in an
article on Telegraph or Telegraphy.
The encyclopedia is the only likely
source to give the difference between
the Morse Code in the U.S. and the
International Code (see Americana, for
example).

      This is another example of some-
thing that rather oddly turns up in De
Sola's Abbreviations Dictionary, though
De Sola does not distinguish between the
different codes.

15-79:   Annual Register covering 1982; Whitaker's Almanack for 1983. Sources such
as Facts on File, Keesing's, New York
Times Index might give the information
but you would not find it so easily.

15-80:   World Almanac, 1983 edition, p. 787 (indexed under Chinese Lunar Calendar,
or Calendars--Chinese Lunar). Possibly also the encyclopedias.

15-81:   To define I.Q., a dictionary would probably be sufficient. But to find out the
tests used in determining I.Q., you would
probably have to go to an encyclopedia
for further information.

15-82:   Encyclopedia year book covering 1982
(e.g., the 1983 Americana Annual's article on publishing).

15-83:   Any dictionary, or a pronunciation book
such as the NBC Handbook of Pronunciation.

15-84:   Statesman's Year-Book (under Union of
Soviet Socialist Republics, then under
Justice, Religion, Education and Wel-
fare--p. 1238, 1982/83 ed.). Possibly
also an encyclopedia although information
may not be up to date.

15-85:   New York Times Index, Facts on File;
almanacs covering 1982, possibly encyclopedia yearbooks covering 1982.

15-86:   Almanacs, indexed under Austria, then
"Economy", or "exchange rates." Statesman's Year-Book, under Austria, then
Economy. For up-to-the-minute information, you might try calling the foreign exchange or international department
of a local bank.

Section 16

YEARBOOK SUPPLEMENTS: STATISTICS

Questions #16/1--16/42

16-1   Under what heading are the almanacs classified in Sheehy? Why?

16-2   What are statistics? Which of the questions that you previously answered through the yearbooks and almanacs are statistical in nature? What types of statistical information are given in these yearbook sources?

Statistical information is included extensively in most of the sources you have examined so far: especially in the almanacs, to a great extent in the encyclopedias and encyclopedia yearbooks, to some extent in news surveys such as Facts on File (and of course in the New York Times itself), and even in the dictionaries (in population figures, for example).
   The next set of sources to examine are examples of those which are specifically devoted to statistical information. In a way they should be considered as supplementary to the unit on yearbooks, because much statistical information (population figures, for example) changes from year to year, and it is very important to have access to information which is as up-to-date as possible. Two of the sources to be examined for statistical information are, in fact, yearbooks. Another is a retrospective source, and one is a bibliographic source. The titles are:

      Statistical Abstract of the United States (CG69)
      Historical Statistics of the United States (CG71, 1CG18)
      County and City Data Book (CG70, 1CG17)
      Statistical Yearbook (of the United Nations) (CG48)
      Statistics Sources (CG52, 1CG9, 2CG13)

16-3   Who publishes the Statistical Abstract?

16-4   The U.S. Census Bureau is the source of a great number of statistics, as well as being responsible for the preparation of the Statistical Abstract. Where would you go to find out what the Census Bureau does, how often a census is taken, how the data from the census are published or made available?

16-5   How often is a major U.S. population census taken? When was the last one taken? Where would you look to find further general information on this last census?

16-6   What is the arrangement of the Statistical Abstract?

16-7   Statistical Abstract of the United States is not called a yearbook or almanac in its title. Is it a yearbook?

16-8   Has anything new been added to the most recent volume of Statistical Abstract? Where would you look to find out?

16-9   Can you find which state had the most elected Black officials in 1979?

16-10   Does Statistical Abstract give only figures or data for the year preceding publication, or does it have retrospective data as well? Can you find, for example, the number of people killed in automobile accidents in 1981? Can you find comparable figures for 1960? What is the source of these figures?

16-11   What is the total estimated cost of the American Civil War? What is the total estimated cost of the Vietnam "conflict"? Are those costs simply the expenses of waging the wars, or are other items included?

16-12   Can you find, in Statistical Abstract, recent figures on the number of librarians currently employed?

16-13   A number of the tables giving statistics on employment (for example, in Statistical Abstract 1982/83, Section 13: Labor Force, Employment, and Earnings, see specifically Table 656 on p. 392 for unemployment insurance) divide the figures by race, usually as "white' and "Black and other." What is meant by "and other?"

16-14   Can you find, in the most recent Statistical Abstract, the total number of new books including new editions published in the United States in the previous year?

16-15   What is the source of these statistics? Knowing the source, what does this lead you to suspect about the types of material included in or excluded from these figures?

16-16   Does the table of new books published, as given in Statistical Abstract, state these omissions for you, or for others who might not even suspect such omissions?

16-17   Does the most recent Statistical Abstract have a figure for the number of books registered for copyright in the previous year?

16-18   In Statistical Abstract 1982/83, the number of monographs (books) registered for copyright in 1981 is given as 119,000, while in Table no. 957, p. 564, New Books and New Editions, published by Subject, the number of new books published is given as 41,434. Are these figures really comparable? Are they really counting the same thing?

16-19   Does the most recent Statistical Abstract list the number of daily newspapers in the United States in the previous year? From what source are these figures taken?

16-20   Statistics are not always easy for the layman to understand, and there are many problems in using and interpreting statistics, even in reading statistical tables correctly. What are some of the problems which may seem evident from the questions you have answered so far? What are some of the things you should look for in using and reading statistical information?

16-21   Is there any general difference between the statistical information given in Statistical Abstract and that given in the almanacs, for example?

16-22   Is all the statistical information given in the Statistical Abstract based on government figures or data?

16-23   Can you find in Statistical Abstract how many books were published in the United States in 1900? If not, where do you go for this information?

16-24   Historical Statistics of the United States exists as a retrospective supplement to the Statistical Abstract. Therefore its scope and arrangement are very similar to the Statistical Abstract itself, and it will be used in much the same way. What retrospective period is covered by this publication? Who is the publisher?

16-25   Will all the statistical tables in Historical Statistics then give figures from 1610 through 1970? For example, are there Consumer Price Indexes back to 1610?

16-26   Can you find out, through Historical Statistics, what the Consumer Price Index is, and how it works?

16-27   What historical statistics do exist for the colonial period? How can you locate them in Historical Statistics? Can you find population figures for the American Colonies? Can you find figures for the amount of tea imported into the Colonies? What is the source of the figures on tea? Can you find the number of slaves brought into the United States? Were all of them actually slaves?

16-28   Another important supplement to Statistical Abstract is the County and City Data Book. What kind of information does it provide? What are its major sources of information? How frequently is it published?

16-29   What is a "metropolitan statistical area" (MSA) or "primary metropolitan statistical area" (PMSA)? How would you locate information on Ann Arbor, Michigan in the County and City Data Book?

16-30   Most of the data included in the County and City Data Book are available in comparable form for all counties or for all cities. For example, what was the percentage of families with income of $50,000 or over in Ann Arbor, Michigan, as compared to Chattanooga, Tennessee (at least in terms of the latest figures available for the latest edition of the County and City Data Book)?

16-31   Do the Statistical Abstract, the County and City Data Book, or Historical Statistics give any international figures, or statistics from other countries? Can you find comparative figures for the percentage of persons under 15 years of age in the U.S. and India?

16-32   Where would you look to find more detailed statistics on the population of India?

16-33   Where would you find general statistics for several countries or areas? Can you find recent figures for the unemployment rate in Japan?

16-34   Does the Statistical Yearbook of the United Nations indicate the sources of its data?

16-35   What is the point in knowing the source or sources for statistical data?

16-36   Statistical Abstract itself contains an extensive listing of statistics sources for further reference.
        (In the 1982/83 volume, see Appendix IV, Guide to Sources of Statistics, p. 924-962.) The next
        title to examine, Statistics Sources, gives further guidance in this area. What is the full title,
        the publisher, and the date of publication?

16-37   What is the arrangement of Statistics Sources?

16-38   Does Statistics Sources list only primary sources of data (e.g., Bowker Company)--that is, the
        organization, agencies, governments, businesses, etc., which collect the data--or also secondary
        sources (e.g., Statistical Abstract, World Almanac) in which statistical data are published?

16-39   Where could you write or call to get figures on poverty?

16-40   Where could you find information on the profits made by drug companies?

16-41   In addition to Statistics Sources, there are a variety of other guides to sources of statistics. Where
        are they listed in Sheehy?

16-42   If you wanted to know more about statistics, such as what they are, how to use them, etc., where
        would you look?

16-1:   CG, Statistics (part of Social Sciences). Probably because a large part of the information they contain is statistical in nature.

16-2:   For a definition of statistics, see any dictionary. Examples of statistical information are the population of Tokyo (#15-62), the Presidential election returns (#15-51), etc. See also the sections on U.S. population, Vital Statistics, Economics, Education, etc.

16-3:   It is a U.S. government publication, specifically the Bureau of the Census of the Department of Commerce. (See title page and Sheehy citation.)

16-4:   Try a general encyclopedia. There may not be an article on the Bureau itself but an article on the Census should give some information. Another more indirect source might be to see if there are any recent government publications (see Section 8) which would be useful. Check in the Monthly Catalog of Government Publications or in the GPO Subject Bibliography which covers the census publications.

16-5:   A U.S. population census is taken every 10 years (see article on Census in Collier's Encyclopedia, © 1983), and the last major census was in 1980. You would expect that an encyclopedia yearbook for 1981 (covering 1980) would have an article on the 1980 census; the 1981 almanacs might also have information.

16-6:   By broad subject grouping, such as population, vital statistics, immigration, education, etc. (see Contents pages) with a very specific index in the back.

16-7:   Yes, because it is an annual publication, containing miscellaneous current and up-to-date information; in this case specifically statistical information. (See definition of yearbook, #15-3.)

16-8:   See Preface (Sheehy annotation would not give it for a recent edition). In general, more social awareness is found in recent editions: coverage of minority groups, etc.

16-9:   1982/83 edition, p. 488, table no. 798, Black Elected Officials, by Office ... States: 1981. That is, as of July 1981 (see note following title of table). Indexed under Black population--elected officials.

16-10:   Yes, some retrospective data for comparison are given. There is no set cut-off date; some tables go back further than others. For example, in Statistical Abstract 1982/83, the index under "Accidents and fatalities--Motor vehicle" lists several page references, and there are a number of tables which give this information in varying forms. See Table 1061 on p. 615: Motor Vehicle Accidents, number and deaths for 1960 to 1981 (1960, 65, 70, 74-81). Total persons killed in 1981: 50,700, total persons killed in 1960: 38,100. There is further breakdown by type of action and vehicle in the accident. The figures are from the National Safety Council, and a specific publication is cited for further reference. Other figures are given in Table 1062 on p. 616, which breaks down the figures by state and cites the U.S. National Center for Health Statistics as a source.

16-11:   Both figures are given in the 1982/83 edition, p. 357, table no. 587 (indexed under Wars, American, total cost of). Be sure to note that the cost of the Civil War is not 7 thousand dollars, but 7 million dollars and is for the Union only; the total estimated ultimate costs listed include all veterans' benefits and payments of interest on war loans as well as the military and national security costs.

16-12:   Yes. In the 1982/83 edition, the index under "Libraries--Employees" (there is nothing under librarians) leads you to tables no. 455 on page 267; no. 509, p. 309 and no. 651, p. 388--Employed Persons, by Race, Sex and Occupation: 1972 and 1978. (Note librarians are grouped together with archivists and curators.)

16-13: In Statistical Abstract 1982/83, see article on "Population," which gives some explanation of methodology, specifically on p. 3 under "Race."

16-14: In Statistical Abstract 1982/83: table no. 957, p. 564, New Books and New Editions Published.... Indexed under Books, etc., in index, or you could find it through the Contents (Communications, then Copyright, Books).

16-15: The sources are Bowker Company publications--Library Journal, Bowker Annual of Library and Book Trade Information, and Publishers Weekly. You already know that the listings in Bowker's Weekly Record exclude certain types of publications--e.g., government publications, most subscription books, dissertations, pamphlets under 49 pages, and periodicals. You might then suspect that these types of publications are probably not included in the statistics from Bowker, and that therefore the figures as given are not strictly representative of all books published. For example, Statistical Abstract itself, although clearly a book, is not represented in the statistics from Bowker because it is a government publication.

16-16: Yes, following the title of the table.

16-17: Statistical Abstract 1982/83: table no. 956, p. 563.

16-18: The table on registration indicates that it includes registrations from residents of foreign countries so that all registrations may not be for books published in the U.S. but only copyrighted here. In addition, you know yourself from the examination of the Catalog of Copyright Entries that many very odd kinds of publications appeared in that listing which did not appear in Weekly Record. Therefore the figures, even though for the same year, cannot really be considered as comparable.

16-19: In Statistical Abstract 1982/83: table no. 951 on p. 561, Newspapers and periodicals: 1979-80 figures are given, as well as some earlier figures. Source is the Ayer Directory. (Indexed under Newspapers and Periodicals--Frequency of publication, or found through Contents: Communications--Newspapers and Periodicals).

16-20: The date is important for timeliness and accuracy; for example, as 1980 census figures have become available, the various reference publications should have begun to reflect these figures instead of earlier 1970 figures. Nomenclature (i.e., what comprises a "book," what comprises "and other," etc.) should be clarified, before you can determine exactly what the figures are telling you, or whether or not the figures are comparable. The source of the information is important, for further reference if necessary, or for general authority and accuracy. For example, you have some understanding about the statistics on books and newspapers because you are familiar with the sources--Ayer's, Bowker --from which they are taken; the figures on automobile accidents might not seem so deceptively simple if you were an insurance agent instead of a librarian. All footnotes or other descriptive or explanatory notes should always be read.

16-21: Statistical Abstract is careful to cite sources, dates, give sufficient explanatory and descriptive data. The almanacs are not always this careful; remember, for example, the wide range of answers found for population data on Tokyo.

16-22: No. The figures on books from Bowker Company and on newspapers from Ayer's, for example, are not government data.

16-23: Some retrospective data are given in Statistical Abstract (see #16-10), but they rarely go back more than a decade or two. In Statistical Abstract 1982/83, the data on books published, Table no. 957, p. 564 (see #16-14), give figures as far back as 1960, but not 1900. The notes for the table direct you to Historical Statistics on the United States for further retrospective information.

16-24: Historical Statistics of the United States goes back to "colonial times" (see title), and actually to 1610 (see Sheehy, CG71). It is not a yearbook, as it is not published annually, and is strictly for retrospective rather than current information. The work itself, most recently published in 1975, covers to 1970 (Sheehy 1CG18). It is published by the U.S. GPO, as is Statistical Abstract.

16-25: Statistics will be given retrospectively only for the years such statistics were kept, so most of the tables will not go back to colonial times. The Consumer Price Indexes (beginning on p. 210) go back to 1800, although not all the breakdowns are available for all years. For example, there were no breakdowns of food into cereals, meats, dairy products, and fruits and vegetables until 1935. The Consumer Price Indexes come up to 1970 in the 1975 ed.

16-26: Yes, see the notes on pp. 191-2 (1975 ed.). Historical Statistics contains much more explanatory material of this nature than does the Statistical Abstract.

16-27: Colonial statistics located in the last chapter (beginning p. 1152, 1975 ed.).
Population estimates, pp. 1168-71.
Tea importation p. 1192 (Series Z473-480). For the source, you have to go to the notes at the beginning of the chapter, looking under the series number.
Slaves pp. 1172-1174 for slave trade (Series Z133-168). See notes on these series (beginning of chapter); that for the slave trade in Virginia notes that until the middle of the 17th century, Negroes came as servants, not as slaves.

16-28: The County and City Data Book presents a variety of statistical information for counties, metropolitan statistical areas, and cities. Descriptive text and source notes are included to help the user interpret the data shown. Most of the statistics are obtained from the latest available censuses and various governments and private agencies. According to Sheehy, it is published "irregularly." (Yet another useful supplement to Statistical Abstract is the State and Metropolitan Area Databook, Sheehy 2CG19.)

16-29: Look in the introductory material and contents pages. See the section entitled "Geographic Concepts and Codes" (p. xix, 10th ed., 1983) for a description of MSA's and PMSA's. Data for Ann Arbor, Michigan, can be found in both Table C: Data for Cities with 25,000 or More Inhabitants by States (p. 650+) and Table D: Data for Places with 2,500 or More Inhabitants by States (p. 812+). Table C has more complete information for those cities which are included. Column headings for the tables can be seen on p. v-xv.

16-30: Check Table C (Data for Cities with 25,000 or More Inhabitants by States).

The cities are arranged alphabetically under state (you must consult more than one page in order to see all of the data presented for each city.) The data on p. 735 indicate that 7.8% of Ann Arbor families (or households) were earning $50,000 or more in 1979. The comparable figure for Chattanooga is 2.8% (p. 785). To determine the source for these statistics you note the item number at the head of the column (98, in this case), and then refer back to the "Source Notes" at the front of the volume. See p. xlviii under "Workers and Money Income" for sources for items C90-106. (10th ed., 1983.)
      Statistical Abstract supplies similar income information (see table no. 715, p. 433, and others, 1982/83 ed.), but it does not break it down by city.

16-31: All are specifically for the United States. The Statistical Abstract does contain a section on comparative international statistics. In the 1982/83 volume, see Section 33; table no. 1520 on p. 861 where some figures on percentages of persons under 15 by country are given. However, the figures for the U.S. are for 1980, and for India are for 1971, so they are comparable only in a general way. See also notes on p. 854 for further comments on comparability regarding the variations in which the data are collected, estimated, defined, etc.

16-32: Some statistical summary for India comparable to the Statistical Abstract of the United States. See Sheehy, same section as that in which the Statistical Abstract appears, under India. For example, item 141: Statistical Abstract, India, (1949+).

16-33: You need an international statistical source, which is likely to be published by an international organization such as the United Nations. See the Statistical Yearbook of the United Nations. This source has no specific subject index other than a country index, so you must use the Table of Contents, checking under likely major subjects. In the 1979/80 edition, the Table of Contents lists a section on Manpower, under which is listed unemployment. See Tables on p. 91+. Statistics are listed by country, alphabetically, and the most recent figures given for most are 1978. The number of unemployed in Japan in 1978 is given as 1,240,000, and the percentage is given as ? ?? (Another important international statistical source is the Demographic Yearbook, Sheehy CG35, 1CG2, also from the United Nations. However, it does not provide information on the unemployment rate in Japan in that it is essentially limited to vital statistics-- births, death, marriages, etc.)

16-34:   Yes, see the notes at the ends of the tables. For example, the unemployment data noted in #16-33 were provided by the International Labour Office (see p. 94). You should also note that the information for Japan was based on labour force sample surveys (see A on p. 94 and the Code column on p. 92 for Japan, 1979/80 edition).

16-35:   See answer to questions #16-20 and #16-21. Knowing the source gives you some idea of the accuracy, authority, impartiality, completeness, comparability, etc., of the data. Even more important, however, it gives you access to the complete raw data on which the statistics or statistical tables are based.

16-36:   Statistics Sources; a subject guide to data on industrial, business, social, educational, financial, and other topics for the United States and internationally. Published by Gale Research Company. Seventh edition, © 1982.

16-37:   Subject (see title), alphabetically. No index so subject listing should be reasonably specific.

16-38:   Both. See preface. See also "Selected Bibliography of Key Statistical Sources" following the preface.

16-39:   Under Poverty: gives U.S. Department of Commerce, Bureau of the Census, with address and an indication of availability of unpublished data. (Statistics Sources, 7th ed., 1982.)

16-40:   Entries under Drugs and Medicine in the alphabetical listing of Statistics Sources (7th ed., 1982) do not really give what you want, as most are related to the cost of drugs, to the number of employees in the industry, etc. Under Pharmaceuticals --Manufacture--Corporation assets and profits (cross reference from Drugs and Medicine), you find that Fortune Directory is a source of published information for this question.

16-41:   Under Social Sciences--Statistics--Compendiums--International Guides and Bibliographies, U.S. Guides and Bibliographies, Indexes and Directories. Some

representative titles are: Guide to U.S. Government Statistics (CG57); Bureau of the Census Catalog of Publications (CG59, 1CG12, 1CG12a, 2CG21); Directory of Federal Statistics for Local Areas; a Guide to Sources (CG77, 1CG21); Directory of Federal Statistics for States; a Guide to Sources (CG78); and American Statistics Index; A Comprehensive Guide and Index to the Statistical Publications of the U.S. Government (CG76, 1CG19).

16-42:   Sheehy lists some dictionaries of statistics (9th ed., p. 481) which might be helpful. Probably a better source would be an encyclopedia article on statistics, and if you are really mathematically ignorant or the whole area of statistics baffles you, then probably one of the encyclopedias such as World Book would be best.

HANDBOOKS AND MANUALS

Questions #17/1--17/83

17-1   What is meant by the term "ready reference" or quick reference? Which of the sources discussed so far, in the entire manual, can be considered as ready-reference sources? Do any seem to lend themselves to this use more than others?

The next set of sources to examine--the handbooks and manuals--are excellent sources for ready-reference use. The handbooks listed here, to be examined and discussed, are only examples from the many available, chosen to represent a certain type or a specific arrangement, etc.:

    Kane: Famous First Facts
    Guinness Book of World Records

    Benét: The Reader's Encyclopedia (BD32)
    Brewer's Dictionary of Phrase and Fable (BD67)

    Bartlett: Familiar Quotations (BD98, 2BD22)
    Stevenson: Home Book of Quotations (BD106)
    Evans: Dictionary of Quotations (BD101)

    Hatch: American Book of Days (2CF12)
    Gregory: Anniversaries and Holidays (1CF15, see CF49)
    Steinberg: Historical Tables (DA47, 2DA7)
    Langer: New Illustrated Encyclopedia of World History (DA42, 1DA15)
    Everyman's Dictionary of Dates (DA36)

17-2.   What is a definition of a handbook? What is the definition of a manual?

17-3   The first two titles--Kane's Famous First Facts, and the Guinness Book of World Records--are representative of a type often referred to as a "curiosity" handbook. What is the basic difference in scope between these two sources? Do they overlap?

17-4   How do they differ in arrangement?

17-5   Who was the first U.S. librarian to be paid for his services?

17-6   Where is the world's remotest inhabited island?

17-7   When was the first photograph taken?

17-8   What authority is there for the facts cited by Kane? Are any sources given? Are sources or authorities cited in Guinness?

17-9   For what is William Horlick famous?

17-10   Can you find out, through Kane or Guinness, what Olav Bjaaland is noted for?

17-11   Who was the first man to reach the South Pole?

17-12   Who is the youngest boxer ever to have won the world heavyweight championship?

17-13   How often are Kane and Guinness up-dated? Is currency important in such books?

17-14   What is the longest bridge in the world, according to Guinness? Do you think this information is still accurate? Where would you go to check on it? What additional or conflicting information can you find? Other than the need for current information, can you see any inherent problem in a question of this nature?

17-15   In the previous question dealing with the longest bridge in the world, would you have considered the encyclopedias as a reasonable source for an answer? In what way would the encyclopedias be useful to you in dealing with this question?

        Both Benét and Brewer are examples of a type often referred to as "literary handbooks," but because of the broad scope of information included, they are very similar in some ways to the curiosity handbooks such as Kane and Guinness. In fact, many other titles listed in Sheehy in the same section in which Brewer is found are also good examples of curiosity handbooks, such as Walsh's Handy Book of Curious Information (BD73); Ackermann's Popular Fallacies (BD66).

17-16   The next two sources are Benét's Reader's Encyclopedia and Brewer's Dictionary of Phrase and Fable. How are these classified in Sheehy?

17-17   What is the difference in scope between Benét and Brewer?

17-18   How are the Benét and Brewer books arranged?

17-19   Benét is considered here as a handbook. Why would it be listed in Sheehy as an encyclopedia?

17-20   Oliver Optic is the pen name or pseudonym for a 19th-century author of many books for boys. He also edited a periodical for children. What is his real name and what is the name of the periodical?

17-21   Charles Dickens was an English novelist, 1812-1879. Could you find information on Dickens in Benét? in Brewer?

17-22   Uriah Heep is a character in a novel by Dickens. What is the name of the novel? What part does Heep play in the novel? Can you find this information in both Benét and Brewer?

17-23   If you came across a reference to Linnaeus' scientific classification system in your reading, could you find an explanation of it in Benét? In Brewer? If you wanted further information, where would you go?

17-24   What does it mean "to wear the willow?" How has this term come about?

17-25   How recently has Benét's Reader's Encyclopedia been revised? Does it seem to put much stress on recent names, allusions, etc.? Would you expect to find James Bond in Benét? in Brewer?

17-26   Nine is often thought of as a number of some mystical significance. Why is it considered mystical? What are some examples of the appearance of the number nine in literature and myth? What are some phrases using the word "nine?" What are the "nine points of the law" (as in, "possession is ...")? Compare entries in Benét and Brewer.

17-27   What does "abracadabra" mean, how is it used, where did it come from?

17-28   Why are Benét and Brewer called "literary handbooks," and classified under "literature" in Sheehy? Why is Benét called a reader's encyclopedia? Are Benét and Brewer limited to literary terms, characters in books, writers, etc.?

17-29   Another type of source related basically to the field of literature and classified under literature in Sheehy are the books of quotations. These are considered here as handbooks, and are used extensively in libraries for ready-reference. Those discussed are only examples of many available. The first two--Bartlett's Familiar Quotations and Stevenson's Home Book of Quotations--are examined here because they show two different approaches to the problem of quotations. How do Bartlett and Stevenson differ in arrangement?

17-30   Locate the quotation "The pen is mightier than the sword" in both Stevenson and Bartlett. How did you go about it? Who is the author of the quote? Is there any difference in the citation given in Stevenson and in Bartlett?

17-31   Would the quotation "The pen is mightier than the sword" be indexed only under pen in these quotation books? Why or why not?

17-32   Can you find a good quotation on foreign opinion of America such as you might use as inspiration for the text of a speech?

17-33   Does Stevenson have any limitations as a source for the preceding question (on quotes on foreign opinion of America)?

17-34   Edmund Burke is listed in the Table of Contents of the Stevenson book. Is this an indication that selections of quotations from his writings will be found in one place, as in Bartlett?

17-35   How would you go about finding the correct words and the title of a poem by John Masefield which you remember only vaguely as being about "the sea?"

17-36   The quotations in Bartlett are arranged by author. Where do quotations from the Bible appear? What, if anything, is done with those quotations which have no attributed author--for example, proverbs? According to the title of Bartlett, proverbs are included; why are they? Is "a stitch in time saves nine" listed in Bartlett?

17-37   Are there any sources which specifically list and index proverbs?

17-38   The latest revision of Bartlett is the 15th edition, published in 1980. What recent, modern writers and other contemporary figures are included in Bartlett? Can you check Stevenson as easily as Bartlett?

17-39   Which of these two books of quotations--Bartlett and Stevenson--has the more useful arrangement?

17-40   The index in the Stevenson quotation book is referred to as an Index and Concordance, and some suggestions for its use are given immediately preceding the index (p. 2420 of the © 1967 edition). What is a concordance?

17-41   If you were searching for a quotation from Shakespeare, and you could not find it in any of the quotation books you had available, where else could you turn?

17-42   Both Bartlett and Stevenson, although recently revised, have long histories. When did they first appear?

17-43   A newer entry on the scene is Evans' Dictionary of Quotations, first published in 1968. How is it arranged?

17-44   Françoise Sagan (French novelist, born 1935) has been quoted as saying "Men have more problems than women." What is the rest of her comment, and is it a quotation from one of her novels?

17-45   Does the Evans quotation book appear to differ from Stevenson in any major way?

17-46   Do the quotation books include as sources only published material, or only literature, or only books?

17-47   What other sources have you examined which would be useful for identifying or verifying quotations?

17-48   When Neil Armstrong stepped from the lunar lander to the surface of the moon at the first moon landing in 1969, he uttered a statement which will be appearing in quotation books of the future. Did he say "That's one small step for man, one giant step for mankind"? Where can you look to check his exact words? Where can you look to find more discussion of the circumstances under which he said them?

17-49 The next set of sources--those concerned with days and dates--are significant primarily for their arrangement: they approach knowledge from a chronological point of view. The first of these, The American Book of Days, is perhaps most similar in scope to the curiosity handbooks. Originally written by George Douglas, this source was revised in a 3rd edition (1978) by Jane Hatch. What is the scope of Hatch?

17-50 How is it arranged?

17-51 Is St. David's Day celebrated in the United States?

17-52 Is the information in Hatch limited only to information about celebrations of holidays and festivals?

17-53 Is the Fourth of July significant for any reason other than the American Declaration of Independence?

17-54 Is there any way in which you can tell from The American Book of Days (Hatch) what local holidays and festivals are celebrated in the southwest of the United States?

17-55 Somewhat comparable to Hatch's American Book of Days is Gregory's Anniversaries and Holidays, which was formerly edited by Hazeltine. How does Gregory compare to Hatch in arrangement and scope?

17-56 If you wanted more reading on St. David and St. David's Day than you found in The American Book of Days, where would you look?

17-57 Where are the Gregory and Hatch books classified in Sheehy?

17-58 Another chronological approach is represented by the next title, Steinberg's Historical Tables. Under what subject is this title classified in Sheehy?

17-59 What is the arrangement of Steinberg? What is the point of the arrangement?

17-60 The American Civil War began in the spring of 1861. What else happened in the world at that same time?

17-61 In Steinberg, under the list for "Western and Southern Europe" for the year 1861, a note is made that "Cavour" died. Can you tell through Steinberg who Cavour was?

17-62 Can you find out, through Steinberg, what was happening in Western Europe at the time of the collapse of the Byzantine Empire?

17-63   In contrast to the bare bones of history given in Steinberg is Langer's New Illustrated Encyclo-
        pedia of World History. How is this source arranged? Can you find out through Langer when
        the Byzantine empire collapsed?

17-64   Can you find out through Langer who Cavour was?

17-65   Where would you find a brief accounting of events of the Communist takeover of Czechoslovakia
        prior to the death of Jan Masaryk, Czechoslovakian foreign minister, in 1948?

17-66   The last of the date books is Everyman's Dictionary of Dates. What is the basic arrangement of
        this source? Is it similar to the other books on days and dates?

17-67   Can you find out the date of the collapse of the Byzantine Empire through the Everyman's Diction-
        ary of Dates?

17-68   Can you find in Everyman's Dictionary of Dates comparative dates for the founding of the major na-
        tional libraries? Can you also find this in Langer?

17-69   One of the confusing points which often arises in discussion of dates is that of the "old style" and
        "new style" calendar or dates. Where could you find a discussion of this problem?

        So far in this section you have examined a few examples of the more generalized types of handbooks:
        curiosity, literary, quotations, dates. There are a vast number of more specialized handbooks and
        manuals available for reference use. A few of these are, for example, The New Emily Post's Eti-
        quette (see Sheehy CF60), Menke's Encyclopedia of Sports (CB230, 1CB69), Robert's Rules of Or-
        der (CJ231, 2CJ106), Scott's Standard Postage Stamp Catalogue (BF118), Occupational Outlook Hand-
        book (CH498). The scope of these sources should be quite self-evident from the titles, and it
        should not be necessary at this point to examine each one individually, although checking the cita-
        tions and annotations in Sheehy for these and other similar titles might be helpful.

        The following questions are to be used as REVIEW for the entire section on handbooks and manuals.
        Keep in mind the last few specialized sources noted above, which you have not yet examined spe-
        cifically. For purposes of this review, do not consider encyclopedias and dictionaries, although
        clearly many of the questions could be answered by using them.

17-70   Where would you look to find a quotation on reading which would be suitable to use on the cover
        of a Great Books reading list you are compiling?

17-71   What is the meaning of the phrase "point of order" which many people seem compelled to shout out
        at intervals during business meetings?

17-72   What is Guy Fawkes Day? Who was Guy Fawkes?

17-73   What is the German title of Thomas Mann's novel The Magic Mountain?

17-74   Where is the wettest place in the world (other than something under water)?

17-75   Who wrote the nursery rhyme "Twinkle, twinkle, little star"?

17-76   What is the order of rank among U.S. government officials?

17-77   What are Movable Feasts and Fasts?

17-78   What does the phrase "the cat's pajamas" mean?

17-79   What are the rules of the game of rugby?

17-80   What was the first national holiday in the U.S.?

17-81   Where would you find a brief discussion of the major historical events in Hawaii prior to the annexation to the U.S.?

17-82   Who is Iphigenia, in Greek Mythology? What is the plot of Euripides' play about Iphigenia?

17-83   How could you find a book that would explain how to build a sauna?

HANDBOOKS AND MANUALS

Answers #17/1--17/83

17-1: See ALA Glossary for definition of ready reference collection. All of the sources studied so far in the manual, including the bibliographic sources, are sources through which factual questions can be answered (e.g., who is the author of a specific book, what is the meaning of a specific word, etc.), and it depends therefore on how easily the fact can be located in the source as to whether it may truly be used as a quick or ready-reference source. Some of the sources --the college dictionaries, the one-volume encyclopedias, the almanacs, for example --because their scope is more factual than in-depth, because they are more portable and therefore perhaps more easily used, because their arrangement tends towards the specific entry or because they are so specifically indexed-- seem to lend themselves more to ready-reference use.

17-2: See ALA Glossary on both. The ALA Glossary tends to define these terms similarly--that is, a handbook as a manual, and a manual as a handbook. The exact definition of a handbook is not really clear, and it is somewhat arbitrary as to what sources are included within this type; some sources seem to be called handbooks mainly because they do not fall into any other category. In practice, the essential feature of a handbook is that it is "handy," compact, concise, set up for reference use rather than reading, usually with extensive information within the limits of its scope, usually concentrating more on basic, known information than on that which is constantly changing. A manual is generally considered more in the how-to-do-it realm, giving guidance, rules, instructions, etc. The terms are often used interchangeably, especially in the titles of publications.

17-3: Kane's is limited to "firsts"; while Guinness concerns itself with longest, shortest, highest, lowest, biggest, smallest, etc., and in fact has comparatively few

"firsts" (more often referred to in Guinness as "earliests"). Furthermore, Kane's is limited to the United States; while Guinness is worldwide. See title pages (neither source is listed in Sheehy).

17-4: Kane is arranged alphabetically by specific item, with various indexes: years, days, names, geographical. Guinness is arranged on a classed basis--for example, all items dealing with the natural world brought together--with a specific subject index.

17-5: Kane, main alphabetical arrangement under Librarian (4th ed., p. 349).

17-6: Guinness: indexed under "Remoteness, islands" or found in the section on "The Natural World," under Land-- Remotest Islands (21st ed., 1983).

17-7: Despite being a "first," you really have to go to Guinness for this one. Kane lists the first photograph taken in the United States (4th ed., p. 463, under Photograph, taken ... in the United States): 1839. Guinness lists the first photograph taken in the world, which was actually earlier, 1826 (21st ed., 1983, under "Photography," which leads you to the section on "Earliest Cameras").

17-8: Kane: See the Preface for comments on this. Some sources are occasionally listed, but as the preface states, these are not necessarily the sources from which the facts are obtained. Guinness: no sources cited, but there are some comments made on the procedures for verifying claimed records.

17-9: Kane, names index. Refers to Milk-- malted milk, and when you look up Milk in the main alphabetical list, you find that Horlick invented the first malted milk....

17-10: Not in Kane and no name index in Guinness.

17-11: According to Guiness: Olav Bjaaland (indexed under "South Pole Conquests").

17-12: Guinness, indexed under boxing.

17-13: Kane is not up-dated very often: 2nd
ed., 1950; 3rd ed., 1964; 4th ed., 1981.
Guinness is up-dated more often (usually
every year). Even so-called "facts" do
change as research brings new information to light, and "records," such as that
of the youngest boxer, change constantly. The publishers have stated that
one-fourth of the records changes with
each year's edition. The kind of facts
included in Guinness are more subject to
change than those in Kane.

17-14: Guinness (1983 ed.), indexed under
bridge, indicates various possibilities,
and here you should immediately see the
inherent problem in this question and
in others like it: the longest bridge
of what type. Possibilities are longest
single span, longest suspension, steel
arch, cantilever, etc. Guinness lists
statistics for all these possibilities.
It does not discuss the differences between the types.
      Since new bridges are always be-
ing constructed, the possibility exists
that this information is out-dated.
Other current sources likely to give
this information would be the almanacs.
World Almanac 1983 (indexed under
bridges), for example, also lists by
type, giving dates, lengths, etc. Like
Guinness it does not discuss the difference between types. It would appear
from both Guinness and World Almanac
that probably what the average unsophis-
ticated-about-bridges person means by
"longest bridge" is longest single span,
with the Verrazano-Narrows Bridge in
New York holding the record.

17-15: Since this is the type of information so
commonly found in almanacs, and since
there is always an element of datedness
involved, it hardly seems worthwhile to
even bother with the encyclopedias.
However, there still remains the unre-
solved problem of the difference between
the various types (single span, suspension, steel arch, cantilever, etc.) of
bridges; finding the answer to this problem may be the real key to determining
the correct answer to the question for
some people, and the difference in types
of bridge construction is one which is
probably best answered from an encyclopedia.
      The Encyclopedia Americana (©

1983, p. 533 of the volume which contains a fairly extensive article titled
"Bridge"), for example, agrees that the
Verrazano-Narrows Bridge has the longest main span in the world, but also
points out that the Mackinac Bridge in
northern Michigan has the longest total
suspended span of any bridge.

17-16: Both are listed under BD: Literature
(in Humanities). Brewer is listed as a
handbook and Benet as an encyclopedia.

17-17: Brewer stresses phrases and terms
(see "to put on the lugs," "as light
as St. Luke's bird," p. 690 of ©
1981 edition). But since phrases can
be interpreted quite broadly, this includes many names of people (Lucy,
St.; Lucy Stoner), places (Lud's Town,
Ludgate, Lutetia), things (lunar month;
lutestring, p. 691, 1981), etc. It has
many similarities to the information
found in the slang and etymological
dictionaries, and some similarities also
to usage sources such as Fowler,
Evans. Benét includes more names of
writers, titles of books, etc. Brewer
includes pronunciation.

17-18: Both are dictionary arrangements, i.e.,
short entries on specific topics listed
alphabetically with all cross-references
within the work itself and no separate
index.

17-19: Possibly because of its title, or its
dictionary arrangement, or the fact
that the information given in its entries is sometimes rather lengthy. This
is a good example of the difficulties in
"classifying" or defining handbooks.

17-20: Benét. Under Optic, Oliver: gives
real name (William Taylor Adams) and
some information. Does not say see
also, but the real name is given in
small capital letters indicating an article also on Adams, and the article on
Adams gives the name of the periodical he edited. It is therefore necessary to look under all possible entries
for the fullest information. (Not in
Brewer.)

17-21: In Benét, which includes author, writers, etc. Not in Brewer.

17-22: Both Benét and Brewer indicate the
name of the novel (David Copperfield)
in which Uriah Heep appears, and both
indicate the kind of generally unpleas-
ant character he represents. Benét

tends to relate this more specifically to the plot of the novel.

17-23:   Both Benét and Brewer have entries; Benet under the name of the man (Linnaeus, Carolus) and Brewer only for his system (Linnaean system). The information given is sketchy, although it might be sufficient for your needs at the moment. For further discussion, you could go to a regular encyclopedia.

17-24:   Brewer (Dictionary of Phrase and Fable). Not in Benét; which does not attempt to include phrases in the same way as Brewer. This is an example of the somewhat confusing arrangement of Brewer; this phrase, to wear the willow, is not listed in strictly alphabetical order, under "to," or even under "wear," but rather "willow" (considered by Brewer as the keyword in the phrase) along with some other phrases also dealing with willow. Brewer tends to group phrases under related keywords. The typography does not make this too clear.

17-25:   Benét had a major revision in 1965. This is not exactly up-to-the-minute revision, of course. There is not a lot of stress on recent material, although it is included (there is a reference for James Bond, and for Ian Fleming, in Benét), probably on the theory that the modern reader will not need an explanation of James Bond as much as he will need one of Oliver Optic. Brewer, although also revised from time to time (most recent, 1981), seems to stress modern items even less than Benét. Brewer ignores James Bond.

17-26:   Both have entries directly under "Nine." Brewer is much more extensive, explains the reason for the mystical significance of nine, includes phrases using the number, explains what the nine points of the law are. Both list many examples of the appearance of the number nine in literature and myth. The Benét account appears to have been taken almost verbatim from Brewer, with some of Brewer left out. See preface to Benét on its relation to Brewer and other such handbooks.

17-27:   See Benét and/or Brewer (entries are almost word for word the same).

17-28:   Neither is limited only to literary information (see #17-23 on Linnaeus), although Benét in particular does heavily stress the literary. They aim to provide handy sources of information on names, words, phrases, allusions of all kinds which the

general reader may come across. The information is extensive in coverage, but limited in depth.

17-29:   Bartlett is arranged by author, chronologically. Stevenson is arranged by subject, alphabetically. Both have an index by authors alphabetically, and an index of keywords alphabetically.

17-30:   For Bartlett, it is necessary to check in the keyword index and then follow up the reference to the page on which the quote appears. For Stevenson, you could either check the keyword index as in Bartlett, or you could look in the alphabetical table of contents for the broad topic of Pen, then Pen and Sword and turn to the page to which that refers you. Both cite Bulwer-Lytton as the author and give the title, act, and scene of the play in which it appears. Bartlett further gives the date of the play, and the author's full name and dates are also given on the same page as the quote. In Stevenson it is necessary to refer to the alphabetical author list.

17-31:   No, it should be indexed under all important keywords (pen, sword, probably mightier). The point is to have as many accesses as possible in case you have the sense but not the correct words; also to provide, in Bartlett's, a subject access under both pen and sword.

17-32:   To use Bartlett for this, you have to look in the index under "America," perhaps also "American," then check out each reference (or those that seem suitable); a tedious and time-consuming process, and besides this only gives you access to those quotations or phrases which specifically refer to America. In Stevenson, you can refer directly to the subject of America--foreign opinion (see Table of Contents) where many quotes on this subject are grouped together.

17-33:   It is limited in terms of current material (latest quote is dated 1931) and international scope (mostly Englishmen and Americans are quoted).

17-34:   No. Edmund Burke is listed in the Table of Contents of Stevenson (as are other writers) as a subject entry. The list of quotations referred to are about Burke, not by him.

17-35:   To use Stevenson for this, you would turn to the sections on "Sea" and on "Ships," and then look through several pages of quotes in each to see if something by Masefield is listed which strikes the right chord in your memory. To use Bartlett, you could turn directly to the section of quotes from Masefield (probably turning first to the author index to find out where Masefield is located in the chronological list).

17-36:   This is not too clear from either the Table of Contents or the introductory material, and the Sheehy annotation is not much help either. If you just root around in the book itself, you find that quotations from the Bible (and from a few other religious sources) are listed at the beginning, following a few items from Ancient Egypt. Anonymous listings, including some nursery rhymes, are put at the end of the author section. For the problem of proverbs, it is not at all clear. Many proverbs of course can be attributed somehow to some author, and thus in Bartlett they would appear under that author rather than anonymously. If you check out "a stitch in time saves nine," through the index, you find that it is listed, unattributed, in a <u>footnote</u> under quotes from Persius, along with the quotation about necessity being the mother of invention. (If you look under the quotes from Petronius you discover that "one good turn deserves another," which would seem to be a good candidate for an anonymous proverb, is in fact attributable to Petronius.) There is almost as much information in the footnotes of Bartlett as there is in the main body of the source; the footnotes <u>are</u> indexed, however.

17-37:   See Sheehy, 9th ed., p. 306. (Indexed under "Proverbs, collections.")

17-38:   Since the authors in Bartlett are arranged chronologically (by birthday), you can check toward the end of the list to see what younger, or contemporary, people are included. (It should not be assumed that all additions to the latest edition will appear at the end of the chronological list, however.) Starting with the years 1899 and 1900 as arbitrary indications of what twentieth-century people are included, you can find in the 15th edition Humphrey Bogart, 1899- (p. 843) and Louis Armstrong, 1900- (p. 1046), etc. Muhammad Ali, Bob Dylan, and Mick Jagger also appear in the 15th. Modern

writers such as Yevtushenko, Jack Kerouac, James Baldwin, Allen Ginsberg, J. D. Salinger, etc., are included.
          Since Stevenson has no chronological list of authors, you cannot check it in the same way, but of course you can check individual authors' names (Kerouac, Baldwin, Ginsberg, etc.) in the alphabetical list.

17-39:   The usefulness of the arrangement depends on the question. The problem is similar to that of the dictionary of synonyms vs. the thesaurus of synonyms (or of slang words). Stevenson brings together in one place all the quotes on one subject, and if you have a problem with essentially a subject approach (foreign opinion of America) then Stevenson, or other quotation books arranged on a similar pattern, are probably most helpful. For an author approach (Masefield), Bartlett is more helpful. For checking on the source of a specific quotation (the pen is mightier than the sword), either one will do; the only problem is to find a quotation book which includes the quotation you are looking for.

17-40:   See ALA Glossary and/or any dictionary. The comments in Stevenson are also helpful. A concordance is essentially a word index, and it is usually done for the works of one author (or for the Bible). It lists all words or all significant words in that author's work, giving references to their specific appearance. It can be used as a source for locating specific citations for quotations if the author is known.

17-41:   Check a concordance of Shakespeare's works if one is available, since a concordance would presumably give you access to all appearances of any keyword and would therefore be much broader. See Sheehy, 9th ed., p. 337 (indexed under Shakespeare, William--concordances); five concordances of Shakespeare are listed.

17-42:   Bartlett in 1855 and Stevenson in 1934 (see Sheehy annotations).

17-43:   Like Stevenson.

17-44:   Evans: see under subject of Men and Women. (Indexed under "women," or under author's name.) Taken from New York Times.

17-45:   It seems to be somewhat more selective

in choice of quotations, and is probably generally more modern. The topics under which quotes are arranged are often quite different than the Stevenson choice, and often more specific (stiff upper lip, Pickwickian, ozymandias, no soap, etc.). Evans also has comments on many of the quotations included (see under Ammunition, Muffett, etc.). In general, the Evans book has a certain charm of its own, not unlike that of his Dictionary of Contemporary American Usage.

17-46: No. The second quotation from Humphrey Bogart (#17-38) in Bartlett was from a movie. The quotation from Françoise Sagan (#17-44) in Evans was from the New York Times.

17-47: Any of the dictionary sources which used quotes as examples, especially the Oxford English Dictionary. The new 1972 supplement to the OED (see #12-42) should provide a useful source for modern quotations.

17-48: The Armstrong quote can be found in the 15th, 1980 edition of Bartlett, and it is correctly given as: "That's one small step for a man, one giant leap for mankind." A discussion of the circumstances can be found in a source giving reasonably full coverage of news events of that year (1969): for example, the 1969 New York Times Index, or an encyclopedia yearbook (e.g., frontispiece of the Collier's yearbook for 1970 covering 1969 is a footprint on the moon with the quotation given but no author noted).

17-49: See the Preface to the Third Edition. Hatch presents, day by day, information about holidays, festivals, and anniversaries in the U.S.; American history; distinguished citizens; religious events; and various celebrations connected with sports, commerce, and local custom. In order to update the 1948 edition, new information has been added on such topics as civil rights and the women's movement.

17-50: By day of the month (e.g., January 26, January 27, January 28, etc.) with an index of subjects and holidays and events.

17-51: Hatch: look first in index under St. David's Day for reference to page number, where you find that it falls on the first of March. The article discusses various celebrations and gives historical and legendary information about St. David.

17-52: No, it includes much historical and bio-

graphical material as well as folklore and custom. See the preface, but better yet see the Contents: first flag of Washington's Army, Millard Fillmore's birthday, first balloon ascension, etc.

17-53: The birthday of Calvin Coolidge and others. American Book of Days, under July 4.

17-54: Only by going through the Contents or the index and choosing those which seem to be appropriate, which would be a very inadequate approach.

17-55: The first part of Gregory is arranged, as is Hatch, by day of the month. The second part is a calendar of movable days. The third part is a bibliographic source, a list of books about holidays divided into several broad categories. There is also a general index. The entries in Gregory are not as full as in Hatch, but Gregory cites sources and further readings, and is generally more international in scope.

17-56: You might find a reference to a source of additional information in Gregory, Part 3, "Books Related to Anniversaries and Holidays."

17-57: CF: Folklore and popular customs, specifically Holidays. (The earlier Douglas ed. of American Book of Days is the edition listed in Sheehy.) A similar book not listed in Sheehy is Chases' Calendar of Annual Events (published annually by the Apple Tree Press, Flint, Michigan). Chases' is an annually published calendar or listing of special days, weeks, and months for the year. It includes religious and national holidays, astronomical phenomena, historical anniversaries, birthdays, fairs, festivals, a variety of celebrations, and miscellaneous information such as Presidential proclamations and time zones.

17-58: DA: History and Area Studies--General.

17-59: Strictly by year, chronologically, with items divided into 6 major classifications per double page. The object is to show the general reader what was going on in a given age in various parts of the world in different fields of activity (see Foreword and Preface).

17-60: Emancipation of the serfs in Russia, Wagner's opera Tannhäuser was produced in Paris, and Hans Christian Andersen's <u>Fairy Tales</u> was published.

17-61:   No.   Steinberg gives only the bare facts, no descriptions, discussions, explanations.

17-62:   No, only if you already happen to know the date of the fall of the Byzantine Empire.   The <u>only</u> access in Steinberg is by date.   There is no index.

17-63:   Chronologically also--by general period (i.e., Prehistoric, ancient, etc.), but within that overall period, broken down geographically (i.e., Paleolithic period-- Europe, Africa, Asia, etc.).   There is a specific index, and you can find Byzantine Empire, collapse of, with references to page numbers (not dates) on which you can find the fall of Constantinople in 1204 and, eventually, the end of the Byzantine Empire in 1453.   (And you can then refer back to Steinberg under 1453 and find out that in 1453, Gutenberg and Fust were printing the Mazarin Bible.)

17-64:   Yes, index under Cavour (Italian statesman), references to several pages which discuss (although briefly) his activity in the unification of Italy.

17-65:   Langer: index under Masaryk.

17-66:   This is an example of a date book with an <u>alphabetical</u> arrangement, similar to a dictionary or encyclopedia.   This is a handbook of miscellaneous information with the stress on events, on dates.

17-67:   Yes, perhaps more easily than in Langer, since you only have to read one short article in Everyman's, instead of skipping through several references and cross-references as in Langer.   The problem in Everyman's is entry.   It does not have an entry under Byzantine Empire, but does have a reference under Byzantium to see Constantinople and Roman Empire, Eastern. The entry for "Roman Empire, Eastern, or Byzantine Empire" is the one you want.

17-68:   In Everyman's under Libraries, modern. Libraries as such not indexed in Langer, although a few specific ones are, but the information is very scattered and therefore more difficult to find.

17-69:   Gregory has a discussion of the problem in the Introduction.   The American Book of Days (Hatch) has a brief discussion under "Calendar" in the Appendices.   Any general encyclopedia also should have in-

formation.   Brief mention in Everyman's in introductory matter under Calendars.

17-70:   Quotation book with subject arrangement --i.e., Stevenson's or Evans'.

17-71:   Robert's Rules of Order, indexed under Point of Order.

17-72:   Hatch's American Book of Days, or Gregory.   Also a mention in Brewer in entry for "Guy."

17-73:   Benet's The Reader's Encyclopedia, under Magic Mountain, The.

17-74:   Guinness, under Natural World-Weather (indexed under weather and rainfall).

17-75:   Bartlett's Familiar Quotations, keyword index under twinkle.

17-76:   Try an etiquette book.   The New Emily Post's Etiquette, 1975 edition, p. 137-46 (under "Official Protocol") gives unofficial guidelines, and has two pages of U.S. officials listed in descending order of rank.   Another possibility, found in the Sheehy 1980 supplement under the subject heading "etiquette" is Protocol: the Complete Handbook by McCaffree and Innis (1CF16).

17-77:   Hatch has a brief note on movable events.   Gregory has a section on movable days.   See Brewer under Feast.

17-78:   Brewer, listed under cat.

17-79:   Encyclopedia of Sports.   (Contents or index under rugby.)

17-80:   Kane's Famous First Facts (under Holiday).

17-81:   Langer's New Illustrated Encyclopedia of World History, check index under Hawaii and follow up references.   You need some discussion of events, so a simple date book would not be sufficient.

17-82:   Brewer's Dictionary of Phrase and Fable. Also in Benet.   Benet is better on the plot of Euripides' play.

17-83:   This is the kind of how-to-do-it information which might be found in a handbook or manual, particularly a manual as it was defined in #17-2.   What you need here is a bibliography or list of how-to-do-it books.   Sheehy lists two such bibliographies under "Recreation

and Sports--Bibliography" (p. 452+, 9th
ed.): How-to-Do-It Books; a Selected
Guide (CB219) and Nueckel's Selected
Guide to Make-It, Fix-It, Do-It-Yourself
Books (CB221). Also listed in Sheehy
are some indexes to periodical articles covering the same area.

Section 18

DIRECTORIES

Questions #18/1--18/53

18-1   Where would you look, in the sources you have already examined, to find out what the Royal Society (of Great Britain) is or does? Where would you look to find out what its current address
is?

The next set of sources deals with information about organizations of all kinds including those not
so well known as to be included in the encyclopedias. These titles also represent a specific type
of source: directories.

    Encyclopedia of Associations (CA67)
    Foundation Directory (CA56/57, CB197, 1CA29, 2CA28)
    Research Centers Directory (CA68/69, EA180/181)
    Yearbook of International Organizations (CK214)
    Guide to American Directories (CH140, 1CH64, 2CH57)

18-2   What is the definition of a directory?

18-3   In other words, a directory is simply a list of names and addresses, such as a telephone directory. It may in addition give other, fuller information. A directory can be a list of either people or organizations (or both); directories of people will be dealt with specifically in the next section, on biographical sources. The directories examined here are concerned with organizations.
        What is an organization? What other words are often used to express the same idea?
Where are most of the directories on your list classified in Sheehy?

18-4   In which of the sources you have previously examined would you expect to find directory information about organizations or associations?

18-5   The first title to examine is the Encyclopedia of Associations published by the Gale Research Company. This source starts right out to confuse the issue by calling itself an encyclopedia instead
of a directory, but in size alone it does appear to be quite encyclopedic. How many volumes are
there for this source, and how is it arranged?

18-6   Does the Encyclopedia of Associations attempt to define the term organization or association, as used
in its titles and included in its scope?

18-7   Which of the following organizations would you expect to find in the Encyclopedia of Associations:
Alcoholics Anonymous, Republican Party, Civil Air Patrol, Television Information Office, American
Library Association, R. R. Bowker Company, American Booksellers Association, American Legion,
Elks Club, American Council of Learned Societies?

18-8   Is there an organization for people who own or are interested in Model T Fords?

18-9   Who is the president of the Amalgamated Flying Saucer Clubs of America?

18-10   Does a source such as the Encyclopedia of Associations need to be revised and brought up-to-date frequently? How is this accomplished with this particular source?

18-11   How is the up-dating service arranged? To check for an organization is it necessary to check each issue?

18-12   When was the International Dance-Exercise Association founded?

18-13   How would you go about getting names and information for all of the various ecology action groups now working to save us from ourselves?

18-14   What are the names and addresses of some organizations from which you can get information on mental telepathy, clairvoyance, ESP, and other psychic phenomena?

18-15   Organizations and associations are excellent sources for current and highly specialized information. Why is it important for a reference librarian to realize this?

18-16   Another useful thing for librarians to remember about organizations and associations is that they publish material--lots of useful, cheap, frequently free materials which will not necessarily appear in the bibliographic sources. Can the Encyclopedia of Associations be any help in a bibliographic way? Can you find through this source what publications, if any, are put out by the Wilderness Society?

18-17   What is the headquarters' address of the National Association for Gifted Children? What does the organization do?

18-18   How would you find out if there is a chapter or branch of the National Association for Gifted Children in your city?

18-19   Where are the headquarters of the AAAS located?

18-20   The next directory is an example of one which is somewhat more specialized: The Foundation Directory. What is the scope of this publication? How is a foundation defined, for inclusion in this source? Does this differ much from a dictionary definition?

18-21   The introduction to the 8th edition of the Foundation Directory states that over 21,000 foundations are presently active in the United States; yet only about one-seventh of these are listed in the directory. What is another limiting factor?

18-22   How is the Foundation Directory arranged? What is the purpose and what are the general assets of the Joseph P. Kennedy, Jr., Foundation?

18-23   Can you find through this source what foundations exist to aid conservation activities?

18-24   Where can you find some comparative figures showing major fields in which foundation grants were given in the 1970's--for example, how much foundation money went to welfare aid as compared to international activities?

18-25   Another directory published by the Gale Research Company is titled Research Centers Directory. How does this differ in scope from the Encyclopedia of Associations?

18-26   How is the Research Centers Directory arranged?

18-27   Is any effort made to cover research centers that were missed by the most recent edition or that were too new to be included?

18-28   What areas of research are presently being carried on at the Parapsychology Laboratory of St. Joseph's University? Are the results published anywhere?

18-29   What further sources of information on psychical research (ESP, etc.) can you find through the Research Centers Directory?

18-30   Encyclopedia of Associations includes basically only organizations of the United States. The next source is titled Yearbook of International Organizations. Would this source list political organizations in France, for example?

18-31   What kinds of organizations are included?

18-32   What international organizations are there in the field of bibliography?

18-33   What publications are put out by the International Federation for Documentation?

18-34   Does an organization exist to study and determine standards on a world-wide basis for various kinds of instruments used for measuring?

18-35   The next title on the list is essentially a bibliographic source for directories. What is the full title of the Guide to American Directories? Does it have any limitations in scope?

18-36   Besides providing a list of directories for librarians, does the Guide to American Directories have any other purpose?

18-37   Can you find a list of manufacturers in the state of Nebraska?

18-38   Is there an international directory of libraries?

18-39   What does the Guide to American Directories list under the heading "bibliographies"?

18-40   Directory information tends to change relatively frequently. Is the Guide to American Directories current?

The following questions are REVIEW questions for directories, and the sources previously covered in Part II of the manual.

18-41   Is sousaphone a word of American origin?

18-42   Which language has the shortest alphabet?

18-43   Antonio Palau y Dulcet is a Spanish bibliographer whose famous Manual del Librero Hispano-Americano (Sheehy AA885) is one of the most comprehensive lists of material published in Spain and Spanish America. When and where was he born?

18-44   Where does the phrase "mad as a hatter" come from?

18-45   Where could you find a map of New York City?

18-46   Where can you find the pronunciation of the word "pusillanimous" given in the International Phonetic Alphabet?

18-47   How many different kinds of dog clubs are there in the United States?

18-48   Where would you find information, perhaps with illustrations, about the assassination of Anwar Sadat in late 1981?

18-49   Who won the Cy Young Award in 1965? What is the award for?

18-50   What is the address of the Keep Britain Tidy Group?

18-51   What is the density of the population in Pakistan?

18-52   Where would you find some general but current information about the Republic of Vanuatu (formerly the New Hebrides)--how big it is, how many people live there, what kind of educational system it has, what kind of commerce it has, if any, etc.?

18-53   Where would you look to find out where you could take your air conditioner to get it repaired?

18-1: An organization as venerable as the Royal Society should be included in an encyclopedia (see Britannica, for example). For the current address, check an almanac (Whitaker's, for example).

18-2: See ALA Glossary. Also see any dictionary, but the ALA Glossary comes closest to a clear explanation of a directory as a specific type of reference source.

18-3: Any dictionary to define organization. A dictionary or synonym book would give other possible words, such as association, society, group. Sheehy lists most general directories under CA: Social Sciences--General Works.

18-4: All of the sources may have some information on organizations or associations. The dictionary and supplementary language sources may have information in the sense that they may define or identify a particular group, and the abbreviations dictionaries are particularly useful in this way. But information would not be extensive. Encyclopedias may give background, purpose, scope, history, etc., for some of the major associations and groups, but would not be likely to give specific directory-type information such as addresses, officers, etc. In the yearbook sources for current information you can often find a lot of directory information on organizations; the almanacs all have special lists of names and addresses; the Statesman's Year-Book is a further source of current information for groups in specific countries. News summaries will of course give information on groups which are active, in the news, or so new they do not yet appear in the more standard sources.

18-5: 17th edition, 1983 has 3 volumes. 1st volume (in two physical volumes) is called National Organizations of the United States; organizations are arranged under broad subject headings, with an alphabetical index of names of organizations and more specific subject headings; 2nd volume is a geographic and executive (persons) index; 3rd volume is an up-dating service, called New Associations and Projects.

18-6: The introduction says it includes non-profit American membership organizations of national scope, plus, selectively, for-profit groups if they are voluntary, non-membership, foreign, international ... citizen action groups, projects and programs. Also included is information about "missing" and inactive and defunct organizations. The terms organization and association are not really defined. Many groups are included in the Encyclopedia of Associations which one might not expect to find there. See the quotation from Alexis De Tocqueville on the page opposite the title page.

18-7: All are there except R. R. Bowker Company, which is a commercial firm (i.e., not non-profit). The Republican Party is represented by the Republican National Committee.

18-8: Yes. Model T Ford Club International, listed in Section 13 (Hobby and Avocational Organizations), and indexed alphabetically under automobile. Also indexed under Model T, and under Ford.

18-9: Encyclopedia of Associations vol. 1, (indexed under Amalgamated, etc.).

18-10: Organizations die and proliferate like people, and even those which continue change officers, addresses, etc. Any directory of organizations is soon outdated. The Encyclopedia of Associations is kept up to date by a periodic supplement (see vol. 3, binder) called New Associations and Projects.

18-11: By broad subject groupings, same as for vol. 1, with an index of names of organizations and keywords. The index cumulates in each issue, so you only need to check the latest for specific organization names.

18-12: See Vol. 3, #2, April 1983 issue (of the 17th, 1983 ed.).

18-13: Check the keyword subject index (which is called an "Alphabetical Index to Organization Names and Key Words," 17th, 1983 ed.). Vol. 1 has only a few under ecology but a lot under conservation (such as Save the Redwoods) or environmental, which have similar purposes.

18-14: Key is to find the proper keyword. These organizations are classed under Section 4, Science, Engineering and Technical Organizations, and indexed under "parapsychology." Once you get to the right group of organizations, there are some marvelous sources: see especially the Association for Research and Enlightenment, which has a library, lends material, does indexing, publishes information, etc. Also see Haunt Hunters, which is a clearing house for such information.

18-15: Reference librarians need not end the search for information or knowledge only with the materials in their own library. Librarians, library users or researchers can be referred to other more complete sources of information.

18-16: Yes, main entries for each organization list publications (often briefly) if applicable. (Another source of this type of information, as noted in Section 1a, is the new Associations' Publications in Print.)

18-17: Indexed under National Association for Gifted Children, and under gifted children. Refers to main entry which gives address, and tells purpose of organization.

18-18: Check your local telephone directory. (Encyclopedia of Associations does not necessarily list local chapters.)

18-19: Problem is to find what AAAS stands for, as Encyclopedia of Associations does not index abbreviations. Go to Acronyms, Initialisms, and Abbreviations Dictionary (also published by Gale) or De Sola Dictionary of Abbreviations from Section 13. Each lists several possibilities, some of which are also found in the Encyclopedia of Associations.

18-20: See preface of Foundation Directory (8th ed., 1981) for scope of the source. Specifies non-governmental and non-profit. Dictionary definitions are not necessarily this limiting.

18-21: Money; they must have assets of $1,000,000 or more or make grants of $100,000 or more to be included.

18-22: Arranged geographically, by state, with indexes by state and city; donors, trustees, and administrators; foundation name; and fields of interest. Foundation Index under Kennedy (Joseph P.), Jr. Foundation, gives "locator number."

18-23: Yes, see fields of interest index.

18-24: See Introduction to Foundation Directory.

18-25: See Introduction, under "Types of Research Units Listed" in 8th ed., 1983.

18-26: Similarly to Encyclopedia of Associations, under broad subject groupings, with alphabetical indexes for keyword subjects, names of the centers, and names of the parent institutions.

18-27: Between editions of the Research Centers Directory, supplementary current information concerning non-profit research activities is published in a periodic supplement entitled New Research Centers (Sheehy CA69 and introduction to source).

18-28: Research Centers Directory, index of research centers under Parapsychology Laboratory.

18-29: Subject index under Parapsychology (cross-reference from psychical). Four centers listed, at least one of which is listed in the Encyclopedia of Associations, 17th ed., 1983.

18-30: It is international in scope in the sense that it lists organizations whose aims or activities are international in character, not international in the sense that it includes all organizations from all countries.

18-31: See introductory matter of the 1983/84, 20th edition: "Types of organizations included."

18-32: See Index under Bibliography International, which lists names of organizations (these can then be looked up in the list of descriptive entries for further information), 1983/84 ed.

18-33: Yearbook of International Organizations, under name of organization (Interna-

tional Federation Documentation) will refer you by reference number to the descriptive entry, which indicates the organization's publications (1983/84 ed.).

18-34: Here you really have to know the word
for measuring instruments: metrology,
which is the subject keyword used in
the Index of the 1983/1984 ed. The
reference number given in the index then
refers you to the descriptive entry for
the International Organization of Legal
Metrology.

18-35: Guide to American Directories; a guide to
the major directories of the United States
covering all trade, professional and industrial categories. Limitations: primarily
American or U.S. publications (11th ed.,
1982).

18-36: See Preface, "designed to aid each type
of business and industry in locating new
markets...."

18-37: Guide to American Directories will give you
the name of another source which contains
such a list: see sections on Manufacturers, geographical arrangement, under
Nebraska.

18-38: See Sheehy. See also Guide to American Directories, under Libraries, look for
one which fits this description. Major
Libraries of the World is one which you
would not expect to find in this source
according to its title. A similar publication, the Directory of Directories (2CH56),
also includes some major foreign directories.

18-39: A really strange collection of things,
many of which hardly seem to fall under
the library-use definition of "directory,"
as given in the ALA Glossary, for example. The Guide uses the broader definition of a directory as being something
which serves to direct or guide, and as
such, bibliographies--which do serve to
direct or guide--are included as directories. There are 34 pages of entries
under "Bibliographies."

18-40: According to the Preface, it is the most
"up-to-date information source in American directories ever assembled in one
volume." However, the Directory of Directories (2CH56), is supplemented by
two issues of Directory Information Service, which is available by subscription.

18-41: Mathews' Dictionary of Americanisms.

18-42: Guinness Book of World Records (under
Language and Literature).

18-43: Born 1867 in Montblanch according to
Espasa (Spanish encyclopedia, Sheehy
AC82), under Palau y Dulcet, Antonio.

18-44: Not from Alice in Wonderland. See
Brewer's Dictionary of Phrase and
Fable, 1981, p. 696, under "mad." This
may sound like a quotation book problem, and actually it is in Evans although
not in Bartlett.

18-45: Encyclopedias are a good source for this
type of thing--see Americana.

18-46: NBC Handbook of Pronunciation.

18-47: Encyclopedia of Associations, Section 13
(Hobby and Avocational Organizations)
under Dog. Or index under "dog" as
keyword.

18-48: Encyclopedia yearbooks, news surveys,
possibly almanacs. See the 1981 Annual Register, for example.

18-49: Almanacs. See World Almanac, indexed
under Cy Young award. The 1983 ed.
tells you who won the Cy Young award
but not why it is awarded. However,
the list for the Cy Young awards is
within a section titled "baseball." With
that information in mind, you can then
read about the Cy Young award in the
baseball section of Menke's Encyclopedia
of Sports (1973 ed.), indexed under
"baseball--Cy Young awards").

18-50: Encyclopedia of Associations is basically
U.S. only. A British almanac such as
Whitaker's should list it.

18-51: Statistical Yearbook of the United Nations.

18-52: Statesman's Year-Book.

18-53: Yellow pages of your local telephone directory.

BIOGRAPHICAL SOURCES: UNIVERSAL

Questions #19/1--19/57

19-1   What is a "biography"?

19-2   Biographical reference sources do not necessarily present entire "lives" of individuals but may be limited only to some very essential facts. What kinds of questions or problems may be considered as "biographical" in nature?

19-3   What sources have you examined so far which give you biographical information?

In other words, all reference/information sources are potentially useful for biographical information. The next set of sources to examine deals specifically with biographical material:

    Webster's Biographical Dictionary (AJ31)
    Chambers's Biographical Dictionary (AJ19)
    New Century Cyclopedia of Names (AJ24)

    International Who's Who (AJ35)
    Current Biography (AJ34)

19-4   The first title on the list is Webster's Biographical Dictionary. Who is the publisher and what else have they published that you are familiar with?

19-5   What was one of the chief differences between Webster's Third unabridged dictionary and Webster's Second, regarding biographical information?

19-6   Is there anything in the title of this first source which might tell you how the source is arranged? Is this in fact the arrangement?

19-7   Can you find out, through Webster's Biographical Dictionary, what Marie Antoinette's full name was and how she died?

19-8   One of the complaints made about Webster's Third was that it doesn't even tell who Jesus Christ was. Does the Webster's Biographical Dictionary? What about Buddha?

19-9   Can you find out, through Webster's Biographical Dictionary, who was nicknamed or known as the "Old Pretender"?

19-10   Can you find out, through Webster's Biographical Dictionary, who invented the chronometer?

19-11   Can you find out anything about Guy Fawkes Day through Webster's Biographical Dictionary?

19-12   Does Webster's Biographical Dictionary include George Washington? Lyndon Johnson? Richard Nixon? John F. Kennedy? Robert Kennedy? Ted (Edward) Kennedy? Ronald Reagan?

19-13   Do the entries in Webster's Biographical Dictionary give bibliographic references, or cite further sources? Are the entries signed by the authors? What authority is given for the information?

19-14   What factors should be considered in determining the scope of a biographical source?

19-15   One of the major problems both in using and in compiling biographical sources is that of deciding who is or who should be included. In determining a "selection policy" (or exclusion policy, as the case may be), what possible factors may be considered?

19-16   What is the scope of Webster's Biographical Dictionary? Are the people included in it limited geographically? By chronological period? Does it include living people as well as those who have died?

19-17   Since Webster's includes only some 40,000 entries (see Preface), it must have some limitations, however. How did the editors decide who to include and who to leave out? What is their "selection policy?"

19-18   In selecting names from such a broad scope for such a comparatively limited list, it is usually considered most difficult to choose from the modern or contemporary names. Why is this?

19-19   Another biographical source similar in scope and arrangement to Webster is Chambers's Biographical Dictionary. The Preface to Chambers is particularly readable and to the point on the problem of selection, making clear that the real choice lies not so much with any objective criteria as with "who is most likely to be looked up."
        Compare the entries in Webster and Chambers on D. H. Lawrence. What are the differences, if any? Does the entry in Chambers appear to be entirely factual or does it offer any value judgments?

19-20   Does Chambers list Washington, Nixon, Johnson, John F. Kennedy, Robert Kennedy, Ted Kennedy, Ronald Reagan?

19-21   What is Robert Dodsley known for? Is there a full-length biography about him?

19-22   Can you find out, through Chambers, who was known as the Old Pretender? Can you find out who invented the chronometer?

19-23   What would seem to be the major differences between Chambers and Webster, if any?

19-24   Do both Webster and Chambers note pronunciation?

19-25   In which of these sources would you find a list of the rulers of Great Britain?

19-26   Can you determine how Webster and Chambers are kept up to date?

19-27   A much older title, Lippincott's Biographical Dictionary (Sheehy AJ29, most recently revised in 1930) supplements the first two titles in a special way. What is the full title of this source, and what does the title tell you about its scope and arrangement?

19-28   In which of the three sources so far--Webster, Chambers, and Lippincott--would you find who Oceanus was?

19-29   Another source somewhat similar to Lippincott's Biographical Dictionary but rather more recently revised (1954) is the New Century Cyclopedia of Names. Using the Sheehy annotation only, how does the scope of this work compare with that of Webster's and Chambers's? How does it compare with Lippincott's Biographical Dictionary?

19-30   Is the New Century Cyclopedia of Names connected with any source you have previously examined?

19-31   James McDougal Hart was a nineteenth-century landscape painter. What particular aspect of land-scape painting was he noted for?

19-32   What is the origin of the use of the name "Gotham" in reference to New York City?

19-33   Sir Oliver Martext is a character in one of Shakespeare's plays, As You Like It. Would you ex-pect to find information about him in any of the biographical sources you have examined so far? Would you expect to find information about him in any of the sources you have examined previous to this section?

19-34   Obviously, all four of the sources so far examined can be considered "retrospective" in scope. Do they also include "current" personalities? Do they attempt to exclude people who are still living?

19-35   The next source is the International Who's Who. Obviously, from the title, its scope is interna-tional, people from all countries. Equally obviously, there must be some limitations on this. Does the book give any indication of the limitations, or of the selection policy?

19-36   Does the International Who's Who include John F. Kennedy? Richard M. Nixon? Ronald Reagan? Wouldn't John F. Kennedy be considered as known outside of his own country? What further limitation is set on inclusion of names? Is there anything in the title which might lead you to think this?

19-37   The International Who's Who then must be considered as a current biographical source, as com-

pared to retrospective. What information is given for those included in International Who's Who?
Where does the information come from?

19-38   What can you find about the educational background of Great Britain's Margaret Thatcher?

19-39   What can you find about the educational background of Elton John (rock star)? What are his
         leisure interests? How about Jane Fonda?

19-40   How often is International Who's Who issued, and how long has it been appearing?

19-41   Are older editions of International Who's Who of any reference value?

19-42   Spyros Kyprianou is the President of Cyprus. Would you expect to find an entry for him in In-
         ternational Who's Who? Would you expect the entry to give you any information on his attitudes
         towards Communism, towards American policies in Cyprus?

19-43   The next source, Current Biography, is one which attempts to provide the kind of detailed and
         discursive biographical information not found in the brief factual entries of the sources you have
         examined so far. Is there anything in the title of this source which further defines its scope?
         What is the publication pattern of Current Biography (that is, how often does it appear)? Who
         is the publisher?

19-44   What are the criteria for inclusion in Current Biography? Are the people who are written up pri-
         marily in the entertainment field, or in government? Are they limited to Americans?

19-45   What is the arrangement of Current Biography? Can you find an article on François Mitterand?

19-46   Who wrote the article on Mitterand? What are the sources of information used? Is there any way
         you can determine its authority?

19-47   The prefatory material in each monthly issue, "About this publication," states that these biographies
         are "objective rather than authorized biographies." What does this mean?

19-48   Colleen McCullough is the author of the best seller The Thorn Birds. How she ever lived in Aus-
         tralia, which is the setting for her novel?

19-49   Wayne Gretzky, professional ice hockey player, was, in 1980, the youngest hockey player ever to
         be voted Most Valuable Player. What other records does he hold? When did he become a profes-
         sional hockey player? Where would you expect to find biographical information on Gretzky, who
         is Canadian?

19-50   Are the articles in Current Biography ever revised or up-dated?

19-51   Information on currently newsworthy people is not always easy to find, especially for those sud-
         denly thrust into the public eye. Question #19-18 noted the problem of choosing from contempo-
         rary names for the universal but limited sources such as Webster's Biographical Dictionary, or
         even the encyclopedias. A source which gives only current coverage, such as International Who's

Who, is of some help here, but the information is limited and the choice of names is perhaps even more limited, to those who have already proved themselves. Current Biography is an attempt to help fill in this gap, but even this extremely useful source is limited to some 300-400 names per year, and there is some delay in getting the material into print. What other sources can you turn to, then, for information on currently newsworthy names?

19-52   For prominent persons who have died, obituaries can be useful because they can cover the entire life of a person. They often include photographs as well. What are some sources of obituaries?

19-53   Biographical information is sometimes difficult to locate for certain persons because they are known by pseudonyms or nicknames. Are there any sources which help to identify the original names behind the pseudonyms?

19-54   Where would you look to find out who is the U.S. ambassador to Indonesia?

19-55   Who invented the ice cream cone?

19-56   Of the biographical sources which you have examined so far, can you make any generalizations about the arrangement of the material, and about the access to the material? What information do you need before you can make use of them?

19-57   Of the biographical sources which you have examined so far, can you make any generalizations about the scope? Do you see any patterns forming in the way the scope of such sources can be limited? Do you see any relationships between the geographical and chronological coverage, and the selection policies for those names included, or between the geographical and chronological coverage, and the amount of information given?

BIOGRAPHICAL SOURCES: UNIVERSAL

Answers #19/1--19/57

19-1:   See any dictionary.

19-2:   Who is A? When was B born? Where was C born? What is D noted for? Where was E educated? Where does F live? and so on.... Also, why did G do such-and-such? When did H do such-and-such? Also, who did such-and-such?

19-3:   Dictionaries if they include names, either separately or interfiled (Webster's Third doesn't, Webster's Second does, etc.). Encyclopedias, especially through the indexes; information may be in some depth for well-known people. Encyclopedia yearbooks, and news surveys, especially for people of very current interest. Almanacs to some extent; they include much information about specific people, but it is not indexed under the specific name of the person--such as winners of the Nobel Prize. Handbooks, especially the curiosity and literary types. Quotation books and bibliographies can also be useful sources of biographical information; it is possible that you might find people listed in these sources who do not appear elsewhere. Directories of organizations, especially if they have "names" indexes.

19-4:   G. and C. Merriam Co.; publishers of Webster's Third International Dictionary, Webster's Dictionary of Synonyms.

19-5:   Biographical information in Webster's Second was given in a special list called a Pronouncing Biographical Dictionary. No biographical information was given in Webster's Third at all unless it was indirectly through a name used as an adjective.

19-6:   Dictionary, therefore possibly the arrangement would be a so-called dictionary type, all entries in one single alphabet.
          Yes, the source is arranged this way--all entries, including cross-references, in a single alphabet.

19-7:   Yes, entry under Marie Antoinette. (© 1980 or earlier printings.)

19-8:   Entries for both Jesus Christ (under Jesus with cross-reference from Christ) and Buddha (under Gautama Buddha with cross-reference from Buddha). These are two of the longer entries in this source.

19-9:   Yes, cross-reference from Old Pretender.

19-10:   No, no subject entries or subject index.

19-11:   Yes, it is mentioned in the entry for Fawkes, Guy.

19-12:   Johnson, Nixon, Kennedy all listed, although information given is sparse. Robert Kennedy is listed within the entry for John F. Kennedy. Ted Kennedy and Reagan are not included at all (© 1980). Washington is listed. However, note the length of the entry for Washington as compared to those for more recent presidents.

19-13:   No bibliographic references are given; for authors, some of their works are cited, of course, but no bibliographic references or further sources for the subject of the entry are given. The entries are not signed. Indication of authority, writers of the entries, sources consulted, etc., are given in the preface.

19-14:   Two main factors: who is listed in it, and how much information is given.

19-15:   Geographical (national, regional, etc.); period (retrospective, current; another way of putting it, with biographical sources, is living or dead); "subject"-- i.e., occupation, profession; also perhaps race, sex, religion.

19-16:   Universal or general scope. No limiting factors such as nationality, period, subject, etc. See Preface, first sentence. As is usually the case, however, American and British names are stressed.

19-17:   The editors admit (see Preface) that the limited size of the source makes necessary a restriction in the names included, and they do not specifically state their criteria for inclusion other than experience (i.e., theirs), objectivity, and a list of sources referred to.

19-18:   See Preface to Webster's on this. The problem is similar to that of the encyclopedia yearbooks or news surveys-- knowing at the moment what is likely to prove most noteworthy.

19-19:   Both give dates, birth information, information on birth and marriage, and titles of some of his books. Chambers gives fuller biographical information on his life, plus further references to biographies, studies, letters, etc. Chambers also gives some evaluative comments on his writing. (See Chambers, © 1968, published by Chambers in Edinburgh, or 1969 published by St. Martin's in New York.)

19-20:   All (Americans) except Reagan are listed in Chambers, basically a British publication, but the location of information depends somewhat on whether you are using the © 1968 edition published in Edinburgh by Chambers or the 1969 edition published in New York by St. Martin's. The Edinburgh, 1968 printing has an Addenda in the front which brings their entries up to date to the presidential nomination in the summer of 1968, and includes Johnson's announcement of retirement, Nixon's winning of the Republican nomination, Robert Kennedy's assassination. It also includes an entry on Hubert Humphrey, who up to that time had apparently not been considered most likely to be looked up. Robert and Edward Kennedy are not given full entries in the main list but are noted in the entry for John. In the 1969 edition published by St. Martin's, these corrections have been incorporated into the main entries, and the entry for Nixon has been further corrected to include his election to the Presidency. Information on all of these tends to be fuller in Chambers than in Webster's. It does not list Reagan because it is not current enough to do so.

19-21:   Chambers; entry is Dodsley. Among other things, he started the Annual Register. A biography (by Strauss) is cited --with the very briefest of bibliographic information--in the Chambers entry.

19-22:   Yes, both through index. Old Pretender listed under Nicknames and Personalities. Chronometer under Science and Industry.

19-23:   Both are universal or general in scope, not limited geographically or by period. Webster has more entries (40,000) compared to Chambers (15,000). Chambers is published in Great Britain and might be considered therefore to stress British names. Chambers, with somewhat less entries, has also fuller entries, gives bibliographic notes; as the preface says, it attempts to be something more than a catalogue of facts. Chambers has a subject index, of sorts.

19-24:   Webster makes a major point of doing this. Chambers does it when it seems necessary.

19-25:   Webster: see special tables at the back.

19-26:   According to Sheehy (see AJ31), Webster historically has practiced a kind of continuous revision, but the 1980 edition does not indicate the revision policy. Chambers has periodically revised editions (1961, 1968/69, etc., as indicated on the verso of the title page).

19-27:   Universal Pronouncing Dictionary of Biography and Mythology. (Title page or Sheehy.) Arrangement is dictionary, all in one alphabet, like Webster and Chambers. Scope also includes mythology, unlike Webster and Chambers. Also puts great stress on pronunciation; Preface and Introduction almost entirely devoted to this problem.

19-28:   Oceanus is a god in classical mythology; therefore only in Lippincott.

19-29:   New Century Cyclopedia of Names expands the idea of "names" to its broadest scope--including names of places, of events, of works of art or literature or music. It includes biographical information, although it is limited in entries to names. Lippincott's is more limited to biographical information but extending this idea to include names of people in mythology, that is people who never lived. Webster and Chambers are more limited yet, to actual people. A similar but more recently published source is Webster's Dictionary of Proper Names (Sheehy BD93); the Sheehy annotation notes that the latter work also includes abbreviations and acronyms.

19-30:   The Century Dictionary and Cyclopedia from Section 12 on dictionaries. See Sheehy annotation.

19-31:   Webster's Biographical Dictionary has

an entry, lists landscape painting only. New Century Dictionary goes further and notes especially sheep and cattle.

19-32:   New Century Cyclopedia of Names, entry under Gotham. Look also at following entry under Gotham, England, for significance of the reference.

19-33:   New Century Cyclopedia of Names. Also in Benet's The Reader's Encyclopedia.

19-34:   All include current personalities and they do not attempt to exclude those who are still living. This is seen easily in Webster and Chambers, who include for example Washington (retrospective), Kennedy (current, but not living), Nixon (current and living). Lippincott and Century are less likely to include very current personalities simply because they are not so recently revised but they do not exclude current or living persons; this can be seen by glancing through the pages and finding many entries with only birth dates given.

19-35:   Foreword (1983-84) indicates "contains biographies of people from almost every country in the world and in almost every sphere of human activity" and "men and women who have achieved international prominence."

19-36:   Nixon and Reagan are included; Kennedy isn't. (Mrs. Kennedy, now Mrs. Onassis, is.) Further limitation is that persons included must be living. This is not stated in the source. The only clue you get is the title: who's who (who is who). (1983-84 ed.)

19-37:   Full date and place of birth, parentage, marriage, children, education, publications, leisure interests, posts held, etc., and address, sometimes telephone number. All information not always given for each entry. Foreword implies information is obtained from subject himself/herself through questionnaires.

19-38:   See entry for Thatcher in International Who's Who.

19-39:   See their entries in International Who's Who.

19-40:   Annually since 1935, according to the Sheehy annotation (AJ35). A similar source with a much shorter publishing history is Who's Who in the World (Sheehy AJ38), first published in 1971-72.

19-41:   Yes, for those persons who have died and have therefore been dropped from succeeding editions. See obituary list in each volume.

19-42:   Yes, you would expect to find Kyprianou listed in International Who's Who, since he fits the criterion of being known outside of his own country. However, the entry will give you only the barest facts of his career and will not tell you anything about his attitudes, beliefs, politics, etc.

19-43:   Current Biography--apparently some stress on current interest. In line with this, it appears in monthly issues, cumulating annually into the Current Biography Yearbooks. Published by Wilson Company.

19-44:   See "About this publication" in monthly issues: people who are prominent in the news, in all areas, internationally. Preface to annual volumes: living leaders in all fields of human accomplishment the world over.

19-45:   Entries arranged alphabetically by name of the person discussed. Monthly and annual volumes include a list of the names classified loosely by profession, also a necrology or list of obituary notices of those who have died since the last issue. There are cumulative name indexes in each monthly issue and each annual volume. The article on Mitterand is found in the 1982 Yearbook volume. Check the index of the last issue and the index of the bound volumes.

19-46:   Articles are not signed, and no writers' or compilers' names are given anywhere. The prefatory matter indicates that sources of information are newspapers, magazines, books, sometimes the biographee, and that careful researching is done. A list of further references is given at the end of each article.

19-47:   That the articles have been written by someone other than the biographee, and that they have been written to be objective rather than to please the biographee.

19-48:   Current Biography 1982 volume.

19-49:   Possibly he would be in International Who's Who, but the information would be sketchy. Because of his recent rise to stardom in professional sports, you might expect an article about him in

Current Biography, and there is in the 1982 volume.

19-50: Minor changes, revisions, etc., are not necessarily made. Some older articles are superseded by new articles reflecting a major change in the biographee's situation. See the 1982 article on Ronald Reagan, President, in contrast to the 1949 and 1967 articles on Ronald Reagan, actor and governor, respectively.

19-51: New York Times Index (see Section 7) for some information and further references on anyone in the news. There is also the New York Times Biographical Service (Sheehy AJ37, 1AJ9), which is a monthly compilation of current biographical information that has appeared in issues of the New York Times. Facts on File and Keesing's may be of some help. Readers' Guide and other periodical indexes may list useful references. Many of the references cited in the Current Biography articles are from periodicals and news magazines indexed in Readers' Guide.

19-52: The New York Times is a good source of obituaries, and they can be identified in the New York Times Index. But to avoid searching through several indexes, or newspapers, for a specific obituary, you can turn to the New York Times Obituaries Index (AJ25, 2AJ12). The two volumes in this series list all of the names for obituaries appearing in the N.Y. Times through 1978. Each entry gives brief information about the person and refers to the original obituary listing. Another helpful source is the Annual Obituary (St. Martin's Press). The 1982 volume of the Annual Obituary contains over 400 entries, with photographs.

19-53: Yes. One notable example is the Pseudonyms and Nicknames Dictionary edited by Jennifer Mossman (2AA18). The second edition of this work has about 90,000 entries with references to sources and brief biographical sketches. (See the title page and preface for the many types of pseudonyms and nicknames included.)

19-54: You have the title, but not the name. You need the name to find it through the biographical sources. Statesman's Year-Book under Indonesia, gives this information, reasonably up-to-date.

19-55: Try Kane's Famous First Facts. Again, you do not have the name; you have

the event, or the fact, so you have to work from that approach.

19-56: Those sources which are specifically biographical in nature are, in general, always arranged alphabetically by the name of the person. They are nearly always in dictionary or directory form (Webster being an example of a dictionary form; International Who's Who being an example of a directory form). Current Biography, because its entries go beyond brief dictionary length into encyclopedic length articles, is perhaps an exception here, but even this source is arranged strictly alphabetically by name of the person. Subject access is non-existent in most of the sources and that which does exist is very limited.

In general, then, the biographical sources are best approached by specific name. It is possible to find subject information in the biographical sources, but sometimes this is best done by using other approaches to get the name, then using the biographical sources for further information.

19-57: All of the biographical sources which you have examined so far have been very broad in scope; universal or general. The only pattern which is forming so far is that of specifically current material (International Who's Who, living persons only; Current Biography, people "prominent in the news") as opposed to retrospective-and-current (Webster's Biographical Dictionary, etc.). The broader the scope is geographically and chronologically, the more the choice of persons included must be limited to the well-known and very noteworthy. The broader the scope is geographically and chronologically, the less information you get about each person included. These patterns and relationships may not seem clear yet, as you have examined only the more general sources. Keep them in mind as you work through the next section.

Section 20

BIOGRAPHICAL SOURCES: NATIONAL AND SUBJECT

Questions #20/1--20/89

The biographical sources which you examined in the previous section were all very broad in scope: general or universal. That is, they included persons from all places, all times. With such a broad basic scope, the principle limiting factor in these sources became a matter of the space available; therefore, limits are put on the number of and which names are chosen, the amount of information given about each name.

20-1   In this section, you will examine sources which are more limited in scope and therefore less limited in information and in the names included. On what basis would you expect these more limited sources to be organized? Think in terms of the patterns of organization of other information/reference sources you have examined. Look in Sheehy and see how the biographical sources are arranged, under what headings they are grouped.

The next set of sources to be examined are:

      Who's Who in America (AJ57)
      Marquis Who's Who Publications: Index to All Books (1AJ4)
      Who Was Who in America (AJ51/52, 1AJ23)
      Who's Who (AJ178)
      Who Was Who (AJ176)

      Dictionary of National Biography (AJ165, AJ167)
      Concise Dictionary of National Biography (AJ166)
      Dictionary of American Biography (AJ41, 1AJ16)
      National Cyclopaedia of American Biography (AJ43/44, 1AJ20, 2AJ16)

      American Men and Women of Science (EA222, CA93, 1EA38, 1CA42)
      Directory of American Scholars (AJ63, 1AJ25, 2AJ15)

      Biography Index (AJ4)

20-2   The major pattern which appeared in the biographical sources examined in the previous section was that some of the sources were limited specifically to current names: e.g., either people who are living (International Who's Who) or people prominent in the news (Current Biography). The first of the national sources to examine, Who's Who in America, fits into this pattern. Who publishes Who's Who in America? How often does it appear? How long has it been published?

20-3   Approximately how many names are there in the most recent edition of Who's Who in America?

20-4   What are the criteria for inclusion in Who's Who in America? In other words, who or what do you have to be to get in? Are only Americans included? What about persons no longer working?

20-5   What information is given in the entries? How is the information obtained?

20-6   Is the information given in Who's Who in America evaluative, or is it purely descriptive?

20-7   If you did not realize that Hodding Carter's first name is actually William, could you still find his entry in Who's Who in America? What do the parentheses around William mean?

20-8   Who's Who in America lists only a small percentage of the total population of the United States. Are there any similar sources which, by narrowing the scope, can provide access to a larger number of people?

20-9   In addition, the annual Marquis Who's Who Publications: Index to All Books lists the names of all biographees appearing in the then current editions of Marquis Who's Who biographical directories and indicates the volumes in which complete biographical information is found. Which directories does the Index to All Books index?

20-10   There are also who's who type sources which narrow their scope according to other criteria. Is there, for example, a who's who type publication devoted to black Americans?

20-11   Is there any usefulness in back volumes or outdated volumes of Who's Who in America?

20-12   Is there any way to get access to those names dropped because of death, other than through the earlier or outdated volumes?

20-13   How is the series of Who Was Who in America arranged?

20-14   If you were trying to locate the entry for Albert Schweitzer in Who Was Who in America, would you have to know the year in which he died in order to find it?

20-15   Who's Who in America goes back only to 1899. Is there coverage of this type prior to this date?

20-16   Do the Who Was Who in America volumes include only entries from the original Who's Who in America series?

20-17   The next title on the list is simply known as Who's Who, and properly it should have been considered prior to Who's Who in America, since it existed prior to the American source. Who's Who is the British counterpart to Who's Who in America. Who publishes Who's Who, and how long has it been appearing?

20-18   How does Who's Who compare to Who's Who in America in format and arrangement?

20-19   How do the two sources compare in scope? Does Who's Who include only Britishers? Are Caspar

Weinberger and Ronald Reagan listed in Who's Who? What are the criteria for inclusion in Who's Who? Are they similar to Who's Who in America?

20-20   What information is given in Who's Who? Is it similar to that in Who's Who in America?

20-21   Does Who's Who have retrospective volumes for the deceased, as does Who's Who in America? What period is covered? Is there an index to the volume?

20-22   Who is the present President of the French Republic? Where would you look to find a brief biographical sketch about him?

20-23   Where would you look to find a similar sketch or information about a minor public official of France?

20-24   So far you have examined current (who-is-who type) and retrospective (who-was-who type) sources for the United States and Great Britain. Are there other retrospective biographical sources organized by country? What other retrospective biographical sources exist for Great Britain?

20-25   The major retrospective biographical source for Great Britain is the Dictionary of National Biography. Although called a "dictionary" in the title, this source is really more of an encyclopedia. What is its scope?

20-26   The Dictionary of National Biography was published in parts over a period of time, much like some of the bibliographic sources. It was later reprinted. The Sheehy annotation may seem somewhat confusing, and the arrangement of the source itself is not always clear. Mainly, it is important to remember that the scope excludes living persons (in other words, includes only those deceased) and that there are a number of supplementary volumes. How many volumes are there to the set, and how is it arranged?

20-27   On what basis are names added to each of the chronological supplementary volumes to the DNB?

20-28   If you wanted to find the biographical article in the DNB on Sir Edward Charles Blount and you did not know in what year he died, would you have to go through all of the volumes?

20-29   Where was Sir Walter Scott born?

20-30   Who wrote the article on Sir Walter Scott (author of the Waverley Novels)? Where would you look to find the qualifications of the author of the article?

20-31   Does the article on Sir Walter Scott give further sources or references?

20-32   What is the Concise Dictionary of National Biography? How is it related to the DNB itself?

20-33   Is there any subject access to the DNB? If you wanted information on the establishment of the Irish Free State, could you find it through the DNB?

20-34   The DNB is a British retrospective source. Would you expect to find a biographical article on John Hancock, signer of the American Declaration of Independence? George Washington? Benjamin Franklin? John Adams? Paul Revere? Daniel Boone? Thomas Paine? Anne Bradstreet (first New England poet)? John Eliot (translated Bible into an Indian language)?

20-35   When was the DNB first published? When were many of its articles written? What advantages and/or disadvantages does this give it as a biographical source?

20-36   An example of the way a contemporary account can be somewhat misleading is in the DNB article for Sir Leslie Stephen himself. The biographical article on Stephen in the DNB and the introductory article on Stephen as editor, in the first volume, both mention his two marriages and the fact that he had two sons, and that one of his sons was a scholar of Trinity College, Cambridge. Both articles were written in the very early 1900's. Neither mentions who his daughters were. One of his daughters is now in fact probably more well-known than her father. Where would you look to find who his daughter is?

20-37   A source similar in purpose to the Dictionary of National Biography is its American version, the Dictionary of American Biography. What is the basic arrangement of this set? How does the arrangement compare to the DNB?

20-38   Is there an abridged version of the Dictionary of American Biography as there is with the DNB?

20-39   How does the scope of the Dictionary of American Biography differ from or compare to that of the Dictionary of National Biography?

20-40   Former President Harry S Truman is certainly a notable American, no longer living. Is he included in the Dictionary of American Biography?

20-41   Would you expect to find articles in the Dictionary of American Biography for John Hancock? George Washington? Benjamin Franklin? John Adams? Paul Revere? Daniel Boone? Thomas Paine? Anne Bradstreet? John Eliot?

20-42   John Burgoyne, William Howe, and Henry Clinton were all generals of the British Army during the American Revolution. Presumably therefore they would not be included in the Dictionary of American Biography (and they are not). Where would you look for biographical information on these men?

20-43   Thomas Hutchinson (born in Boston) was governor of the Massachusetts Bay Colony at the time of the Boston Tea Party and was loyal to the Crown during events preceding the Declaration of Independence. He was succeeded as governor by General Thomas Gage (born in England) who later became commander-in-chief, for a brief time, of the British forces in North America. Would you expect these men to be included in the Dictionary of American Biography? in the Dictionary of National Biography?

20-44   Who wrote the article on Hutchinson in the DAB? Are bibliographic references given?

20-45   Is the biographical information given in the Dictionary of National Biography and the Dictionary of American Biography limited to factual, objective information, or is it evaluative as well? Does this have any relationship to the importance of finding out who wrote the articles?

20-46   How does the bibliographic information given in the DNB and the DAB compare with that given in the other retrospective sources you have examined, Who Was Who in America and Who Was Who?

20-47   In general, articles in the Dictionary of American Biography are thorough, scholarly, reliable, signed, with bibliographic references. One limitation to the source, however, is that it covers really only the major names in American retrospective biography (approximately 16,000, according to the Preface of the Concise DAB, 2d ed., 1977). What other retrospective sources for American biography are available?

20-48   How does the scope of the National Cyclopaedia of American Biography compare to the DAB, according to Sheehy?

20-49   What is the arrangement of the National Cyclopaedia? Look at the source itself, not at the Sheehy annotation, and see if you can figure it out.

20-50   Anna P. Dinnies was an American poet, quite minor. What can you find out about her through the National Cyclopaedia?

20-51   Does the index to the National Cyclopaedia give you any access to the material other than by personal name? If you were doing research on the history of printing in the United States, would the National Cyclopaedia be helpful to you?

20-52   Actually, the National Cyclopaedia is not so impossible to use as it may appear at first glance, but it is somewhat more complicated than the other biographical sources. What is its primary use?

20-53   Is there a retrospective biographical source for Australians, which is scholarly, definitive, gives information in depth, and is reasonably recently published?

20-54   So far, you have seen that the biographical sources are organized, like bibliographic sources, on a national basis, current vs. retrospective. For example, if you needed information on a contemporary Belgian scientist, where would you look?

20-55   In what further way can biographical sources be limited in scope, thus expanded in coverage? If you didn't find the contemporary Belgian scientist in the who's who for Belgium type of source, how else could you approach the problem?

20-56   The next few sources are examples of subject-limited biographical sources. There are some subject lists which have a general or universal scope, but these are examples which further fit into the pattern of division along national lines.
         The first of these, American Men and Women of Science, is another multi-volume source. What is the basic arrangement? Does this biographical source appear on an annual basis? How is it updated? What sciences does it include?

20-57   What information is given for each entry, and how is the information obtained?

20-58   What are the criteria for inclusion in American Men and Women of Science? Is it limited to living persons only?

20-59   What about the humanities? Where could we expect to find information on the historian Arthur S. Link, for example?

20-60   The next title is Who's Who in American Art. What does this title tell you about the source, without even looking at it? What can you guess about the arrangement and scope of the source, without looking at it? Would you expect to find and can you find information about Andrew Wyeth in this source, without bothering to read through the preface, introduction, check the Sheehy annotation, etc.?

20-61   The data given on Wyeth in Who's Who in American Art are limited to bare facts. Where might you find an article discussing his life and activities?

20-62   Where are American Men and Women of Science and Who's Who in American Art classified in Sheehy?

20-63   What is the name of a professional biographical dictionary or directory for librarians?

20-64   Sheehy has a section, AK, titled Genealogy, following the section on Biography. What is genealogy?

20-65   What bibliographic sources do you have thus far which will give you access to other biographical publications?

20-66   The next title is one which specifically guides you to further sources of information: The Biography Index. Who is the publisher of this source? What is its publication pattern?

20-67   What is the scope of Biography Index? How does it differ from the Readers' Guide? Could you find biographical material through the Readers' Guide?

20-68   Biography Index indexes currently published magazines and books. Does this mean that only living persons, or persons of current interest will appear in this source? Would Biography Index list Martin Luther? Martin Luther King? Coretta King? Elton John? John Lennon? Plato? Ronald Reagan?

20-69   Can you find out, generally, through Biography Index, who Plato was?

20-70   A Current Biography article on John McEnroe was published in 1980, but he has been much in the sporting news since then. What recent biographical material or magazine articles have appeared about him?

20-71   Is there any point in checking the Readers' Guide as well as Biography Index for material on John McEnroe?

20-72   What is the title of a recently published full-length biography of Katharine Hepburn, American actress?

20-73   Would Biography Index give you access to current studies of the work of Galileo?

20-74   If you were searching for a biography of Albert Einstein suitable for an elementary school student to read, would Biography Index be of any use to you?

20-75   Does Biography Index have any subject access at all? If you were doing research on the problem of modern museums, would Biography Index be of any use to you?

20-76   Biography Index includes a "Checklist of Composite Books Analyzed." What does this mean? Why is this list included?

20-77   A source somewhat similar to Biography Index is the Biography and Genealogy Master Index. What is the complete title of this work? How does it differ from Biography Index? Who publishes it?

20-78   How would you deal with the following question: where was John Biddle born?

20-79   If you don't know anything and can't get a clue about John Biddle, what would your procedure be? Where would you start? Is there any relationship between the scope of the source and your likelihood of finding a particular name in it?

The following questions can be used as REVIEW for the biographical sources; keep all of the other previously examined sources in mind, however.

20-80   What is Vanessa Redgrave's telephone number?

20-81   Where would you find a fairly lengthy and authoritative article on John Baskerville, an English printer and typefounder, which includes the comments of some of his contemporaries about him?

20-82   Who is the present Governor General of New Zealand?

20-83   Becky Sharp appears in the novel Vanity Fair by Thackeray.   Where would you look to find information about her?

20-84   How much does Dustin Hoffman pay per month for his New York apartment?

20-85   What factor led Henry Clay Folger to develop his book collecting interests?   How did he make his money?

20-86   Who was the first governor of Illinois?

20-87   Where would you find information on the life of Captain Bligh of the H.M.S. Bounty?

20-88   What are the names of some people who are currently interested in the study of flying saucers or other unexplained aerial phenomena?

20-89   Rootabaga Stories is the name of a book of tales for children.   Who wrote it?

BIOGRAPHICAL SOURCES: NATIONAL AND SUBJECT

Answers #20/1--20/89

20-1: Biographical sources tend to be organized on a <u>national</u> basis. Sheehy lists first general and international works, then works for the United States, then works for other countries, arranged alphabetically by name of country.

This is very similar to the way <u>bibliographic</u> sources are organized. Just as complete universal bibliographic sources are difficult if not impossible to achieve, universal biographical sources tend to be very limited in information. Fuller coverage can be obtained on a national basis.

In a way, we can say that all reference sources are organized, broadly, on a national or geographical basis. Dictionaries, for example, are organized by language, which is similar to a national or geographical division. Most encyclopedias are general or universal in coverage, but they tend to stress material of the country or language in which they are published, therefore, we think of them as American, British, German, etc. It is really more correct to say that most reference sources are <u>published</u> on a <u>national</u> basis and therefore tend to have a geographical or language bias which makes them most useful from a national or geographical approach. However, the national biographical sources are more clearly <u>limited</u> in scope to national coverage.

20-2: Publisher: Marquis-Who's Who, Inc., Chicago.
<u>Appears</u>: biennially (every two years).
<u>Published since</u>: 1899
(See title page and Sheehy annotation.)

20-3: See Preface. 1982-83 edition: 75,200 names.

20-4: See Preface and "Standards of Admission." Many people are included automatically by virtue of their position; others are selected based on "noteworthy achievements that have proved to be of significant value to society." All selections are supposedly based on the "application of objective criteria." Some

non-Americans are included despite the title (leading government officials of Canada and Mexico, for example). A new feature is a Retiree Index of persons whose names have been deleted from the main list because they have retired from active work.

20-5: Information given is similar to that in International Who's Who: name, birth, parents, marriage, family, education, positions held, membership in organizations, publications, address. In general, information is obtained from the biographies themselves. Some data are gathered by the publisher if the biographee fails to furnish them, in which case an asterisk follows the sketch (see the Preface and Table of Abbreviations).

20-6: Purely descriptive, objective, though some of the sketches are now appended with an italicized statement, "Thoughts on my Life." This statement, according to the Preface of the 1982-83 ed., "reflects those principles, goals, ideals, and values that have been guidelines for success and high standards."

20-7: Some cross-references are given in the main alphabetical list, including that from Carter, Hodding to Carter, (William) Hodding, III. For the explanation of the parentheses, see "Alphabetical Practices" in the prefatory matter.

20-8: Yes, and with the organizational pattern still on a geographical basis. Sheehy lists several regional who's who sources, published by Marquis and following the same format of the main source (see items AJ58, 59, 60, 61); Sheehy (p. 214) also notes that state publications are available although not listed there. Who's Who in America now includes a list of the individuals whose sketches appear in one of the Marquis regional directories (see the Preface).

20-9:   See the "Contents" section of the latest edition of the Index to All Books.

20-10: Yes, see Sheehy 1AJ27: Who's Who Among Black Americans. The 1980-81 edition of this work provides biographical information for about 16,000 black Americans having "reference value." This work can be located by searching through the appropriate section of Sheehy (General Reference Works--Biography) or by checking the index. (Who's Who Among Black Americans is indexed in the Sheehy supplement under "Afro-Americans, biography.")

20-11: See Sheehy annotation for AJ57. Some names are dropped because of deaths and some names are dropped for reasons other than death (these reasons not being clearly stated); information on those persons would of course be available only in earlier editions. Some entries in current editions have had to be shortened for space considerations, and reference may be made to earlier editions (see explanation of symbols in the Table of Abbreviations).

20-12: Names dropped because of death are found in Marquis' series called Who Was Who in America. (See Sheehy annotation under Who's Who in America.)

20-13: There are (as of 1983) seven volumes divided chronologically (i.e., 1897-1942, 1943-1950, etc.), which are compilations of the original sketches from Who's Who in America, 1899+. Each volume is arranged alphabetically by name of person, just as the current or contemporary volumes are.

20-14: No; there is a cumulative index for all volumes in the most recent volume.

20-15: Marquis has also published a "Historical Volume," covering 1607-1896, on the same plan but using original research since there were no volumes of Who's Who in America to draw on for that time.

20-16: See Preface to vol. 6 (1974-76): "... for the first time a Who Was Who in America volume will contain ... biographees ... whose listings were in publications other than Who's Who in America." It also now includes sketches of recently deceased "world notables." Some entries, in the addendum, represent names overlooked in the original Who's Who in America series, as well as corrections and deaths received too late to

be added to the main alphabetical list.

20-17: Published in London by Black (U.S. edition by St. Martin's Press), since 1849. (See Sheehy annotation.)

20-18: In arrangement they are similar; in format they are similar although Who's Who is smaller. Who's Who is published annually, while Who's Who in America appears biennially.

20-19: In scope the sources are similar. Who's Who includes names of important people other than Britishers--Weinberger and Reagan, for example (1983 ed.). In fact, a recent review indicated that Who's Who is becoming more international. The criteria for inclusion in Who's Who are not stated, as they are in Who's Who in America, except to say that one does not have to pay for the privilege.

20-20: Information given in both is similar, almost entirely limited to objectively stated facts. (See #20-6 for the one exception for Who's Who in America.) Who's Who tends to include recreations, and the various parts of the entry (education, publications, etc.) are clearly set out by the use of italic type.

20-21: Yes, see Who Was Who. Who Was Who goes back only to 1897, although Who's Who itself goes back to 1849. There is now a separately published index to the first seven volumes (1897-1980) of Who Was Who. This facilitates searching for an entry when the date of death is not known.

20-22: You would have to go to some source such as Statesman's Year-book to find the name of the present President. Statesman's Year-book 1982/83 lists François Mitterrand as the President. He is not listed in Who's Who in America, 1982-83, but he is in Who's Who, 1983. (See #20-19.)

20-23: Look for a who's who in France type of source. Sheehy, under France--Contemporary, lists one, Who's Who in France (AJ152).

20-24: See Sheehy, biography section under Great Britain, where several sources are listed. The first is Dictionary of National Biography.

20-25: All noteworthy inhabitants of the British Isles and the Colonies, exclusive of living persons (see Sheehy annotation). "From the earliest times to 1900" (title page of vol. 1), with supplements to 1970. The DNB itself has no real preface explaining its scope.

20-26: The basic arrangement is under name of person with entries all in one alphabetical list (dictionary). There are 22 basic volumes covering "earliest times to 1900"; the first 21 are one alphabetical list, the 22nd volume includes additions of persons who died too late for inclusion in vols. 1-21. Thus vol. 22 forms a kind of supplement to the "beginning to 1900" set. Then there are several supplementary volumes for the twentieth century, divided chronologically, each arranged alphabetically as is the basic set.

20-27: On the death of the biographee, as with the Who Was Who volumes.

20-28: There is a cumulative index in the last of the supplementary volumes (1961-1970 published in 1981) which gives all names in the supplementary volumes plus birth and death dates. This tells you that Blount died in 1905 so you can check the 1901-11 volume.

20-29: The problem here is which Sir Walter Scott; there are six Walter Scotts listed in the main set of the DNB, two of them "Sirs." The last listed, author of the Waverley novels, is probably the best known.

20-30: The article is signed L.S. and you must refer back to the list of contributors in vol. 1 (or in the same volume in some older editions) to find that the author is Leslie Stephen. Stephen is actually one of the editors of the DNB, and you could find out more about him by reading the article on him in the DNB itself; he died in 1904 and is therefore in the first of the 20th century supplementary volumes.

20-31: Yes, many further sources are listed. The DNB is particularly helpful for bibliographic references.

20-32: The concise DNB is an abridged version of the DNB, with the articles themselves shortened or abstracted. All names from the DNB for which "substantive" biographical information is given are included. Some errors are corrected. (See Preface to vol. 1 of the Concise DNB.) It serves then as an index to the larger DNB as well as a smaller and less expen-

sive version.

20-33: There is a subject index of sorts (similar to that in Chambers's Biographical Dictionary) in the back of the second volume of the Concise DNB. You could use it to check under Ireland, then Irish Free State, then find names of persons presumably active in that field, and look at the articles under their names.

20-34: The DNB claims to include "noteworthy" Americans of the Colonial period. Of the names listed, only Paine, Bradstreet, and Eliot are included in the DNB. These three were born in England, and the others were not, which may explain their inclusion.

20-35: Originally published from 1885 on and therefore written at that time or earlier (see Sheehy annotation). It has the disadvantage of being by now out-of-date in some respects, not reflecting current scholarship and discoveries. (Some revision and corrections are found in the Concise DNB.) However, it has the great advantage of giving what are nearly contemporary accounts of the people included, or accounts based on contemporary views.

20-36: Webster's Biographical Dictionary, under Stephen, Leslie, refers to his two daughters by their first names and refers you to the entries for their husbands, through which circuitous means you can find that one daughter was writer Virginia Woolf. Chambers's Biographical Dictionary is somewhat clearer, in the entry for Stephen, Leslie, that Virginia Woolf is one of his daughters. At the time the DNB articles were written, of course, she was still a very young woman and not well known as she is now. There is a DNB article for Virginia Woolf herself (she died in 1941).

20-37: Like the DNB, it is arranged alphabetically by the name of the person. It was first published in 20 volumes plus two supplements and an index. Five more supplements have brought it up to date through 1965. There is one alphabetical list in the basic set, then another alphabetical list in each of the supplements.

A reprint edition was published in 11 volumes. Each volume of this reprint edition contains two of the original volumes, and volume 11 consists of three supplements, extending cover-

age through 1950. An Index to the reprint edition was published in 1974 and
covers volumes 1-10 and the first five
supplements. Another Index was published in 1981 by Scribners and covers
volumes 1-10 and all seven supplements.

20-38: Yes, Concise Dictionary of American Biography; follows essentially the same
pattern as the Concise DNB.

20-39: The DNB is essentially a biographical
source for Britishers, and the DAB is
essentially a source for Americans. See
Preface of source for statement of scope.
The DAB (like the DNB) excludes living
persons. It is restricted to those persons who have actually lived in the
United States (or in the territory now
known as the United States) although
not restricted to those born in the United
States. It specifically excludes British
officers who served in the colonies after
independence was declared (i.e., those
not on our side). Included, within these
restrictions, are those who have made
some significant contribution to American
life.

20-40: No. He died in 1972, and the DAB coverage only goes up to 1965.

20-41: Yes, all are included.

20-42: All three are included in the Dictionary
of National Biography.

20-43: Both Hutchinson and Gage are in the
DAB and in the DNB. (Both left the
colonies for England prior to the Declaration of Independence.)

20-44: As in the DNB, articles are signed with
initials (contributors identified in the
front of each volume of the DAB). Also as in the DNB, extensive bibliographic
references are given for the articles.

20-45: In general, DNB and DAB entries are
evaluative as well as factual. As examples, see the articles in both sources on
Hutchinson, particularly the final paragraphs. See also the entry on Melvil
Dewey in the Concise DAB. In any
source where value judgments are given,
it is important to know who wrote the
material, who is giving the judgment,
what are his/her qualifications for doing
so.

20-46: The Who Was Who volumes, as do the
current who's who type, basically give
strictly objective statements of fact

(see #20-6). The information is quite
limited compared to that found in the
encyclopedic type entries of the DNB
and DAB.

20-47: See Sheehy, same section as the DAB.
Also the Sheehy annotation for the DAB
itself compares the scope of the DAB to
two other major retrospective sources,
Appleton's Cyclopaedia (AJ40) and the
National Cyclopaedia of American Biography (AJ43/44, 1AJ20, 2AJ16).

20-48: National Cyclopaedia is much more comprehensive, less limited and selective.
(See Sheehy annotation.)

20-49: The National Cyclopaedia is a good example of a thoroughly confusing source.
All of the biographical sources examined
so far have been arranged alphabetically
by the name of the person. Looking at
the single volumes of the National Cyclopaedia shows no obvious rationale behind the arrangement of the material.
It is not alphabetical, and not obviously chronological. Since it is a biographical source, and since there are clearly
separate entries each headed with the
name of a person, the need is for some
sort of access by personal name, preferably alphabetically, and the obvious
thing to look for, then, is an index of
some sort. Each volume has a separate
index, but there are more than 50 volumes, so checking each volume would be
a tedious task. Again, the obvious thing
to look for is some sort of cumulative index.

According to the Sheehy annotation
(AJ44), a cumulative index was published
in 1969, then published again in a revised version in 1971. According to the
Sheehy supplement (1AJ20), a 3rd index
was published in 1975; this cumulative
index goes through v. 54 of the numbered series and v. "L" of the lettered
or current series. A 4th cumulative index (2AJ16), published in 1979, supersedes earlier indexes and covers the numbered or permanent series through v.
58 and the lettered or current series
through v. "M."

20-50: Look in the 1979 4th Index under Dinnies, Anna P., which refers you to vol.
13, p. 149, where you find the entry
for her with biographical information.

20-51: There is subject access as well as name
access through the index. For example, there are extensive references under the heading of "Printing," plus some

see also references to other related subject headings.

20-52:   It is useful primarily for its comprehensiveness; see Sheehy annotation. The entries are more extensive than in Who's Who, for example. It includes living persons so provides more current coverage. It has some subject access. For a work which has a coverage similar to that of the National Cyclopaedia, in that it includes living persons, you may wish to take a look at Webster's American Biographies by Van Doren and McHenry (Sheehy 1AJ21). Its biographies are "full-scale" in that they provide more than the basic facts, and they average about 350 words each.

20-53:   See Sheehy, biography section, under Australia: for example, AJ79 and 1AJ33, the Australian Dictionary of Biography. Note that this source, unlike most of those you have examined, has a basic chronological arrangement.

20-54:   In a current (who's who type) source for Belgium.

20-55:   Subject limitations; i.e., lists of scientists, artists, musicians, etc.

20-56:   The basic arrangement is alphabetical by name. It is issued irregularly rather than annually (12th ed., 1971; 13th ed., 1976; 14th ed., 1979; 15th ed., 1982). The major multi-volume part of the set covers the "Physical and Biological Sciences"; there has been a section for the "social and behavioral sciences not included in the major compendium," but it was left out of the 15th ed. because of limited acceptance. See Sheehy annotation for a list of major fields included.

20-57:   Same type of factual achievements as is listed in who's-who-type sources: education, degrees, positions, membership, specific scientific fields of interest (see entries themselves). The information is obtained from the biographees themselves through questionnaires; again, similar to the who's-who-type sources (see Preface).

20-58:   Criteria listed in Preface. The source does not clearly state it is limited to living persons only, but its nature (the fact that the information is based on questionnaires filled in by the biographees, for example) dictates that it is probably limited in this way.

20-59:   There is an entry for Link in the Directory of American Scholars, 8th ed., 1982 (Sheehy AJ63, 1AJ25, 2AJ15). This work provides biographical coverage of scholars in the humanities similar to the coverage provided by the two preceding titles.

20-60:   This is a who's who type source, therefore probably limited to living persons and giving the basic factual data obtained from the biographee himself; no evaluative comments or discursive treatment of his work. It is limited to Americans and Canadians and Mexicans and limited (not to artists) to people working in the field of art, artists, administrators, historians, educators, collectors, librarians, critics, curators and dealers. You can assume it will be arranged alphabetically by name of person. You can expect to find Andrew Wyeth listed there, and you will find him in the W's as you would expect (15th ed., 1982). The one thing you can't assume is that the source will be revised or issued every year, and you should therefore check the date of publication to see how recent it is. (Revised biennially, according to Sheehy.)

20-61:   Try Current Biography; periodical indexes.

20-62:   Under the subject (i.e., C: Social Sciences, E: Pure and Applied Sciences, BE: Fine Arts), then under biography; not in the Biography (AJ) section.

20-63:   Check Sheehy under the subject area of librarianship (AB), then under Biography. The most recent listed is titled the Dictionary of American Library Biography (Sheehy 1AB13), but it is limited to deceased persons. Who's who type directories include A Biographical Directory of Librarians in the United States and Canada (AB88) and Who's Who in Librarianship and Information Science (AB93). A more recent who's who type directory, Who's Who in Library and Information Services, was published by the American Library Association in 1982.

20-64:   See Sheehy, 9th ed., p. 234.

20-65:   Sheehy, any of the national bibliographic sources with subject access (under names of biographee as subject, or checking under Biography itself as the subject), any of the periodical indexes. See #19-51.

20-66: Wilson Company. It appears quarterly and cumulates each year, then every three years.

20-67: See Prefatory Note in quarterly issues, or Sheehy annotation. Biography Index lists or indexes biographical material appearing in periodicals, books, etc. The Readers' Guide indexes only periodicals; Biography Index indexes books as well, plus some periodicals not indexed in Readers' Guide. Biographical material could be located through the Readers' Guide, indexed under the name of the person as subject.

20-68: All persons, all times.

20-69: Yes, if you find an entry for him. See September 1979 to August 1982 volume. Entries give dates and brief identifying label (i.e., Greek philosopher).

20-70: See Biography Index cumulations and issues since 1980.

20-71: Biography Index duplicates, for biographical material, what is in Readers' Guide. But Biography Index appears only quarterly, and Readers' Guide appears twice a month, thus Readers' Guide might give you more current access for periodicals, in addition to a broader scope of materials than you would find indexed in Biography Index.

20-72: See Biography Index under Hepburn, November 1983 issue, or cumulation which includes this). Separately-published biographies are listed, or indexed, in Biography Index.

20-73: Yes, see Sept. '79-Aug. '82 volume under Galilei, Galileo.

20-74: Yes, juvenile literature is included and so noted. See Sept. 1979-Aug. 1982 volume, for example.

20-75: Biography Index has a kind of subject access in its "index to professions and occupations." You could, for example, check under "Museum directors and curators" in each issue for names of specific people, then check the main index itself under these names for articles or other biographical material about them. The biographical material, if at all extensive, would undoubtedly contribute something to your research.

20-76: These are books containing "composite" biographical material--that is, not limited only to one person--which are analyzed or specifically indexed in Biography Index. For example, Nancy Levinson's First Women Who Spoke Out (published by Dillion Press in 1983) is indexed or analyzed in the August 1983 issue; that is, the book is cited, giving the pertinent pages, under the names of each of the women whose lives it covers. These books are listed in the Checklist so that libraries may use it as a purchasing guide; it may be frustrating to have the index if you do not have the books or periodicals in which the information is located.

20-77: The complete title is: Biography and Genealogy Master Index: A Consolidated Index to more than 3,200,000 biographical sketches in over 350 current and retrospective biographical dictionaries. Unlike Biography Index, its coverage is restricted to biographies appearing in biographical dictionaries. It is published by Gale Research.

Related sources also published by Gale Research include: Performing Arts Biography Master Index, Biography Almanac (essentially an abridged version of BGMI), and Bio-Base (a microfiche format index which includes all of the entries in BGMI plus over 500,000 additional ones).

20-78: You need to know more than just the name of the person. In the first place, there are no doubt many, many John Biddles. Which do you want? In the second place, you need to know what source to turn to first, so you should have some idea of the time period of the person, and some idea of his nationality. In library reference work, you would ordinarily expect to get some sort of clue from the inquirer about the particular person he/she is searching for. Hopefully, your own reading and general knowledge background might be helpful. You can also make some assumptions or guesses; for example, from the name it would seem reasonable that John Biddle is English or American.

20-79: Start with the universal sources, work through national, regional, special, subject, etc. Work from broadest scope to narrow scope. The broader the coverage of the source, the less insignificant names it will include.

Another option might be to check in the Biography and Genealogy Master Index. It does include John Biddle;

in fact, the 1980, 2d. ed. lists 15 John
Biddles. So your search will still be
difficult unless you have some idea of
which John Biddle you want.

20-80:   Curiously enough, this information is
given in the entry for Redgrave in the
International Who's Who.

20-81:   Dictionary of National Biography.

20-82:   Statesman's Year-Book will give fairly recent information.

20-83:   New Century Cyclopedia of Names; Reader's Encyclopedia.

20-84:   This is the kind of information which frequently appears in Current Biography
articles. But unless the article is recent,
this information may well be out-of-date.

20-85:   Dictionary of American Biography.

20-86:   Try an encyclopedia, under Illinois.

20-87:   Captain Bligh was actually a real person;
the novel Mutiny on the Bounty was
based on a real incident. There is an
article on Captain (William) Bligh in the
Dictionary of National Biography.

20-88:   Try directories of organizations, such as
Encyclopedia of Associations, under flying saucers as subject entry, to get
names of officers.

20-89:   Title of literary work, see New Century
Cyclopedia of Names. See also Reader's
Encyclopedia. See also BIP, title volume, where you will of course find it only if it is still in print.

GEOGRAPHICAL SOURCES: GAZETTEERS AND GUIDEBOOKS

Questions #21/1--21/85

21-1   What is the arrangement of Sheehy's Guide to Reference Books?

21-2   If you were looking in Sheehy for material on a specific subject (for example, education), where would you look?

21-3   In which of these major divisions have most of the bibliographic and reference sources which you have examined so far been classified?

21-4   In what ways have the bibliographic and reference sources which you have previously examined been general rather than subject sources?

21-5   The final sections of this manual cover geographical sources. How are geographical sources classified in Sheehy?

The geographical sources, then, can be examined as examples of sources within a subject field, as well as basic reference sources. The first set of titles to examine is:

   Wright and Platt: Aids to Geographical Research (CL5)
   Brewer: The Literature of Geography (CL1)

   Columbia Lippincott Gazetteer of the World (CL56)
   Webster's New Geographical Dictionary (CL61)

   California (American Guide Series) (see CL268)
   Hotel and Motel Red Book (CL270)

21-6   Geography is treated as a subject area in Sheehy, but is included in many reference textbooks and library school reference courses as part of the basic or general or non-subject areas. In what ways is geography a part of general, as opposed to subject, reference work?

21-7   What is the study of the field of geography? Where would you look for a simple definition? Where would you look for a fuller description, with some discussion of the major divisions or branches of the field and some information on its historical development?

21-8   Geography is classified in Sheehy as part of the social sciences. How would you find out how geography is classified in a library collection? Why is it important to know how a subject field is classified in a library collection?

21-9   Which sources that you have previously examined have included geographical information, including maps?

21-10   Does Sheehy give any general background on the subject of geography--what it covers, how it is related to other fields, etc.?

21-11   Sheehy lists bibliographies and other reference sources for geography in Section CL. Does Sheehy attempt to list all such sources? Does Sheehy attempt to be comprehensive for subject areas? What is the scope of Sheehy's Guide to Reference Books, especially in relation to the subject fields?

21-12   Where do you look, then, for more comprehensive and specialized coverage of the subject field?

21-13   Wright and Platt is listed in Sheehy as a "guide." Since there are many kinds of guides used in reference work, perhaps a better designation for this particular type of source is "guide to the literature." What is a guide to the literature?

21-14   Probably the best way to see what a guide to the literature is, is to examine one. Wright and Platt's Aids to Geographical Research is an excellent example of a guide to the literature. What is the purpose of the Wright and Platt book? What is its scope? What is one major drawback to its use?

The next series of questions is designed to show you how to approach geography (and therefore any other subject) as a subject area, by using guides to reference sources (such as Sheehy), guides to the literature of a specific subject (such as Wright and Platt, and Brewer), and what you have already learned throughout this manual regarding types of sources. These questions (through #21-39) can be answered with the aid of Sheehy, Wright and Platt, and Brewer; it is not necessary to have access to the specific geographical sources noted throughout the answers.

21-15   What are some of the main topics or divisions into which the study of geography is divided?

21-16   Do Wright and Platt or Brewer give any information about how geographers work? what kind of facts, data, information they deal with? what geographical research attempts to do or to discover or to explain?

21-17   Do Wright and Platt or Brewer make any suggestions as to how the student of or researcher in (or librarian in) the field of geography might go about exploring the literature of this subject?

21-18   Do Wright and Platt or Brewer give any general guidance on the ways in which geographical materials are most likely to be arranged?

21-19   Do Wright and Platt or Brewer discuss ways in which libraries may be used in the search for geographical information? (Remember that Wright and Platt was written for geographers, not librarians.) Are other collections of material, besides libraries, suggested for use?

21-20   Do Wright and Platt or Brewer discuss or suggest ways in which people and organizations may be used in the search for geographical information? (Note the name of the organization responsible for the publication of Wright and Platt itself; see title page.)

21-21   Do Wright and Platt or Brewer list any <u>bibliographies of bibliographies</u> in the field of geography?

21-22   What access do you have, through the national bibliographic sources studied in Part I of this manual, to information on <u>current U.S. or English</u> geographical publications?

21-23   Using Sheehy, can you find any bibliographies <u>currently</u> published (i.e., on an on-going basis as are CBI, BPR, etc.) which are specifically limited to geographical publications?

21-24   Sheehy, of course, does not indicate whether these current sources are in fact <u>still</u> currently appearing. Where would you check to find out?

21-25   What access do you have, through the national bibliographic sources, to <u>retrospective</u> geographical publications?

21-26   Are there any bibliographies specifically limited to geographical materials which do give better <u>retrospective</u> coverage?

21-27   Does Sheehy list bibliographies specifically on the subject of phytogeography (plant geography)? on agricultural geography? on population geography? Does Wright and Platt? Does Brewer? Which appears to be more useful for the specialized aspects of the subject: Sheehy or a guide to the subject literature?

21-28   Where would you look, in the sources you have examined in other parts of this manual, to find the titles of some <u>periodicals</u> in the field of geography?

21-29   Is there a <u>list of periodicals</u> limited specifically to those in the field of geography?

21-30   Is there a periodical <u>indexing and/or abstracting service</u> (similar to Readers' Guide) limited to geographical materials?

21-31   What access do you have to <u>government publications</u> in the field of geography?

21-32   Other than bibliographies, what <u>types</u> of reference sources have you examined so far?

21-33   The examples you examined of these types of reference sources have been of a general nature, not subject-limited. The same types of sources exist in the subject fields, and their scope (within the limits set by the subject) and arrangement tend to be similar to the general sources you have already examined, so that once you know or assume the existence of such sources, you already know how they can be used and for what kinds of information they will be most useful.

How would you find out what dictionaries, for example, exist in the subject field of geography?

21-34   Can you tell, from checking in Sheehy, what is the title of the most basic, most useful dictionary of technical terms in the field of geography?

21-35   You could find in the general encyclopedia an article on geography itself, what it consists of, some history of its development, etc. Where would you look to find out what is currently being done in this field?

21-36   What kind of handbooks are there in the field of geography?

21-37   Is there a directory of organizations for geography?

21-38   The directories for geography seem to list both people and organizations. Are there any biographical sources for the field other than these? Where would you look for current biographical information on geographers living and working in the field today?

21-39   The types of reference sources which you have examined throughout this course are found also in the subject field of geography, as they are in most subjects. In addition, a subject field tends to have types of sources peculiar to that particular field, related to the kinds of information and the need for approaches to information peculiar to that particular field. To understand these specialized types of sources, it is often helpful to have some knowledge about the subject area itself and what kind of work is done in it.
         Sheehy lists four specialized types of sources for geography. What are they?

21-40   Atlases will be taken up in a separate section, but the other specialized sources for geography will be examined in this section of the manual. The first special type is the gazetteer. What is a gazetteer?

21-41   Is there anything in the title of the Columbia Lippincott Gazetteer which indicates its scope? its arrangement?

21-42   How up-to-date is the Columbia Lippincott Gazetteer? How important is it for such sources to be up-to-date?

21-43   Would you expect to find all of the following in the Columbia Lippincott Gazetteer: Iran, Moscow, Hainan Island, Thames River, Stonehenge, Mount Kilimanjaro, Niagara Falls, Botswana?

21-44   What does the Columbia Lippincott Gazetteer give as the population for Aiea, Hawaii? What does the entry itself have to say about the location of Aiea? What does T.H. stand for? What is the date for the population figure given?

21-45   Is this information brought up to date in any way in the Columbia Lippincott Gazetteer?

21-46   Where would you find information on the latest census figures for Aiea?

21-47   The scope of the Columbia Lippincott Gazetteer is world-wide, but it must have some limitations in what it can include. As the universal biographical sources attempted to limit their scope by including only the most "important" names, does Columbia Lippincott attempt to limit its scope by, for example, the relative size of the place it lists?

21-48   The title of the next source is Webster's New Geographical Dictionary. Is it in fact then a dictionary or a gazetteer? How current is it? How is it kept up to date?

21-49   Who is the publisher of Webster's New Geographical Dictionary?

21-50   What is one of the chief differences between Webster's Third unabridged dictionary and Webster's second, regarding geographical information?

21-51   Webster's New Geographical Dictionary is obviously, by size alone, more limited in scope than Columbia Lippincott. What kind of limitations has it set on the places it includes?

21-52   Does Webster's New Geographical Dictionary include Botswana? recent population figures for Aiea, Hawaii? What about Zimbabwe?

21-53   What is the county seat of Sequatchie County, Tennessee, according to Webster's New Geographical Dictionary?

21-54   How old is the city of Katmandu, and what of interest can be seen there? Compare Webster's and Columbia Lippincott.

21-55   Where would you find a more recent population figure for Katmandu?

21-56   What kind of industry, if any, is there in the town of Poggio Rusco in Italy? What is the population?

21-57   Where is Yezo or Yeso?

21-58   What is the difference between the name Yezo and Hokkaido?

21-59   Webster's New Geographical Dictionary includes only U.S. towns with population of 2,500+; Columbia Lippincott includes only incorporated towns listed in 1950 census. Neither includes New Tazewell, Tennessee. Where else could you look, of the sources previously examined, to find the location, population, and general information on manufacturing and industry, if any, for New Tazewell, Tennessee?

21-60   How many islands are there in the Philippine Island group? Can you find information showing the relative size and placement of the major islands? Can you find the location of Calayan Island, in the Philippines? Compare Columbia Lippincott and Webster's.

21-61   In general, does the Columbia Lippincott Gazetteer have maps? Can you locate Calayan Island on any map through the information given in the entry in Columbia Lippincott?

21-62   Where was the ancient country or territory of Phoenicia located? Is there now a geographical area called Phoenicia?

21-63   What are the major differences between the Columbia Lippincott Gazetteer and Webster's New Geographical Dictionary?

21-64   The ALA Glossary defines a gazetteer simply as a geographical dictionary. Is this strictly accurate? For example, can you find in either the Columbia Lippincott or Webster's definitions of such terms as mountain, ocean, pond, sea-level, estuary, desert, topographic?

21-65   Where would you look to find definitions of such terms? For example, where would you look to find out the difference in the use of the word "river" and "stream" to geographers?

21-66   Where is the Mohave Desert located in California, according to the gazetteers? Is that the correct spelling for the name?

21-67   The spelling of geographical names often varies, and problems arise in knowing which is the correct or approved spelling, and in knowing what variants exist under which the place may be listed in a gazetteer or identified on a map. Is there any official way in which such problems are resolved?

21-68   What are the two agencies which are concerned with the problems of variance of spelling of American and English place names? What publications are available which present their decisions?

21-69   Where would you look to find the meaning or origin of the word mojave (or mohave) in the name Mojave Desert?

21-70   The next type of specialized source for geography taken up in Sheehy is the atlas. Atlases will be examined in the next section. The fourth of the specialized sources in Sheehy is the "guidebook." What is the definition of "guidebook" as it is used in this context?

21-71   There are several series of guidebooks available (e.g., Baedeker's, Muirhead's, Nagel's, Fodor's, etc.) noted in Sheehy but Sheehy does not attempt to give specific listings for the individual titles in these series or for guidebooks not published in such series. Is there any specialized bibliographic source for guidebooks?

21-72   If you became intrigued by the Columbia Lippincott Gazetteer's description of Katmandu in Nepal, and you decided you wanted to visit there, where could you find further information on the city, the interesting spots to visit, hotels to stay in, etc.?

21-73   If you were trying to decide whether you should get a Fodor or Nagel or Baedeker guidebook for Great Britain, where would you find some comparative discussion of the information given in each, recency, etc.?

21-74   One of the best known, although very old, series of guidebooks is the American Guide (see Sheehy CL268). This series includes guides to each of the states, as well as some cities and some regions. The next title to examine--California; a Guide to the Golden State--is from this series. When was this guide originally published, and when was the latest revision?

21-75   In what way does this guidebook give information useful to tourists? Can you find out through it whether or not you can visit San Simeon, William Randolph Hearst's former estate? how you get into the movie studios and how you can see the TV programs in Los Angeles? what motels and hotels you can stay at near Disneyland? how old the Golden Gate Bridge is?

21-76   Does this guidebook give any historical background on the state, as well as information of purely current interest?

21-77   Where is the town of Petaluma located within California? Is there any special industry there? What does the name mean?

21-78   If you were planning to visit California, and wanted to do some reading about the state before your trip, would this guidebook be useful to you?

21-79   What is the difference between the information given in a guidebook and that given in a gazetteer? How are guidebooks of use to a library?

21-80   Does the American Guide series' book on California give you room rates for the Ahwanee Hotel in Yosemite National Park?

21-81   Is the Hotel and Motel Red Book a comprehensive listing of all hotels and motels in the world?

21-82   What is the approximate price of a double room in the Concorde Hotel in Tel Aviv?

21-83   Is there a Holiday Inn in Tulsa, Oklahoma?

21-84   If you were planning a meeting of approximately 1,000 people in Los Angeles, what hotels could provide you with a banquet room which would seat all your guests, an auditorium or meeting room which would seat all your members, plus movie and slide projectors and a P.A. system?

21-85   Where would you look to find out train schedules and prices for a trip from Chicago to Los Angeles?

GEOGRAPHICAL SOURCES: GAZETTEERS AND GUIDEBOOKS

Answers #21/1--21/85

21-1: See Contents page. Five major divisions: A, General Reference Works; B, Humanities; C, Social Sciences; D, History and Area Studies; E, Pure and Applied Sciences.

21-2: Under the section for that specific subject; for education, in the major division C for Social Sciences, then in section CB for Education.

21-3: Nearly all have been in the major division A, General Reference Works. A few (especially in the sections on yearbooks and almanacs, handbooks and manuals) have been classified in subject areas; for example, the statistics sources in section 16 under Social Sciences--Statistics.

21-4: In scope, they have covered all (or at least most) of the subject areas. Most of the sources have not been limited to or primarily limited to one subject area, or even one broad subject area such as science. In some of the sections of this manual, you have examined a few examples of specifically subject limited sources, such as American Men and Women of Science and Who's Who in American Art in the biographical sources.

21-5: As a subject area, Section CL, major division of Social Sciences.

21-6: Geographical questions and problems, like biographical questions, are frequently encountered in general library reference work: questions like where is X, how big is Y, how many people are there in Z, what is the climate of A, what is the capital of B, what are the principle cities of C, etc.

Geography is an extremely broad subject field, overlapping, contributing to, and being dependent upon many other subject disciplines, especially in the sciences and social sciences (anthropology, history, geology, mathematics, etc.).

21-7: A general dictionary for a simple basic definition; an encyclopedia for a general

basic discussion. All three major adult encyclopedias have articles on geography.

21-8: You need to know how, or where, a subject is classified in a library collection so that you can know generally where in the building the material itself is located and can be found. The same knowledge will tell you generally where the reference material on a subject field can be found in the library's reference collection.

To find out how the subject is classified in the library, you can check the two basic subject classification schemes used in libraries: Dewey (Dewey Decimal Classification and Relative Index, see Sheehy item AB160) and Library of Congress (Outline of the Library of Congress Classification, plus detailed schedules for each class, see Sheehy AB157).

In LC, for example, geography is classified, with anthropology and recreation, in G--following history (C, D, E and F) and preceding Social Sciences (H) which puts it generally in the area of Social Sciences. The geography categories go from G through GF, including major divisions of geography--general (with such sub-divisions as voyages and travel, adventures/shipwrecks/buried treasure, polar regions, etc.) atlases, maps, mathematical geography, cartography, oceanography, anthropogeography and human ecology.

In Dewey, geography and history are in the last of the 10 major classes (900), general geography being specifically in 910, with divisions for historical geography (911), then atlases and maps, etc. (912), then divisions by area (ancient world, modern Europe, modern Asia, etc.). This classification separates geography from the other social sciences but shows its relationship to history.

21-9: Some of the dictionaries (Webster's 2nd unabridged, for example, but not Webster's 3rd unabridged; especially Random House, etc.).

All of the encyclopedias--articles on major countries and cities, etc., references in the indexes to specific place names. Good pictorial representations of all kinds, including maps. Foreign encyclopedias especially good for information on foreign countries or place names.

Encyclopedia yearbooks to some extent and news summaries to some extent, especially for up-to-date geographical changes, new place names, population figures, etc.

Almanacs have some maps, some specific information and place names (the curiosity and literary handbooks in particular).

As with biography, every source is a potential source of geographical information if only indirectly. For example, a bibliography about Thailand will include sources of geographical information on Thailand.

21-10: No, only a few paragraphs at the beginning of Section CL specifically on library needs in the field.

21-11: For Sheehy's scope, see Preface. Sheehy is selective, not all-inclusive.

21-12: In the opening paragraphs on CL: Geography, Sheehy suggests using "guides." Specifically suggested are Wright and Platt's Aids to Geographical Research and Brewer's The Literature of Geography. These two titles are among the first listed in Sheehy for geography, under "General Works--Guides."

21-13: ALA Glossary has no such entry, and the term is too specialized for general dictionaries. Guides to the literature are basically bibliographic sources, but the most useful guides are more than simply lists of sources; they are also bibliographic guidebooks, handbooks, manuals, giving some information about the subject field and guidance in use of the material.

21-14: See Wright and Platt, Introduction, first paragraph. Purpose: to serve advanced students and professional workers in geography. Scope: observations on the nature of geographical studies, general discussion of published aids to geographical research, selected lists of bibliographies, etc.; not references to primary works but information guiding one to other works which will open up the literature.

The major drawback to Wright and Platt is that it is out-of-date (1947), as

noted by Sheehy. Brewer's The Literature of Geography, 2d ed., 1978, Sheehy 2CL1 (the questions in this manual are based on the 1st ed., 1973), is similar and more recent, but still not quite as good as Wright and Platt as an example of a really classic guide to the literature. Both Wright and Platt and the more up-to-date Brewer will be used here as examples of "guides to the literature" for the field of geography. Remember in using Wright and Platt that the lists of titles of specific sources will be dated; the sources listed there will still exist, but newer sources are now available. The introductory and general materials are generally not dated.

There are other guides to the literature of geography--see Sheehy CL1-CL5.

21-15: See Wright and Platt, Contents, II: Topical Aids (historico-geographical, physical geography, mathematical geography, phytogeography, urban geography, etc.). See Brewer, chap. 1: "Definition." See also the general encyclopedia articles on geography, and to a limited extent, see the Dewey and/or LC classification schemes under geography.

21-16: Wright and Platt: Introduction, sections titled "Field work and indoor work," "Geographical description and interpretation," also "Aids to geographical field research," "Aids to geographical study indoors."

Brewer: chap. 1, section titled "Channels of Communication," also chap. 8, The History of Geography and Geographical Thought, and chap. 9, Geographical Techniques and Methodology.

21-17: Through the use of bibliographic sources. In Wright and Platt: Introduction, section titled "Bibliographic Aids." In Brewer: chap. 1, sections titled "Bibliographic structure" and "Searching the literature."

21-18: Wright and Platt: Introduction; "Classification and arrangement of the material in bibliographic aids." Brewer: chap. 2, The Organization of geographical literature in libraries.

21-19: Wright and Platt: See Introduction, "Guides to collections." Wright and Platt does not give any discussion of use of the card catalog, library classification schemes, reference and circulation policies, etc., which are found in some other literature guides. Also suggested are museums, botanical and zoological gardens. Brewer does discuss card catalogues briefly in chap. 2.

21-20:   Wright and Platt: See Introduction, section titled "Guides to Individuals and Institutions"; see also list of people, institutions, organizations in the Appendix (badly out of date now, of course, but still useful as an example of what kind of information can be found in a guide to the literature). Wright and Platt was published "for the American Geographical Society." Other than what was suggested in #21-16, Brewer does not appear to discuss this in the same way that Wright and Platt does.

21-21:   Wright and Platt: Under General Aids, Geographical Bibliographies: Bibliographies of geographical bibliographies.
     Brewer: chap. 3, section titled "Literature guides and bibliographies of bibliographies." (Note that Brewer, in discussing the datedness of Wright and Platt, comments: "Unfortunately none of the more recent guides is equivalent in terms of either breadth or detailed annotation.")

21-22:   Any bibliographic record with subject access: Subject Guide to Books in Print, American Book Publishing Record, and BPR Cumulative, Subject Guide to Forthcoming Books, Cumulative Book Index, NUC (1983+ subject access), for example.

21-23:   Sheehy--under Geography, Bibliography, Current, lists several, including Current Geographical Publications (CL23), Bibliographie Géographique Internationale (CL24), etc.

21-24:   Ulrich's Periodical Directory; Irregular Serials and Annuals.

21-25:   Those with subject access: American Catalogue and U.S. Catalog (preceding CBI); Evans; American Book Publishing Record back to 1876. (Nothing really very satisfactory prior to the 20th century.)

21-26:   See Sheehy-- Geography, Bibliography, titles listed CL6-CL22. See Wright and Platt, General Aids, Geographical bibliographies, retrospective ... (p. 58+). See Brewer, chap. 3, "Geographical Bibliographies" (p. 39+).

21-27:   Wright and Platt, in the section on "Topical Aids," lists bibliographic

sources under various subjects such as plant geography, agricultural geography, etc. Brewer, in chap. 11 on Human Geography, has a section on population geography which includes bibliographic sources. Sheehy lists under bibliographies, for Geography, only those dealing with the overall subject. Other bibliographies may be found under related subjects, such as agriculture, botany, etc.

21-28:   Ulrich's International Periodicals Directory.

21-29:   Sheehy--Geography, Bibliography, Periodicals, lists two such lists (Harris' Annotated world list of selected current geographical serials in English, French, and German, CL31, and Harris and Fellman's International list of geographical serials, CL32).
     Wright and Platt, and Brewer both give a short list with discussion.

21-30:   Sheehy lists Geo Abstracts (CL27). It is not clear from the annotation whether this includes books, and/or periodical articles or what. Other items noted for question #21-23 include periodical articles as well as books.

21-31:   Try Newsome or Leidy subject guides; neither may have entries for geography as such but should have related entries (maps, travel, surveying, climatology, agriculture, etc.).
     Try U.S. GPO Subject Bibliographies for related topics: maps, states of the U.S. and their resources, national parks, census publications, etc.
     Brewer has a chapter (7) on such publications.

21-32:   Dictionaries, encyclopedias, yearbooks or annuals, handbooks and manuals, directories (organizational and biographical).

21-33:   Check Sheehy, then further check a guide to the literature, such as Wright and Platt or Brewer. Sheehy is sometimes easier to work with since it is organized according to these general types of sources and follows the same pattern you have used for learning the general sources. However, the sources in Sheehy are selective and therefore it may be necessary to use other guides as well. It is also useful to realize that the distinction between the types of sources is not always completely clear, and one guide may classify a title as a handbook while another guide may classify it as a dictionary, etc.

21-34:   Sheehy, under Geography, lists dictionaries and encyclopedias together, making no clear distinction between the two types. There are four titles in English which appear to be limited to technical geographical terms. Annotations for all of them indicate that either Monkhouse's Dictionary of Geography (CL41) or Stamp's Glossary of Geographical Terms (CL35) are probably the fullest.

21-35:   A yearbook or annual of some sort. Sheehy does not list items which clearly fall into this category for geography. A regular encyclopedia yearbook might be helpful. Brewer lists, under "Directories and yearbooks" in chap. 3, the Geographisches Taschenbuch (see Sheehy CL50, under "directories").

21-36:   Sheehy lists one on Deserts of the World (CL45). Wright and Platt list some titles which might fall into this designation under "General Geographical Manuals" (p. 7+). Brewer lists some useful items in chap. 9 on Geographical Techniques and Methodology.

21-37:   Sheehy, under Geography--Directories, lists Orbis Geographicus (CL52), which appears to be a comprehensive directory of organizations, institutions, and people in the field, and is updated periodically. Another title, Geographisches Taschenbuch (CL50), listed under Directories is called a handbook in the annotation, and appears every two years with reports of expeditions, etc., so could serve as a yearbook type of source for current developments. It also lists organizations and people.

21-38:   Sheehy lists nothing which quite does this, at least currently. You could consider a broader scope--e.g., social sciences. See section CA in Sheehy, Social Sciences--General--Biography, which refers you to American Men of Science which includes persons in the social sciences as well as the physical and biological sciences, and as such specifically includes geographers. (It will not however give you access to those persons working in geography unless you know their names.)

21-39:   Following the section headed "General Works," listing guides, bibliographies,

dictionaries and encyclopedias, handbooks, and directories, Sheehy lists: Gazetteers (General, then U.S., then by country); Geographical names and terms (the same); Atlases (with extensive sub-divisions); Guidebooks (basically only general and U.S.).

21-40:   See ALA Glossary, or a regular dictionary, or the paragraph in Sheehy (p. 576-7) under "Gazetteers," or the first paragraph of the Preface to the next source to examine, the Columbia Lippincott Gazetteer.

21-41:   Scope is "of the world." The word Gazetteer in the title, meaning dictionary of geographical place names, indicates that its arrangement will probably be (dictionary-type) in one alphabetical list.

21-42:   The Columbia Lippincott Gazetteer was published in 1952, with a 1961 supplement added to the back of the volume in the 1962 printing. See Sheehy (CL56); see title page, verso of title page, and page facing title page of the source. Some geographical information will remain the same but much will change.

21-43:   All are included except Botswana, an independent African nation established in 1966 and therefore too recent for even the 1961 supplement of Columbia Lippincott. Mount Kilimanjaro is entered as Kilimanjaro. The gazetteer lists not only names of countries and cities and towns, but all geographical features, such as rivers, oceans, deserts, waterfalls, etc., also historical features such as Stonehenge.

21-44:   The entry, under Aiea, lists it as population 3,714, located in Oahu, T.H. T.H. stands for Territory of Hawaii (see abbreviations list in front matter), which immediately shows it is out of date. The front matter also lists a "key to population figures" which shows, under Hawaii, that 1950 figures have been used.

21-45:   Yes, in the 1961 supplement. There is no entry for Aiea as such. The entry for Hawaii in the supplement brings it to statehood (1959). A list of 1960 Census population figures for U.S. cities, arranged by state, is also given in the supplement; here you can find Aiea with 11,826 population in 1960.

21-46: 1980 Census; try 1981 or later almanacs
        for latest census figures.

21-47: See Preface. Columbia Lippincott claims
        to list all U.S. cities and incorporated
        towns listed in the 1950 census; the 1960
        census list in the supplement is limited
        to places of 1,000 or more population.

21-48: Since a gazetteer is defined generally
        as a geographical dictionary, Webster's,
        by its title, falls into the category of
        gazetteer. It was last published in 1980
        and according to the Preface, "the limita-
        tions of revisions and the magnitude of
        change made it desirable to review critical-
        ly the entire work and recompose the book."

21-49: G. and C. Merriam Co., publishers of
        Webster's Third New International Dic-
        tionary, Webster's New Dictionary of
        Synonyms, Webster's Biographical Dic-
        tionary.

21-50: Geographical information in Webster's
        Second is given in a special list called
        a Pronouncing Gazetteer. No geograph-
        ical information is given in Webster's
        Third at all unless a proper name is used
        as an adjective.

21-51: See Preface. Stresses United States and
        Canada. Has specific minimum population
        figures (varies with the country) for
        inclusion, with some exceptions; U.S.
        cities must have 2,500+ population.

21-52: Botswana has a full entry with map.
        Aiea is listed with population of 12,560
        (1970 census figures). Zimbabwe, the
        site of ruins, is listed; Zimbabwe, the
        correct name of the country, is listed
        with a cross-reference to the article on
        Rhodesia (the name of the country until
        1979). (© 1980.)

21-53: Webster's New Geographical Dictionary
        (© 1980) under Sequatchie, refers to "ta-
        ble" at Tennessee; under Tennessee,
        table lists all counties of the state and
        gives their county seat. (Columbia Lip-
        pincott gives name of county seat in entry
        for Sequatchie County.)

21-54: Columbia Lippincott gives a much more
        extensive description than Webster's of
        its background, the temples, palaces,
        and pilgrimage sites there. Webster's
        merely locates it. Columbia Lippincott
        gives its population according to 1920
        figures; Webster's (© 1980) lists popula-
        tion figures from a 1971 preliminary cen-
        sus.

21-55: Try recent almanacs, Statesman's Year-
        Book.

21-56: Not in Webster's (too small). In Colum-
        bia Lippincott. Macaroni manufacturing.
        Population given is 2,705, but since
        this is for the 1936 census (see "Key to
        Population Figures" in front) this is hard-
        ly reliable at this point.

21-57: Northernmost island of Japan, Hokkaido.
        Webster's has cross-references to Hok-
        kaido from both Yezo and Yeso. Colum-
        bia has cross-reference from Yezo only.

21-58: Columbia Lippincott entry explains that
        the island was called Yezo (and varia-
        tions on that), then renamed Hokkaido
        following restoration of imperial power
        (1968). Webster's gives similar informa-
        tion.

21-59: Try Ayer's Directory of Publications
        (see section 5), which includes descrip-
        tions of all the places in which the news-
        papers listed are published.

21-60: Both Columbia Lippincott and Webster's
        have an entry for the Philippine Islands
        and give the number of islands. Colum-
        bia Lippincott has discussion about the
        relative size and placement of the is-
        lands, but only Webster's has a map (on
        page 948 of the 1980 edition, and ap-
        parently not referred to in the article
        itself on pages 946-7) which gives that
        information easily and visually. Calayan
        Island (north of Luzon) can be located
        on the Webster's map. Both Columbia
        Lippincott and Webster's also have a
        separate entry for Calayan Island tell-
        ing where it is located, but only through
        the map in Webster's can you see its
        location.

21-61: Columbia Lippincott has no maps; Web-
        ster's has some. The entry in Columbia
        Lippincott for Calayan Island gives geo-
        graphical coordinates (latitude and longi-
        tude) which would allow you to locate
        it on other maps in other sources.

21-62: Phoenicia is not a meaningful geographi-
        cal name for the modern world, but
        both Columbia Lippincott and Webster's
        have entries for it giving its meaning
        in historical terms.

21-63: Columbia is larger, has more entries and
        tends to give more information for en-
        tries. Webster's is more selective in
        entries, primarily directed to American
        users. Webster's is more up-to-date;

Columbia is out-of-date in many respects. Columbia is more expensive. Webster's has maps.

21-64: No. These gazetteers are more accurately called dictionaries of places. They list only place names and define only actual place names. They do not define technical terms in the field.

21-65: Use a technical dictionary (see answer to #21-34). For example, A Glossary of Geographical Terms, edited by Sir Dudley Stamp (Sheehy CL35), under "river," gives the definition according to the OED and Webster's, then comments on these definitions according to geographical usage.

21-66: Both Columbia Lippincott and Webster's give cross references from Mohave Desert to Mojave Desert. Webster's indicates that both spellings are permissible, but Mojave preferred. Columbia Lippincott lists other place names, similar in location, for which the spelling Mohave is apparently preferred.

21-67: See Preface to Columbia Lippincott Gazetteer which discusses this problem. The second group of specialized geographical sources in Sheehy--Geographical Names and Terms--deals with this area. It is also discussed in Wright and Platt in the section titled "Spelling of Geographical Names" (see table of contents).

21-68: United States Board on Geographic Names; for publications see Sheehy CL118/19. Permanent Committee on Geographical Names for British Official Use; for publications see Sheehy CL115/116/117. (Also in Wright and Platt, p. 78+, with more information and some references to periodical articles explaining the work of these agencies.)

21-69: Sometimes the origins or meanings of words used in place names will be given in dictionaries, especially if the name is a commonly used one or if the word is used in other ways than just as a place name. Origins may be given in gazetteers. Some meanings or origins are given in the place name "decisions" lists put out by the U.S. Board on Geographic Names. In addition, there are specialized sources which exist just to describe place names in terms of their meaning or origin. These are listed in Sheehy specifically by country, following the general sources which give official decisions on place names. Sheehy gives no source specifically for

California, but does list American Place Names by Stewart (CL123), which would answer this question. Another possibility is bibliographic: Sealock, Sealock and Powell's Bibliography of Place-Name Literature (CL120; 3d ed. published in 1982), which might lead you to a source which would answer the question. "Mohave/mojave" can also be found in Mathews' Dictionary of Americanisms (see Section 13).

21-70: See ALA Glossary. See also a general dictionary, since guidebook in this sense is a very common word. Sheehy does not specifically define the term, other than to indicate that guidebooks are prepared specifically for travelers or tourists.

21-71: See Sheehy under "Guidebooks--Bibliography": Neal's Reference Guide for Travelers, published in 1969 (CL267), Nueckel's Selected Guide to Travel Books, published in 1974 (1CL68). A newer such source is Heise and O'Reilly's Travel Book: Guide to the Travel Guides, published by Bowker in 1981.

21-72: A guidebook for Nepal should do this. See Neal or Nueckel for possibilities.

21-73: Sheehy is a little help (see general paragraphs preceding list of guidebooks, 9th ed., p. 595-6). Neal may be of more help here, although now outdated. An even better way would be to examine these guidebook series yourself, to see which gave the general information you wanted, and which most appealed to you in format, style, etc. If possible, locate and examine one or two examples from these series. A bookstore or a public library is probably one of the easier places in which to do this.

21-74: Originally published 1939, complete revision 1967 (see verso of title page).

21-75: The guidebook does give this type of information, which you can find most easily through checking the index (for San Simeon, Disneyland, Golden Gate Bridge). The information on the movie and TV studios is not indexed, and can be found in the chapter on the city of Hollywood, rather than in the chapter on Los Angeles. This guidebook does not attempt to offer detailed information on motels, accommodations, prices, opening times, etc., thus it does not become dated as quickly as those guidebooks which rely heavily on this type of tourist information.

21-76:   Yes, much historical background is given,
          one of the especially useful features of
          the American Guide series; see Part I:
          California, from past to present.

21-77:   See index for reference to specific infor-
          mation.

21-78:   Yes, extensive lists of further reading;
          see Appendices. A more recent guide
          that one would expect to have some trav-
          el information on California is Posts'
          Travel in the United States: A Guide
          to Information Sources (Detroit, Gale
          Research, 1981).

21-79:   See Sheehy, paragraphs preceding the
          list of guidebooks (9th ed., p. 595-6).

21-80:   The Ahwanee Hotel is mentioned (see in-
          dex) but no room rates, times, etc.,
          given. For this information, the next ti-
          tle, the Hotel and Motel Red Book, would
          be useful.

21-81:   No, only members of the American Hotel
          and Motel Association. See "How to use
          RED BOOK ..." on p. T2 of the 1983-84
          ed.

21-82:   Hotel and Motel Red Book: Near & Mid-
          dle East, then Israel, then Tel Aviv,
          then Concorde Hotel; prices given; ad-
          vertisement is noted (1983-84 edition, p.
          912).

21-83:   Yes, see Hotel and Motel Red Book un-
          der Oklahoma, then Tulsa.

21-84:   See Hotel and Motel Red Book, "Meeting
          Planners Guide" section, using index
          under California, then Los Angeles.

21-85:   The Official Guide of the Railways (Shee-
          hy CL272), which is published eight
          times a year, gives schedules and prices
          for all trains in the United States, in-
          cluding commuter railroads, plus for Can-
          ada, Mexico, and selected European coun-
          tries. Sheehy also lists a similar source
          for airlines (see "Timetables," 9th ed.,
          p. 596).

Section 22

GEOGRAPHICAL SOURCES: ATLASES

Questions #22/1--22/85

22-1   How would you go about determining who wrote the following: "As soon as men begin to talk about anything that really matters, someone has to go and get the atlas?"

Atlases are a very specialized type of reference source which can provide a wealth of information, both general and geographical, if carefully used. The atlases listed here for examination in this section are only a selection of many available:

>   Rand McNally Cosmopolitan World Atlas (CL219, 2CL39)
>   Hammond Medallion World Atlas (CL207, 2CL35)
>   Goode's World Atlas (CL204)
>   Rand McNally Commercial Atlas & Marketing Guide (CL218a)
>   Times Atlas of the World, Comprehensive ed. (CL201, 1CL53, 2CL40)
>   Times Index-Gazetteer of the World (CL57)

22-2   What is an atlas?

22-3   What are the criteria on which you should judge an atlas? What things should you look for in examining an atlas?

22-4   Since an atlas is basically a collection of maps, it is also helpful to have some understanding of maps in general. What is a map? Is there any difference between "map" and "chart"? Where would you look to find the origin of the word "map"?

22-5   What is cartography?

22-6   If you wanted to get some background information on maps and map-making--for example, if you were a librarian suddenly put in charge of a collection of maps and/or geographical material-- where would you go for help?

22-7   What types of maps are available? What can be shown by means of a map?

22-8   The first atlas to be examined is the Rand McNally Cosmopolitan World Atlas, published by Rand McNally and Company in Chicago. One of the items you have checked for in nearly every source examined is the date of the source, to know how current the information is and how frequently it is revised. What is the date of the atlas you are examining? What is the revision policy for the Cosmopolitan?

22-9   What is the scope of this atlas, according to its title and according to the table of contents? It is published in the United States; is it an atlas only for the United States?

22-10   How much of this atlas is devoted to the United States? How does this compare with the space given to the rest of the world?

22-11   Although world-wide in scope, half of this atlas is devoted to coverage of the United States. Is this surprising?

22-12   What is the general arrangement in this atlas? Is it alphabetical? Is the map for Alaska between that for Africa and that for Australia?

22-13   What kind of maps are found in the Cosmopolitan World Atlas? Can you find a map which shows the political boundaries of Laos? Can you find a relief map showing elevation and mountainous areas of Laos? Can you find a map which shows population density of Laos? How are these maps grouped? Are all the various kinds of maps dealing with Laos or Asia grouped together?

22-14   What are map projections? Are these explained in this atlas?

22-15   On the political map of Cambodia, Laos, etc., is the type of map projection used indicated? Could you find out through the atlas how this particular projection is formed?

22-16   Why is it important to realize the type of projection used in a map and to know how the projection is formed?

22-17   On this same map, is the scale indicated? What is meant by "scale" in maps? In what ways can the scale of a map be represented or indicated?

22-18   The scale of the map of Cambodia and Laos, etc., is 1:8,000,000. The scale of the map following, of India and Pakistan, etc., is 1:16,000,000. Is the scale of the map for Cambodia larger or smaller than that of the map of India? Is the map of Cambodia therefore more detailed or less detailed than the map of India?

22-19   Locate the map for Rhode Island in the Cosmopolitan. Is the scale of that map larger (and therefore capable of being more detailed) than the map of Laos?

22-20   Is there anything in the Cosmopolitan by which you can compare Laos to Rhode Island in size, in area?

22-21   Can you also compare the population? Are dates given for the population figures? Is anything shown to indicate the source of all this information?

22-22   Are the maps themselves, in the Cosmopolitan, dated? How can you tell if they have been revised
         or brought up to date in any way?

22-23   How would you go about locating New Tazewell, Tennessee on a map in this atlas?

22-24   On the same map, locate the town of Rutledge, just south of New Tazewell. Is this town larger or
         smaller than New Tazewell? What is the name of the railroad line which runs through New Tazewell?
         What is the name of the river which runs north of New Tazewell?

22-25   What is the population of New Tazewell? What is the source of these figures?

22-26   Does the index of the Cosmopolitan World Atlas include all the names which appear on all of the maps
         within the atlas? Does it include any names not appearing on the maps within the atlas?

22-27   Does the Cosmopolitan World Atlas consist only of maps and an index to those maps?

22-28   Is this additional information available only in the atlas or is it available also in other sources?

22-29   In general, what or who does the Cosmopolitan cite as its authority/ies? Does it list editors or
         consultants? Does it cite or acknowledge sources?

22-30   Another atlas similar in scope, size, etc., to the Rand McNally Cosmopolitan, and published by
         another well-known mapping company, is the Hammond Medallion World Atlas. How recent is this
         atlas? Can you tell anything about its revision policies? Are the maps dated? Is Botswana or
         Zimbabwe included?

22-31   What is the scope of the Hammond Medallion World Atlas? How much of it, comparatively, is
         devoted to the United States?

22-32   Does the Hammond Medallion atlas include political, physical, and topical maps? How are the maps
         arranged? Is it similar in arrangement to the Rand McNally Cosmopolitan? Look at the maps for
         Alaska and for Brazil, for example.

22-33   Is there a map in the Hammond Medallion showing population distribution for the world?

22-34   What is the scale of the political map which shows Laos? How does it compare to that in the Cos-
         mopolitan?

22-35   Is the projection of the map indicated? Is that type of projection explained in the atlas itself?

22-36   There are indexes for each separate political map in Hammond's Medallion atlas. Is there a cumu-
         lated or general index?

22-37   Can you locate New Tazewell, Tennessee, in this atlas? Is the population given?

22-38   Once you have located New Tazewell, on the Tennessee map (method similar to that used in Cosmopolitan), do you see any differences between the maps in the Hammond Medallion and those in the Cosmopolitan?

22-39   Does the atlas give any sources for the information it includes, such as population figures and other statistics?

22-40   Does Hammond's Medallion atlas have supplementary gazetteer or encyclopedia information as the Cosmopolitan does?

22-41   The next atlas to examine, Goode's World Atlas, is an example of a school atlas that is also useful because of its handier size. Who is the publisher of Goode's?

22-42   Presumably then Rand McNally maps are used, probably some of those included in the Cosmopolitan. What would have to be done to the Cosmopolitan maps if they were to be used in Goode's (or vice versa)?

22-43   What is the revision policy for Goode's?

22-44   To be useful as a school atlas, what would you expect this particular atlas to stress?

22-45   Does Goode's provide these things? How does it compare with the Cosmopolitan in this respect?

22-46   Does Goode's have a general index? Are population figures included? Is any special information included? How are the places located on the maps?

22-47   Does Goode's contain a lot of supplementary or encyclopedic type information?

22-48   Does Goode's stress the United States as much as the Cosmopolitan does?

22-49   The next atlas is an example of a rather specialized atlas, and one which is extremely useful for its very detailed coverage of the United States--the Rand McNally Commercial Atlas and Marketing Guide. What is the scope of the Commercial Atlas? How much of it is U.S.? Is there any world coverage?

22-50   What is the purpose of the Commercial Atlas?

22-51   How up to date is the Commercial Atlas? How is it kept up to date?

22-52   What information does the Commercial Atlas give you about cities and towns in the U.S.? See sample index entry in the introductory material (for the 6th section, page 114 of the 1983 ed.).

22-53   What else can you find out about New Tazewell, Tennessee, through the Commercial Atlas? How does this compare to what you could find in the Ayer Director of Publications (see #21-59)?

22-54   What is the date of the population figures given in the Commercial Atlas?

22-55   The last atlas to examine, but by no means the least, is the Times Atlas of the World, Comprehensive Edition. Where was this atlas published? Who made the maps?

22-56   When was this atlas last published and what is its previous history?

22-57   What is the scope of this atlas? What is the coverage given to the United States? Is there a full map for California? Where was this atlas originally published?

22-58   How is the atlas arranged?

22-59   Does the Contents list in this atlas give you any information that is helpful in making comparisons of the maps themselves, without even seeing the maps?

22-60   Can you find a map for Perth, Australia which shows Guildford Road and locates the Parliament House?

22-61   How does the map for London compare with that for Paris? for New York City?

22-62   Can you locate the British Museum on the map of London?

22-63   Locate the map for Laos. Are both political and physical maps given? How does the scale compare with that of the other atlases? Is the projection given?

22-64   Are the projections and scales explained in the atlas?

22-65   Is New Tazewell, Tennessee, found in the Times Atlas?

22-66   Could you find New Tazewell, Tennessee, on a map in the Cosmopolitan Atlas from the information given in the index of the Times Atlas?

22-67   One of the problems with the five-volume Mercury Edition of the Times Atlas was that each of the five volumes had its own index and there was no cumulative or general index for the entire atlas. This was remedied in 1965 when the Times Publishing Company put out the Times Index-Gazetteer of the World. Although this is a gazetteer, and so listed in Sheehy, it is being examined here in conjunction with the atlases because it differs considerably in scope and use from the other gazetteers. In what way does it differ?

22-68   What is the purpose of giving latitude and longitude?

22-69   The Times Index-Gazetteer thus serves as an index to any atlas or any map. Where is Guy Fawkes located?

22-70   Does the Times Index-Gazetteer list Botswana? Zimbabwe? Rhodesia? Timbuktu? Brussels, Belgium? Stonehenge? Phoenicia?

22-71   How many place names are given in the Times Index-Gazetteer? How does this compare with other sources, such as the Columbia Lippincott Gazetteer? the Times Atlas?

22-72   Honey Creek, Wisconsin, is listed in the Times Index-Gazetteer but not shown on the Times Atlas maps. Can you locate it on a map in any of the other atlases? Would you expect that it would not be indexed in the other atlases?

22-73   Is there an atlas devoted specifically to the Philipppines?

22-74   Are there any bibliographic sources for atlases? for maps? Where would you look to find them?

22-75   Are there any sources which evaluate atlases comparatively as with encyclopedias?

22-76   What is a globe? What is the particular usefulness of a globe as compared to maps?

The following questions can be used as REVIEW for the geographical sources.

22-77   Where is Clayton, Missouri, and how big is it?

22-78   Pitcairn Island is in the Pacific Ocean, and is about two miles long. Where can you find a map of it which shows the location of Bounty Bay and Pt. Christian?

22-79   Where can you find a pictorial representation of the world's climates?

22-80   What is a Mercator projection?

22-81   Where would you look to find the names and addresses and price ranges of some places to stay overnight in Kennebunkport, Maine?

22-82   Where can you find a map showing major military installations in the entire United States--that is, a map which will show you clearly where such installations are concentrated?

22-83   What does the word "holm" mean in the name of the city Stockholm (Sweden)?

22-84   Is Niagara Falls the biggest waterfall in the world?

22-85   Where could you find a map showing the location of the Bibliothèque Nationale in Paris and some information on what hours it is open during the summer?

GEOGRAPHICAL SOURCES: ATLASES

Answers #22/1--22/85

22-1: Quotation books. Rudyard Kipling wrote it.

22-2: See ALA Glossary, or any dictionary, or technical dictionary in geography (question #21-34).

22-3: See Sheehy, outline guide for examining atlases, in paragraphs preceding list of atlases (9th ed., p. 587).

22-4: See ALA Glossary on map and chart for library-related definition. See any dictionary. See technical dictionary for geography (as in #21-34). For origin, see Oxford English Dictionary. (A Glossary of Geographical Terms, edited by Stamp, quotes OED on origin as well as giving definition.)

22-5: See any dictionary.

22-6: Start with one or more articles from the general encyclopedias. Wright and Platt has some rather specialized information (p. 83+). Follow up bibliographic references in encyclopedias for further reading. Find some periodicals (through Ulrich's?) which deal with the subject and make a habit of perusing them from time to time.

22-7: Wright and Platt divides them into locational (those with which most people are familiar) and topical (those which show specialized aspects such as population, railways, resources, vegetation, climate, etc.).
 Locational maps are also called political (showing boundaries and places); or physical or topographic (showing landforms, physical features, relief, etc.).
 Topical maps are also called thematic maps. Atlases which are devoted to specific and specialized themes (such as a climatological atlas) are found in the subject areas.

22-8: The date should be given on the title page and/or the verso of the title page in the copyright statement. Rand Mc-

Nally and Company has been publishing atlases under the general name of "Cosmopolitan World Atlas" since 1949 (see Sheehy). A new edition came out in 1971 and is discussed in the Sheehy annotation (CL219). It would appear that, as with other major and expensive reference sources kept in print over a period of years, this publication has had some moderate form of continuous revision with some up-dating in new printings. Other new editions came out in 1978 (2CL39) and 1981 and are basically very similar to the 1971 edition. Information has been up-dated in the latest editions. The 1981 edition is subtitled the Census Edition and contains some 1980 U.S. Census data. The 1971, 1978, or the 1981 edition can be used for these questions. Note in the Sheehy annotation that Rand McNally has published a series of other atlases of varying sizes derived from the Cosmopolitan. Another Rand McNally atlas, the New International Atlas (2CL37), not part of the Cosmopolitan series, is also highly recommended.

22-9: World Atlas, Contents lists the world, Europe, Asia, Africa, etc., as well as the United States.

22-10: You can tell this most easily from the table of contents. The atlas contains approximately 125 pages of "World Reference Maps," of which about half are devoted to North America and all but 15 pages of that to the United States. The same general proportion of U.S. to world information is true for the other sections of the atlas.

22-11: It shouldn't be by now, since nearly all the reference sources you have examined here--even though worldwide or universal in scope--tended to emphasize information for the country in which they were published. This "bias" is probably most easily seen in the atlases.

22-12: See Contents. Not alphabetical. Maps are grouped by geographical regions. World first, then Europe (including individual maps for British Isles, Italy, etc.), Asia (including regional maps of two to five countries), etc. Maps for individual states are grouped under the United States which is under North America.

22-13: Cosmopolitan has political and physical maps. The major map section consists of political maps and includes under Asia a map showing Cambodia (Kampuchea in the 1981 ed.), Laos, Vietnam, Thailand, and Malaysia together, giving political boundaries and locations of cities and towns, etc. In the 1971 edition, a shorter set of physical maps emphasizing landforms (mountains, etc.) follows the political maps. In the 1978 and 1981 editions these are the "environment maps" preceding the political maps. There are no topical or thematic maps, and no map showing population density in Laos. The 1978 and 1981 editions include U.S. travel maps.

22-14: Map projections are ways by which the earth's curved surface is portrayed on a flat (map) surface. See Contents for reference to the pages in the Cosmopolitan introductory section in which projections are explained and illustrated.

22-15: Projection indicated at the bottom of the page of the map; types of projections discussed and illustrated in the introductory material of the atlas. This specific projection is included.

22-16: To understand the extent to which distortion may occur in the map.

22-17: Scale is the relationship of the size of an area on the map to the area it represents. It also is discussed in the introductory material to the Cosmopolitan World Atlas. It can be represented or stated in three ways:
        fractional or numerical, or sometimes called natural: 1:8,000,000;
        written or word: 1 inch = 126 statute miles;
        graphic or linear or bar: divisions of the bar showing the stated distance.
The scale on the map in the Cosmopolitan is shown in all three ways.

22-18: As the lower number of the fraction decreases, the scale becomes larger. As the scale becomes larger, the amount of detail which can be given increases. The scale of the map for Cambodia is larger than that for India, therefore more detail can be given in the map for Cambodia. This can be seen visually also, since part of Laos and most of Thailand appear in the far right side of the map of India and Pakistan, etc., and they are obviously smaller than they appear in the map which features them.

22-19: The map for Rhode Island is on the same page as the map for Connecticut, and therefore not in alphabetical order and is most easily located by using the Table of Contents. The scale for the Rhode Island map is larger (1:731,000 or 1 inch=11.5 statute miles) than that for Laos (1:8,000,000).

22-20: See World Political Information Table, following the maps. Laos is listed as 91,429 square miles; Rhode Island as 1,214 square miles.

22-21: Total population and population density (per square mile) are also given. Populations figures are "estimated"; nothing is said about what this estimate is based on. No source is indicated for any of the information.

22-22: No, the maps themselves are not dated. You can check for revisions and updating only if you know something significant you can check for. For example, look at the map of Africa to see if Botswana (new name as of 1966) is shown. Is Nauru (in the South Pacific) shown as an independent nation (as of 1968)? Is Tonga (also in the South Pacific) shown as a member of the British Commonwealth (as of 1970)? Is East Pakistan shown as Bangladesh? Is Rhodesia shown as Zimbabwe (as of 1979)? The National Geographic Atlas of the World (Sheehy CL211, 1CL54), another recommended atlas, provides its buyers with a yearly update supplement which might indicate these kinds of changes.

22-23: Turn to general index of place names in back, alphabetical, find New Tazewell, Tennessee, which refers you to "C10, 117." For help in interpreting this, see "Explanation of the Index and Abbreviations" just preceding the index. The page number of the map is 117. The location on the map is C10; the letters are given on the right side (the C somewhat obliterated by the map in this instance) and the numbers along the top of the middle section (Tennessee being split in half in order to get it on the page). Follow C across and 10 down and then poke about a bit for New Tazewell, somewhat to the southwest of the C10 intersection.

22-24: Rutledge and New Tazewell are both represented by dots of approximately the same size, but Rutledge is an open circle. To discover the significance of this, it is necessary to turn back to the introductory section which explains "Map Symbols" and the index reference system. This tells you that dots of the same size represent the same sized cities or towns and that an open dot is a county seat. The railroad is shown but not identified on this map, and the river is the Powell River. The features noted in light blue letters are not easily read.

22-25: Population figures for cities, towns, counties, and states in a special section following the U.S. maps. The source of the figures in the 1981 edition is the 1980 U.S. Census.

22-26: See "Explanation of the Index and Abbreviations." Only "important" names from the maps are given. Some names are included that were not on the maps, signified by an *.

22-27: No, there is a large section of "Geographical Facts, Figures and Information about the World and the United States." (This is divided into a U.S. section and a world section in the 1981 edition.)

22-28: It is also available (although in different forms) in other sources--encyclopedias, almanacs, statistical sources, for example; also in gazetteers and guidebooks.

22-29: No editors or consultants listed. Sources cited (see Introduction) only in the most general way. The U.S. Census is generally referred to for U.S. population figures. Apparently, the publisher's name is to be considered the primary authority for this work.

22-30: Hammond published new editions of the Medallion World Atlas in 1971, 1979, and 1982. Some sort of moderate form of continuous revision or up-dating appears to be practiced; maps are not dated, but some up-dating has been done. See Botswana in the 1971 and 1979 editions; and Zimbabwe in the 1979 edition. Note in the Bhooly annotation (CL207) for

the Medallion atlas that Hammond, like Rand McNally, publishes a series of atlases of varying sizes with the same general content as the Medallion; the Ambassador version is specifically noted.

22-31: Scope is world wide. Of 324 pages of maps, over 130 pages, or at least one-third, are devoted to the United States.

22-32: The types of maps included are not clear from the Contents, although the arrangement is. It is strictly geographical, the world first, then Europe, then Asia, etc. This is similar to the New Cosmopolitan.
      Looking at the map(s) for Brazil (South America), you find 4 pages, including a political map, a topographic (physical) map, a topical map showing agriculture, industry and resources, plus detailed maps for the capital city, and southeastern area, a highway map for that area, an index for states, cities, towns, general area, population, etc., information for the country, a picture of the flag, and an indication of where Brazil is in relation to the rest of South America. The same general plan is followed for Alaska. Thus, the Hammond Medallion atlas does include political, physical, topical (some) maps, and they are grouped together by area.

22-33: Not on a world-wide basis. It is shown for general regions, such as Europe (p. 7), Asia, etc.

22-34: Map for Burma, Thailand, Indochina, and Malaya, p. 73-4. The scale of the political map is shown in the linear bar only and is somewhat difficult to compare with the Cosmopolitan without actually measuring the two bars. (The scale is approximately the same.)

22-35: Type of projection noted on the map. Projection discussed following the index, p. 475+.

22-36: General index, called "World Index" or "Index of the World," at end of map section. It includes names not found in the individual indexes, and presumably all those found in the individual indexes.

22-37: New Tazewell, Tennessee, is listed in the world index and in the individual index for Tennessee. Population given only in the individual index, not in the general index. Zip code given in both.

22-38:   Hammond Medallion is easier to distin-
         guish county boundaries, easier to read
         name of river; but at the same time
         less information is given--railroad line
         not indicated, for example.

22-39:   See Gazetteer-Index of the World in the
         front, which is an attempt to give
         sources but not specific enough to be
         much help. Slightly more specific sources
         are listed in "Sources and Acknowledgments."
         It does however, indicate whether figures
         are from official censuses or otherwise,
         and the date.

22-40:   Yes, but not as much. Some terms,
         distance table, statistics at the end of
         the atlas. Some of this type of informa-
         tion given with each set of maps for each
         country or state.

22-41:   Rand McNally and Company, publishers
         of Cosmopolitan. In fact, the atlas is
         often cited as Rand McNally Goode's
         World Atlas.

22-42:   Reduced in size to fit pages (or vice
         versa).

22-43:   More or less continuous revision. See
         verso of title page for list of copyright
         dates. Sheehy annotation says "frequent-
         ly revised."

22-44:   General information on how to use an at-
         las and maps. Topical or thematic maps
         showing rainfall, population, resources,
         vegetation, trade, transportation, etc.

22-45:   Yes. Introduction is good and covers a
         lot of needed general information on pro-
         jections and scale, etc. Extensive topical
         or thematic maps for the entire world.
         Cosmopolitan had nothing in the way of
         thematic maps.

22-46:   Yes, there is a general index in the
         back. Population figures not given.
         Some pronunciation given. Places are
         located by giving page of map, and geo-
         graphical coordinates (latitude and
         longitude).

22-47:   Very little in comparison to the Cosmo-
         politan, for example. Some comparisons
         (islands, mountains, etc.), principle
         countries with area and population, glos-
         sary of foreign geographical terms.

22-48:   No, more on rest of the world.

22-49:   Most of it is U.S. There is some world
         coverage but not nearly as much as in

the other atlases you have been examining. Maps for other parts of the world
appear to be mostly for simple reference.

22-50:   Purpose is perhaps best given in the
         title--commercial atlas and marketing
         guide. According to the Introduction,
         it "... brings current economic and geo-
         graphic information together in a refer-
         ence work designed to provide both max-
         imum statistical coverage and authorita-
         tive interpretation of business data.
         The atlas employs maps, tables, and
         charts for the presentation of materials."
         Primarily for business firms who need
         information on the best market areas
         for particular types of goods, what kind
         of supply routes (post offices, railroads,
         etc.) are available, where the shopping
         is done, what the size of the population
         is, what type of people live there (col-
         lege age, military families, etc.).

22-51:   Annual revision (see cover and title
         page, also see Sheehy annotation). Li-
         braries "subscribe" to this atlas; this
         is actually a rental system--the atlas
         belongs to Rand McNally and is returned
         to them each year and a new revised
         issue received (see front cover).

22-52:   Sample entry in the 1983 edition is for
         the hypothetical city of Rand and in-
         dicates the extensive information given
         in this atlas. In this way, it is similar
         to a gazetteer and in fact goes beyond
         the information given in most gazetteers
         for small places.

22-53:   The index entry (1983 ed.) tells you
         that it is in Claiborne County, has a
         post office, at least one bank, is incor-
         porated, can be located (E-20) on the
         map of Tennessee, the zip code is 37825,
         the elevation is 1,472 ft., 449 m. and
         the population is 1,192 (1980). Refer
         to the sample entry as noted in #22-52
         and to the code at the bottom of the
         page for the entry for New Tazewell.
         Information is similar to what you might
         find in Ayer's.

22-54:   See Introduction and Explanation. In
         addition to figures from the 1980 cen-
         sus, it provides estimates of population
         beyond the 1980 figures, thus it is al-
         ways reasonably up to date.

22-55:   Published in the U.S. by Times Books.
         Maps by John Bartholomew and Son,
         Ltd., Edinburgh (verso of title page).

22-56:   1983. For history, see Foreword or

Sheehy annotation. Based on the five-volume edition called the Midcentury Edition, published 1955-59. The Comprehensive Edition, in one volume, was first published in 1967.

22-57: Scope is world-wide. The United States gets about 12 plates out of 123, much less in proportion than in other atlases you have examined. There is no state map for California. California is shown in two two-page maps for Pacific Coast. (Texas and Alaska do each have double-page spreads, however.) This is not an American-made atlas. It was originally published in Great Britain.

22-58: Similarly to most of the other atlases: by geographical area (world, followed by Orient, etc.). All maps including thematic or topical maps for an area are together.

22-59: The Contents list gives the scales of the maps as well as the plate numbers, so that you can make an instant comparison of the general coverage you can expect to get. For example, the map of the U.S. is 1/12,500,000; those for the northwest, southeast, etc., regions are all at 1/2,500,000, showing much more detail.

22-60: Inset map for Perth (scale 1/250,000) on plate for Australia West.

22-61: London and environs, scale of 1/100,000. Paris the same. New York City smaller (1/250,000). See Contents.

22-62: Only if you know where to look for it. It is shown on the map. It is not indexed, however.

22-63: See list of States, Territories, and Principal Islands of the World in the front; lists Laos, map at plate 25. Scale is 1/5,000,000--larger than Cosmopolitan or Medallion. Projection (Mercator) is given.
    Maps in Times are physical or topographic with political (boundaries, cities, etc.) overlaid.

22-64: No, not as in the other atlases you have examined.

22-65: See index, on map plate 105, locator reference D1.

22-66: Yes. Times Index gives geographical coordinates (latitude and longitude) which can be used on any map which shows latitude and longitude

22-67: See Foreword. Intentionally not a descriptive gazetteer-index. Purpose is comprehensive, quick, handy locational guide. Place names only give larger area (i.e., country, state, etc.) plus latitude and longitude, plus reference to maps in the Times Midcentury Edition for those names which appear on the maps in that atlas.

22-68: So that a place can be located on any map which gives parallels and meridians. See Foreword. (See also question #21-61.)

22-69: Three Guy Fawkes listed in Times Index-Gazetteer. One is a river in Tasmania, with reference to a map in the Times Midcentury Edition (no geographical coordinates given). One is an island in the Galapagos Islands, not located on a map in the Times atlas but geographical coordinates given. The third is a city or town in Australia, also not located on a map in the Times atlas but geographical coordinates given.

22-70: Timbuktu and Brussels cross-referenced from English version to vernacular version (Tomboucton and Bruxelles respectively). Botswana and Zimbabwe not listed (too early, 1965). Rhodesia is listed, though no longer the correct name of the country. Stonehenge listed (still exists as a place). Phoenicia not listed except as a town or city in New York state (historical place which no longer exists). The Foreword of the Times Index-Gazetteer is particularly good to read on the problems of name changes, spelling variations, etc.

22-71: Times Index-Gazetteer lists 345,000 place names (see Foreword and Sheehy). Columbia Lippincott: 130,000. Times Atlas, Comprehensive edition: 200,000.

22-72: You can locate it on other maps through the geographical coordinates. It may be indexed in other atlases, especially those with strong coverage for the U.S. Using the Hammond Medallion atlas map for Wisconsin, you can locate the point for the geographical coordinates, which would actually put Honey Creek in Michigan, rather than in Wisconsin. Honey Creek is located in the Hammond Medallion atlas (see index) in the inset map for the Milwaukee area in the upper right of the Wisconsin map.

22-73: See Sheehy, section on Atlases--National

and Regional--Philippines.

22-74: See Sheehy: Geography--Atlases--Bib-
liography (on both maps and atlases):
Lock's Modern Maps and Atlases (CL166),
Alexander's Guide to Atlases (CL165,
1CL45), and International Maps and Atlases in Print (1CL47). A source too new
to be listed in Sheehy is Kister's Atlas
Buying Guide (Phoenix, Oryx Press,
1984). It is similar in format to Kister's
Dictionary Buying Guide and Encyclopedia
Buying Guide (see Sections 12 and 14).

22-75: See the reviews in ALA's Booklist (Reference Books Bulletin). See some of the
bibliographic sources for atlases (#22-
74). See also Kister.

22-76: See any dictionary. A globe is an accurate visual representation of the world's
surface, as opposed to the distortion of
the various map projections. Globes cannot give any information which cannot also
be found through maps, but they have a
special visual impact and effectiveness
which enhances the information found
through maps and atlases.

22-77: Gazetteers, atlases, perhaps encyclopedias
or dictionaries. May need to check something continuously brought up to date such
as Ayer Directory of Publications or Rand
McNally Commercial Atlas for recent population figure.

22-78: Times Atlas is a likely choice since it gives
very detailed maps.

22-79: An atlas, particularly one which has good
thematic maps. Goode's has a thematic
map on world climatic regions.

22-80: See almost any atlas which gives illustrated
discussion of projections, such as Goode's.

22-81: Hotel and Motel Red Book, possibly a guidebook for that region.

22-82: Rand McNally Commercial Atlas has such
a map.

22-83: See lists of geographical equivalents or
foreign geographical terms in supplementary
material in most of the atlases.

22-84: Problem is similar to that of the bridges.
What do you mean by biggest? longest?
highest? widest? most water? Some atlases have lists of waterfalls in "world
facts" sections in the back, but usually
list only highest. Gazetteers have entries for Niagara Falls but are not com-

parative. Almanacs, as usual, are most
helpful here since they tend to give lots
of comparisons. Try also Guinness Book
of World Records.

22-85: Guidebook for Paris, or guidebook for
France which includes Paris. (A French
encyclopedia might help but might not
give recent information.)

Section 23

REVIEW OF PART II

Questions #23/1--23/60

This section is a review of Part II: Basic Reference Sources, Sections 12-22.

In this review, you should follow the same procedure used in Section 11 (Review of Part I): you can either search out the specific answers in the sources, or simplify the process by deciding which source(s) you would use to answer the question, or use a combination of both methods. What you do should depend on how much time you have and how much practice and review you think you need.

In either case, you should begin by deciding which source or sources to use. Think in terms of the type of information required by the questions and the type of sources available. In deciding which source(s) to use, think first of the type of source (generic name) and then a specific title (brand name) which is an example of that source and which would--because of its scope and arrangement--be likely to give you the answer to that question.

For many of the questions, there may be several possible sources in which you could find the answer. This is even more true of the sources in Part II than for the bibliographic sources in Part I. You should try to think of as many possibilities as you can, because you may find yourself working in a library which will not have all of the sources studied in this manual. Also, you cannot rely on the specificity of the general reference sources in the same way that you can with the bibliographic sources. For example, if you are searching for the price of a book, you can be reasonably sure that a source which claims to include price, such as BPR or CBI, will in fact include that information for all the items listed. If you are searching for a fact such as a man's birthplace, you cannot be at all sure that the biographical sources will include that information for all persons listed; you may have to check further in other sources also giving biographical information.

However, in this review section, you should again assume that you have available all of the sources studied in the manual, and you should then think in terms of which would be the best or the most likely source to use and why. Think in terms of the existing pattern or structure of the available reference sources. For example, the general encyclopedias will in fact frequently provide factual answers for a large proportion of reference questions. But in using the encyclopedias for such factual material, you always have to consider the problems of how accurate, how up-to-date, how detailed, etc., the information is. There may be other more direct, more current, more easily used sources.

As before, if you find that you are not really sure which source(s) you should choose, and why, then it may be that you need more practice in and use of the sources to clarify your understanding of them. Try searching out the answer to the question in various likely sources, and see if this procedure helps you to compare the usefulness and scope of the sources.

Throughout Part II of the manual, no specific suggestions were given for making the kind of review charts which you made for the bibliographic sources. If you have not made any such charts or brief comparative notes, you might find it useful now to review the material by going over the sections, noting down the various types (generic names: i.e., unabridged English language dictionary, usage book, synonym dictionary or synonym thesaurus, general adult American encyclopedia, encyclopedia yearbooks, directory of organizations, etc.) of sources, then noting down the kinds of information for which those sources are most useful (i.e., definition of words in English language, etc.), then trying to remember, or coordinate from the list in the List of Sources of this manual, various specific titles which are examples of types of sources.

Then turn to the review questions, trying to answer them, without the aid of your notes. There are plenty of review questions for practice.

23-1   Where would you find a discussion of recent developments in organ transplants (e.g., heart, kidneys, etc.) in the past few years?

322

23-2   How does a computer work?

23-3   What is the origin of the word Hoosier, and is it used to mean Indiana or someone from Indiana?

23-4   When and where was movie actor James Garner born? Is that his real name?

23-5   Where would you look to find the titles of some biographies about nurses for a student interested in nursing as a career?

23-6   What are the major retail sales areas of the United States? How are these distributed geographically throughout the country?

23-7   Where would you find statistics on coffee production in the Philippines in the early 1960's?

23-8   John Jones (not a made-up name) was the personal physician of Benjamin Franklin and wrote an article about Franklin's last illness. Where would you find further information about Jones' education and career with further bibliographic references, and which would probably also include a reference to the article on Franklin?

23-9   Swaziland is an African nation which became independent in 1968. What was its previous history? What kind of government does it currently have? Does it have an ambassador to the United States and if so, who is currently in that post?

23-10   What are some well-known statements or comments which have been made about patriotism?

23-11   A word currently much used is "parameters." What exactly does it mean?

23-12   What is the difference between whom and whomever?

23-13   How large is the Oritani Motor Hotel in Hackensack, New Jersey?

23-14   Where would you find information on the exact date, extent of damage, area covered, etc. for a recent earthquake in Southern California?

23-15   Where can you find information about Zoroaster?

23-16   What is a word which is similar in meaning to "negotiate" but is not quite so formal?

23-17   Where would you find information on television writer Andy Rooney? Where does his work appear besides on "60 Minutes?" How did he get his start in television? What are some of the topics he has written about?

23-18   What were the names of the original states of Germany before its division at the end of World War II? What are the present states of the (West) German Federal Republic?

23-19   What is the present form of government in the West German Federal Republic, and who is its head?

23-20   What is the meaning of the word "saucefleme," used in the 15th century (Middle English)?

23-21   Who said "It is not observed that ... librarians are wiser men than others"?

23-22   What is the OAS, an organization active in Algeria?

23-23   Where would you find a list of books on fortune telling?

23-24   Where would you find a short bibliography on folk music?

23-25   If you were asked to conduct a meeting, where would you find information on what order of business to follow?

23-26   How many and what railroads serve Peoria, Illinois?

23-27   What is the name of the long-suffering female in Chaucer's A Clerk's Tale?

23-28   Where would you find comparative figures showing the number of telephones in the United States in the late 1800's, early 1900's, mid-1900's?

23-29   What was Ikhnaton, an Egyptian king of the 14th century, noted for?

23-30   If your small boy was interested in the weather and wanted to set up a weather observation station in your yard, where could you look to help him? What if he wanted to know specifically how an anemometer works?

23-31   What does "cockamamie" mean (as in, What is this cockamamie school all about anyway)?

23-32   A well-known German bookseller is the firm of Otto Harrassowitz, presently located in Wiesbaden. Can you find out anything of the earlier history of this firm?

23-33   Henry Green is the pseudonym of an English novelist. What is his real name?

23-34   Where would you find some statistics on the consumption of tobacco products in the U.S., and on the changes, if any, in cigarette smoking habits in the U.S. in recent years?

23-35   What are the names and addresses of some places to stay overnight in New Orleans?

23-36   What is the meaning of the word "cubomancy?"

23-37   Truman Capote is the author of the book Music for Chameleons.   What is his address?

23-38   Where would you look to find a pictorial representation of the major food-producing areas of the
         world?

23-39   What is the origin of April Fools' Day?

23-40   Where can you find an explanation of "new math" for a confused "old math" parent?

23-41   Where can you find a reproduction of Masolino's painting called "Banchetto di Erode"?

23-42   Where is Madison, Wisconsin, located? What is it known for? Is there any major industry or manu-
         facturing there? What is its approximate population?

23-43   Where would you look for clarification of the usage of "Junior," "II," "III," etc. for a man given
         the same name as his father or blood relatives?

23-44   What does the Center for Interest Measurement at the University of Minnesota concern itself with?

23-45   Who invented the ball-point pen?

23-46   What is the origin of the phrase "First catch your hare?"

23-47   Where would you look to get some ideas for decorating a school bulletin board for the month of
         June?

23-48   Who or what or where is Chandra?

23-49   In what year did Albert Schweitzer win the Nobel Peace Prize?

23-50   What is the purpose of the group which calls itself Fly Without Fear? Who are its current officers,
         and where can you write to them?

23-51   Where would you find useful information for someone who wanted advice on purchasing an encyclo-
         pedia for his home?

23-52   Specifically where are the Mexican volcanoes of Ixtacihautl and Popocatepetl, and how do you pro-
         nounce them?

23-53   Where would you find a list of various natural disasters (floods, fire, earthquakes, etc.) for the
         past year or so?

23-54   Where would you look to find the date of the first climbing of Mount Kilimanjaro?

23-55   Where would you find a detailed map of New Guinea?

23-56   Where would you find some historical and descriptive information about Nevada, giving details about the interesting things to see and do there?

23-57   To whom could you write to get really up-to-date information on research in the development and testing of pesticides?

23-58   What is the author and title of a recently-published biography of Henry Kissinger?

23-59   What are some slang terms having to do with being exhausted, tired out (e.g., "beat to the socks")?

23-60   What is the source of: "Better is the end of a thing than the beginning thereof"?

23-1: Encyclopedia yearbook (Americana Annual, Collier's Year Book, Britannica Book of the Year), probably under "medicine." This source would probably not be available yet for the past year, but would be available for the few years preceding last year. Other sources, such as New York Times Index or Facts on File which would give news of such developments, could also be used and would be available for the past year, but they do not really give a "discussion" and since you must search in them under various headings (e.g., kidney transplants) in various issues (weekly or semi-monthly) they are not really as convenient for a general view as the encyclopedia yearbooks.

23-2: General information, fuller than a dictionary would give: general encyclopedia, Britannica, Americana, Collier's--depending on level of comprehension of person who wants to know. Perhaps even a children's encyclopedia would be useful (World Book, Compton's).

23-3: Historical or etymological dictionary: Mathews' Dictionary of Americanisms. General dictionary might also give it.

23-4: Biographical information; this sort can be easily found in almanacs. World Almanac and Information Please both give Garner's birth date and place and his real name. Possibly also Current Biography.

23-5: Bibliographic source for biographies: Biography Index, which has an "occupations" index and indicates juvenile books.

23-6: Atlas, specifically in this case the Rand McNally Commercial Atlas--the only source you've had so far which is really likely to answer this quesiton.

23-7: Statistical source with international scope: Statistical Yearbook of the United Nations.

23-8: Biographical source with encyclopedic-type information and bibliographic references, for American no longer living: Dictionary of American Biography. General encyclopedia might be used but probably would not be so extensive on such a minor figure. National Cyclopaedia of American Biography would be likely to include him but not likely to include bibliographic references.

23-9: Current information needed--Statesman's Year-Book is best as it should answer all these questions and more, and should be comparatively current. Almanac may also be useful but unlikely to give name of ambassador.

23-10: Quotation book; in this case, probably one with a subject approach such as Stevenson's Home Book of Quotations would be easiest to use.

23-11: General dictionary; the more recent, the better.

23-12: This is a usage problem. The dictionaries, especially the unabridged, may give some help, but a fuller discussion would be found in the supplementary sources specifically covering usage, such as Fowler's Dictionary of Modern English Usage or Evans' Dictionary of Contemporary American Usage.

23-13: Travel/tourist information; guidebook or accommodations directory; Hotel and Motel Red Book should do it.

23-14: News summary service (Facts on File or New York Times Index).

23-15: Name given only, perhaps not clear whether this is a real person, myth or literature, whether living or dead, or what area. Start with universal sources, such as Webster's Biographical Dictionary, New Century Cyclopedia of Names, or a general encyclopedia. General dictionaries (Webster's 3rd under Zoroastrianism).

23-16: Synonym. Dictionary may be helpful, but a better source would be those which specifically cover synonyms, and in this case, one which tries to "discriminate" between meanings of words (Webster's New Dictionary of Synonyms) rather than one which simply lists synonymous words.

23-17:   Current biographical information on currently popular figure. More than just basic biographical data as given in Who's Who in America. Current Biography is a likely source. If not there, try Biographical Index for references to magazine articles, etc.

23-18:   See Webster's New Geographical Dictionary or Columbia Lippincott Gazetteer under Germany. Encyclopedia probably would also be helpful.

23-19:   See most recent Statesman's Year-Book or an almanac.

23-20:   Dictionary which includes words not in current usage. Oxford English Dictionary under saucefleme; Century Dictionary under sausefleme.

23-21:   Quotation book, can be answered through key-word type index; Bartlett's Familiar Quotations or Stevenson's Home Book of Quotations.

23-22:   Abbreviations or acronym source (Acronyms, Initialisms, and Abbreviations Dictionary, for example). Might be in dictionaries, might also be in encyclopedias. (Sounds from the way the question is phrased as if it is a geographical problem; however, since it deals with an organization, it cannot be answered through the geographical sources.)

23-23:   Bibliographic source: encyclopedias might be useful but perhaps an even better source would be How-To-Do-It Books or Nueckel's Selected Guide to Make-It, Fix-It, Do-It-Yourself Books.

23-24:   General encyclopedias usually include short bibliographies or lists of references for major articles. Americana, Collier's, Britannica, perhaps World Book or Compton's depending on reading level you wanted.

23-25:   Manual covering this specific topic: Robert's Rules of Order.

23-26:   Official Guide of the Railways, if you had it. Another useful and current source for this information is the Rand McNally Commercial Atlas. Some other atlases might show railway routes but would not necessarily be as current or detailed enough to show Peoria.

23-27:   Literary handbook: Benét's The Reader's Encyclopedia. You have the name of the literary work and need a source which will give you some general information on plot and characters. Biographical sources not helpful as you need the name, but do not know it.

23-28:   Statistical source: Historical Statistics of the United States.

23-29:   Biographical source with universal scope, limited information: Webster's Biographical Dictionary or Chambers's Biographical Dictionary. Try general dictionaries.

23-30:   Children's encyclopedia: World Book or Compton's.

23-31:   Slang term not in general dictionaries-- see special dictionaries of slang. Probably easier to use one with dictionary arrangement such as Wentworth and Flexner's Dictionary of American Slang.

23-32:   Foreign (German) encyclopedia for details on minor item. Try Brockhaus Enzyklopaedia or Meyers Enzyklopaedisches Lexikon.

23-33:   Literary handbook; Benét's The Reader's Encyclopedia.

23-34:   Statistical source: probably Statistical Abstract of the U.S., perhaps used in conjunction with Historical Statistics of the U.S. This sort of thing can often be found in the almanacs also.

23-35:   Tourist/travel information; guidebooks and accommodations directories. Hotel and Motel Red Book.

23-36:   General dictionary.

23-37:   General, very current biographical information on comparatively "noted" American, living: Who's Who in America.

23-38:   An atlas for pictorial representation, in map form. Goode's World Atlas has a lot of thematic maps.

23-39:   Source which deals with holidays: Gregory's Anniversaries and Holidays, or Hatch's American Book of Days. Literary handbooks might also be useful.

23-40: Encyclopedia. Children's encyclopedias perhaps even better on this than those for adults, not because material is "written down" but because the children's encyclopedias do try to include general information helpful to parents as well as to children.

23-41: Foreign encyclopedia for minor things which might not be in general American encyclopedias. Enciclopedia Italiana is both Italian and noted for art reproductions.

23-42: Probably a gazetteer for this one. An atlas would locate it (through the index, then looking at a map) and would probably give the population, but would not give information on industries, etc. Webster's New Geographical Dictionary should be current. Ayer Directory of Publications would also help.

23-43: General dictionary or usage book might be helpful; but probably a better source would be a manual on etiquette, such as The New Emily Post's Etiquette.

23-44: Directory of organizations, specifically the Research Centers Directory.

23-45: Sounds like a biographical approach but since it is subject-access rather than name-access, the biographical sources may not be much help. This is actually one of those "curious" facts to be found in Kane's Famous First Facts. "Who invented" is often synonymous with "first." An encyclopedia might also be helpful.

23-46: Sounds like a quotation book, but in this case the phrase is not really a correct quotation but somewhat of a corruption, so the quotation books don't help. Brewer's Dictionary of Phrase and Fable.

23-47: Gregory's Anniversaries and Holidays, Hatch's American Book of Days, or Chases' Calendar of Annual Events.

23-48: Try New Century Cyclopedia of Names, since it may not be clear whether this is biographical, geographical, or literary.

23-49: You can approach this from two ways: biographical under Schweitzer or subject under Nobel Peace Prize. Almanacs list such prizes with past winners and this is probably the quickest route. Universal sources such as Webster's Biographical Dictionary or encyclopedias might be best for biographical approach; Schweitzer is dead and internationally known.

23-50: Directory of organizations: Encyclopedia of Associations.

23-51: Encyclopedia Buying Guide and/or "Reference Books Bulletin" in Booklist.

23-52: Source which locates geographically and gives pronunciation: Webster's New Geographical Dictionary. Columbia Lippincott Gazetteer would probably give pronunciation also. NBC Handbook of Pronunciation would probably give pronunciation but would not locate. Dictionary giving geographical information might also be useful.

23-53: Almanacs are useful. Both World Almanac and Information Please have lists, although they are not easy to find. You can use the New York Times Index but you have to know what the disaster is in order to locate information about it; there is no list, as such, under "disasters."

23-54: Several possible approaches; gazetteers might do it (Webster's does in 1972 edition, doesn't in earlier editions; Columbia Lippincott does); encyclopedias might do it; date books (Everyman's Dictionary of Dates includes it).

23-55: Atlas. Probably Times Atlas of the World, since it is excellent for relatively large-scale maps of world coverage.

23-56: Encyclopedia might be useful, but better would be a guidebook for the state of Nevada, such as one in the American Guide series.

23-57: See Encyclopedia of Associations, Research Centers Directory—subject approach.

23-58: Bibliographic source for biography: Biography Index, under Kissinger as subject.

23-59: Dictionary specializing in slang terms—either a dictionary-arrangement (Wentworth and Flexner: Dictionary of American Slang) or thesaurus arrangement (Berrey and Van den Bark: American Thesaurus of Slang) would be helpful, but in this case, since you are not after the meaning of a specific word, but rather a general list or group of words, the thesaurus approach would be better.

23-60: Quotation book, using keyword index. (Ecclesiastes 7:8.)

INDEX OF SOURCES

This index represents those titles which appear in the List of Sources, pp. v-xiii of this manual. The sources are listed under only one entry (whether author or title), that which is given in the source list. Following each title is a reference (e.g., AA612) to its listing in Sheehy's Guide to Reference Books (9th edition), where complete bibliographic citations may be found. For those titles not in Sheehy, further bibliographic information is given following the title.

Index references given here for each title are to the numbers of the questions (and/or answers) in the manual which cover that particular title (e.g., 1a/14-21; this means section 1a, questions 14 through 21). References were made for the primary discussion of each source, and not necessarily for appearances of the title in the compare and contrast questions, or in the review questions in each section or in Sections 11 and 23. Some titles were discussed only briefly in the text of the question sections, rather than in specific questions/answers; for these, references have been made to page numbers (e.g., p. 14) rather than question numbers.